KLEINE ERZÄHLUNGEN UND IHRE MEDIEN

REIHE
KULTUR.WISSENSCHAFTEN

Herausgegeben vom Bundesministerium für
Bildung, Wissenschaft und Kultur

BAND 8.1

HERBERT HRACHOVEC
WOLFGANG MÜLLER-FUNK
BIRGIT WAGNER
(HG.)

Kleine Erzählungen und ihre Medien

TURIA + KANT
Wien

Bibliografische Information Der Deutschen Bibliothek
Die Deutsche Bibliothek verzeichnet diese Publikation in der
Deutschen Nationalbibliografie; detaillierte bibliografische
Daten sind im Internet über http:/dnb.ddb.de abrufbar.

Bibliographic Information published by Die Deutsche Bibliothek
Die Deutsche Bibliothek lists this publication in the Deutsche Nationalbibliografie;
detailed bibliographic data is available in the
internet at http:/dnb.ddb.de.

ISBN 3-85132-370-X

VERLAG TURIA + KANT
A-1010 Wien, Schottengasse 3A / 5 / DG 1
info@turia.at • www.turia.at

Inhalt

Einleitung

Kleine Erzählungen begleiten und strukturieren unseren Alltag wie die großen, und neben dem Satz *the medium is the message* gilt auch, dass Medien vor allem Speicher einer unübersehbaren formalen und inhaltlichen Vielfalt von Erzählungen sind. Auch Vorwörter und Einleitungen pflegen gern den narrativen Gestus, indem sie die Leserschaft nicht nur vorausdeutend auf den Inhalt des Buches einstimmen, sondern in der Rückwende dessen Entstehungsgeschichte erzählen. Sie erfüllen damit eine klassische Funktion des Narrativen, nämlich die der Legitimation; daneben befriedigen sie auch die Lust am Episodischen. Wir wollen uns diesen Gestus nicht verwehren und zunächst ein wenig zurückblicken; unsere Entstehungsgeschichte ist jedenfalls auch Teil der Institutionalisierungsgeschichte von Kulturwissenschaft und *cultural studies* an den österreichischen Universitäten.

Der vorliegende Band präsentiert die Ergebnisse der Ersten Internationalen Graduiertenkonferenz, die im April 2002 an der Universität Wien stattgefunden hat und deren Durchführung vom Forschungsschwerpunkt Kulturwissenschaften/Cultural Studies des österreichischen Bundesministeriums für Wissenschaft, Bildung und Kultur finanziert worden ist; ebenso hat das Bundesministerium die Publikation dieses Bandes ermöglicht. In diesem Zusammenhang danken wir Christina Lutter sehr herzlich; ebenso danken wir Markus Arnold, Anna Babka, Karl Brunner und Andrea Griesebner, die uns bei der Vorbereitung und Durchführung der Konferenz entscheidend unterstützt haben. Das Konzept der Graduiertenkonferenz ist dem Ziel verpflichtet, der transdisziplinären Forschung im Bereich der deutschsprachigen Kulturwissenschaften und der angelsächischen Tradition der *cultural studies* einen Raum *innerhalb* der Universität zu geben, einen ersten Institutionalisierungsschritt zu setzen, was im internationalen Vergleich keineswegs selbstverständlich ist; darüber hinaus handelt es sich um ein Instrument der Förderung junger Wissenschaftlerinnen und Wissenschaftler (in einer Forschungslandschaft, die nicht eben reich an Graduiertenförderung im Bereich der Humanwissenschaft ist).

Diese erste von insgesamt vier Konferenzen konzentrierte sich auf zwei Forschungsfelder, denen im Rahmen des *cultural turn*, der kulturellen Wende in den Humanwissenschaften entscheidende Bedeutung zukommt:

einerseits Konzepte des Narrativen und andererseits neue Ansätze im Bereich der Medienforschung.
Narrative Konzepte spielen als Konstruktionsformen von Identität und Kontinuität in vielen Wissenschaftsdisziplinen eine zentrale Rolle: in der Philosophie im Zusammenhang mit dem »Ende der großen Erzählungen« (Lyotard), in der Psychoanalyse und Psychologie, in den Geschichtswissenschaften und natürlich in der Literaturtheorie, die in den vergangenen Jahrzehnten – nicht zuletzt im Gefolge des Strukturalismus – ein überaus differenziertes Instrumentarium für die Analyse von Erzählungen entwickelt hat, das mittlerweile medienspezifisch auf die Analyse von Filmen und anderen Bildmedien übertragen und erweitert worden ist. Heute stellt die Theorie des Narrativen über die angestammten Bereiche der literarischen Prosa hinaus ein wichtiges Werkzeug der kulturellen Analyse dar: denn Erzählungen gibt es nicht nur in der Kunstform Literatur; vielerorts stiften sie Sinn, Kontinuität und Dauer, konturieren ›Identität‹ und konstruieren individuelle und kollektive Erinnerung.
Wie der Begriff der Kultur, so sind auch jene der Medien und des Narrativen keineswegs eindeutig und fordern zu vielfältiger methodologischer Anstrengung heraus. So führen die Autorinnen und Autoren dieses Buches exemplarisch vor, wie unterschiedlich die Annäherungen an das Thema Medien sein können: narratologisch, semiotisch, anthropologisch, medienhistorisch, technikgeschichtlich. Auch der narrative Komplex ist äußerst vielschichtig und lädt zu vielfältigen Analysemethoden ein; Erzählungen lassen sich auf den verschiedensten Ebenen unterscheiden: im Sinn einer Typologie von Geschichten, durch ihre ästhetische Komposition (Fokus, Stimme), durch verschiedene Genres und Inszenierungsformen. Zentral ist in diesem Band die Verbindung der beiden Forschungsbereiche, die allzu oft nebeneinander bestehen und zu selten auf die Ergebnisse und methodologischen Ansätze des jeweils anderen zurückgreifen und sich mit ihnen so auseinander setzen, dass transdisziplinäre Fragestellungen sinnvoll werden.
Die Beiträge spannen einen Bogen von der Antike bis zur Gegenwart, wobei die bunte Medienwelt unserer Gegenwart den Schwerpunkt bildet. Sie machen deutlich, dass und wie der mediale Wandel auf die Beschaffenheit der Narrative auf allen Ebenen – Inhalt, Form, Fokus, Inszenierung – zurückschlägt und somit den symbolischen Raum von Kulturen modifiziert, zugleich auch die Art und Weise, wie Identität und Alterität modelliert, gebrochen oder dekonstruiert werden. So analysiert der Text von Roger Bromley, eines Vertreters der englischen *cultural studies,* die medialen Möglichkeiten der Generierung von Solidarität im Zeitalter der Globalisierung, während sich die Romanistin Vittoria Borsò am Beispiel von Flauberts *Salammbô* noch einmal dem Medium der Schrift sowie dem Span-

nungsverhältnis von Visualität und Narrativik zuwendet. In ihrer markanten Differenz führen die beiden Texte die Bandbreite des theoretisch und auch politisch Möglichen im Feld der heutigen Kulturwissenschaften vor. Mit dem medialen Wandel richtet sich nämlich die Aufmerksamkeit zunehmend auf die Art und Weise, wie kleine (und große) Erzählungen sich im Feld der Kultur formieren und situieren und diskursive Praktiken erzeugen, die das Feld des Politischen prägen.

Bei der Auswahl der Beiträge ging es uns nicht zuletzt darum, das theoretisch zu fundierende Verhältnis von Medien und Narrativen in verschiedenen Anwendungsbereichen zu beleuchten und die historische Dimension einzuschließen, die in nicht wenigen aufgeregten Medientheorien unberücksichtigt bleibt. Kartographie im Fernsehen, Photographie, Experimentalfilm, CD-Rom und Internet, aber auch die metaphorische Medialität einer mittelalterlichen Mystikerin, das Medium Buch im Zeitalter der Reformation, die medienästhetische Arbeit mit archäologischen Quellen, *oral history* und Gedächtnispolitik, die mehrfache narrative Kodierbarkeit von dokumentarischem Filmmaterial, die Analyse von ›enzyklopädischen‹ Romanen, die ästhetische Konfiguration der Ovidschen Metamorphose als ›Kippbild‹, dies alles illustriert die thematische Vielfalt, die in der theoretischen Engführung von Medialität und Narrativität liegt, und die methodischen Möglichkeiten, die genannten Phänomene zu analysieren.

Als Anwendungsformen kulturwissenschaftlicher Theoriebildung können die Aufsätze dieses Bandes zum besseren Verständnis des Zusammenhangs von medialem und kulturellem Wandel beitragen. Es wäre voreilig, jedweden kulturellen Wandel deterministisch auf die Veränderung der medialen Gegebenheiten in einer Kultur zurückzuführen, aber umgekehrt stellt das Mediale selbst einen integralen Bestandteil kultureller Analyse dar. Gewiss sind auch andere als die hier privilegierten methodischen Zugriffe im neu entstandenen, kulturwissenschaftlich geweiteten Feld der Humanwissenschaften sinnvoll und notwendig; jedenfalls aber sind die Forschungsfelder Narrative und Medien für die Analyse symbolischer Räume konstitutiv; sich mit ihnen auseinander zu setzen, scheint unhintergehbar zu sein und gestattet es den Humanwissenschaften, politische Fragen auf eine neue Weise zu formulieren: nämlich als Frage nach der Logik der Medien, der Artikulation ihrer ›Botschaften‹ und der Wirkungsweise der kleinen und großen Erzählungen im symbolischen Raum von historischen und gegenwärtigen Kulturen.

Die politische Dimension der Kulturwissenschaften lässt sich über die explizite Diskussion politischer Themen (Globalisierung, Gedächtnispolitik, Nahostkonflikt, *gender*-Politik) hinaus aus ihrem methodischen Selbstverständnis begründen. Denn die kulturelle Wende in den Humanwissenschaften impliziert, dass Kulturanalyse niemals eine bloß neutrale

Beschreibung des symbolischen Feldes, sondern auch eine Intervention in diesem darstellt. Kulturwissenschaft zielt nicht zuletzt auf eine Politik der ›Form‹. Es kommt darauf an, wer wie und wo erzählt. Und auf das mediale Format der Erzählungen.

Wien, im März 2003
Herbert Hrachovec, Wolfgang Müller-Funk, Birgit Wagner

Cultural Studies und Medienwissenschaften

Narratives for a Journey of Hope: Stories of Global Transition

ROGER BROMLEY

I should like to start with a dogmatic statement about globalization:

> The secular project of increasing material well-being throughout the whole world by means of extended capital accumulation [has] failed to deliver on its promises. It could not satisfy human wants, needs and desires nor liberate time and space for emotional and intellectual development. It promised unlimited consumerism ... as a path for the pursuit of happiness but delivered at best lopsided and at worst fraudulent benefits. It produced substantial wealth and empowerment for the few [perhaps 20% of the world; RB] and disillusionment, repression, misery and degradation for the rest. (Harvey, 2000: 193)

I see narrative as a practice of symbolic representation through which people construct meaning. If, as has been argued, over the past twenty years or so, globalization has meant ›the intensification of consciousness of the world as a whole‹ (Robertson, 1992: 8) and ›the »global« increasingly exists as a cultural horizon within which we (in varying degrees) frame our existence‹ (Tomlinson, 1999: 30), then how can we produce narratives which will enable us to interpret and understand this? In particular, a response is needed to the neo-liberal economic ›genre of discourse‹ that has come to dominate the narration of the global, silencing other voices and making witnessing impossible. As globalization in its current form extends its power and domination, offers itself as the model to which all others must be made analogous, is assimilative and appropriative in countering heterogeneity and alterity, what part can narrative play in producing versions of the ›global‹ which are dialogical, unconditional, inherently ethical, resistant to appropriation, and openly engaged with the distant and the different?
How can we intervene in the form of symbolic projects which are ›reflexively sustained in relation to rapidly changing circumstances, on a local and global scale‹ (Giddens, 1991: 215)? It is this reflexive process that I first wish to highlight. If our relation to the world is being transformed by digitalisation, the Internet, and the electronic media, what implications does this have for our traditional assumptions about narrative form? How,

given this technological mediation and image overkill, can narrative intervene by devising other ways of telling which render ›issues of distant moral concern congruent with individual, locally situated lifeworlds‹ (Tomlinson: 179)? This will be the core question running through my argument.

What new kinds of narrative codes can be developed? It is partly a technical question – a matter of techniques and formal strategies – but it is mainly an ethical one. How can narrative strategies make image and information flows – in what Castells calls a ›a new symbolic environment‹ – interactive and dialogical. The distance to be overcome is both physical/geographical and moral. To help shape some kind of response to these questions I want to focus upon three contemporary texts, a film by the Austrian director Michael Haneke: *Code Inconnu* (2000), and two books of photography by the Brazilian Sebastiao Salgado called *Migrations* and *The Children* (both 2000), in which he documents the epic displacement of the world's people at the close of the twentieth century. Without for one moment questioning the uniqueness of the Holocaust, what I shall be arguing is that the displacement of the world's people, the genocide and ethnic cleansing of the past decade or so urgently require their own forms of narratable remembrance in order, in Ricoeur's words, ›to give memory a future‹. As Simone Weil said: ›there are only two services which images can offer the afflicted. One is to find the story which expresses the truth of their affliction, the words which can give resonance through the crust of external circumstances to the cry which is always inaudible … why am I being hurt?‹ (quoted in *The Spectre of Hope*, 2001)

One of our tasks is to think through the consequences for narrative of changes in mediation brought about by globalizing processes, to find the story:

> The evolution of media has decreased the significance of physical presence in the experience of people and events … Now physically bounded spaces are less significant as information is able to flow through walls and across great distances.
> As a result, where one is has less and less to do with what one knows and experiences. Electronic media have altered the significance of time and space for social interaction. (Meyrowitz, 1985: vii -viii)

Not only electronic media, one might add, but also travel. Fifty years ago, China was 5000 miles away from Britain. Today, it is still 5000 miles away but, whereas in 1952 it was a two-week journey by air, today it is eleven hours. Hence, a photographer, Salgado, was able to chronicle the 1990s by travelling to 43 countries in six years. How has a film director, like Haneke, used this time-space compression, thematically and technically?

Narrative is always a speculative discourse, a discourse of possibility, hope and the future: it is not prescriptive, even if teleological, but re-scriptive, conjectural and also, perhaps, with an element of risk, of the not known. It is hypothetical, rather than being subject to empirical practice or positive knowledge. There is also a trace of vision, of seeing, in the very idea of the speculative. In this way, we might like to think of film, or photography, as not representational but speculative/perspectival. As globalization has been brought about, mainly, by the reconfigurations of space and time produced by a particular phase of capitalism, how can narrative map its own reconfigurations?

If it is, above all, the capitalist production of space which is the dominant mode of reconfiguration, how can narrative – classically seen as temporal and diachronic – develop a spatial and synchronic dialectic? How can the distant, the incomplete, and the displaced be properly brought together? How can this ›de-materialized‹ space be re-materialized as part of a political and ethical narrative? How can the seemingly contradictory existence of de-materialized space with a high degree of cultural interpenetration produce a narrative which sustains profound changes in modes of thought and understanding? Everyone is being ›pulled into the orbit of capital‹ (a theme of *Code Inconnu*) ›while large sections of the world's population [are rendered] permanently redundant in relation to the basic dynamics of capital accumulation‹ (Harvey: 68).

›Possibility‹, Ernst Bloch commented, ›has had a bad press. There is a very clear interest that has prevented the world from being changed into the possible‹ (in Harvey: 258). A loss of hope, the sense that there is no alternative, has characterised many responses to globalization which is why I have called this chapter, ›Narratives for a Journey of Hope‹, and want to focus upon two very different narrative interventions which give possibility a future, but not in any naïve or sentimental fashion. Both operate with alternative modes of thought and understanding using different media, different resources and technical strategies:

> Visionary thought is not inherently millenarian, perfectionist, or utopian (in the vulgar sense of the term). It need not and does not ordinarily present the picture of a perfected society. But it does require that we be conscious of redrawing the map of the possible and desirable forms of human association and designing new practical arrangements to embody them. (Unger, 1987: 359-60)

So perhaps it would not be too fanciful to describe what I am asking for as a redrawing of the map of the possible and desirable. Unger uses the concept of ›structure transforming conflicts‹ which well describes Haneke's film and Salgado's photographs. He also speaks of ›freeing sociability from script‹, another of the functions of the texts in question. The challenge remains, however, to transform signifiers of hope into grounded, material referents. These texts do this, I shall argue, by the ways in which they are shaped by continuous processes of struggle, without closure, and by identifying agencies and processes of change for constructing the future.

The children in the classroom at the beginning and end of the film constitute in their deafness and muteness the possibility of other modes of signifying, productively freeing themselves from the always already known script of the spoken and the heard. Above all, they can see and they co-inhabit unself-consciously a multicultural space. The film's prologue is set in this classroom of deaf-mute children. Against a large, white background a little girl is miming something as she crouches down and reacts with surprise. Her classmates sign a number of possible interpretations – each arising perhaps from their own preoccupations – but cannot work out her mime. This indicates at the outset that there is no simple correlation between signifier and signified, and that decoding is something which will have to be extended into the context of the whole ensuing narrative. This scene is the first of forty-six micro-narratives which constitute the cinematic text. We cannot enter the world of that child directly, or experience her meaning, but can only develop an ethical sensitivity, an empathy (a partnership even) which recognises her, not as a deaf child, but as an experiencing other, a signing/signifying subject.

This links with Haneke's idea of taking the spectator as a partner in the narrative process. The fragments of the film signify a before and an afterwards and belong to the world from which the spectator enters the cinema and to which she/he will return. Haneke recognises the limits and imperfections of cinema as a means of expressing reality, and sets up his camera accordingly. The last five scenes are without any dialogue and the only sound is insistent drumming by the deaf schoolchildren. In the final shot of the film another child from the same class is also seen miming and, because mute, making a series of sounds which are not quite words. It is this state of ›not quite words‹ at the end of the film which prompts the thought that articulation now begins again, but this time it involves the refiguring of our existence as we return from narrative text to action.

As partners in the cinematic process, we have a lot of hermeneutic work to do. I will give a brief example. On the Metro, Anne, an actor, is verbally abused and spat upon by two Arab teenagers who both flirt with and taunt her, referring to her class position and possible contempt for them. In this long, unedited sequence we see Anne being made very insecure and frightened by this treatment. Finally, she is defended by a middle-aged Arab man, ashamed of their behaviour. The scene is tense and threatening and the young Arab males are presented very negatively. This micro-narrative/fragment requires us to extend our perception into a larger context of French colonial history, Arab immigration (and the presence of French-born people of Arab origin and the generational conflict that can produce), and the situation of Arab youth in the banlieues of Paris – under-educated, unemployed, racialised. As Mary Dejevsky observes:

> In big French cities such as Paris and Lyon, it is possible for the city-dwellers never to have anything to do with the banlieues, or those who live in them, and vice-versa. There is a ›comfortable France‹ and an ›uncomfortable France‹ and the paths of the two need never cross.

Extending this metaphorically, one might say that there is a ›comfortable‹ Europe (which we inhabit) and an ›uncomfortable‹ Europe (the former Eastern bloc) in *Code Inconnu* and, with Salgado's work, a ›comfortable‹ world and an ›uncomfortable‹ world (4/5ths of the globe). Through narrative their paths do cross and they are brought into conflict and exchange. The Arab, the African (Amadou and his family) and the Rumanian illegal immigrant (Maria) might initially be seen from the outside and the viewpoint of the comfortable spectator, as stereotypes (›typical‹ one shopkeeper says of Amadou), troublemakers, deviants, others: denizens of the ›uncomfortable‹. Amadou's arrest and Maria's deportation remind us, in Scott Lash's terms, that ›the institutions of totality, including law, politics and history, can only judge the individual as a Universal I‹ and cannot address the ›other as marginal – as the beggar, stranger, widow, orphan – [who] overflow the categories of totality‹ (Lash, 1996: 93).

What the film does is produce a series of ›overflowing‹ micro-narratives (little narratives), inlines and deep profiles, which enable us to journey into the spaces of the disadvantaged, in all their complex and contradictory habitations, and not just as reversed, and romanticised, stereotypes. Similarly, Salgado's photographs are, at first glance, drawn from the now-familiar, almost stock images of war zones, sites of dispossession and displacement, or of people in flight across borders. Salgado sees the documentary photographer as a vector connecting the different realities of people around the world. By contextualizing the photographs, he enables the viewer to live with this world, take it in, to visit in the complex sense of being a guest in someone else's space, travelling to that location, and also of seeing/viewing, observing and examining: a micro perspective is offered. This is one of the powers of narrative, this ›being a guest in someone else's space‹, visiting and travelling. In both cases, moral distance is converted into narrative proximity and ethical possibility. These ›stereotypes‹:

> Occupy a very disadvantaged position in the hierarchy of media power structures… Even when they appear on screen, they do so largely in silent and often marginal roles [and are rarely] given the opportunity of giving their own point in their own words. (Hargreaves in Morley: 164)

Maria, for example, is first seen seated in the bottom right corner of the screen – the iconic beggar – and she is silent throughout the first two scenes of her humiliation, apprehension by the police, and deportation. She, and those like her, are fundamentally alien, othered, seen from the privileged western perception. What Haneke and Salgado do is to re-locate these figures in a global, post-colonial narrative: they are the bearers of our own cultural anxieties and fears. They are also, of course, carriers of stories and are given space to become active/voiced subjects/participants in their own narratives, however partial and fragmented – they become hosts, if you like. All Haneke's films, in form and content, are opposed to the current media industry. He believes the spectator must be given the possibility of participating in the film, and not simply be a passive consumer authorised only to ingest spoon-fed images but, rather, the very person who completes the film. In the same way, his ›migrants‹ are invested with narrative agency and forms which, rather than seeing them as object or image, offer the possibility of recognition and ›authorship‹, empowerment. Every identity ›is mingled with that of others in such a way as to engender second-order stories which are themselves intersections between numerous stories. We are literally entangled in stories‹ (Ricoeur, 1996: 6).

Code Inconnu is not, despite the comments of some critics, about something as banal as the impossibility of communication but very much about the ways in which narrative of a particular kind can open up the possibilities of communication, but not in the readily available forms. The film is concerned with population changes in the richer countries – multicultural societies – and as such, Haneke argues, could be set in any comparable large European city. Paris is the primary location of the film in all senses of the word. It is cosmopolitan, the bearer of traces of a colonial history, a global city, a site of consumerism, and a migrant space.

Three core families in the film are linked by the opening incident, but also by situation. Jean and George's father is a struggling farmer; Maria and Amadou's ›root‹ families in Rumania and Mali, respectively, are also in rural locations. Nevertheless, Amadou's little sister in Paris asks ›where is Africa?‹ and the birth of a calf in Maria's home village is carried out under instructions from a relative in Rome by mobile phone. No simple or absolute distinctions are possible, but increasing urbanisation and the global rural exodus are themes in the film. The families are also linked by intergenerational conflicts. Amadou – a teacher of deaf children – eats in the same restaurant as the middle-class professionals, Anne and George, and his family think he spends too much time with white people; his father returns to Mali; Jean runs away from the farm and refuses to prepare himself to inherit it; Maria and her daughters clash; she is let down by a fellow-immigrant. The ethnic ›others‹ are not romanticised but seen in complex and conflicted locations – a combination of roots and routes. Maria, in particular, is tracked at a number of levels. We enter her humiliation and poverty, her evacuation from spaces of identity and meaning. In the opening scene, which precipitates much of the following action, Jean throws his food wrapper into her lap as a sign of contempt for her begging. When she is deported, the over-bright colours of the aircraft and the insistent glamour of the air hostesses contrast with her dull, shapeless clothing and her silence. At home, family life is far from idyllic. She returns to Paris, at high cost and considerable risk, partly to earn money to send back to the village but partly one feels, as an escape: the migrant's inchoate dream of possibility. We see the life behind the face and follow a trajectory from iconic, tabloid figure to a heterogeneous narrative profile.

Anne is a film and theatre actor. She is fully competent in the realm of the egological and the performative – the simulated – but in her relations with George, and in her confusion and failure to act in respect of an abused neighbouring child, she is shown as incapable of empathy (entering the child's narrative time and space) or of action. However, she breaks out of her walled-in, image-bound world by aborting George's child (whether this is true, or metaphorically so, we never know) and changing the code of her apartment to finally exclude him when he returns from one of his frequent trips abroad.

George is a key figure, a proxy for the conventional filmmaker, expropriating and exploiting images. He finds life easier in the war zone – ›over there, it's simple, here life is complicated; there, it's hard at first, then you get into the swing of things‹. Rarely ›here‹, as the photographer ›there‹ he is indifferent to the situation and only its image-potential engages him. Detached in all senses of the word – the first world voyeur – he steals/appropriates other people's tragedies. The images he sends back, in the letter-tape, are contextless – ›I tried writing often, but gave up; I didn't know what to say‹ – they lack any narrative momentum. Back in Paris, in Anne's apartment, George is seen assembling his camera. The sequence is reflected throughout in a full-length mirror, suggesting the narcissism of the image-trader. At one point, George poses in front of the mirror as if to film himself or to arrange himself as ›the photographer‹, a role or pose – the consumer of images. Later, in the Metro, he takes a series of portraits surreptitiously – a series of objects or images, non-consensual unlike Salgado's subjects allowing themselves to be photographed. He is unresponsive and irresponsible, monological and unethical.

Both Haneke and Salgado attempt to give back their stories to the ›always already narrated‹ so that they can narrate. In both cases, it is an ethical project, a telling against the initial, pre-scripted story. As has been noted, Anne, the film actor, and her boyfriend, George, a war photographer, are part of the image industry (Anne even lives next door to a cinema), a self-enclosed, self-absorbed relationship: over-aestheticized and separated from the realm of the ethical. There are brief excerpts of films being made within the film, revealing the role of editing in illusion, manipulation and deception.

In each case, the director and photographer are figures who ask rather than tell, producing episodic narratives which can/must be continued, completed by others: ›to rewrite the event-without-a-witness into witnessing, and into history‹ (Kearney: 58). Narrative as witness is a concept I would wish to hold onto. In Salgado's case, especially, his work testifies to, is witness of, the unspeakability and inaccessibility of the immediate or originating event while insisting on ›the absolute necessity of speaking‹. The process is what I would call, not representational, but *situational* in the sense that it both sites (locates) and cites (calls to mind/summons or arouses), and offers a space in which narrative can emerge in such a way that a new political imaginary can be constructed, the mobilisation of a fresh cognitive and ethical ordering.

Why so many photographs, we might ask? Would not a sample be representative? In Mozambique alone, Salgado came across 350,000 children displaced from their parents. Something that Judith Miller said of the Holocaust is apposite here and is at the heart of much of what I have been saying: ›And only in understanding that civilized people must defend the one, by one, by one … can the Holocaust, can the incomprehensible, be given meaning‹ (in Kearney: 62). This ›one, plus one, plus one‹ is a feature of both the film and the photographs. Both Haneke and Salgado *singularise* in this way, through empathy, a mode of exchange facilitated by narrative. Sensationalised images pull people to look at them and then move on, narratives pull them and keep them.

In Salgado's case, the question ›who are these people?‹ takes time to answer, to come inside their lives. People, he says, come to your lens as they would to a microphone. You assume a large responsibility with the people that you photograph, to tell their stories – they call you, as he expresses it, ›to picture‹; an attempt to narrate, we might want to add, from the point of view of the addressee, the person customarily addressed. This, he says, is not in order to create a bad conscience, guilt or compassion even in the first world viewer, but to extend our range of vision and understanding. Speaking of the children he photographed, he said they emerge from groups as individuals through the lens; through their eyes they are presenting themselves: ›I am here. This is me. I exist.‹ They know they are looking at the world and so they address a question: ›what are you? You out there in the world? Or, perhaps, is there anything else out there?‹

The response to this: ›Here I am‹ might be linked with ideas developed by Levinas, in particular the inauguration into responsibility, the threshold of freedom and self-conscious subjectivity, what Levinas calls ›the very possibility of the beyond‹. In this process, we are called upon to respond to the vulnerability of the other, to act as the one-for-the-other, the stranger, the widow, the orphan. It is a call for an ethical response to an other who cannot be recognised within any shared cultural or political context: ›The strangeness of the Other, his [sic] irreducibility to the I, to my thoughts and possessions, is precisely accomplished as the calling into question of my spontaneity, as ethics‹ (Levinas, 1969: 43). Identity has its source in the engagement with radical otherness resistant to the grasp of appropriation, rather than in the reduction of the other to the same (like George's photography, perhaps) in the form of re-presentation which assimilates everything so that nothing may remain other to it. For Levinas, the *encounter* (and I think of narrative very much as an encounter) – with, in our case, Salgado's subjects, Haneke's ›others‹ – is with ›the Stranger who disturbs the being at home with oneself‹, the zone of the ›comfortable‹ referred to earlier. The other is always incommensurable with my self, *excessive* to representation (precisely, Haneke's point, hence the fades and wipes, the inconclusive, the non-appropriative techniques). The I is put into question by the encounter and the other is ›maintained and confirmed in his [sic] heterogeneity as soon as one calls upon him‹ (Levinas, 1969: 69).

Berger says, at one point in the television programme ›The Spectre of Hope‹ (Arena, BBC Knowledge, December, 2001), ›the priorities according to which we perceive and react to the world might be changeable‹. It is this possibility of change which narrative promises and is connected with the idea of hope. The eyes of the children, the photographs, interpellate us, in the sense that they interrupt or break in upon our unreflexive, ›comfortable‹ narratives but also they hail us, appeal to or entreat us; above all, perhaps, they petition us. This interpellation breaks up unity and continuity and establishes a relation of separation and transcendence. In similar fashion, Haneke's film interpellates us by its technique of incompleteness and its heterogeneity. *Code Inconnu* is sub-titled ›incomplete tales of several journeys‹ and the episodic structure of fragmented sequences (many of which begin halfway and end inconclusively, followed by a wipe – a black screen) disturb, unsettle our ›comfortable‹ linear viewing habits. They put down markers or stakes and invite us to enter the fragment and construct our own continuities and narrative consequences. It should be noted also that the journeys referred to are not only those which take place within the film's diegesis.

At the beginning of Salgado's collection of ninety photographs, *The Children*, there is a dedication: ›This book is dedicated to all the children who look at these photographs and are moved to think about the lives behind the faces‹. Salgado works within a tradition of what has been called concerned, or ethically evaluative, photography and it is precisely this process of being moved to think about the lives behind the faces which characterises ›concerned‹ narratives: they have a mobilisation effect in the following sense – emotional (›being moved‹), cognitive and reflective (›to think‹), and ethical: opening up to the world beyond the faces, the scenes, the text: ›In encountering the stranger-neighbour, I may be *called back* to the ethical from my immersion in the ontological; I may be interrupted in my being‹ (Shildrick, 2002: 91). If I may risk a generalisation, the narrative I am speaking of is one which *interrupts* being, and opens up ›the ethical perspective of the inter-human‹, the recognition that the other is also in relation to others. In Levinas's terms, what justice enables is ›a society where there is no distinction between those close and those far off‹, a point related to what I said at the beginning about making issues of distant moral concern congruent with locally situated lifeworlds. Sara Ahmed has stressed the need to pay attention to the particularity of *modes of encounter* as a way of accounting for the multiplicity of others, opening up the question of elsewhere and otherwise: ›One's infinite responsibility begins with the particular demands that an other might make, but the particularity of my response cannot fulfil my responsibility‹ (Ahmed, 2000: 147). If exposure in the face of alterity is the very condition of becoming then, I would argue, that the narratives I have been discussing are precisely such *modes of encounter* described by Ahmed.

What Haneke does is produce a form of narrative which builds-in its own disruption, it is interruptive almost in the sense used by Levinas (questioning structurally the existing forms of cinematic storytelling) as part of its repertoire of possibilities. He constructs a series of discontinuously narrated communities (Anne, her boyfriend George, his brother Jean and their father; Amadou and his family; Maria and her family; the Arabs in the Metro) with their own singularity and yet also interpenetrating. Its framework is born, he says, not on the screen but in the viewer's mind. It is an *allusive* technique. By using sequence shots and reducing editing, he is trying to eliminate the manipulation of the time factor. In a sequence or a fixed shot, we are in real time. The continuous recording of shots opens up the film to the spectator, and renders the process less ›filmic‹, illusory and structurally exclusive. Shots, Haneke says, should not flaunt their complexity. The questions which motivated and triggered the film project were: can reality be represented? is the fragment the aesthetic response to the incomplete nature of our perceptions? can allusion replace description? is that which is off-camera more precise than that which is on? to the observer, what makes the represented object real, credible or, more precisely, worthy of being believed?

As spectators, rather like the way we receive Salgado's photographs, our task is to take the film in, ingest it, as part of a narrative process of accessibility and reception. A question arises as to whether everything is narratable. Often an event in its immediacy is not narratable/speakable/sayable, as the discursive resources for mediation are not available or are inadequate (think of people rendered speechless by trauma) – the code is unknown. One of the challenges of radical narrative – whatever form it takes – is the quest for discursive adequacy or appropriateness: the intersection of the aesthetics of representation with the ethics of memory and witness. In Ricoeur's words: ›Forgiveness is a sort of healing of memory, the completion of its mourning period. Delivered from the weight of debt, memory is liberated for great projects. Forgiveness gives memory a future‹. Narratives can be both healing and liberating, emancipatory. This is why I used the phrase ›narratives for a journey of hope‹ in my title, because I see films like *Code Inconnu* and photographic works like Salgado's as being constituted by an ethical narrative imagination; resources, in Raymond Williams' memorable phrase, for a journey of hope – a possible future. Narrative aids this process by its synchronising capacity, by bringing the ›unspeakable‹, the ›inexperienced‹ (that which has not yet entered into reflexivity) into narratable experience. Speaking of Holocaust survivors, Terence Des Pres said:

> Whoever comes through will take with him the burden of speaking for others. Someone will survive and death will not be absolute. This small pledge ... is intensely important to people facing extinction .... In the survivor's voice the dead's own scream is active. (in Kearney: 167)

This ties in with the idea of *witness* and the need to produce narratives which imagine ›constantly that there is a witness to all we do and say and that, moreover, this witness is not a passive observer, but someone who relies upon us. In order to be reliable, we must feel needed; for us to feel needed, this Other must be needed‹ (Sennett, 1998: 146). It is this ›reliability‹ which helps to shape what I have called the ethical narrative imagination and the witness is the addressee, or the addressee if s/he could speak.

Looking at the photographs in *Migrations* of genocide, torture, dead bodies, rape and ethnic cleansing in Rwanda, Bosnia, Kosovo, Afghanistan and Mozambique, it is difficult not to simply despair or to respond to the photographs only at an aesthetic level: ›what a beautiful set, or décor, what a well-chosen moment or great composition‹. This would be to respond to the instant or the fragment, to have lost all sense of tragedy. Obviously, we do not photograph genocide, rape or the process of ethnic cleansing, only fragmentary outcomes. To become aware of the full life inside the tragedy – its past, present and future – it is necessary to enter into narrative, so that ›the dead's own scream is active‹. There are also photographs in the book of survivors, children in particular, and, as Berger says, this is connected with the idea of hope; the point about hope is that it is something which actually occurs in very dark moments.

People are in flight but they are also in transition and what they have with them is just a small slice of hope and it is with this hope that they are trying to reach another stable position in life. They allowed themselves to be photographed, Salgado says, because they wanted their plight to be known: the purpose of his work. Consciously, or not, by allowing themselves to be photographed – a passive process – they were entering actively into a dialogue, with an unknown other, and with a possible future: a narrative of adaptation, of possible mobilisation.

Salgado came to understand that everything that happens on earth is connected. The photographs provide this connectivity – a point of narrative intersection – between a world of need and a world of excess. Taken together, they form a troubling image of our world at the turn of the millennium. Even though the photographs in the book (more than 400) are organised into four chapters, photographs in one chapter have echoes in another. This echoic effect, this resonance, is also a feature of Haneke's film in which the opening, eight-minute sequence located in a Paris boulevard unites almost all aspects of the film, installs the locus of connectivity. Both texts are concerned with the movement of people, the reorganisation of humankind by globalization. We cannot, as Salgado says, afford to look away but have to create a new regimen of coexistence.

This leads me back to a point made much earlier about the need for narratives which, by analogy with the Holocaust, create an accelerated/ speeded-up and compressed record/memory through narrative, of all kinds, of our contemporary situation. As Salgado remarks:

> Everywhere I travelled, the impact of the information revolution could be felt. Barely a half century ago, the world could say it ›did not know‹ about the Holocaust [it probably took almost thirty years to achieve, what I would call, full ›narrative currency‹ RB]. Today, information – or at least the illusion of information – is available to everyone. Yet the consequences of knowing are not always predictable. Television informed the world of the massacres in Rwanda or the mass expulsions of Bosnians, Serbs or Kosovars almost as they were taking place, but these horrors nonetheless continued. (Salgado, *Migrations* 2000: 10)

How, in other words, given the information revolution can the ›necessary‹ of globalization be rendered *contingent* through alternative narrative currencies? If globalization is a view of the world that claims that there is no alternative (we have reached the end of history?), then narrative must respond to this change in scale, time and space by opening up to history and complex dimensionality. Once again, Ricoeur is of value here: ›By remembering and telling, we not only prevent forgetfulness from killing the victims twice; we also prevent their life stories from becoming banal ... and the events from appearing as necessary (Ricoeur, in Kearney: 172). Just another image of famine and disaster, switch over; just another hard-luck story of a bogus asylum-seeker, turn the page.

In another context, Ricoeur uses the concept of the circle of threefold mimesis: (1) the prefiguring of our life-world as it seeks to be told (for example, the child coming to the lens); (2) the configuring of experience into text in the act of telling (the process of narrative encoding); (3) the refiguring of our existence as narrative identity and the return, in the form of reflection and rememoration, from narrative text to action (the cultural, social and political consequences). As Couze Venn puts it, the third mimetic relation refers back to the first by way of a transformative praxis applied to the second (Venn, 2000: 100). It is this creative retelling – ›life is always *on the way* to narrative‹ (Kearney: 133) – which leads me to think about narrative not as invention but as *intervention*. In his introduction to *The Children*, Salgado points out that every year, ›UNICEF publishes an alarming report about the state of children in the world. In disheartening detail, it spells out the health, educational, and housing deficits that affect hundreds of millions of children around the world‹ (Salgado, *The Children*, 2000: 9). His book of photographs attempts no such analysis, he says, but merely shows ninety children from different parts of the globe on a particular day in their lives. It is a ›snapshot‹, in a sense: ›They look beautiful, happy, proud, pensive and sad. For a brief moment they were able to say ›I am‹. It is this moment that I would call the moment of narrative which calls upon me to respond but does not prescribe my response. This might be thought as ›the call of the ethical‹. The photograph confers recognition and the ›I am‹ constitutes the onset of subjectivity. But, from the configuration of the text in the act of telling (I am) it is also necessary to travel back from the narrative to the UNICEF reports and the larger political/global narrative of action.

Narrative is not a form of action (poetry makes nothing happen, Auden said), nor is cultural studies, but when we conclude our hermeneutic activity, our academic papers, we have not finished, because then begins the mobilisation, the impulse (an application of sudden force causing motion) to action. It is also the moment when we should be moved to think about the lives behind the faces. I should like to finish with what I would call an ›interpellative‹ poem by the Argentinean poet, Juan Gelman (quoted in *The Spectre of Hope*, 2001):

We have to pass from the kingdom
Of need to the kingdom of freedom
From that of theology
To that of religion
From capitalism to life
From the economics of poetry
To the poetry of economics,
From hunger to you.

REFERENCES

Ahmed, Sara, Strange Encounters: Embodied Others in Post-Coloniality, London, 2000

Berger, John and Salgado, Sebastiao, in: The Spectre of Hope, Arena, BBC Knowledge, December 2001

Dejevsky, Mary, The angry sound of the suburbs, in: The Independent, 26 October, 1995

Giddens, Anthony, Modernity and Self-Identity: Self and Society in the Late Modern Age, Cambridge, 1991

Haneke, Code Inconnu, 2001

Harvey, David, Spaces of Hope, Edinburgh, 2000

Kearney, Richard, On Stories, London, 2002

Lash, Scott, Postmodern Ethics and the missing ground, in: Theory, Culture and Society, 13 (2): (1996), S. 91-105

Levinas, Emmanuel, Totality and Infinity: An Essay on Exteriority, Pittsburgh, 1969

Meyrowitz, Joshua, No Sense of Place: The Impact of Electronic Media on Social Behaviour, New York, 1985

Morley, David, Home Territories, London, 2000

Ricoeur, Paul, Reflections on a New Ethos for Europe, in: Kearney (ed.), Paul Ricoeur. The Hermeneutics of Action, London, 1996

Robertson, Roland, Globalization: Social Theory and Global Culture, London, 1992

Salgado, Sebastiao, The Children, New York, 2000

Salgado, Sebastiao, Migrations, New York, 2000

Sennett, Richard, The Corrosion of Hope, New York,1998

Shildrick, Margrit, Embodying the Monster, London, 2002

Tomlinson, John, Globalization and Culture, Cambridge, 1999

Unger, Roberto, False Necessity: Anti-necessitarian Social Theory in the Service of Radical Democracy, Cambridge, 1987

Venn, Couze, Occidentalism, London, 2000

Schriftkörper und Bildmaterialität – Narrative Inszenierungen und Visualität in Gustave Flauberts »Salammbô«

VITTORIA BORSÒ

»Photographie: Détrônera la peinture (v. daguerréotypie)«
Gustave Flaubert: »Dictionnaire des idées reçues«

BILD UND SCHRIFT: PLÄDOYER FÜR EINE ÄSTHETIK DER MATERIALITÄT

Eine Mediengeschichte zu schreiben, die unabhängig von der Kohärenz der alphabetisierten Gesellschaft, von der Kohärenz der großen Erzählungen des Abendlandes und von den Mythen des Humanismus sein sollte, war eines der Ziele von Friedrich Kittlers archäologischer Vorgehensweise. Das Interesse von Kittler und seiner materialistischen Medienarchäologie war historisch, nicht ästhetisch. Hingegen besteht in Frankreich ein von der Phänomenologie angeregtes Interesse hinsichtlich der Materialität des Bildes. Dieses Interesse hängt mit der Problematisierung des Sehens und der narrativen Interpretation des Bildes als Semantik einer Bildersprache zusammen.[1] Mit der Krise der narrativen und ikonologischen Interpretation des Bildes reagierte man auf die Krise des Sehens, zu der die technologischen Umbrüche um die Jahrhundertwende geführt haben.[2] Das Bild kann nicht mehr vornehmlich als visuelle Diskursivität gelesen werden, die in einer Tiefendimension verborgen ist. Methodologisch gilt also auch für das Bild die Aufforderung, jenen Prozess umzukehren, der die Oberflächenstruktur durchbohrt, als wäre diese lediglich der durchsichtige Vermittler einer Botschaft. Es bedarf für das Bild einer Methodik der Analyse weg von einem etwaigen, verborgenen Denkinhalt hin zur graphischen Oberfläche. Es geht deshalb im Folgenden um eine Theorie des Bildes, die die Spezifik der visuellen Manifestation unabhängig vom Bildgedanken bzw. von einem narrativen Inhalt in den Vordergrund stellt, und es geht auch um die narrativen Konsequenzen einer solchen Theorie der Bildlichkeit.

Unter anderem Roland Barthes hat Lektüren problematisiert, die das Bild als Träger der Evidenz gesellschaftlicher Inhalte interpretieren, denn solche Lektüren gehen auf Kosten der jeweiligen Bildmanifestation. Spuren dieser Kritik findet man bei Barthes schon seit seinen frühen Artikeln zum Fotogramm in den Filmen von Eisenstein bis hin zu »La chambre claire«, seiner Schrift zur Fotografie. Die nicht ganz systematisch ausgesprochene Grundlage von Roland Barthes ist die phänomenologische Interpretation der Visualität durch Maurice Merleau-Ponty, auf dessen Philosophie das neue Textualitätskonzept im Rahmen der *Tel-Quel*-Gruppe, die dekonstruktivistische Arbeit an der Wahrnehmung seitens des »Nouveau Romans« und die Unterscheidung zwischen »Augen« und »Blick« durch Jacques Lacan zurückgehen. Zu nennen wären auch die Entgrenzung des Verhältnisses von Subjekt und Objekt seitens der französischen Philosophie von Gilles Deleuze, die Dekonstruktion der Gleichsetzung von Vernunft und Sichtbarkeit seitens Derridas, die Aufdeckung der Allianz von Sichtbarkeit und Macht seitens Foucaults und die Interpretation derselben im Sinne der phallo-oculo-zentristischen Grundlagen der abendländischen Philosophie durch Luce Irigaray, um nur einige zu nennen. Ohne mich in die philosophische Debatte vertiefen zu wollen, werde ich versuchen, den Spuren jener Theorie des Bildes nachzugehen, die das Bild nicht – oder nicht nur – als Repräsentation eines Bildgedankens, eines narrativen Inhalts erfasst, sondern auch der Spezifik der visuellen Bildmanifestation gerecht wird. Das dynamische Verhältnis von Bildlichkeit und Narrativität sowie die sich daraus ergebenden narrativen Räume können so in den Blick genommen werden.

Die Theorie des Bildes steht u. a. im Kontext der Visualistik, jener in den letzten Jahren aus den Bildwissenschaften entstandenen Wissenschaft, die die Wahrnehmungsmodi durch das im Abendland zentrale Organ des Auges thematisiert hat. Die Grundlegung meiner nachfolgenden Überlegungen findet sich in denjenigen Texten, die die Erfahrung der modernen Kunst philosophisch verarbeiten. Gemeint sind z. B. die verschiedenen Schriften über das Auge im Kontext des Surrealismus, insbesondere seitens »dissidenter« Autoren wie Georges Bataille.[3] Die Krise der Sichtbarkeit betrifft auch moderne Traumtheorien. Anhand der Traummanifestation haben sowohl Michel Foucault als auch Jean-François Lyotard mit unterschiedlichen Referenzen eine ähnliche Kritik an der diskursiven Interpretation des Traums als Träger eines Bildgedankens vollzogen. Die Interpretation des Bildes als Abbild, d. h. als Reproduktion eines Referenten, als ikonologisches Bedeutungselement, entspricht der Interpretation des Traums im Sinne der Traumdeutung, jener deutenden Arbeit, die die Traummanifestation dem Traumgedanken unterordnet und die Figurationsleistung untergräbt. Darin liegt auch die Kritik der Traumdeutung Sigmund Freuds durch den frühen Foucault, so z. B. in seiner 90 Seiten langen Einleitung zu Binswangers existentialistischer Traumtheorie.[4] Foucault stellt fest, dass der Traumgedanke das Ende des Bildes und der Traumarbeit bedeutet. Aus ähnlichen Gründen kritisiert Jean-François Lyotard in seiner Dissertation »Figure, Discours« (1971) Lacans linguistische Auffassung des Unbewussten. In jenem Kapitel, in dem er sich mit dieser Problematik beschäftigt, bezieht er Stellung zugunsten der Figur (»Le parti pris du figuré«). Der Begriff der »Figur«[5] betont die Materialität und ihre sensuelle Dichte, bei der die Erkenntnis sekundär ist. Die Figur entspräche jenem Teil der Theorie Freuds, der sich mit der Darstellbarkeit befasst. Diese werde zerstört, wenn man das Unbewusste auf einen Diskurs reduziere oder wenn man nach dem Dargestellten und nicht dem Darstellungsgeschehen suche.[6] Das Bild werde hierbei vergessen. Hingegen dürfe ein Bild nicht gelesen werden, wie Semiotiker es heute überall tun, so Lyotard. Denn das Bild verlangt vom Blick, dass er die Wege und Umwege geht, die vom Künstler vorgezeichnet sind (1971:14/15). In der Materialität des Bildes ist die Tätigkeit des Traumsubjekts aufgehoben, das auf die Zensur reagiert und sich als optisch bestimmtes »vis-à-vis« dramatisch konstituiert und durch die Traumarbeit materiell am Leben erhält. Anstelle von »Bedeutung« und »Diskurs« lenkt deshalb Lyotard die Aufmerksamkeit auf »Text« und »Figur«.

Am Beginn der modernen Krise des Sehens stehen inter- und transmediale Interferenzen von Text und Bild, sowie synästhetische Kreuzungen, die die Wahrnehmung irritieren. Eine technologisch fundierte Medienanthropologie des Bildes und der Schrift sowie ihres Wechselverhältnisses soll von diesen Experimenten und von der Problematisierung des Sehens ausgehen. Es ist leicht nachvollziehbar, dass mit der Visualität[7] auch diejenigen mimetischen Kunst-, Medien- und Texttheorien hinterfragt werden, die das Bild als Abbild (im Sinne Walter Benjamins) behandeln.

MATERIALITÄT DES BILDES UND NARRATIVITÄT

Die Krise des Sehens an der Schwelle der Jahrhundertwende (zum 20. Jahrhundert) ist von der Krise der narratologischen Bedingungen romanesker Texte begleitet. Dabei spielt das Verhältnis zwischen der Fotografie und den Künsten ebenso eine Rolle wie die Umformung der Wahrnehmungsbedingungen durch das neue Medium der Fotografie, die – wie seit Walter Benjamins Theorie der Reproduktion bekannt ist – auch im Medium der Schrift keineswegs zur Stärkung der Mimesis, sondern umgekehrt zur Infragestellung derselben führt.[8] Statt des organischen Abbilds eines ganzen Weltabschnittes wird die Romanschrift zum fragmentarischen Experiment, das nicht mehr die Welt, sondern das Sehen, das Wahrnehmen des Anderen zum Thema hat. Ich möchte dies anhand jenes vermeintlich realistischen Schriftstellers zeigen,[9] den die »Nouveau Romanciers« als Vorläufer erkannt haben: Gustave Flaubert. Zuerst skizziere ich aber eine Theorie des Bildes, die das Bild nicht allein als semantischer Träger der Narrative versteht. Vielmehr soll die Phänomenologie des Bildes als ein Prozess der Subjektkonstitution definiert werden. Für diesen Prozess, durch den das Subjekt sein Verhältnis zum eigenen Körper und zum Anderen regelt, dient das Bild als Medium. Die Prozesse des Blickes verlaufen deshalb über eine Konstellation von Subjekt, Medium,[10] Körper und Differenz[11].

In einem Aufsatz mit dem Titel »Visualisation et langage« aus dem Jahre 1967 kritisiert Roland Barthes die Interpretation des Bildes im Sinne der Koiné-Annahme seiner Ikonizität, als sei die Ikonizität eine supralinguistische, anthropologische Konstante mit unmittelbarer semantischer Evidenz. Barthes spricht von der Akkulturation des Bildes, die dann eintritt, wenn man das Bild den sozialen Diskursen und dem diskursiven Denken zuordnet. Eine solche Funktion des Bildes nennt Barthes eine Art »sozialer Wehrdienst«. Gewiss, das Bildzeichen kann als bedeutungstragendes Element einer Bildersprache, einer visuellen Diskursivität, gelesen werden, insofern auch Bildzeichen der Kodifizierung seitens der Kultur und des *common sense* unterliegen, syntagmatisch verbunden werden, Makronarrative bzw. narrative Diskurse generieren und an der Zirkulation der Kommunikation partizipieren. Juri Lotman hat z. B. in diesem Sinne die Sprache des Kinos analysiert und Christian Metz eine psychoanalytisch fundierte Semiotik des Kinos entwickelt, bei der die Narrativität die Spezifik des bewegten Bildmediums darstellt. Eine ganze Debatte über das narrative Wesen des Kinos habe sich auf dieser Basis entwickelt, eine These, deren Herrschaft erst durch die bahnbrechende Studie von Gilles Deleuze zu »L'image temps« (1985) gebrochen werden konnte. In der Tat hat die temporalisierte Struktur der subjektiven Wahrnehmung auch eine andere Theorie des Bildes eingeleitet. Das Verhältnis von Subjekt und Objekt wird bei der *image-temps* nicht durch eine statische, raum-zeitliche Konstellation geregelt, sondern ist vom Zeitfluss der subjektiven Erfahrung abhängig, einem Zeitfluss, der seit der Moderne auch die Alterität des Subjektes impliziert. Die Modi des raumzeitlichen Gefüges erklären auch die unterschiedlichen Funktionen der Fotografie nach Walter Benjamin: einerseits als Reproduktion und Abbild, wobei die Präsenz des Referenten sowie ein mit dem Subjekt homogener Raum angenommen werden; andererseits als »Zeugenschaft« des Verlustes einer vorgängigen Zeit, die als Differenz in das Bild eingeht. Hier ist das Bild die allegorische Figur der Zeitlichkeit. Durch Letztere wird Roland Barthes in »La chambre claire« auch das fotografische Bild definieren. Deswegen impliziert eine Theorie des Bildes auch eine bestimmte Theorie des Subjektes, das durch die Visualität sein Verhältnis zum Anderen und zur Differenz konstituiert.[12] Dass die Visualität eine Art Scharnierstelle zwischen dem Subjekt und dem Anderen darstellt, ergibt sich auch aus der potentiellen Polysemie von Bildern. Bilder sind – wie die Zeichen selbst – zunächst indeterminiert. Sie werden erst durch den diskursiven Kontext fixiert, in den sich das Subjekt einschreibt. Dabei wird in der raumzeitlichen Dynamik auch jene Konstellation definiert, in der sein Verhältnis zur Alterität und zur Differenz bestimmt wird. Gerade die Indetermiertheit, Rauheit, Widerspenstigkeit der heterogenen Materialität des Bildes sind Zeichen der subjektiven Expressivität (nach Roland Barthes der »dritte Sinn«), die Friktionen im System der »images«, d. h. der Abbilder gesellschaftlicher Diskurse, provoziert. Wir kommen somit zum Problem der Visualität.

VISUALITÄT: SCHARNIER ZWISCHEN SUBJEKT, ANDEREM UND DER DIFFERENZ

In seiner V. Cartesianischen Meditation erwähnt Edmund Husserl das Bild »Analyse der Empfindungen« von Ernst Mach, und zwar im Zusammenhang mit der Alterität des Leibes. Das Bild von Mach selbst illustriert die Unmöglichkeit, zur gleichen Zeit die gesamte Konstellation des Blickes, d. h. die zwei heterogenen Räume des Sehers und des Gesehenen, zu fokussieren. Der Seher und das Gesehene – das Subjekt und das Objekt – können sich nicht denselben Repräsentationsraum teilen. Thema des Bildes von Mach ist das Sehen selbst sowie die Fremdheit des Leibes im Hinblick auf das Sehen. Husserl wird diese Spur nicht weiter verfolgen; erst Maurice Merleau-Ponty und auf dessen Basis auch Jacques Lacan thematisieren den Unterschied zwischen dem Auge als Dispositiv kultureller Deutungen, in dem der Leib abwesend ist, und dem Blick als ein Ereignis, das erst über die Leiblichkeit des Subjektes erlebbar wird.[13] Das Sichtbare ist eine Projektion des kulturellen Auges, das selbst blind ist. Auf der Metaebene wird im Bild von Mach die Blindheit im Auge des Betrachters reflektiert. Dieses Bild zeigt das, was das objektive Sehen verdeckt. Darüber hinaus ist es auch die Darstellung einer Urszenerie der Konstellation des Blickes sowie seiner Rahmung, seiner möglichen, veränderlichen Gerichtetheit und seiner Bedeutung als Träger des Verhältnisses zwischen Subjekt und Objekt. Die Visualität konstituiert also einen Raum,[14] in dem das Verhältnis des Subjekts zu seiner Alterität ebenso geregelt ist wie sein Verhältnis zur Fremdheit des Leibes, so das Fazit von Husserl anhand des Bilds von Mach.[15] In der späteren Phase der Phänomenologie beschreibt Merleau-Ponty (»Le visible et l'invisible«, Paris 1964) die Beziehung des Subjekts und des Objektes, zwischen denen sich der Blick als ein durch die Schwelle der Leiblichkeit vermitteltes Verhältnis zur Fremdheit und zur Differenz ereignet. Merleau-Ponty verbindet die Fremdheitserfahrung des Leibes mit dem Problem der Visualität und hebt die Qualität des existentiellen Leibes als Chiasmus zwischen schauendem Subjekt und wahrgenommenem Objekt hervor. Tatsächlich ist im selben Körper das Auge zugleich betrachtendes Subjekt und betrachtetes Objekt, die Hand ist fassender Agens und gefasster Gegenstand. Der Leib ist ein der Vernunft fremdes Subjekt und das Objekt von diskursiv komponierten und vom Auge beherrschten Körperbildern. Das Ereignis des Blickes und die paradoxale Erfahrung des Leibes als Subjekt und Objekt des Blickes problematisieren die Sicht- und Erkennbarkeit der Dinge bzw. die visuelle Kompetenz des Subjektes. Es wird deutlich, dass die Visualität vom Verhältnis des Subjektes zu seiner Differenz abhängig ist. Was man mit den Augen erkennt, sind nur Darstellungen *von* Körpern entsprechend der Doxa *über* den Körper; die Leiberfahrung bleibt dabei jedoch jenseits des Diskursiven und Erkennbaren, schreibt sich aber in die Schrift oder in das Bildmedium als Differenz zum Diskursiven ein. Diese Differenz äußert sich als Leerstelle oder als Überschuss, als Brechung oder Friktion.[16] Sie macht sich durch Verneinung des Diskursiven (etwa durch Leerstellen) oder durch transgressive Formen bemerkbar.[17]

DAS SEHEN DES EXPRESSIVEN SINNS UND DIE ARRETIERUNG DER ERZÄHLTEN ZEIT

Die Körperlichkeit schreibt sich also nicht in die Semantik des Bildes, sondern in die Expressivität von Bildern ein, jene Dimension, die Roland Barthes bei der Analyse einiger Fotogramme von »Oktober« (1927), dem Film von Eisenstein, als den *sensus obtusus* oder »dritten Sinn« bezeichnet hat. Der Semantik des Bildes schreibt Barthes eine Abbildfunktion zu: Das Bild fungiert dabei als ikonisch vermittelter Referent einer diskursiven Sprache oder einer narrativen Einheit »Sprache minus Körper«.[18] Ich erinnere hier an die Hauptthesen des Essays zum »dritten Sinn«. Ebenso wie die Denotation und Konnotation funktionieren Abbilder – mit Paul de Mans Begrifflichkeit ausgedrückt – persuasiv und nicht allegorisch. Sie sind phatische Kanäle, also unsichtige Transportmittel einer Botschaft. Dagegen sei der sogenannte dritte Sinn *obtusus*, d. h. resistent gegenüber dem denotativen und konnotativen Sinn, den Barthes *obvius* nennt. Letzterer ist einsichtig, er ist Träger der Sichtbarkeit der Dinge innerhalb der Ordnung der Sprache und des Diskurses. Der *sensus obtusus* sei wie ein »fard«, eine Schminke, die das Material sichtbar macht und den Weg zur semantischen Auflösung des Bildes versperrt. Er ist in seiner Expressivität ähnlich dem »grain du réel«, d. h. der Spur eines Realen, das nur im sprachlichen Überschuss sichtbar wird. Deshalb ist der dritte Sinn auch nicht mit dem Referenten gleichzusetzen. Dies wird besonders im Zusammenhang mit dem »grain de la voix« deutlich. Der »grain« ist etwas raues, was die Wahrnehmung irritiert, wie die raue Stimme, die das Indiz der Leiblichkeit ist. Es ist etwas, was im Zusammenhang mit der Visualität und der Fotografie *punctum* heißen wird. Wie das Mal auf der ansonsten perfekten weißen »Haut« klassischer Statuen, so stellt auch das *punctum* die Differenz im Schönheitsideal dar. Aus der Zeitlichkeit im Zusammenhang mit der Fotografie gewinnt Roland Barthes die These der doppelten Wahrnehmbarkeit von Fotografien: einmal als *studium*, d. h. als Projektion der kulturellen Dispositive (etwa der sozialen Anatomien des Körpers) und zum anderen als Erfahrung eines Differenzzeichens jenseits des Diskurses, das das Subjekt punktiert, ja verletzt (zum Beispiel im Sinne der Spur eines einmaligen Augenblickes in der leibhaften, subjektiven Erfahrung). Diese beiden Momente implizieren verschiedene Konstellationen in Bezug auf den Betrachter: Beim *studium* ist das Subjekt ein Agens, das das Andere durch die Projektion kultureller Muster vereinnahmt,[19] beim *punctum* ist es »Objekt«, das vom Fremden »angeblickt« und »getroffen« wird. Eine solche Expressivität arretiert das referenzillusionistische Kontinuum der Narration, macht das Bild in der Zeit instabil und lässt es ambig erscheinen. Im Kino erfolgt die Arretierung des narrativen und realistischen Diskurses durch Einrahmungen und Vor-Bilder wie Großaufnahmen, die das Bild vom narrativen Diskurs isolieren und einen »régime physique, affectif, intense« verursachen (Bonitzer, 1985:89).[20] Die Isolierung des Bildes, wie sie Roland Barthes mit den Fotogrammen von »Oktober« durchgeführt hat, gibt dem Bild seine vordiskursive Instabilität, Unidentifizierbarkeit und Unentscheidbarkeit zurück. Dies erfolgt einerseits wegen der Ablösung vom narrativen Kontext, andererseits wegen dem Einbruch der Zeit in das Bild, weil der durch die Einstellung betonte Rahmen auf das »off« und damit auf die anderen Zeitstellen jenseits des Bildes verweist. Der Blick findet in den fremdbleibenden Heterogenitätszeichen einen Widerstand. Das Heterogene führt tatsächlich zu einer potentiellen Krise der Gestalt des Objektes und zur Irritation der Identität des Sehenden, aber auch zum Bewußtsein über die automatisierten Einstellungen des kulturellen Auges.

Bei dieser antimimetischen Theorie des Bildes hat der Blick einen anderen Status. Er ist nicht, wie das Auge, das Dispositiv, mittels dessen sich das Subjekt durch die Erkenntnis der Welt (und ihre Vereinnahmung) ermächtigt; das Subjekt findet vielmehr an der Oberfläche des Materials einen Widerstand und eine Grenze. Die Rahmung des Gegenstandes durch den Blick wird als »Einstellung« selbst zum Gegenstand und somit sichtbar und analysierbar. Tatsächlich ist in der experimentellen Kunst und Literatur seit dem Beginn des 20. Jahrhunderts das Bild keine Kompetenzsprache mehr; es fungiert nicht mehr als »Fenster-zur-Welt«;[21] das Bild wird vielmehr opak[22]; das Reale befindet sich weder an der Oberfläche, noch in einem Tiefensinn, sondern anderswo, an einem Ort, den der Blick nicht zu erreichen vermag. In der experimentellen Kunst werden Realitäts-»Einstellungen« durch das Bild in Frage gestellt. Das »Reale« ist von der Darstellung abwesend, es schreibt sich nur durch indirekte Spuren in das Darstellungsgeschehen ein, wie z. B. durch die vom Zugriff des Blickes autonom bleibende Expressivität. Ich meine jene Autonomie vom anthropologischen Blick, den die *Nouveau Romanciers* versucht haben, in Szene zu setzen.

NARRATIVE RÄUME: ÉCRITURE ALS FORM DES MEDIUMS SCHRIFT

Wie für das Bild müssen auch verschiedene Formen des Mediums Schrift differenziert werden.[23] Wenn die Schrift ein Medium ist, d. h. ein an sich indiskretes und undifferenziertes Phänomen, so sind Sinngenerierungen eine nachträgliche Performanz, in der das Subjekt auch seine Identität konstituiert. Nur unter identitätsstabilisierenden Voraussetzungen ist – ebenso wie das Bild – auch das Geschriebene eine »Kompetenzsprache«, über die das Subjekt vollkommen verfügen kann. Hier sind Einschreibungen Speicherungshilfsmittel, die dem phonologischen Dogma unterstehen, das Jacques Derrida mit der Mythologie der Stimme verbunden hat. Jene Form der Schrift jedoch, deren Materialität nicht dem Dogma der *phoné* untersteht, ist nicht Träger einer »parole pleine, présentée à soi et maîtresse de soi«, sondern Raum für die Einschreibung von Differenzen.[24] Dabei muss die Materialität[25] jenseits symbolischer oder semantischer Botschaften in den Blick genommen werden.[26] Roland Barthes hat die Phänomenologie einer solchen Schrift des Körpers mit der kulturellen Fremdheit, mit anderen Raumkonfigurationen und medialen Bedingungen, in Verbindung gebracht. Erst wenn die Zeichen stumm sind, die Orientierung im Raum offen bleibt, wie dies für einen Europäer im Kontakt mit der ihm fremden japanischen Kultur geschieht, wird die Materialität der graphischen Gestalten der Schrift sichtbar. Auf diese Weise – und nicht im Sinne der Epiphanie einer abstrakten Illumination – interpretiert Roland Barthes auch die Gedichtform des Haikus.[27] Barthes betont in Bezug auf den Dreizeiler die sensomotorischen Eindrücke und die optischen (und akustischen) Gestalten, die Gilles Deleuze in »L'Image-temps« (1985) für den Film des italienischen »Neorealismo« und für die »Nouvelle Vague« festgestellt hat.

Das oben Festgestellte gilt auch für das Narrative, und es geht hier nicht darum, einen neuen Paragone-Streit zu entfachen und das Erzählen zugunsten des Bildes zu verabschieden. Es soll vielmehr jene Form der Schrift und des Bildes identifiziert werden, die nicht allein als Dispositiv

für die Projektion gesellschaftlicher Makro-Narrative dient und bei der die Ikonizität und das Sichtbare mehr sind als nur ein Bildschirm, auf den Großformationen gesellschaftlicher Diskurse projiziert werden. Denn im verzeitlichten Raum der Materialität der Schrift erfolgen mit der Möglichkeit der Wiederholung und der Veränderung[28] auch Transkriptionen von Subjektivität, von Differenzen und Fremdheiten sowie von der Heterogenität des Kulturellen, wie schon Roland Barthes anhand von *Sarrazine*, dem Roman von Balzac, gezeigt hat.
Die Medialität der Schrift und des Bildes steht somit im Zusammenhang mit zwei grundlegenden Formen: einerseits mit einer Form, die Gemeinschaftssinn (*common sense*)[29] vermittelt – wobei die Massenmedialisierung von Kommunikation auch der Verbreitung »erfahrungsloser« Informationen Vorschub leistet, wie Walter Benjamin am Beispiel des beginnenden Journalismus festgestellt hat[30] –, andererseits mit einer Form, die zum Ausdrucksraum von Differenz und Fremdheit wird. Hier gilt die Stimme (im gesprochenen Medium) als Indiz und (in der Schrift) als Metapher einer irreduziblen Eigenheit, der Eigenheit des Leiblichen, die nicht Identität, sondern vielmehr ein partikuläres Idiom ist. Es sind störende, fremde, kontingente und zufällige Fremdheiten, die in symbolische Sinneinheiten einbrechen und Identitätssysteme perturbieren. Auch im Roman-Text ist der Zusammenhang von Leiblichkeit und Visualität zu bedenken, jene in Text- wie in Bildmedien mächtige Scharnierstelle zwischen Identität und Alterität.

SICHTBARKEIT, SCHRIFT UND NARRATIVE HETEROTOPIEN. *MISE EN SCÈNE* DER FREMDHEIT IN FLAUBERTS »SALAMMBÔ« ALS INKOMMENSURABILITÄT DES GESEHENEN

Im «Dictionnaire des Idées reçues» heißt es unter »Orientaliste«: »Homme qui a beaucoup voyagé«. Die Reise ist in der Tat mehr als nur die Anwendung eines dokumentarischen Erforschens der Kulturen des Orients nach der orientalistischen Mode, die sich im Anschluss an die archäologischen Entdeckungen und im Zuge positivistischer Geschichtswissenschaften etabliert hatte. Flauberts Metapher der Reise für den Orientalisten ist eine Metapher für den Schriftsteller selbst.[31] Schreiben heißt auch für Flaubert, sich de-platzieren, den Ort der Identität verlassen.[32] Reisen ist mithin Metapher für die *écriture*, insoweit Schreiben die Beschäftigung mit »Alterität« und »Differenz« ist. Deswegen folgt dem sog. realistischen Roman *par excellence* (»Madame Bovary«, 1857) ein Roman über antike Kulturen des sog. Orients (»Salammbô«, 1862), Kulturen, die Flaubert schon seit der im Jahre 1849 entstandenen ersten Fassung von »La tentation de Saint Antoine« (1874) beschäftigen. Die ferne Kultur, deren historische Fremdheit auch monumentalistisch rekonstruiert wird, soll nach der scheinbaren Nähe des bürgerlichen Realismus die Inkommensurabilität des Gegenstandes der Schrift wiederherstellen.

Der Roman konfrontiert mit einer Reihe narrativer Inkohärenzen und widersprüchlicher Gattungsmerkmale: Das historische Gemälde hat gigantische Dimensionen und bleibt zugleich fragmentarisch, vermag also nicht eine historische Synthese zu präsentieren; für die bürgerliche Kritik ist die mythische Aura des Fernen disfunktional.[33] Die epische Breite wird von der Wucherung des brutalen Details übertönt, die Imagination des Bösen überwiegt, die Massenszenen und das Gemetzel des Kampfgeschehens lassen sich in keine sinnhafte Botschaft kohärent einbinden. Vielmehr wird der Text durch exzessive Details zu einem im Hinblick auf die Mimesis opaken, jedoch expressiven Medium, das den Historismus bei weitem hinter sich lässt – etwa bei den zwei Szenen des Grauens vorchristlicher Barbarei, dem Holocaust der Kinderopferungen zu Ehren des Sonnengottes Moloch oder dem Massaker der barbarischen Söldner. Diese Ereignisse werden zwar von den historischen Quellen ebenfalls nachgewiesen (etwa Polybius), jedoch nicht im Zusammenhang mit dem ersten punischen Krieg. Der Historismus verwandelt sich hier in eine Quelle des Inkommensurablen. Die scheinbare *impassibilité* des rituellen Details rekonstruiert das Faszinosum und Tremendum des Mythos als eine Form des Unvordenklichen.[34] Die groteske Fremdheit der Gewalt korreliert ihrerseits mit dem Faszinosum des zentralen Ereignisses,[35] welches wiederum das Erotische und das Sakrale ebenfalls als vorchristliche Form des »unreinen Heiligen«, des Heterogenen, rekonstruiert, in dem Georges Bataille die einzige moderne Form des Heiligen gesehen hat.[36]

Es handelt sich um die erotische Begegnung der zentralen Figuren, die den Motor der *histoire* darstellen: Salammbôs Sehnsucht nach Mâtho, dem Führer der Barbaren, ist eine höchste Form der Transgression, weil sie, Salammbô, Tochter des Hamilkars, auch eine der Göttin Tanit geweihte Priesterin ist; er, Mâtho, stellt seinerseits für sie das absolut Andere, das Tremendum dar, ja die Inkarnation der Todesgefahr, der Zerstörung selbst. Die erotische Verausgabung führt tatsächlich zur letzten Konsequenz, zu dem Tod. Mit der erotischen Metapher für das Andere entspricht Flaubert zwar den Konventionen des Orientalismus, gerade die Heterogenität der transgressiven Handlung unterscheidet jedoch die Liebesszenen Salammbôs von den kodifizierten orientalistischen Liebeszenen und auch von den entsprechenden Szenen bei »Madame Bovary«, mit der doch Salammbô das melancholische und durchaus romantisch konnotierte Temperament gemeinsam hat. Die Übertretung des Heiligen geschieht hier durch das Sichtbarwerden und durch die Inbesitznahme des Schleiers der Göttin Tanit, die anzusehen verboten ist, eine Übertretung der Sichtbarkeit, die sprachlich durch heterogene Exzesse konnotiert ist. Diese Exzesse verletzen den Blick, wohingegen in der orientalistischen Ikonographie das voyeuristische Auge den Schleier durchdringt, sich des in Halbsicht ausgestellten Anderen aneignet und sich selbst ermächtigt.[37] Darüber hinaus ist das Heilige durch die Heterogenität und Promiskuität – zwischen Maschinen, Tier und Mensch, sowie Tod und Leben – im ursprünglichen Sinne von *sacer* evoziert, das Heiliges und das Böses zugleich bedeutet.[38] Die Fremdheit des Anderen und die Heterogenität des Heiligen transgredieren die ikonographische Vereinnahmung der anderen Welt, die mit den orientalistischen Konventionen ebenfalls zitiert wird. Jene Dimension des Eros wird in diesem Roman verwirklicht, die den Anderen in seiner Fremdheit erfahrbar werden lässt,[39] wodurch das erotische Subjekt bewegt, depotenziert, entrückt und entgrenzt wird, wie dies in modernen Theorien des Heiligen von Caillois zu Bataille hervorgehoben wird. Die ironische Inszenierung der Stereotypen demontiert den Orientalismus, während die Expressivität des Heterogenen Spuren einer Existenz hinterlässt, die jenseits der Diskurse über den Orient Bestand hat. Diese doppelte Dimension des Eros – als bürgerliche Domestizierung des Anderen und als transgressive Verletzung des Selbst – entspricht der doppelten Funktion des (kulturell und historisch) Fremden im gesamten Roman. Die Beschreibung jener Welt hat zwar ihren Ausgangspunkt im Okzident (in den Ängsten, Begehren und Fantasien des Okzidents), jedoch so, dass das Material der *écriture* mit dem Überschuss der Beschreibungen, den Paradoxa der beteiligten Diskurse von Historismus und Orientalismus, sowie den Transgressionen jene Undurchdringlichkeit der *matière* hervorbringt, in der die Körperlichkeit und die existentielle sowie historische Fremdheit des anderen Subjekts aufgehoben ist. Angesichts der Erfahrung dieser Fremdheit ist das kognitive Subjekt trunken, *égaré*. Das, was sich durch die Heterogenität der Narrative in der Visualität ereignet, ist eine Umkehrung der Konstellation zwischen Subjekt und Objekt. Wie beim *punctum* der Fotografie, wird das Subjekt zum »beeindruckten«, verletzten Objekt eines sich der Sichtbarkeit entziehenden Fremden.

Die *mise en abyme* denunziert in »Salammbô« den Eurozentrismus des orientalistischen Diskurses und entmachtet zugleich diesen Diskurs durch die Konfrontation mit einer sich der Vereinnahmung durch das Auge entziehenden fremden Welt. Mit einem bisweilen touristischen Blick werden die Barbaren auf der einen Seite durch rassische Stereotypen dargestellt; der Orient ist eine Art »Dictionnaire des idées reçues«,[40] eine Projektion von Stereotypen des Okzidents;[41] auf der anderen Seite gleichen sie einer gigantischen Ansammlung von Differenzen; in ihnen werden Heterotopien inszeniert, jene Kreuzungen heterogener Diskurse, die quer zu den Wissens-

systemen stehen.[42] Diese Beschreibungen enthalten Spuren der (historisch) fernen Welt, deren »positivistisch« recherchierte Details nicht in das Ganze einzubinden sind. Der Orientalismus Flauberts wird dadurch auf eine metakritische Dimension gehoben. Die durchaus als dekonstruktiv einzuschätzende Textarbeit ist mit der heutiger postkolonialer Texte vergleichbar.[43] In dieser Hinsicht geht bei »Salammbô« das in der Materialität des narrativen Textes implizierte heterogene Wissen auch über die kritischen Versuche von Said hinaus, der den Orientalismus durch authentische, autochthone Ausdrucksformen sog. »orientalischer« Kulturen zu überwinden versucht, bleibt doch das Ziel einer authentischen Beschreibung der Kulturen im alten Diskurs von Identität und Alterität. Flaubert zeigt zwar, dass die »Essenz« des Orients eurozentrische Diskurse sind, dass aber jenseits ihrer Grenzen etwas »anderes« existiert, das die Identität des eurozentrischen Subjektes bedroht, es folglich – ganz im Sinne der Betroffenheit durch das »punctum« der Fotografie – irritiert und bewegt.[44]
In der Konstellation zwischen dem Selben und dem Anderen, dem Eigenen und dem Fremden (zwischen dem »wir« und »den anderen«), die vom Roman inszeniert wird, lassen sich verschiedene Verfahren identifizieren, die die Blicke umkehren und vom Anderen her auf den Ort des Sprechersubjekts richten. Die Sprache Flauberts macht deutlich, dass sie eine Wieder-Gabe von Diskursen ist,[45] also keine Aussage über den Anderen, sondern eine Inszenierung des Selbst ist. Sie ist durch Ironie durchkreuzt, jene »romantische« Ironie, die – wie Paul de Man gezeigt hat (1971) – eine sich selbst spiegelnde Falte in die Sprache des Subjektes einschreibt. Ironiesignale sind bei Flaubert bekanntlich Kausalsätze.[46] Die Ironie lokalisiert den Ort des Sprechers »Salammbôs« im Frankreich des *Second Empire* und wendet sich gegen diesen. Der Erzähler scheint nicht verbergen zu wollen, dass die »barbarischen« Bräuche von Karthago als dem Erzfeind Roms, der *sottise* und auch *cruauté* des Bürgertums auffällig ähnlich sind; ebenso verhält es sich mit dem Merkantilismus der Priester des Moloch und der Hypokrisie der katholischen Kirche; auch die Ähnlichkeit des antiken Despoten Hamilkar mit dem *Empereur* der Franzosen bleibt nicht verborgen, der die demokratischen Hoffnungen der Revolution von 1848 niedergeschmettert hatte u.s.w.

a. Perspektivismus als Opazität des Gegenstandes: Grenzen und Chancen der Sichtbarkeit

Die Sichtbarkeit wird im Prinzip auch schon in »Madame Bovary«, dem realistischen Roman *par excellence*, dadurch problematisiert, dass der Blick auf die Welt durch eine jeweils personale Perspektive mediatisiert ist und jenen Perspektivismus einleitet, der über André Gide[47] zur Kritik des Realismus durch den »Antiroman« der »Nouveaux Romanciers« führen wird. Und bereits bei »Madame Bovary« zeigt sich, dass die Sprache kein offenes Fenster zur Welt ist, sondern eher jenes opake Medium, das den Blick auf das Sichtbare inszeniert und seine Determinanten (den Bildschirm und die Rahmung) dekonstruiert. Dieses Prinzip ist auch der Komplexität und Vielschichtigkeit der sog. realistischen Romane von Flaubert inhärent[48] und erklärt, dass Flaubert von den »Nouveaux Romanciers« – von Nathalie Sarraute zu Alain Robbe-Grillet – als Vorläufer der Kritik des Realismus gehuldigt werden konnte. Das Paradoxon der Sichtbarkeit ist auch in der Malerei des sog. Realismus signifikant. Ich verweise auf das berühmte Bild von Courbet mit dem Titel »L'atelier du peintre, allégorie réelle«, das Courbet als Manifest in der alternativen Ausstellung von Bildern des Realismus während der Pariser Weltausstellung 1855 zeigte. Das Thema dieses Gemälde ist nicht die äußere Welt, sondern der Blick des Künstlers. Die »realistische« Landschaft, die der Maler erschafft, ist dort keineswegs die Abbildung der sich vor den empirischen Augen des Malers befindlichen realen Welt, sondern die Begegnung mit der Idee der Muse und mit ihrem Körper, der den im Mittelpunkt der Gesellschaft stehenden Dichter inspiriert.[49] Die Darstellung der »Welt« ist zwar opak. Die Grenzen der Sichtbarkeit sind aber auch ihre Chancen: Durch die Selbstbezüglichkeit wird das Medium selbst als Vermittler zwischen Erzählen und Welt sichtbar; auch die Subjektivität des Blickes sowie die Passagen über die Körperlichkeit des Subjektes werden erkennbar.

b. Visualität: Bewegliche Gerichtetheit der Blicke und topologische Indeterminiertheit

Flauberts Perspektivismus hatte schon bei »Madame Bovary« zu einer (axiologischen) Indeterminiertheit geführt, die das eigentliche Skandalon des Romans war: Die Unterscheidung zwischen Gutem und Bösem war nicht mehr möglich, so die Begründung für die Verurteilung Flauberts seitens des Richters. Diese Unmöglichkeit der Differenzierung ist nun auch auf der mimetischen Ebene das zentrale Moment dieses sog. historischen Romans: Der Blick wechselt zwischen verschiedenen Fokalisatoren. Mal blicken die Barbaren auf die hoch zivilisierte Kultur Karthagos und sind durch ihre Exzesse erstaunt, mal verhält es sich umgekehrt. Analog zu einer selbstreflexiven Kamera, bei der das Medium, der Bildschirm und die Rahmung sichtbar werden, inszeniert auch hier der Blick durch verschiedene Formen der Fokalisation sich selbst als Medium. Das Staunen der Barbaren beim Anblick der durch die zivilisierte Kultur Karthagos vollzogenen Massaker gestaltet die Inkommensurabilität der Gewalt noch expressiver. Die politisch und rituell stark kodifizierte Zivilisation Karthagos ist dabei mit den im Chaos lebenden Barbaren selbst austauschbar, so auch in der Szene der Massaker der Söldner oder der Kinderopferungen durch lebendiges Verbrennen in den von gierigen Flammen erfassten Öffnungen des Molochs. Die Ununterscheidbarkeit dekonstruiert die Opposition zwischen Zivilisation und Barbarei. Eine klare Differenzierung des Blickes in »wir« und »die anderen« ist nicht mehr möglich. Diese Austauschbarkeit der Blicke wird durch die Heterogenität der Symbolik gestützt, deren markantes Beispiel die Szene der gekreuzigten Löwen ist, welche eine blasphemische Ähnlichkeit mit der Ikonographie der Kreuzigung Christi aufweist und die historische Achse der kulturkritischen Perspektive auf die Gegenwart verlängert.[50] Jenseits des historistischen Details der Löwenopfer als symbolische Zerstörung des politischen Feindes Roms (in den Quellen gilt der Löwe für Karthago als Symbol des verhassten Roms) konnotiert der Überschuss der Beschreibung eine gefährliche Nähe zum Christentum.

c. Kulturelle und historische Ferne als Inszenierung der Inkommensurabilität des Fremden

»Salammbô« potenziert die Wahrnehmung des Fremden durch die historische Fremdheit. Das »Abenteuer« der Narrative in diesem Roman ermöglicht es, das »Tun« des Subjektes im Umgang mit dem Anderen zu beobachten. Zum einen haben wir bezüglich *Salammbô* wie auch bezüglich der »Voyage en Orient« festgestellt, dass die Repräsentation des Orients eine Projektion von Stereotypen des Okzidents ist – auch Flauberts Darstellung des Orients sagt vielmehr über die Imagination, Träume und Ängste der Franzosen des *Second Empire* als über die andere Kultur aus –, zum anderen wird durch den Versuch, die historische Fremdheit zu rekonstruieren, auch die Grenze der Darstellbarkeit des (kulturell und historisch) Fremden unterstrichen. Dieser Roman verbindet also Orientalismus und Historismus in fruchtbarer Weise, indem er beide in ihrem Telos herausfordert. Diese Herausforderung geschieht über die Visualität. Der Roman stellt die Frage nach der Sichtbarkeit des kulturell und historisch Fremden und nach dem narratologischen Umgang mit seiner Darstellung. Ähnlich wie die Fotografie ist auch dieser Roman paradoxal. Er ist Abbild eines Wissens über die Realität und zugleich die Auflösung dieses Wissens in einer fremd werdenden Heterogenität, in der lediglich Fragmente erkennbar bleiben; er ist Wiedergabe und Inszenierung, Reproduktion und Montage zugleich. Ähnliches gilt für die Episteme, die sich mit der neuen Technologie, der Fotografie, ergeben, wie sich anhand der orientalistischen Reisen darstellen lässt. Das Fremde soll positivistisch und fotografisch erfasst, ethnographisch kartographiert werden. Gerade aber aus Flauberts »Voyage en Orient« und den »Carnets de Voyage« von Maxime du Camp und Flaubert wird ersichtlich, dass die Reise zwar dokumentarisch vorbereitet wird, jedoch die Visualisierung des Orients vornehmlich eine Inszenierung vom Platz des Eigenen aus ist.[51] Bei Flaubert zeigt sich aber auch, dass sich andererseits der Blick bei der Wahrnehmung des Fremden mit den Grenzen des *studiums* konfrontiert sieht.

Die narrativen Verfahren im Zusammenhang mit der Visualität bewirken in diesem Roman, dass die Zeichen kein Identitätssystem konstituieren. Das Heterogene verhindert, dass das Differente als empirische Gestalt gesehen werden kann. Das Differente bleibt Prozess, es gerinnt nicht zu einem Signifikat in einem System von Oppositionen, die den Ort der Identität des Wahrnehmenden, den *origo* seiner Rede, affirmieren. Vielmehr bleibt die Differenz ein unabgeschlossenes (differenzielles) Prinzip, das die Identität des Sehenden irritiert. Der scheiternde Versuch, die heterogenen Bilder zu identifizieren, konfrontiert den Leser mit den eigenen axiologischen, kognitiven, erkenntnistheoretischen und ethischen Einstellungen. Dies führt auch zu einer destruktiven Arbeit auf axiologischer Ebene: Das Monsterhafte der beschriebenen Welt wird zum Bestandteil der Zivilisation. Die Wildnis ist in der Zivilisation,[52] das wilde Denken ist die andere Seite der Rationalität (Lévi- Strauss). Damit erreicht Flaubert eine Form des Exotischen, das die Blickrichtung des Anthropologen kritisch auf das Selbst zurückwirft, eine Literaturform, die im 20. Jahrhundert durch Michel Leiris und Victor Ségalen erreicht wird.[53] Wie beachtlich die Ergebnisse der Textarbeit sind, wird deutlich, wenn man bedenkt, dass gegen Ende des Jahrhunderts der durch Maurice Barrès kollektiv ausgedehnte »Egotismus« eines nationalen Ichs die anderen Kulturen als »barbarisch« ausgrenzt.[54] Dagegen legen die im Roman inszenierten Blicke die Ambivalenz der französischen Kultur offen, die sich zwischen dem aufkommenden Nationalismus und der exotischen Anziehung durch die kolonialistisch eroberten und in Weltausstellungen bestaunten Fremden befindet.

In unserer Analyse der Materialität des Textes haben wir einen Widerstreit zwischen Visualität und Narrativität festgestellt:

Die visuelle und textuelle Materialität des Romans erzeugt einen Raum des Widerstandes gegen den Versuch des Lesers, die als »natürlich« angenommenen Konstellationen von Identität und Alterität im Text wiedererkennen zu wollen. Die Narrative, anhand derer das Subjekt seinen *origo* bestimmt und Position zum Anderen bezieht, wird zu einem dynamischen Raum, in dem diese Position erst als Prozess erarbeitet werden muss. Der Prozess inszeniert eine – zwischen dem Subjekt und den Dingen bewegliche – Blick-Konstellation, die die jeweiligen Einstellungen (zur Welt, zum Selbst und zum Anderen) sichtbar macht. Die Dynamik der Bilder macht erst den Blick, seine Offenheit oder aber Ausgrenzungskraft, sein Bewusstsein oder die Delegierung an das Regime des gesellschaftlich geführten Auges bewusst.

Das widerstreitende Verhältnis von Visualität und Narrativität führt zu beträchtlichen Ergebnissen. Die Materialität des Mediums der Schrift ist eine Provokation für die Epistemologie des Realismus ebenso wie für die der Gattung des Historischen Romans:

Was den realistischen Roman betrifft, so lässt sich für »Salammbô« eine ähnliche These aufstellen, wie sie bei Jorge Luis Borges, der mit höchster Virtualität Heterotopien von Diskursen zum Zentrum seiner eigenen Narrative gemacht hat, hinsichtlich »Bouvard et Pécuchet« zu lesen ist: Der letzte Roman von Flaubert habe, so Borges, der späteren Forschung eine Falle gestellt; die diskursive Inkohärenz zwinge den Leser, Position zu beziehen und den eigenen Standort offen zu legen. Jene Literaturwissenschaft, die den Roman als nicht gelungenen Versuch des Realismus kritisiert hatte, wurde von der topologischen Indeterminiertheit des Romans gezwungen, die eigenen mimetischen Interpretationszwänge zu offenbaren.[55]

Als historischer Roman setzt sich *Salammbô* kulturkritisch mit Geschichtsdarstellungen auseinander. Dieser Roman verwirklicht den perspektivischen Modus, den sich Carlo Ginzburg in einem kürzlich erschienenen Interview[56] für den Historiker gewünscht hat:

> C'est un renversement du point de vue traditionel: l'objet regarde le créateur, et il y a de l'étrangeté dans ce regard [...]. Faire de l'histoire, c'est rendre le passé le plus étrange possible.

Ginzburg bezieht sich exakt auf die in unserer Analyse des »historischen Romans« Flauberts beschriebene phänomenologische Perspektive, die durch die auf Maurice Merlau-Ponty und Roland Barthes zurückgehende Metaphorik des Blickes zu erfassen ist: Durch die materielle (mediale) Verfremdung schaut das historische Objekt den Schöpfer mit fremdem Blick an. Erkenntnisfördernde Narrative der Geschichte wären also solche, die die Vergangenheit – ähnlich wie die Kreuzigungsszene in »Salammbô« – so fremd wie möglich darstellen.[57]

In seinem Interview spricht Carlo Ginzburg mit Bezug auf das aktuelle politische Phänomen Italiens (Silvio Berlusconi) von der Dringlichkeit einer solchen Arbeit an der Wahrnehmung. Angesichts der sich heute aufdrängenden »Realität der Bilder« ist es dringlich, das Auge vom Medium zu trennen und jene Blicke zurückzugewinnen, die uns unsere eigene Position bei Inszenierungen und Interfaces bewusst machen. Dazu braucht man eine Phänomenologie des Bildes, die es erlaubt, das Unbehagen am Sichtbaren und Unsichtbaren länger auszuhalten.[58]

ANMERKUNGEN

[1] Auch die neuere Literaturwissenschaft stellt die traditionelle Hermeneutik in Frage, die von den *litterae* abstrahiert, und strebt die Umkehrung des Lesens an, weg vom Denkinhalt hin zum Buchstaben. Bernhard Teuber hat z. B. mit diesem methodischen Vorgehen eine neue Lektüre der Mystik unternommen (vgl. Teuber, Bernhard, Sacrificium litterae: Allegorische Rede und mythische Erfahrung in der Rede des heiligen Johannes am Kreuz, München 2002).
[2] Vgl. Körner, Hans, »Keine Benennungen«. Wols: Bildmaterial, Bildbegriff und die »richtige Einstellung« des Betrachters, in: Andrea von Hülsen-Esch, Jean Claude Schmitt (Hg), Die deutsch-französische Kolloquienreihe zur »Methodik der Bildinterpretation« 1998-2000. Ein Erfahrungsbericht aus deutscher und französischer Perspektive, Bd.1-2, Göttingen 2002, Bd. 1, S. 259-303.
[3] Neben »Histoire de l'œil« von Georges Bataille (Oeuvres Complètes, T. I) ist auf den in der Zeitschrift »Documents« (No.4, Septembre 1929) erschienenen Artikel zu »Œil« hinzuweisen. Dieser Essay ist der Teil des »Dictionnaire«, mit dem Bataille eine Art »extraction lexicographique«, d. h. eine Entnahme der Organe aus ihrem scheinbar »natürlichen«, organischen Zusammenhang vollziehen wollte. In die gleiche Richtung ist auch der Text »Le gros orteil« zu situieren. Batailles (wie auch Artauds) Anliegen war es, durch die Annäherung heterogener Dinge in der Sprache auch die in der kulturellen Anatomie des Abendlandes bestehenden Hierarchien zwischen dem Kopf als dem höherwertigen Sitz der Vernunft einerseits und den Sinnen andererseits zu dekonstruieren und eine offene Topographie des Körpers nachzuzeichnen. Ich verweise in diesem Zusammenhang auf die Essays von Denis Hollier, La prise de la Concorde suivi de Les dimanches de la vie. Essais sur Georges Bataille, Paris, insbesondere »L'œil pinéal«, S. 157f.
[4] Vgl. Borsò, Vittoria, Foucault und Binswanger der Traum, der Tod und der Andere, in: Heinz, R./ Tress, W. (Hg.), Traumdeutung. Zur Aktualität der Freudschen Traumtheorie, Wien 2001, S. 117-128.
[5] Die lateinische Etymologie des Begriffes »figura« geht auf lat. »fingere« (bilden, formen, gestalten) zurück, mit dem Marcus Terentius Varro die Tätigkeit des Bildhauers, des »fictor« bezeichnete. Zu erwähnen ist Varros historisches Bilderbuch (mit dem Titel »imagines«), in dem 700 Bilder bedeutender Griechen und Römer, jedes mit einem Epigramm, dargestellt waren.
[6] Ähnlich wie Foucault, wendet sich Lyotard gegen das Verständnis des Traums als Diskurs: »L'œil, c'est la force. Faire de l'inconscient un discours, c'est omettre l'énergétique. C'est se faire complice de toute la ratio occidentale, qui tue l'art en même temps que le rêve« (Lyotard, a.a.O, S. 14). Mit der Definition des Auges als »Kraft« schließt Lyotard an Merleau-Ponty an, wobei das Energetische, besonders durch Lacan, auf den Blick bezogen wird (siehe weiter unten).
[7] Ich unterscheide zwischen Visualität und Sichtbarkeit (oder »Visibilität« als Entlehnung aus dem Latein). Ersteres meint allgemeine Phänomene, die den »Visus«, den Gesichtssinn, betreffen; zweiteres zielt auf die Transitivität des Gesichtssinns zum Objekt hin (»visibilia«). Im ersten Fall stehen die Handlungen des Subjektes in Bezug auf den Gesichtssinn, im zweiten die Dinge im Zentrum, die sich möglicherweise der Sicht öffnen.
[8] In seiner Untersuchung der Narrative in der aktuellen Mediengesellschaft weist Wolfgang Müller-Funk auf die mit der Avantgarde verbundenen Krise der traditio-

nellen Erzählformen hin. Diese Krise betrifft die Erfahrung der Zeit, den Modus des Erinnerns und die Konstruktion des Selbst; als Gegenbewegung sei in den Massenmedien der Rückgriff auf die von der Avantgarde negativ sanktionierten Evidenz des Bildes sowie auf Gattungen (wie das Melodrama) und auf die aristotelische Mimesis zu konstatieren, weil die (durch Adorno als naiv-episch kritisierten) linearen Erzählformen orientierend wirken (vgl. Müller-Funk, Wolfgang, Die Kultur und ihre Narrative: eine Einführung, Wien 2002, S. 29, 31). Durch die Hinwendung zu den Bildmedien wird die Sichtbarkeit überhaupt erst mit einem doppelten Diskurs belegt; einerseits einem Vertrauen hinsichtlich der ikonischen Evidenz von Bildern, andererseits einem Krisendiskurs mit Bezug auf die mimetischen Implikationen des Bildes (vgl. auch Müller-Funk, Wolfgang 2002, S. 31). Der Krisendiskurs der Moderne trage indes »das Kainsmal der ›différance‹ (Derrida)« in sich, so auch Müller-Funk anhand der Rezeption der einflussreichen Medienkritik Benjamins (2002, S. 22).

[9] Für den Übergang vom Realismus zur Moderne vgl. Baskakov Alexej, Vom Realismus zur Moderne: die Darstellung des antiken Orients in »Salammbô« von Gustave Flaubert und »Joseph und seine Brüder« von Thomas Mann, Würzburg 1999.

[10] Jacques Lacan unterscheidet im Medium, durch das die Blicke vermittelt werden, zwei miteinander verbundene Dimensionen: den Bildschirm und die Rahmung, die auch die Einstellung des Betrachters implizieren. Bildschirm und Rahmen, und damit die Art der Einstellung zum Gegenstand, werden erst in Verbindung mit einem selbstbezüglichen Material (mit selbstbezüglichen ästhetischen Formen und Inszenierungen) sichtbar. Wird die Einstellung erkennbar, so ist der Blick potentiell selbstreflexiv und beweglich. Bleiben Bildschirm und Rahmung unsichtbar, so sieht das Auge nach dem Blickregime der dem Medium mitgegebenen (gesellschaftlichen) Einstellungen. Auf der Grundlage dieser Modi (das dem Medium aufgegebene Auge und der aktive und selbstreflexive Blick) analysiert Žižek die Blickregie des Hollywood-Kinos (Žižek, Slavoj, Lacan in Hollywood, Wien 2000). Für Jacques Lacan ist auf das »Séminaire XI« hinzuweisen (vgl. auch Lacan, Jacques, Die Spaltung von Auge und Blick, in: Das Seminar von Jacques Lacan, Buch XI, Weinheim/Berlin 1980, S. 73-126).

[11] Zur terminologischen Klärung ist zu unterscheiden zwischen Alterität und Differenz. Den Begriff der »Differenz« benutze ich im Sinne von »différance«, d. h. im Sinne eines unabschließbaren Prozesses des Differierens (Derrida, L'écriture et la différence, Paris 1967), während mit Alterität der Fall gemeint ist, in dem die Differenz bei der Differenzierung von Identität und Alterität zum Stillstand kommt. Die Alterität wäre dabei eine Projektion des Anderen vom System des Eigenen aus. Weiterhin unterscheide ich im Sinne von Bernhard Waldenfels zwischen dem Anderen und dem Fremden, Ersteres enthalten im kognitiven System des Eigenen, Letzteres eine Andersheit, die den Horizont des Verstehens überschreitet (Waldenfels, Bernhard, Der Stachel des Fremden, Frankfurt/Main 1998).

[12] Die Tragweite der Untersuchungen von Blickkonstellationen im Verhältnis zur Alterität und Differenz zeigte sich u. a. bei der Analyse der Sichtbarkeit in der Lyrik des deutschen Expressionismus. Vgl. Borsò, Vittoria, La invisibilidad de lo real y la expresión de la escritura, in: Sileno 10, Felix Duque (Hg.), (2001), S. 50-60.

[13] Vgl. Jacques Lacan, Seminaire *XI*.

[14] Dass die Visualität ein Ereignis, ist das die Welt konstituiert, zeigt auch Rolf Nohr im Zusammenhang mit der Kartographierung des Raums im Fernsehen, wobei er vom Bühlerschen Modell der Orientierung im Raum (Ich-, Hier-, Jetzt-Origo) ausgeht. Vgl. seinen Beitrag im vorliegenden Band.

[15] Vgl. Waldenfels, Bernhard, Nähe und Fremde des Leibes, in: Behrens, Rudolf, Roland Galle (Hg.), Menschengestalten. Zur Kodierung des Kreatürlichen im modernen Roman, Würzburg 1995, S. 11-24.
[16] Zu Roland Barthes' Theorie und Praxis der *écriture* vgl. Ette, Ottmar, Roland Barthes. Eine intellektuelle Biographie, Frankfurt a. M. 1998.
[17] Der Hiatus zwischen Sichtbarkeit und Unsichtbarkeit, zwischen Empirie der Körpersysteme und Erfahrung des Leibs ist Teil einer im 19. Jahrhundert sich verschärfenden Dualität von positivistischen Systemen und Alteritäts- bzw. Fremdheitserfahrungen. Aber besonders die experimentelle Kunst und Literatur zu Beginn des 20. Jahrhunderts geben Zeugnis vom Misstrauen der Schriftsteller gegenüber dem Bild, insoweit es als Stütze der mimetischen Funktion der Kunst dienen kann. Vgl. auch Müller-Funk, 2002, S. 31.
[18] Vgl. Barthes, Roland, De la parole à l'écriture, in: Ders., Le grain de la voix: entretiens 1962-1980, Paris 1981, S. 10-13.
[19] Wie Foucaults Analyse der Mikrophysik der Macht gezeigt hat, ist das Subjekt als den kulturellen Diskursen unterworfen, also als sub-jectum anzusehen (vgl. u. a. Foucault, Michel, Introduction à l'usage des plaisirs (Bd. II der Histoire de la Sexualité) Paris 1984).
[20] Pascal Bonitzer sagt über die Großaufnahme, dass sie »induit directement un régime pictographique de l'image de cinéma« (1985:89). Godard wird mit den »Vor-Bildern« der Malerei im Film Passion ähnliches tun (vgl. Paech, Joachim, Passion oder die Einbildungen des Jean-Luc Godard, Frankfurt/Main 1989). Das in diesem Sinne charakterisierte expressive Bild führt die »Nouvelle Vague« zu einem explizit antimimetischen Moment des Kinos.
[21] Vgl. Krämer, Sybille, Sprache, Sprechakt, Kommunikation, Frankfurt/Main 2001.
[22] Im erwähnten Buch zur Figur betont Lyotard die Opazität des Zeichens, d.h. die Intransitivität der Figur hinsichtlich der Sichtbarkeit und der Erkenntnis des Anderen, eine Qualität, die dagegen dem Symbol zugeschrieben wird (Lyotard, a.a.O., S. 13).
[23] Auf der Grundlage des Mediumbegriffs von Luhmann habe ich versucht, verschiedene Formen des Schriftmediums zu differenzieren. Vgl. Borsò, Vittoria, Gedächtnis und Medialität: Die Herausforderung der Alterität«, in: Vittoria Borsò / Gerd Krumeich / Bernd Witte (Hg.), Medialität und Gedächtnis. Interdisziplinäre Beiträge zur kulturellen Verarbeitung europäischer Krisen, Stuttgart, S. 23-53.
[24] Derrida, Jacques, L'écriture et la différence, Paris 1967. Zu den jüdischen Wurzeln jenes Verständnisses der Schrift, das die Präsenz durch die Differenz ersetzt, verweise ich auf die von Gerhard Sellin und François Vouga herausgegebene Monographie, die die biblische Eschatologie vom (toten) Buchstaben her und nicht vom (lebendigen) Wort entsprechend der platonischen Tradition deutet (Sellin, Gerhard, François Vouga (Hg.), Logos und Buchstabe. Mündlichkeit und Schriftlichkeit im Judentum und Christentum der Antike, Tübingen 1996.)
[25] Dietmar Kamper situiert die Leiblichkeit in der Materialität der Schrift, die er als »vor-schriftliche« (im Sinne von vorsymbolische und diskursive) Form des Graphischen bezeichnet (vgl. Kamper, Dietmar, Zur Soziologie der Imagination, in: Hans Ulrich Gumbrecht/Ludwig Pfeiffer (Hg.), Schrift, München 1993, S. 193-200).
[26] Vgl. hierzu Borsò, Vittoria, Der Körper der Schrift und die Schrift des Körpers. Transpositionen des Liebesdiskurses in europäischer und lateinamerikanischer Literatur, in: Borsò, Vittoria et al., Schriftgedächtnis – Schriftkulturen, Stuttgart 2002, S. 323-342.

[27] Barthes, Roland, L'Empire des signes, Paris 1970.

[28] Dieses Prinzip stellt für Judith Butler die Grundlage ihrer Konzeption der Performanz, durch die sich das Subjekt trotz der Zwänge des Diskurses konstituiert (z. B. Butler, Judith, Körper von Gewicht. Die diskursiven Grenzen des Geschlechts, Frankfurt a. M. 1995, besonders S. 51-84, 189-219).

[29] In Anbetracht der Notwendigkeit des »common sense« für den gesellschaftlichen Gemeinschaftssinn erfasst Müller-Funk mit dem »common sense« ein Phänomen, das hinsichtlich der Makronarrative über die negativen Konnotationen der Theorie Roland Barthes‹ (und des Poststrukturalismus) hinausgeht: »Dieser symbolisch-narrative Gemeinbestand einer Kultur lässt sich als das begreifen, was einer Kultur »Stabilität verleiht und ihr die Härte gegen Devianz« ermöglicht. Dabei kann man den *common sense* als ein Insgesamt der in einer Kultur verfügbaren, nicht-impliziten, in den Zustand der Selbstverständlichkeit versetzten Wissensbestände begreifen oder aber auch als ein eigenes Symbolsystem, das mit anderen (Wissenschaft, Religion) in Interaktion steht, aber durchaus eigenen Gesetzmäßigkeiten folgt« (Müller-Funk, a.a.O., S. 155).

[30] So Walter Benjamin in »Über einige Motive bei Baudelaire«: »Die Krisis der künstlerischen Wiedergabe, die sich so abzeichnet, lässt sich als integrierender Teil einer Krise in der Wahrnehmung selbst darstellen«. Vgl. Benjamin, Walter, Über Einige Motive bei Baudelaire, in: Ders., Gesammelte Schriften. Unter Mitwirkung von Theodor W. Adorno und Gershom Scholem, hg. von Rolf Tiedemann und Hermann Schweppenhäuser, Bd. I.1: Abhandlungen. Frankfurt a. M., 1991, S. 605-653, hier S. 645.

[31] Vgl. Grivel, Charles, Reise-Schreiben, in : Gumbrecht, Hans Ulrich, Ludwig K. Pfeiffer (Hg.), Materialität der Kommunikation, Frankfurt a. M. 1998, S. 615-634.

[32] So heißt es zum Beispiel in Flauberts »Voyage en Orient«: »Je voulais sortir de chez moi, de mon moi, aller n'importe où,, partout, avec la fumée de ma cheminée et les feuilles de mon acacia« (Flaubert, Gustave, Voyages, T. II, Paris 1948, S. 16).

[33] Schon Froehner (aus der Sicht der Altertumswissenschaften und der Archäologie) und Sainte Beuve (wegen der ästhetischen Verstöße durch die Darstellung des Schrecklichen) hatten die historische Glaubwürdigkeit des Romans bemängelt. In ähnliche Richtung geht auch die Kritik der traditionellen Literaturgeschichtsschreibung, etwa von Thibaudet (Histoire de la littérature française de 1789 à nos jours, Paris 1969), für den es Flaubert nicht gelingt, das Prinzip des realistischen Romans nach Lukács zu verwirklichen, nämlich die antike Welt näher zu bringen. Akzeptiert man das Mimesis-Postulat, so kann die Rettung des Romans nur durch das ästhetizistische Paradigma erfolgen, wie es z. B. durch Corrada Biazzo Curry geschieht: »Flaubert voulait écrire une oeuvre gratuite, qui se tint debout par la seule force du style« (Description and Meaning in Three Novels by Gustave Flaubert, New York 1999, S.107). Man muss hingegen der neueren Forschung zu diesem Roman zustimmen, die die Interpretation im Sinne des historischen Romans oder im Sinne der Gesellschaftskritik als einseitig ansehen (z. B. Friedrich, Sabine, Die Imagination des Bösen: zur narrativen Modellierung der Transgression bei Laclos, Sade und Flaubert, Tübingen 1998; Ley, Klaus (Hg.), Verborgene Lektüren. »Salammbô« und der zeitgenössische historische Roman in England, in: Ders. (Hg.), Flauberts »Salammbô« in Musik, Malerei, Literatur und Film. Aufsätze und Texte, Tübingen 1998, S. 3-36; Yee, Jennifer, La »Tahoser« de Gautier et la »Salammbô« de Flaubert: L'Orientale et le voyage au-de la de l'histoire, in: Australian Journal of French Studies. 36,2 (1999), S. 188-199). Auch meine Analyse geht über die falsch gestellte Frage

nach dem Realismus und dem historischen Roman hinaus. Das grundsätzliche Problem der kulturellen und historischen Alterität wird im Roman miteinander verknüpft. Die Konstruktion des kulturell und historisch Fremden durch den Text verbindet sich mit dem Ziel Flauberts einer indirekten Kritik gleichermaßen am realistischen wie am historistischen Paradigma.

[34] Flaubert selbst bekennt sich zu den sich als engagiert aufklärerisch begreifenden zeitgenössischen Historikern wie etwa Jules Michelet (»Histoire romaine«) und Ernest Renan. Als historischer Roman soll »Salammbô« eine Art Antipode zu dem für die französische Gattung konstitutiven englischen Roman wie etwa in der »Early Church Novel« darstellen und veranschaulichen, welche Reaktionen auf allen Ebenen eintreten, wenn die Ordnung in einem bestimmten Augenblick durch das Einbrechen einer äußeren Kraft gestört wird (Ley 1998, S. 18 f.).

[35] Vgl. die entsprechende Untersuchung von André Stoll, Sous la tente du barbare: L'Espace de la seduction dans »Salammbô« de Flaubert, in: Bauer, Roger, Fokkema, Douwe (Hg.), Actes du XIIe congres de l'Association Internationale de Littérature Comparée, 1988 Munich, III: Espace et frontières dans la littérature (suite), München 1990, S. 146-152.

[36] Ich beziehe mich auf »L'Erotisme«, Paris 1957.

[37] Zur Bedeutung des Schleiers als mythischer Gründungsfigur der Schwelle zwischen Bekanntem und Unbekanntem (vgl. z. B. Vonessen, Franz, Der Mythos vom Weltschleier, Anaios Bd. IV, No.1 (1962) S. 1-31).

[38] Nicht selten konnotiert Flaubert die Heterogenität durch die Übertretung der Ordnung des Natürlichen bei der Verbindung von Leben und Tod oder Mensch und Maschine. Dies betrifft sowohl die Kultur Karthagos (z. B.: »On avait, dans les bâtiments des Syssites, douze cents esclaves nubiles, de celles qu l'on destinait aux prostitutions de la Grèce et de l'Italie, et leurs cheveux, rendus élastiques par l'usage des onguents, se trouvaient merveilleux pour les machines de guerre«, 1970, S. 292) als auch die Barbaren (»Un redoublement de fureur animait les Barbares. On les voyait au loin prendre la graisse des morts pour huiler leurs machines«, 1970, S. 292). Beides tritt übrigens im Kapitel zum Gott Moloch auf, dessen Beschreibung selbst durch die heterogene Verbindung von Mensch und Maschine konnotiert ist und eine expressionistische Filmdarstellung (z. B. *Metropolis* von Fritz Lang) in Erinnerung ruft.

[39] Vgl. Waldenfels, Bernhard, Cultura propria e cultura estranea. Il paradosso di una scienza dell'estraneo, in: Paradigmi, Anno X, no. 30 (Settembre-Dicembre 1992), S. 643-663; Der Stachel des Fremden, Frankfurt a. M. 1998; Topographie des Fremden, Studien zur Phänomenologie des Fremden 1, Frankfurt a. M. 1999.

[40] Siehe z. B. die Beschreibung der Barbaren im Kapitel »Le festin«. Auch die erste Beschreibung von Salammbô in diesem Kapitel entspricht den Stereotypen des orientalistischen Schönen.

[41] Z. B. »C'était une mode gauloise adaptée par le Suffète au besoin de la situation; les Gaulois se crurent devant une ville de leur pays. Ils attaquèrent avec mollesse et furent repoussés« (1970, S. 295). Es handelt sich um ein ausgezeichnete Beispiel sowohl für die Austauschbarkeit der Gegner als auch für die ironische Funktion der Projektion von Autostereotypen bei der angeblichen Darstellung der »Barbaren«.

[42] Foucault, Michel, Les mots et les choses, Paris 1966 und La bibliothèque fantastique, in: Raymonde Debray-Genette et al., Travail de Flaubert, Paris 1983, S. 103-122.

[43] Darauf weist auch E. L. Constable hin: »In questioning Said's own generalization,

I suggest that Flaubert uses the function of detail, the relation of part to whole in *Salammbô*, as a hyperbolic imitation, and critique, of Orientalism's cumulative, synthesizing use of details« (Constable, Edward L., Critical Departure : Salammbô's Orientalism, MLN, 111 (1996), S. 625-626, hier S. 627). Flaubert, wie die »Post-Said«-Kritiker inszenieren dagegen heterogene Kulturen (298); und weiterhin: »Instead, he finds an abundance of exotic details, distinctions, precisions, and characteristics, an overwhelming materiality of signifiers« (299).

[44] Ganz regelmäßig findet sich in den »Voyages« im Zusammenhang mit dem Blick auf die unbekannte Kultur der Übergang vom *studium* des Orients, das Flaubert deutlich als Zitat bürgerlicher Stereotypen markiert, zu Blicken, bei denen das anfänglich souveräne Subjekt mit dem Tod konfrontiert und betroffen ist. So z. B. die Beschreibung der Visionen auf der Nil-Fahrt, bei der zunächst das Auge das Bekannte sieht: »notre raïs Ibrahim, accroupi à la turque« oder »le second tenait la barre tout en fumant son chibouk de bois noir« (1970, S.16). Die Übergänge zur Betroffenheit gehen von der Auflösung der realistischen Landschaft in geradezu impressionistischen Farbflecken (»Sur l'autre rive, à gauche, c'était une teinte rose; plus c'était rapproché de terre, plus c'était rose. Le rose allait montant et s'affaiblissant, il devenait jaune, puis un peu vert; le vert pâlissait et, par un blanc insensible, gagnait le bleu qui faisait la voûte sur nos têtes, puis se fondait la transition (brusque) des deux grandes couleurs«) bis hin zur stellenweisen Auflösung der Syntax, wobei die Auflösung von der plötzlichen Assoziation mit dem Grab begleitet wird: »Danse des matelots. – Joseph à ses fourneaux. – Barque penchée. – Le Nil au milieu du paysage. – Nous sommes au centre. – Les bouquets de palmiers à la base des pyramides de Sakkara semblent comme des orties au pied des tombeaux« (1970, S. 17).

[45] Bachtin, Michail, Esthétique et théorie du roman, Paris 1975.

[46] Vgl. Friedrich, Sabine, Die Imagination des Bösen: zur narrativen Modellierung der Transgression bei Laclos, Sade und Flaubert, Tübingen 1998; Klaus Ley, Verborgene Lektüren. »Salammbô« und der zeitgenössische historische Roman in England, in: ders. (Hg.), Flauberts »Salammbô«, in: Musik, Malerei, Literatur und Film. Aufsätze und Texte, Tübingen 1998.

[47] Ich beziehe mich z. B. auf die in »Les faux monnayeurs« implizite Romantheorie, auf die u. a. Lucien Dällenbachs Begriff der *mise en abyme* zurückgeht (Le récit spéculaire: essai sur la mise en abyme, Paris 1977).

[48] Vgl. auch den Hinweis von Klaus Ley hinsichtlich des bereits in »Madame Bovary« verfolgten Plans der Sprengung der bürgerlich-abendländischen Seh- und Erlebensgewohnheiten (1998, S. XI).

[49] Vgl. Borsò, Vittoria Körperbilder und Leiberfahrung in der Literatur der Moderne, in: Genge, Gabriele (Hg.), Sprachformen des Körpers in Kunst und Wissenschaft, Tübingen/Basel 2000, S. 159-173.

[50] Die Kreuzigungsszene der Löwen durch die Karthager ist eine auch von der Forschungsliteratur stets zitierte Kernstelle. Neben der Blasphemie konfrontiert die Expressivität des Bildes mit dem Monströsen einer jeden. Die Beschreibung wird außerdem durch den Blick der Barbaren fokalisiert (»Ainsi se vengeaient les paysans carthaginois quand ils avaient pris quelque bête féroce; ils espéraient par cet exemple terrifier les autres. Les Barbares, cessant de rire, tombèrent dans un long étonnement. ›Quel est ce peuple‹, pensaient-ils, ›qui s'amuse à crucifier des lions'« (1970, S. 54).

[51] Bei dem für die Gattung der »Voyage en Orient« einflußreichen Gérard de Nerval (»Voyage en Orient«, 1853) wird der Orient vor allem auf der Basis memorisierter

(fiktionaler) Prätexte visualisiert. Auch bei Nerval lässt sich – wenn auch weniger häufig – das Scheitern des »studiums« vor der Inkommensurabilität des Faszinosums feststellen. Ähnlichen Fragen widmet sich u. a. die zur Zeit in Arbeit befindliche Dissertation mit dem Titel »Blick(e). Orientalismen in französischer Literatur des 19. Jahrhunderts« von Susanne Stemmler, Düsseldorf.

[52] Ich beziehe mich auf Freuds Darstellung der (gewaltsamen) Alterität der Zivilisation in »qTotem und Tabu«, aber auch in »Der Mann Moses und die monotheistische Religion«. Vgl. hierzu die Analyse von Bernd Witte (Witte, Bernd, Sigmund Freuds »Der Mann Moses« und die jüdische Tradition, in: Borsò, Vittoria, Krumeich, Gerd, Witte, Bernd (Hg.), Medialität und Gedächtnis. Interdisziplinäre Beiträge zur kulturellen Verarbeitung europäischer Krisen, Stuttgart und Weimar 2001, S. 55-68).

[53] Vgl. hierzu auch Todorov, Tzvetan, Nous et les autres, Paris 1989. Angesichts dieser Befunde geht der Roman über die Ästhetisierung des Bösen hinaus, denn im Roman fehlt die Möglichkeit zur Situierung des (ästhetisch) Guten in einer autonom vom moralischen Diskurs bestehenden Gewalt. Die Welt »Salammbôs« ist nicht – im Sinne Nietzsches (1886) – jenseits von Gut und Böse. Vielmehr partizipiert jede Instanz, jede Figur, an dem politischen, institutionellen oder moralischen Bösen. So z. B. der Sklave, der als Diener zum Despot und Sklaventreiber wird, so Schahabarin, der Priester des Tanit, oder Salammbô selbst, welche einer Phèdre gleich, dem Mond geweiht und der Sonne verfallen ist.

[54] Ich verweise auf die Analyse der Ambivalenz in den Texten von Barrès durch Susanne Stemmler (Stemmler, Susanne, Unter dem Blick der Barbaren. Erinnerung und Alterität bei Maurice Barrès, in: Borsò, Vittoria, Krumeich, Gerd, Witte, Bernd (Hg), Medialität und Gedächtnis. Interdisziplinäre Beiträge zur kulturellen Verarbeitung europäischer Krisen, Stuttgart und Weimar 2001, S. 69-98) und auch auf die Dissertation von Susanne Stemmler.

[55] Vgl. Jorge Luis Borges, Vindicación de Bouvard et Pécuchet, in: ders., Prosa completa, Bd. 1, Barcelona 1980, S. 205-210.

[56] Interview mit Antoine de Baecque in: Libération, 10.2.2002, S. 40-41.

[57] Ähnlich argumentiert Ley in Bezug auf »Salammbô«. Vgl. Klaus Ley, a.a.O.,1998, S. X-XI.

[58] Das Unbehagen an der Kultur ist jene Seite, die jede Narrative begleitet, so Müller-Funk am Beispiel des Falls Caspar Hauser: »Kultur lässt sich als der Prozess begreifen, der das Unheimliche und Entsetzliche zum Verstummen zu bringen trachtet. Das ist der tiefste Antrieb aller Geschichtenerfinder rund um den jungen Mann mit dem falschen Namen: Würde die Erzählung gefunden und mit ihr der richtige Name, der die unverwechselbare individuelle Rolle im Ablauf des unbekannten, mysteriösen Geschehens symbolisch markiert, dann ließe sich eben jenes unerträgliche Unheimliche beseitigen, zumindest zur Ruhe bringen«. Ich verweise auch auf die im gleichen Zusammenhang stehenden Hinweise hinsichtlich des »horror vacui« bei der Ablehnung der Malerei der klassischen Moderne (Müller-Funk 2002, S. 150-151).

Narratologischer Auftakt

»Erzählerische Unzuverlässigkeit« in Literatur und Film

Anmerkungen zu einem Begriff zwischen Narratologie und Interpretationstheorie

TOM KINDT

Die kulturwissenschaftliche Diskussion hat sich in den letzten Jahren verstärkt dem Problem des Erzählens zugewandt.[1] Wer Kulturen verstehen will, dies ist in den ›cultural studies‹ mittlerweile die opinio communis, der kommt um eine Beschäftigung mit dem Phänomen des Erzählens nicht herum; denn narrative Prozesse sind für die Organisation und Tradierung von Wissen und mithin für die Entwicklung von Kulturen von grundlegender Bedeutung. So einhellig in aktuellen kulturwissenschaftlichen Studien gefordert wird, daß dem ›cultural turn‹ der geisteswissenschaftlichen Disziplinen ein ›narrative turn‹ zu folgen habe, so geschlossen wird in ihnen zugleich davon ausgegangen, daß für ein solches Vorhaben keine entscheidende Unterstützung von dem Bereich textwissenschaftlicher Theoriebildung zu erwarten sei, der seit den 1960er Jahren mit den Problemen des Erzählens beschäftigt ist: von der Narratologie.[2] Als ein Forschungsfeld, das seinen Namen, seine Ausarbeitung und Durchsetzung dem Strukturalismus verdankt, wird die Erzähltheorie von Seiten der Kulturwissenschaft entweder als konzeptionell zweifelhaft oder als methodologisch unzulänglich eingestuft.

Die konzeptionellen Vorbehalte gegenüber der Narratologie lassen sich daran ablesen, daß diese auch in den meisten derjenigen kulturwissenschaftlichen Untersuchungen vernachlässigt wird, die sich mit Fragen der narrativen Gestaltung von Texten befassen; wenn das Erzählen in der Kulturwissenschaft zum Thema wird, dann wird in der Regel auf rhapsodische Überlegungen von Walter Benjamin oder Jean-François Lyotard zurückgegriffen, nicht aber auf systematisierende Versuche wie die von Gérard Genette oder Gerald Prince. Die methodologischen Zweifel an der Narratologie zeigen sich in den vielen Vorschlägen zu einer kontextualistischen Neuausrichtung der Erzähltheorie, die in den letzten Jahren vorgebracht wurden. Die traditionelle Narratologie, so der Tenor dieser Vorschläge, stelle nicht die Mittel bereit, um die komplexen Probleme historischer und mithin auch kulturwissenschaftlicher Untersuchungen lösen zu können; die Narratologie müsse darum aus einem Instrumentarium für die strukturale Analyse von Texten in eine Theorie für deren funktionale Interpretation in kulturellen Kontexten umgestaltet werden.[3]

Die folgenden Überlegungen sollen dazu anregen, Kulturwissenschaft und Erzähltheorie in anderer Weise zueinander ins Verhältnis zu setzen, als dies aufgrund jener Bedenken bislang geschehen ist. Die bisherigen kulturwissenschaftlichen Stellungnahmen zur narratologischen Tradition übersehen fast ausnahmslos, daß die Erzähltheorie sich längst von ihrer strukturalistischen Herkunft emanzipiert hat und mittlerweile in Textdeutungen und Literaturgeschichten sehr heterogener Ausrichtung zumeist als Heuristik fungiert.[4] Wird die Narratologie im Sinne dieser Verwendung als ein bloßes ›toolkit‹ verstanden, verlieren die gegenüber ihrer Nutzung innerhalb der Kulturwissenschaft vorgebrachten Vorbehalte ihre Grundlage. In heuristischer Funktion kann die Narratologie im Rahmen kulturwissenschaftlicher Studien bedenkenlos eingesetzt werden, denn eine entsprechende Verwendung setzt weder ein Bekenntnis zum Strukturalismus noch eine Umgestaltung der Erzähltheorie in eine Interpretationstheorie voraus. Soll ein Begriff(szusammenhang) der narratologischen Diskussion in kulturwissenschaftlichen Kontexten heuristisch verwendet werden, muß lediglich geklärt werden, ob er sich tatsächlich in dieser Weise nutzen läßt.[5]

Diese Anmerkungen zum Verhältnis von Kulturwissenschaft und Erzähltheorie sollen im folgenden durch die Beschäftigung mit einem Begriff veranschaulicht werden, der in den vergangenen Jahren zu zahlreichen Stellungnahmen herausgefordert hat: mit dem Begriff des »unzuverlässigen Erzählers«.[6] Meine Überlegungen gliedern sich in zwei Teile: In einem ersten Abschnitt möchte ich die Skizze einer Klärung des Konzepts vorlegen; ihr Ansatzpunkt wird der Kontext der Begriffsprägung sein, ihr Ziel eine Modellierung des Begriffs, die ihn für eine als Beschreibungssprache verstandene Narratologie nutzbar macht (1). Die Hinweise, die sich aus der Explikation für die Diskussion des Begriffsgebrauchs ergeben, werde ich im zweiten Teil durch einen kurzen Blick auf die Verwendbarkeit des Konzepts zur Analyse filmischen Erzählens zu verdeutlichen versuchen (2).

1. UMRISSE EINER EXPLIKATION DES BEGRIFFS »ERZÄHLERISCHER UNZUVERLÄSSIGKEIT«

»Sie glauben doch wohl nicht, daß ein Arsch wie ich eine Geschichte ordentlich erzählt, oder?«[7] Mit diesen Worten beginnt der Erzähler von Stephen Frys Roman *Das Nilpferd* seinen Bericht und er scheint so schon in seinem ersten Satz offenzulegen, was Normalleser und Literaturwissenschaftler gemeinhin mühevoll selbst herausfinden müssen: ob man sich auf die Angaben eines Narrators verlassen kann, ob er als »zuverlässig« oder »unzuverlässig« einzustufen ist. Natürlich gibt Frys Erzähler mit seiner Bemerkung nur scheinbar Auskunft über seine »Zuverlässigkeit«, um tatsächlich in subtiler Weise die Komplexität der Bestimmung narrativer Vertrauenswürdigkeit zu veranschaulichen: Wenn man Frys Narrator glaubt, daß auf ihn kein Verlaß ist, warum sollte man ihm dann seine Eingangsbemerkung abkaufen? Und sofern man ihm, wie er es nahelegt, mißtraut, was macht man dann mit seinem Hinweis auf die Berechtigung solcher Vorbehalte?

Aus dieser Komplexität erklärt sich neben der Hartnäckigkeit, mit der das Konzept des »unzuverlässigen Erzählers« seit seiner Prägung in Wayne C. Booths *Rhetoric of Fiction* von 1961 diskutiert wird, auch die Fragestellung, an der sich die Debatte orientiert: Die Diskussion beschränkt sich weitestgehend auf die Frage der Operationalisierung von Booths Begriff, auf die Charakterisierung von Verwendungsbedingungen oder die Chancen einer Nutzung des Konzepts im Bereich der Filmanalyse. Versäumt wurde und wird dabei, was der Beschäftigung mit der Frage nach der Verwendung des Begriffs eigentlich vorauszugehen hat – dessen Explikation.[8]

Es sind zwei grundlegende, bislang aber kaum beachtete Eigenheiten von Booths Auseinandersetzung mit dem Phänomen »unzuverlässigen Erzählens«, bei denen eine Explikation des Begriffs ansetzen sollte: Zum einen gilt es den engen Zusammenhang zwischen Booths Bestimmung »erzählerischer Unzuverlässigkeit« und dem Ziel einer Rhetorik literarischer Normenvermittlung zu berücksichtigen, das er in seiner *Rhetoric of Fiction* in Fortführung des Ansatzes der Chicago School of Criticism verfolgt (1.1). Zum anderen darf nicht übersehen werden, daß Booths Verwendung des Konzepts nicht immer mit dessen Definition in Übereinstimmung steht (1.2).

1.1. Booth hat immer wieder betont, daß es ihm in *The Rhetoric of Fiction* um eine spezifische Form der Beschäftigung mit literarischen Erzähltexten zu tun war – um die Bestimmung der Techniken nämlich, mit denen in der Epik Wertvorstellungen vermittelt werden.[9] Im Nachwort zur zweiten Auflage seines Buches hat er dessen Anspruch noch einmal ex negativo umrissen:

> [T]his book [...] does not provide a complete ›theory of fiction‹, or a ›structuralist typology of narrative possibilities‹, or a developed doctrine of ›textuality‹, let alone of ›intertextuality‹. It does not, indeed it does not, develop an adequate ›Rezeptionstheorie‹, or an anatomy of criticism, or even a poetics of fiction. It is not a systematic science of anything, not even of ›narratology‹. And the list could go on.[10]

In der Booth-Rezeption sind solche Hinweise kaum beachtet worden; man hat die *Rhetoric of Fiction* zumeist umstandslos als Beitrag zur Narratologie gelesen und die von Booth eingeführten Begriffe im Bedarfsfall in den je eigenen Ansatz übernommen. Nicht gesehen wurde dabei, daß viele der Konzepte von Booth so eng mit dem Vorhaben einer rhetorischen Literaturbetrachtung korreliert sind, daß sie sich nicht ohne weiteres in jeden beliebigen literaturwissenschaftlichen Ansatz integrieren lassen. Zu diesen Konzepten zählt aufgrund seiner Definition auch der Begriff des »unzuverlässigen Erzählers« – Booth bestimmt ihn so:

»For a lack of better terms, I have called a narrator *reliable* when he speaks for or acts in accordance with the norms of the work (which is to say, the implied author's norms), *unreliable* when he is not.«[11]

Der Grund für die begrenzte Verwendbarkeit des Begriffs ist leicht zu sehen: Das Konzept »erzählerischer (Un-)Zuverlässigkeit« läßt sich im Gegensatz zu den meisten narratologischen Begriffen nicht in Untersuchungen mit unterschiedlicher interpretationstheoretischer Ausrichtung verwenden, weil es mit Hilfe des »impliziten Autors« bestimmt wird. Die Begriffsverwendung ist damit an eine Instanz gebunden, die für eine spezifische Sicht der Bedeutung literarischer Werke steht; wer das Konzept gebraucht, legt sich mit anderen Worten auf einen bestimmten Ansatz der Textinterpretation fest.[12]
Will man dies vermeiden und den »unzuverlässigen Erzähler« als Konzept einer interpretationsheuristisch ausgerichteten Narratologie erläutern, darf man bei der Begriffsbestimmung weder auf den »impliziten Autor« noch auf eine entsprechende interpretationstheoretische Kategorie wie den »Autor«, den »Rezipienten« o. ä. Bezug nehmen.[13] Man muß vielmehr versuchen, das Konzept so zu fassen, daß es als ›neutral‹ im Hinblick auf Interpretationstheorien klassifiziert werden kann. Dies läßt sich erreichen, indem Booths ›verfängliche‹ Definition in eine Art ›offenen Term‹ umformuliert wird, in einen Bestimmungsvorschlag, der auf die parenthetische Erläuterung zum Werkbegriff verzichtet: Der Erzähler in einem literarischen Werk ist *zuverlässig*, wenn er ausdrücklich für dessen Normen eintritt oder in Übereinstimmung mit ihnen handelt; er ist *unzuverlässig*, wenn dies nicht der Fall ist.
Die Modifikation der Begriffsbestimmung erweitert die Anschließbarkeit des Konzepts, indem sie dessen Zuschreibung als Aspekt einer umfassenden Textauslegung charakterisiert, die potentiell mit dem jeweils gewählten Interpretationsansatz variieren kann.[14]

1.2. Betrachtet man neben Booths Definition auch seine Verwendung des Begriffs »erzählerischer Unzuverlässigkeit« in der *Rhetoric of Fiction*, wird eine weitere Schwierigkeit deutlich, die sich im Zuge der Auseinandersetzung um das Konzept noch verschärft hat: Der Bestimmung zufolge wird einem Erzähler mit der Klärung seiner »Zuverlässigkeit« ein Platz in dem als Wertordnung verstandenen Werkganzen zugewiesen. In Booths exemplarischen Textanalysen geht es jedoch weniger um die moralischen Standpunkte von Narratoren als vielmehr um die prinzipielle Wohlgeformtheit ihrer Narration. Es kann hier dahingestellt bleiben, ob Booth die Ereigniswiedergabe in Erzählungen nur deshalb so genau untersucht, weil er die normative Vorbildlichkeit ihrer Erzähler überprüfen will, oder ob er nicht unter der Hand einen zweiten Begriff »erzählerischer (Un-)Zuverlässigkeit« einführt. In der Diskussion des Konzepts ist es jedenfalls durch das Festhalten an Booths Begriffsbestimmung und die gleichzeitige Ausrichtung an seinen Anwendungsbeispielen zu einer solchen Differenzierung der Begriffsbedeutung gekommen: Wenn die »Zuverlässigkeit« eines Erzählers geklärt werden soll, dann wird sowohl gefragt, ob er für das Werk, in dem er spricht, *axiologisch repräsentativ* ist, als auch untersucht, ob er die Geschichte, von der er berichtet, *mimetisch adäquat* wiedergibt.

Es ist leicht zu sehen, daß kein zwingender Zusammenhang zwischen diesen beiden Fragen besteht: Erzähler, die von einer Geschichte oder Welt adäquat berichten, müssen in normativer Hinsicht nicht für das Werk stehen, dessen Bestandteil sie sind. Und ein Werk kann in seinen Leitwerten durch seinen Erzähler repräsentiert werden, auch wenn dessen Rede narrative Seltsamkeiten birgt. Hinter dem Begriff des »unzuverlässigen Erzählers« verbergen sich also zwei gleichermaßen intuitionsgesättigte Konzepte, die hinsichtlich ihrer Zuschreibung voneinander logisch unabhängig sind. Das aber heißt, daß eine explikative Präzisierung des Begriffs zwei Spielarten »erzählerischer (Un-)Zuverlässigkeit« unterscheiden muß.[15]

Ich kann hier keine eingehende Herleitung der nachstehenden Erläuterungsvorschläge liefern; im vorliegenden Zusammenhang müssen die folgenden Hinweise genügen: Das erste Explikat stellt eine weniger mißverständliche Version von Booths Definition dar. Das zweite Explikat versucht eine Vorstellung auf den Begriff zu bringen, die bislang nur in Listen von Indikatoren für »erzählerische Unzuverlässigkeit«[16] und Verfahren zu ihrer Validierung[17] zum Ausdruck gekommen ist – die Vorstellung, daß für eine gerechtfertigte Zuschreibung des Konzepts zwei Bedingungen erfüllt sein müssen: Eine Ausdrucksverwendung setzt zum einen die Ermittlung textueller Anomalien und zum anderen die Bestimmung einer narrativen Konzeption voraus, die jene Eigenwilligkeiten motiviert.

Explikat 1 – *axiologisch (un-)zuverlässig*: Der Erzähler eines Abschnitts A eines literarischen Textes T ist *axiologisch zuverlässig*, wenn er ausdrücklich für die Leitwerte$_A$ eintritt oder in Übereinstimmung mit ihnen handelt; er ist *axiologisch unzuverlässig*, wenn dies nicht der Fall ist. (Es kann gelten A = T.)

Explikat 2 – *mimetisch (un-)zuverlässig*: Der Erzähler eines Abschnitts A eines literarischen Textes T ist *mimetisch zuverlässig*, sofern es keinen als Bestandteil einer Strategie beschreibbaren Anlaß gibt, an der Angemessenheit seiner Präsentation der $Geschichte_A$ (oder $Welt_A$) zu zweifeln; er ist *mimetisch unzuverlässig*, wenn dies nicht der Fall ist. (Es kann gelten A = T.)[18]

Es wäre zweifellos sinnvoll, die Unterscheidung zwischen »axiologisch« und »mimetisch unzuverlässigen Erzählern« weiter zu differenzieren. Vor allem für das Konzept »mimetischer Unzuverlässigkeit« erscheint eine Spezifizierung wünschenswert – etwa hinsichtlich der ›Dimensionen‹, in denen Geschichten unangemessen wiedergegeben werden[19], oder hinsichtlich der ›Reflektiertheit‹, mit der Erzähler zweifelhaft berichten[20]. Im vorliegenden Zusammenhang muß auf einen entsprechenden Versuch verzichtet werden.

2. ÜBERLEGUNGEN ZUR ATTRIBUTION DES BEGRIFFS »ERZÄHLERISCHER UNZUVERLÄSSIGKEIT«

Für die Charakterisierung der Verwendung des Konzepts »erzählerischer (Un-)Zuverlässigkeit« ergeben sich aus der Explikation zwei Aufgaben: Es sind einerseits die Bedingungen näher zu erläutern, die den Definitionen zufolge erfüllt sein müssen, damit ein Erzähler als »axiologisch« oder »mimetisch (un-)zuverlässig« eingestuft werden kann. Dies ist – wie bereits gesagt wurde – eine Fragestellung, die in der Debatte um den Begriff eingehend behandelt worden ist. Andererseits hat die Analyse des Begriffsgebrauchs genauer zu bestimmen, was in den Erläuterungsvorschlägen mit dem Konzept des Erzählers gemeint sein kann. Die abschließenden Hinweise werden sich auf die Diskussion dieser zweiten Frage beschränken – denn von ihrer Klärung hängt es entscheidend ab, ob sich das Konzept der »(Un-)Zuverlässigkeit« nicht allein in Untersuchungen zur Epik, sondern auch in solchen zu anderen narrativen Medien wie etwa dem Film nutzen läßt.

Daß sich hinter dem Begriff des Erzählers in den umrissenen Erläuterungen Unterschiedliches verbergen kann, ist nicht auf den ersten Blick zu sehen; man kann es sich aber mit Hilfe von Marie-Laure Ryans Unterscheidung zwischen »personal« and »impersonal narration« leicht vergegenwärtigen: Von »personal narration« spricht Ryan, sofern es in einem Erzähltext Hinweise darauf gibt, daß er als Rede einer Erzählerfigur zu verstehen ist. Mit »impersonal narration« hat man es ihr zufolge dann zu tun, »when the narrator's discourse presupposes only one property: the ability to narrate a story«[21]. Vor dem Hintergrund dieser Unterscheidung lassen sich die Voraussetzungen der Begriffsverwendung wie folgt bestimmen: Um das Konzept »axiologischer (Un-)Zuverlässigkeit« zuschreiben zu können, ist das Vorliegen von »personal narration« erforderlich; die Begriffsverwendung setzt eine Instanz voraus, die sich vom Werk unterscheiden und im Vergleich mit ihm in axiologischer Hinsicht evaluieren läßt. Das Konzept »mimetischer (Un-)Zuverlässigkeit« ist in seiner Verwendung nicht in dieser Weise restringiert. Es kann gleichermaßen im Fall von »personal« oder »impersonal« erzählten Texten zur Anwendung kommen, da seine Zuschreibung lediglich das Vorliegen von narrativen Anomalien und die Möglichkeit ihrer strategischen Motivierung erfordert – beide Bedingungen können auch durch Erzählungen erfüllt werden, die keine psychologischen Indizien für einen Narrator enthalten.

Nach diesen Vorklärungen kann man nun grundsätzlich angeben, ob und wie sich das Konzept der »(Un-)Zuverlässigkeit« im Gebiet der Filmanalyse nutzen läßt, ohne sich mit der Grundsatzdiskussion zum Erzählerbegriff aufzuhalten. Filmisches Erzählen kann prinzipiell sowohl in »axiologischer« wie in »mimetischer« Hinsicht (un-)zuverlässig sein. Die axiologische Variante setzt dabei voraus, daß ein Film oder einzelne seiner Sequenzen erkennbar die Sichtweise einer extra- oder intradiegetischen Figur wiedergeben; die mimetische Variante hängt nicht von einer solchen Bedingung ab. Man hat also von drei grundlegenden Formen filmischer Unzuverlässigkeit auszugehen: von axiologische Inkongruenz bei personaler Narration, von mimetischer Inadäquatheit bei personaler Narration und von mimetischer Inadäquatheit bei impersonaler Narration.[22] Die obigen Definitionen lassen sich nun wie folgt variieren:

Explikat 1' – *axiologisch (un-)zuverlässig*: Der Erzähler eines Abschnitts A eines Films F ist *axiologisch zuverlässig*, wenn er ausdrücklich für die Leitwerte$_A$ eintritt oder in Übereinstimmung mit ihnen handelt; er ist *axiologisch unzuverlässig*, wenn dies nicht der Fall ist.

Explikat 2" – *mimetisch (un-)zuverlässig*: Der Erzähler/das Erzählen eines Abschnitts A in einem Film F ist *mimetisch zuverlässig*, sofern es keinen als Bestandteil einer Strategie beschreibbaren Anlaß gibt, an der Angemessenheit seiner Präsentation der Geschichte$_A$ (oder Welt$_A$) zu zweifeln; er/es ist *mimetisch unzuverlässig*, wenn dies nicht der Fall ist.

Wie die Bedingungen der Begriffszuschreibungen zu verstehen sind, welche der Grundformen von Unzuverlässigkeit im Film auch tatsächlich umgesetzt werden und welche weiteren Subtypen der Erzählweise Beachtung verdienen – auf all dies kann ich hier nicht mehr eingehen. Ich hoffe aber, für entsprechende Diskussionen zumindest den Boden bereitet zu haben.

ANMERKUNGEN

[1] Mit den Ausdrücken ›kulturwissenschaftlich‹ und ›Kulturwissenschaft‹ beziehe ich mich im folgenden auf die seit etwa einem Jahrzehnt unternommenen Versuche, die Geisteswissenschaften im deutschsprachigen Raum nach dem Vorbild der ›cultural studies‹ neu auszurichten, vgl. zu diesem Vorhaben etwa Böhme/Scherpe 1996. Ich muß hier auf eine Kritik dieser Versuche verzichten, vgl. hierzu Müller 1997.

[2] Vgl. zur Geschichte der Narratologie den Abriß in Prince 1995.

[3] Zu den Anfängen der gegenwärtigen Auseinandersetzung um eine kontextualistische Narratologie vgl. Chatman 1990. Beispiele für die Forderung nach einer Neuausrichtung der Erzähltheorie liefern Lanser 1986, 1988 und 1999, Fludernik 1996, Herman 1997, 1999 und 2001 und Darby 2001. Einen Überblick über die Beiträge zur Modellierung der postklassischen Narratologie geben Fludernik 2000 und Nünning 2000.

[4] Eine heuristische Funktionalisierung der Narratologie hat sich nicht nur in der literatur- und medienwissenschaftlichen Praxis immer wieder bewährt; sie wird überdies von vielen bekannten Vertretern der traditionellen Erzähltheorie explizit unterstützt: Genette etwa versteht sein narratologisches Instrumentarium als »eine Entdeckungshilfe und ein Werkzeug der Beschreibung« (Genette 1994, 190), und Franz K. Stanzel ist überzeugt, daß sich seine erzähltheoretischen Konzepte »für die Analyse des einzelnen Erzählwerks« und mithin als »Dienerin der Literaturkritik und Interpretation« nutzen lassen, gerade weil sie ein »System sowohl der denkbaren als auch der historischen Erzählformen« (Stanzel 1991, 300) entwerfen sollen.

[5] Vgl. hierzu ausführlich Kindt/Müller 2003.

[6] Einen Überblick über den Forschungsstand geben Nünning 1998 und Currie 1995. Interessant unter kulturwissenschaftlicher Perspektive sind vor allem Spence 1998, Fludernik 1999 und Zerweck 2001.

[7] Fry 1994, 9.

[8] Zur Konzeption der Explikation von Begriffen vgl. die Hinweise bei Carnap 1951, 1-18, Pawlowski 1980, 157-198 und Danneberg 1988, 50-64.

[9] Zu den Ursprüngen und Grundzügen von Booths Projekt einer Rhetorik literarischer Texte vgl. Booth 1982 und Kindt/Müller 1999, 277-280.

[10] Booth 1983, 404.

[11] Booth 1961, 158f. Hervorhebung im Original.

[12] Vgl. hierzu Kindt/Müller 1999, 284-287. Hintergrund einer solchen Sicht des »impliziten Autors« sind die Überlegungen zum Aufbau von Interpretationstheorien in Danneberg/Müller 1984. – Einen Überblick über die Diskussionen um den Begriff des »impliziten Autors« liefert Nünning 2001.

[13] Dies tut etwa Nünning, wenn er vorschlägt, die »(Un-)Zuverlässigkeit« von Erzählern an dem ›Abstand‹ zu bemessen, »that separates the narrator's view of the world from the reader's or critic's world-model and standards of normalcy« (Nünning 1999, 61). Vgl. zu diesem Vorschlag auch Nünning 1998 und Zerweck 2001.

[14] Anders ausgedrückt: Dem Erläuterungsvorschlag zufolge hängt es u. a. von den jeweils leitenden Vorstellungen über die interpretative Bestimmung der Bedeutung eines literarischen Werks ab, ob der Narrator eines Textes als »zuverlässig« oder »unzuverlässig« zu charakterisieren ist.

[15] Es ist bislang erst in zwei Studien versucht worden, die beiden umrissenen Spielarten »erzählerischer Unzuverlässigkeit« zu unterscheiden, vgl. Martinez/Scheffel

1999, 100-107 und Phelan/Martin 1999, 88-109. Daß der Verzicht auf eine entsprechende Differenzierung die Beschäftigung mit Booths Konzept erheblich beeinträchtigt, läßt sich etwa anhand der Ergebnisse und Vermutungen ablesen, zu denen Jahn 1998, Baah 2000 oder Zerweck 2001 gelangen. Zur Kritik an den Ausführungen von Jahn vgl. Yacobi 2001.

[16] Vgl. hierzu etwa Nünning 1999, 64f.

[17] Vgl. vor allem Yacobi 1981 sowie die Diskussion ihrer Vorschläge in Diengott 1990.

[18] Die Unterscheidung zwischen Texten (T) und Textabschnitten (A) läßt die beiden Erläuterungsvorschläge zweifellos etwas umständlich erscheinen; sie ist aber nötig, um eine sinnvolle Anwendung des Begriffs »erzählerischer (Un-)Zuverlässigkeit« sowohl auf extra- als auch auf intradiegetische Erzähler zu ermöglichen, vgl. dazu Genette 1994, 162-165.

[19] Vgl. Wall 1994, 38 oder Nünning 1998, 11f.

[20] Vgl. Riggan 1981 oder DeReuck 1990, 300.

[21] Ryan 1981, 518.

[22] Realisiert wird von diesen Spielarten unzuverlässigen Filmerzählens freilich zumeist nur die figural zurechenbare Spielart einer problematischen Ereigniswiedergabe – sei es in intradiegetischer Form wie in Hitchcocks *Stage Fright*, sei es in extradiegetischer Form wie in David Finchers *Fight Club*.

BIBLIOGRAPHIE

Baah, Robert, Rethinking Narrative Unreliability, in: Journal of Literary Semantics 28. Jg. (1999), S. 180-188.

Böhme, Hartmut, Klaus R. Scherpe (Hg.), Literatur und Kulturwissenschaft. Positionen, Theorien, Modelle, Reinbek bei Hamburg 1996.

Booth, Wayne C., The Rhetoric of Fiction, Chicago 1961.

– Between Two Generations: The Heritage of the Chicago School, in: Profession 82 Jg. (1982), S. 19-26.

– Afterword to the Second Edition: The Rhetoric in Fiction and Fiction as Rhetoric: Twenty-One Years Later, in: W. C. B, The Rhetoric of Fiction, 2. Aufl., Chicago 1983, S. 401-457.

Carnap, Rudolf, Logical Foundations of Probability, Chicago 1950.

Chatman, Seymour, What Can We Learn from Contextualist Narratology?, in: Poetics Today 11. Jg (1990), S. 309-328.

Currie, Gregory, Unreliability Refigured: Narrative in Literature and Film, in: Journal of Aesthetics and Art Criticism 53. Jg. (1995), S. 19-29.

Danneberg, Lutz, Zwischen Innovation und Tradition: Begriffsbildung und Begriffsentwicklung als Explikation, in: Christian Wagenknecht (Hg.), Zur Terminologie der Literaturwissenschaft, Stuttgart 1988, S. 50-68.

Danneberg, Lutz, Hans-Harald Müller, Wissenschaftstheorie, Hermeneutik, Literaturwissenschaft. Anmerkungen zu einem unterbliebenen und Beiträge zu einem künftigen Dialog über die Methodologie des Verstehens, in: Deutsche Vierteljahrsschrift für Literaturwissenschaft und Geistesgeschichte 58 Jg. (1984), S. 177-237.

Darby, David, Form and Kontext: An Essay in the History of Narratology, in: Poetics Today 22. Jg. (2001), S. 829-852.

DeReuck, Jenny, Etching »Inconscience«: Unreliability as a Function in Narrative Situations, in: Journal of Literary Studies 6 Jg. (1990), S. 289-303.

Diengott, Nilli, Narratology and Feminism, in: Style 22. Jg. (1988), S. 42-51.

– Reliability in Narrative: Some Theoretical Issues, in: Language and Style: An International Journal 23. Jg. (1990), S. 369-378.

– Implied Author, Motivation and Theme and Their Problematic Status, in: Orbis Litterarum 48. Jg. (1993), S. 181-193.

Fludernik, Monika, Towards a »Natural« Narratology, in: Journal of Literary Semantics 25 Jg. (1996), S. 97-141.

– Defining (In)Sanity: The Narrator of the *Yellow Wallpaper* and the Question of Unreliability, in: Walter Grünzweig und Andreas Solbach (Hg.), Grenzüberschreitungen: Narratologie im Kontext. Transcending Boundaries: Narratology in Context, Tübingen 1999, S. 75-95.

– Beyond Structuralism in Narratology: Recent Developments and New Horizons in Narrative Theory, in: Anglistik. Mitteilungen des Deutschen Anglistenverbandes 11. Jg. (2000), S. 83-96.

Fry, Stephen, Das Nilpferd. Roman, Zürich 1994.

Genette, Gérard, Die Erzählung, mit einem Nachwort hg. von Jochen Vogt, München 1994.

Herman, David, Scripts, Sequences, and Stories: Elements of a Postclassical Narratology, in: PMLA 112 Jg. (1997), S. 1046-1059.

– Narrative Theory as a Cognitive Science, in: Narrative Inquiry 11. Jg. (2001), S. 1-34.

Herman, David (Hg.), Narratologies: New Perspectives on Narrative Analysis, Columbus 1999.

Jahn, Manfred, *Package Deals*, Exklusionen, Randzonen: das Phänomen der Unverläßlichkeit in der Erzählsituation, in: Ansgar Nünning (Hg.), *Unreliable Narration*. Studien zur Theorie und Praxis unglaubwürdigen Erzählens in der englischsprachigen Erzählliteratur, Trier 1998, S. 81-106.

Kindt, Tom, Hans-Harald Müller, Der »implizite Autor«. Zur Explikation und Verwendung eines unstrittenen Begriffs, in: Fotis Jannidis u. a. (Hg.), Rückkehr des Autors, Tübingen 1999, S. 273-287.

– Narrative Theory and/or/as Theory of Interpretation, in: Tom Kindt und Hans-Harald Müller (Hg.), What Is Narratology?, Berlin, New York 2003 [im Erscheinen].

Lanser, Susan S., Toward a Feminist Narratology, in: Style 20. Jg. (1986), S. 341-63

– Shifting the Paradigm: Feminism and Narratology, in: Style 22. Jg. (1988), 52-60.

– Sexing Narratology: Toward a Gendered Poetics of Narrative Voice, in: Walter Grünzweig und Andreas Solbach (Hg.), Grenzüberschreitungen: Narratologie im Kontext. Transcending Boundaries: Narratology in Context, Tübingen 1999, S. 167-183.

Martinez, Matias, Michael Scheffel, Einführung in die Erzähltheorie, München 1999.

Müller, Hans-Harald: »Aus den fremdartigsten Säften zusammengebraut«. Die verlorene Einheit der Philologie im Medium der Kulturwissenschaft – Zwei Legenden, in: Frankfurter Rundschau (2.9.1997), Nr. 203, S. 12.

Nünning, Ansgar, Unreliable, Compared to What? Towards a Cognitive Theory of *Unreliable Narration*: Prolegomena and Hypotheses, in: Walter Grünzweig und

Andreas Solbach (Hg.), Grenzüberschreitungen: Narratologie im Kontext. Transcending Boundaries: Narratology in Context, Tübingen 1999, S. 53-73.

– Towards a Cultural and Historical Narratology: A Survey of Diachronic Approaches, Concepts, and Research Projects, in: Bernhard Reitz und Sigrid Rieuwerts (Hg.), Anglistentag 1999 in Mainz. Proceedings, Trier 2000, S. 345-373.

– Totgesagte leben länger: Anmerkungen zur Rückkehr des Autors und zu Wiederbelebungsversuchen des »impliziten Autors«, in: Literaturwissenschaftliches Jahrbuch 42 Jg. (2001), S. 353-385.

Nünning, Ansgar (Hg.), *Unreliable Narration*. Studien zur Theorie und Praxis unglaubwürdigen Erzählens in der englischsprachigen Erzählliteratur, Trier 1998.

Pawlowski, Tadeusz, Begriffsbildung und Definition, Berlin, New York 1980.

Phelan, James, Mary Patricia Martin, The Lessons of »Weymouth«: Homodiegesis, Unreliability, Ethics, and *The Remains of the Day*. In: David Herman (Hg.), Narratologies: New Perspectives on Narrative Analysis, Columbus 1999, S. 88-109.

Prince, Gerald, Narratology, in: Raman Selden (Hg.), The Cambridge History of Literary Criticism, Vol. 8: From Formalism to Poststructuralism, Cambridge 1995, S. 110-130.

– Narratology, Narratological Criticism and Gender, in: Calin-Andrei Mihailescu und Walid Harmaneh (Hg.), Fiction Updated: Theories in Fictionality, Narratology, and Poetics, Toronto 1996, S. 159-64.

Riggan, William, Picaros, Madmen, Naïfs, and Clowns. The Unreliable First-Person-Narrator, Oklahoma 1981.

Ryan, Marie-Laure, The Pragmatics of Personal and Impersonal Fiction, in: Poetics 10. Jg. (1981), S. 517-539.

Spence, Donald P., Das Leben rekonstruieren. Geschichten eines unzuverlässigen Erzählers, in: Jürgen Straub (Hg.), Erzählung, Identität und historisches Bewußtsein, Frankfurt/M. 1998, S. 203-225.

Stanzel, Franz K., Theorie des Erzählens, 5. Aufl., Göttingen 1991.

Wall, Kathleen, *The Remains of the Day* and its Challenges to Theories of Unreliable Narration, in: Journal of Narrative Technique 24 Jg. (1994), S. 18-42.

Yacobi, Tamar, Fictional Reliability as a Communicative Problem, in: Poetics Today 2. Jg. (1981), S. 113-126.

– Package Deals in Fictional Narrative. The Case of the Narrator's (Un)Reliability, in: Narrative 9 Jg. (2001), S. 223-229.

Zerweck, Bruno, Historicizing Unreliable Narration: Unreliability and Cultural Discourse in Narrative Fiction, in: Style 35. Jg. (2001), S. 151-178.

Alles auf Anfang

Anmerkungen zu Chris Marker, *La Jetée* (1962)

STEFANIE DIEKMANN

I. NÄHER UND FERNER

Von wo aus wird erzählt? Und: In welche Richtung? Wo setzt die Erzählung ein? Wohin bewegt sie sich? Ist der ihr eingeschriebene Blick einer, der in die Vergangenheit geht, oder geht er in die Zukunft?
All das sind, so könnte man meinen, einfache Fragen, aber das stimmt nicht; nicht hier. Eher rufen sie etwas von der Verwirrung wach, die *La Jetée* auszulösen vermag, gleich am Anfang, wenn die Erzählerstimme Anstalten macht, den ersten Teil dieses Narrativs innerhalb einer fiktiven Zeitordnung zu sistieren.

This is the story of a man marked by an image from his childhood. The violent scene that upset him, and whose meaning he was to grasp only years later, happened on the main jetty at Orly, the Paris airport, sometime before the outbreak of World War III.[1]

Sometime before the outbreak of World War III, kurz vor Ausbruch des dritten Weltkriegs. Etwa zu jener Zeit, heißt es, habe sich zugetragen, was gleich darauf in einer kurzen Folge von Bildern vor Augen gestellt werden wird, scheinbar retrospektiv und aus großer Distanz; dabei ist, was hier zum Bezug genommen wird, niemals geschehen. Dieser Krieg hat noch nicht stattgefunden, weder 1962, als Marker seinen Film fertigstellte, noch vierzig Jahre später im April 2002, jedoch könnte man sich vorstellen, daß er damals (siebzehn Jahre nach Hiroshima und Nagasaki, ein Jahr vor Dallas, einige Monate vor oder nach der Kubakrise) unmittelbarer bevorzustehen schien als heute.
Das Ereignis ist nicht näher gerückt, es hat sich vielmehr entfernt. Was sich als Frage der Zeit darstellte (ein halbes Jahr vielleicht, vielleicht auch ein Jahrzehnt), ist mit den Jahren nicht eingeholt worden, die Katastrophe ferner anstatt näher, und das, obwohl die Zeit fortgeschritten ist, stetig darauf zu, jedenfalls von damals aus betrachtet. Man könnte von diesem An-

fang lernen, unter anderem, daß eine linear angelegte Bewegung (eine Bildfolge, eine Lebensgeschichte, ein Bericht von sukzessiven Zeitreisen nach Eintreten der Apokalypse) nicht notwendig dorthin führt, wohin man es erwartet. Nicht in die Zukunft beispielsweise. Nicht in größere Nähe zu dem, was noch kommen sollte, oder in größere Distanz zu dem, was einmal war, sondern geradewegs in die Vergangenheit, zurück an den Anfang, die eine Begebenheit, aus der dann alles Weitere entstand. Von *La Jetée* erzählen heißt zwangsläufig auch: sich mit einer paradoxen Erzählstruktur befassen.

II. SICH STERBEN SEHEN

Das Paradox: Nicht, daß einer zum selben Zeitpunkt an zwei Orten gewesen zu sein scheint (eine klassische Rätselaufgabe der Kriminalliteratur), sondern daß sich an einem Ort auf einmal zwei Zeitebenen verschränken, genauer: daß einer diesen Ort als Kind und als Mann aufgesucht hat, und daß die Wege der beiden sich dort kreuzen, als sei zwischen dem ersten und dem zweiten Besuch keine Sekunde vergangen, als hätte das Kind auf den Mann, der Mann auf das Kind gewartet, oder als gäbe es hier statt zwei Zeitpunkten nur einen einzigen (in den Worten des Skripts: *a twice-lived fragment of time*), in dem ein und derselbe Protagonist in zweifacher Gestalt zugegen ist.

Orly, Sunday. Parents used to take their children there to watch the departing planes. On this particular Sunday, the child whose story we are telling was bound to remember the frozen sun, the setting at the end of the jetty, and a woman's face.
Nothing sorts out memories from ordinary moments. Later on they do claim remembrance when they show their scars. That face he had seen was to be the only peacetime image to survive the war. Had he really seen it? Or had he invented that tender moment to prop up the madness to come?
The sudden roar, the woman's gesture, the crumpling body, and the cries of the crowd on the jetty blurred by fear.
Later, he knew he had seen a man die.

Das Rollfeld von Orly, auf das der Protagonist aus *La Jetée* auf seiner letzten Reise durch die Zeit zurückkehrt, ist der Ort, an dem er den Tod findet und zugleich längst gefunden hat. Er erkennt das buchstäblich im letzten Augenblick. Was die Rückkehr evident macht, dem Zeitreisenden ebenso wie den Zuschauern, ist, daß jener *hier starb*, mit dem Einsetzen der Erzählung, als das Ereignis aus der Sicht des Kindes entfaltet wurde. Der Schauplatz einer allerersten Begebenheit (genauer: der ersten, die der Reisende im Gedächtnis behält) begegnet wieder als einer, an dem – simultan – ohne Verzögerung – immer schon – auch das Letzte geschieht, geschehen ist, da *La Jetée* den Tod ebenso in die Zukunft wie in die Vergangenheit setzt.

(H)e understood there was no way to escape Time, and that this moment he had been granted to watch as a child, which had never ceased to obsess him, was the moment of his own death.

In einem Augenblick vorüber: Die Formel resümiert das Leben des Zeitreisenden ziemlich exakt. Dennoch scheint der Film auch von anderem zu erzählen, einer älteren und einer jüngeren Vergangenheit etwa, von Amnesie, Gedächtnisleistungen und einer erzwungenen Erinnerungsarbeit. Daß er davon erzählt, läßt vermuten, daß zwischen dem Blick des Kindes und dem Tod des Mannes doch ein Abstand gewesen sein könnte, Zeit genug für etwas wie eine Lebensgeschichte, aus der später einige Fragmente wiederauftauchen; aber woher kommen diese, und wie wären sie einzupassen zwischen zwei Momente, die in Wahrheit ein einziger sind, Lebensanfang und Lebensende gleichsam verschränkt?
Ich wurde geboren und *Ich starb*. Louis Marin nannte dies einmal die zwei undenkbaren Aussagen eines jeden autobiographischen Textes, zwei Fälle von eigentlich unmöglicher Erkenntnis.[2] Wenigstens die zweite Aussage jedoch ist eine, die von dem Mann, der sich am Ort seines längst vergangenen Todes wiederfindet, getätigt werden könnte; allerdings scheint er über die Umstände seines Sterbens lange Zeit nicht ausreichend orientiert.

III. VERTIGO

Antizipiert würde eine solche Situierung (*ich starb – damals, an diesem Ort, zu diesem oder jenem Zeitpunkt*) durch eine Reminiszenz, die Marker etwa in der Mitte seines Filmessays ansiedelt. *Hier wurde ich geboren* sagt Madeleine Elster zu Scottie Ferguson in Hitchcocks Film *Vertigo* (1958), und: *Hier bin ich gestorben*, wobei sie die Zeitpunkte ihrer Geburt und ihres Todes, *Hier* und *Hier*, auf den Jahresringen eines jahrhundertealten Baumes markiert. Wenn *La Jetée* diese Szene wiederholt, wird sie sich verwandelt haben, denn diesmal ist es der männliche Protagonist, der vor den Augen seiner Begleiterin die zeitliche Bestimmung vornimmt, und auch die Auskunft, die den Verweis erklärt, ist nicht mehr ganz dieselbe wie zuvor.

They walk. They look at the trunk of a redwood tree covered with historical data. She pronounces an English name he doesn't understand. As in a dream, he shows her a point beyond the tree, hears himself say, »This is, where I come from ...«

Von hier komme ich, sagt der Protagonist, den man aus der Zukunft in die Vergangenheit zurückgeschickt hat. Er deutet dabei auf einen unbestimmtem Ort außerhalb der Jahresringe, i. e. außerhalb des Zeitgefüges, das sich in diesen dargestellt findet. Wollte er hingegen den genauen Wortlaut des *hier geboren* und *hier gestorben* wiederholen, so wären zwar die Worte dieselben, nicht aber die deiktische Geste, da ihm nichts zu tun bliebe, als zweimal auf denselben Punkt zu verweisen, während in Madeleines Eintrag eine zeitlich-räumliche Distanz abgemessen wird.

Dort sterben wollen, wo man geboren wurde, auch: dort sterben, wo man als Kind einmal gewesen ist. Der Wunsch ist in literarischen und filmischen Erzählungen recht häufig formuliert worden, ein Grundmotiv, wenn man so will, indes behandelt es der Film *La Jetée* ein wenig anders als gewöhnlich. Der Unbekannte, der statt einer Flucht in die Zukunft die Rückkehr auf das Rollfeld von Orly und damit den Tod wählt, tut dies nicht nur, um einen Ort wiederzusehen, den er als Kind besuchte. Er stirbt auch in der vergangenen Gegenwart seiner Kindheit, das heißt: zu einer Zeit, als er noch Kind ist, jedoch ereilt ihn der Tod eben nicht im Kindesalter, sondern vor den Augen des Kindes, als Mann. Die Erinnerung daran begleitet ihn sein Leben lang und ganz am Ende veranlaßt sie ihn, *dorthin* zurückzukehren, diesmal endgültig.

Zweimal wird der Ort des Todes übrigens auch in *Vertigo* aufgesucht, ebenso wie sich der Tod selbst in diesem Film zweimal ereignet, beide Male vor den Augen desselben Zeugen. Dieser jedoch ist nicht identisch mit der Person, die zu Tode kommt. Die, die sterben muß, und der, der dies beobachtet, sind zwei verschiedene bei Hitchcock; tatsächlich lassen sich sogar die beiden Tode der Protagonistin in einen vorgetäuschten und einen wirklichen trennen, von denen der zweite dem Spuk von Wiederkehr und Wiederholung ein Ende setzt und den zweimaligen Zeugen auf etwas brutale Weise von einer temporären Verwirrung kuriert. Der Schwindel, den der Titel *Vertigo* verspricht, ist so groß nicht, oder jedenfalls geringer als in *La Jetée*, wo Beobachtung und Tod zur Sache eines einzigen werden, der einmal sieht und einmal stirbt, beides auf derselben Szene, in einem Moment, von dem nur mitgeteilt wird, er habe ihn zweimal durchlebt. In die Strukturen der Sequentialität sind solche Tode nicht einzuordnen, ganz im Gegensatz zu den zweien aus *Vertigo*; allerdings ließen sich anstelle von Madeleine und Ferguson durchaus andere Figuren finden, die sich vergleichbar paradoxen Erfahrungen ausgesetzt finden wie der Zeitreisende von Orly, dessen Sterben sich als eine große Paraphrase auf den Begriff des *déjà vu* gestaltet.

Die Autoren Bierce (in *Die Brücke über den Eulenfluss*[3]), Blanchot (in *Der Wahnsinn des Tages*[4]), Borges (in *Das geheime Wunder*[5]), Golding (in *Pincher Martin*[6]) haben aus dem Moment des Todes ähnlich erstaunliche Geschichten entwickelt: Berichte von seltsamen Aufschüben, Retardierungen oder Reprisen, für die die zeitliche Ordnung des Erzählten eigentlich keinen Platz bereithält; Tode, die überlebt, übersprungen, rückgängig gemacht, aufgeschoben oder mehr als einmal in Szene gesetzt werden; Bewegungen durch Zeit und Raum, die sich auch retrospektiv nicht ordnen lassen. Selten (nie) ist die zeitliche Ordnung dieser Geschichten so übersichtlich wie in jenem mythischen Narrativ, in dem für die Dauer eines nicht endenwollenden Moments vor den Augen des Sterbenden noch einmal sein Leben in Bildern oder Bildausschnitten vorbeizieht. Was *La Jetée* mit diesem narrativen Konzept verbindet, ist der Umstand, daß auch bei Marker vom Augenblick des Todes aus erzählt wird, nur geschieht das eben nicht in einer chronologischen Rückblende, sondern in Sprüngen und Schleifen und ohne daß der letzte Moment von Anfang an als solcher kenntlich gemacht wäre.

VI. MEDIENTECHNISCHES

Das Prinzip einer Narration in Ausschnitten behält Marker indes bei. *La Jetée* ist ein Film, der sich als eine Reihe von Einzelaufnahmen präsentiert, ein Filmessay, der sich den Anschein des Fotografischen gibt; im Vorspann steht: *un photo-roman*. Erzählt wird Bild für Bild, das heißt: fast immer disjunktiv, diskontinuiert, in unbewegten Tableaus, die gelegentlich mit Geräuschen (Motoren, Stimmen) unterlegt sind und ansonsten überlagert durch *voice over* oder Musik. Der Ton löst sich vom Bild, die Bilder voneinander, der halluziniert bruchlose Ablauf, der gewöhnlich die filmische Wahrnehmung kennzeichnet, ist hier deutlich zäsuriert, in Standbilder zersetzt, ergänzt um die Stimme von außerhalb, die aus Bildern und Bildfolgen die Teile einer Erzählung macht, ohne dabei die Vereinzelung der Aufnahmen aufzuheben.

In dieser Geschichte um Lücken – Erinnerungslücken, Zeitlöcher oder -tunnel, Dunkelheiten, Passagen, etc. – erhält der Raum zwischen den Bildern gewissermaßen allegorische Qualität, gerade weil man eines so gut wie das andere in ihm sehen kann: den blockierten nicht weniger als den aufgelassenen Übergang; das verdeckte ebenso wie das fehlende, das verlorene oder das ersetzbare Erinnerungsbild; die unwiderrufliche oder (ganz im Gegenteil) die zeitweilige, zwischenzeitliche Fragmentierung des Narrativs. *La Jetée* ist nicht dazu eingerichtet, dergleichen Ambivalenzen durch eingängigere Konstruktionen oder unmißverständliche Kennzeichnungen zu ersetzen. Weder nimmt der Film eine Vereindeutigung vor noch legt er nahe, dies retrospektiv zu versuchen.

Gelegentlich scheinen sich die Abstände zwischen den Bildern zu verringern; in solchen Momenten sieht *La Jetée* beinahe aus wie andere Filme. Abläufe beschleunigen sich, Bewegung oder doch eine Idee von Bewegung entsteht, Sequentialität, die nicht nur eine des Materials ist, sondern bspw. die einer Geste oder eines Vorgangs. Man kennt dergleichen Effekte, wenn auch vor allem aus Filmen, die sehr viel später gedreht werden, so etwa *Ein Z und zwei Nullen* (1986) von Peter Greenaway, der die Funktionsweise eines Mediums in vergleichbarer Weise ausstellt, indem er seine Protagoni-

sten aus tausenden von Einzelaufnahmen eine ganz eigene Serie von Lehrfilmen (Darstellungen der organischen Dekomposition) zusammensetzen läßt. Film führt hier Film vor, oder auch: Film betreibt Mimikry am Film – und zitiert dabei jenes Stück Mediengeschichte, nach dem die Fotografie als Vorform des Kinos figuriert, das statische Bild sich zum bewegten erst entwickelt. Etwas von den protofilmischen Bildstrecken eines Eadweard Muybridge findet sich bei Greenaway, aber auch bei Marker, der die Sequenzen aus *Human* oder *Animal Locomotion* in den Aufnahmen vom letzten Lauf seines Zeitreisenden evoziert.[7]
Meist jedoch bleiben die Aufnahmen gegeneinander abgesetzt. Sie stehen für sich, flüchtig genug, oder besser: mit verhaltener Insistenz. Insistenz (die von Eindrücken, Bildern, etc.) ist ein Thema des Films und ebenso sein Prinzip, das allerdings wenig offensiv und eher wie beiläufig durchgesetzt wird. Ein wenig erinnert die Abfolge der unbeweglichen Tableaus auf der Leinwand an eine Diavorführung (diese moderne und doch zugleich schon wieder anachronistische Spielart der *ars memoria*), ein wenig an die Betrachtung von Fotoalben, die Marker ohnehin in mancher Hinsicht als Modelle gedient haben könnten. Die Ordnung des Materials in Bildgruppen, die Einteilung loser Formationen von Aufnahmen mit demselben Schauplatz, Thema oder Gegenstand kennzeichnen den Film wie die allbekannten Erinnerungsbücher.

V. DAS ALBUM

Man könnte die Bilder ordnen und vorführen, fast so, wie man die Bestände des gewöhnlichen Fotoalbums präsentiert. (Eines oder mehrerer: Da die Szenarien sehr verschiedene sind, die Motive in vielen Fällen verstörend, ließen sie sich kaum in einem einzigen Band versammeln.) Dies sind die Bilder vom Ausflug nach Orly. Dies einige Aufnahmen aus dem zerstörten Paris. Hier: Fotos, die den Verlauf des ersten Experiments dokumentieren, mit dem die Reise des Protagonisten in die Vergangenheit vorbereitet wurde. Dann: Ein Foto, das dazwischen geraten ist und in keines der Konvolute einsortiert werden kann. Dann: Bilder aus Friedenszeiten, Bilder aus der Zeit nach der Katastrophe. Später die Bilder vom Besuch in einem Museum; es war der letzte gemeinsame Ausflug, und ich erinnere mich, daß wir lange vor dem Schaukasten mit den ausgestopften Tieren standen. Zeigen, erzählen, kommentieren: Das Grundmuster, das die Handhabung aller Fotoalben bestimmt, kennzeichnet auch die Sequenzen aus *La Jetée*.
Deutlicher noch werden die Affinitäten zum alltäglichsten Requisit memorialer Kultur, wo sich der Fokus von der *narratio* zur *memoria* verschiebt. Das Fotoalbum, angeblich einer jener Gegenstände, die man in Zeiten der

Katastrophe als besonders kostbaren Besitz behandelt (das erste, was man aus dem Feuer holt; das letzte, was aus dem leichten Gepäck aussortiert wird), kann dazu dienen, Bilder von einer Zeit in eine andere zu retten, sie zu bewahren, zu konservieren, wo die Welt, die sie abbilden, von Zerstörung bedoht ist oder bereits ausgelöscht. Ähnlich funktioniert allem Anschein nach das Gedächtnis des Protagonisten in *La Jetée*, mit dem allerdings wesentlichen Unterschied, daß hier die geretteten Bilder weniger umstandslos verfügbar sind, als es beim Album der Fall ist und auch nach ihrer Manifestation eine gewisse Unklarheit über ihren Status bestehen bleiben wird.

The camp police spied even on dreams.
This man was selected from among a thousand for his obsession with an image from the past.
Nothing else, at first, but stripping out the present, and its racks.
They begin again.
The man doesn't die nor does he go mad. He suffers.
They continue.
On the tenth day, images begin to ooze, like confessions.

Am zehnten Tag der Versuchsreihe, so die Auskunft, beginnen Bilder auszusickern, wie Geständnisse. Welche Behandlung der Versuchsperson, welche Methoden der Nötigung dem vorausgegangen sind, wird nicht erklärt, jedoch scheint deutlich genug, daß es eine Weile dauert, bis das Bildmaterial preisgegeben (zugänglich gemacht) wird. Die Freisetzung erfolgt zögerlich, und das ändert sich auch nicht, als aus den Bildern etwas wie eine Geschichte zu entstehen beginnt und mit der Geschichte etwas wie eine Vergangenheit.

Ausschnitte aus dem imaginären Album des Protagonisten von *La Jetée*: *A peacetime morning. A peacetime bedroom. A real bedroom. Real children. Real birds. Real cats. Real graves.* Roland Barthes sagte einmal, jegliche Fotografie sei auch eine Beglaubigung von Präsenz, eine (wie es scheint) unabdingbare Bestätigung, »daß die Sache dagewesen ist«[8]. Mehr noch als für andere Fotos, kann dies für die fotografischen Standbilder dieser Sequenz geltend gemacht werden, die nicht so sehr als Bilder eines vergangenen oder verlorenen Wirklichen zu betrachten wären denn als Bilder einer Wirklichkeit, von der bis zuletzt nicht klar sein wird, ob es sie je gegeben hat. Daß die Sache dagewesen sei, ist eine Möglichkeit, über die in *La Jetée* nicht unbedingt Gewißheit herrscht, und die Beweiskraft des Bildes ist keineswegs so evident, wie von Barthes beschrieben. Um so deutlicher aber tritt in den Aufnahmen der *wirklichen* Zimmer und *wirklichen* Lebewesen jene Macht zutage, die das fotografische Medium noch unter den Bedingungen der Ungewißheit behält: das Vermögen, eine Welt existent zu setzen.[9]

Eine Welt und eine Geschichte. Ebensowenig, wie sich etwas Endgültiges über den Status jener Wirklichkeit aussagen ließe, die nur in ein paar Erinnerungsbildern (aber sind sie das tatsächlich?) existiert, bietet sich diese Perspektive in der Liebesgeschichte, die vielleicht schon einmal stattgefunden hat, vielleicht aber auch nicht, die erinnert wird oder imaginiert oder geträumt – oder schlichtweg erfunden. Auch mit dieser Möglichkeit hat der Zeitreisende bei seinen Begegnungen mit der geliebten Gestalt zu rechnen.

It was the starting point for a whole series of tests, in which he would meet her at different times. Sometimes he finds her in front of their markings. She welcomes him in a simple way. She calls him her Ghost.
As for him, he never knows whether he moves toward her, whether he is driven, whether he has made it up, or whether he is only dreaming.

Es könnte sein, daß die Begegnungen, die sich hier als Teil einer gelebten Vergangenheit präsentieren, nichts anderes sind als in vergangener Zeit Geträumtes und Phantasiertes, phantasierte Vergangenheit auch oder der Traum einer Geschichte, die sich aus einem Bild entspinnt, das von jenem Nachmittag am Rande des Rollfelds datiert. Dieses Bild wieder-finden und den Tod finden, sind vollkommen simultane Erfahrungen in einem Film, der das eine, einzige, obsessiv festgehaltene Bild im übrigen nicht zeigt, und wenn doch, dann ohne es kenntlich zu machen. Ein wenig erinnert auch dies an Barthes, der in seinem Buch über die Fotografie eine vergleichbare Politik des Zeigens und Nicht-Zeigens betrieb, indem er das Foto, um das sein ganzes Narrativ organisiert scheint, aus der Erzählung heraushielt, es nicht zeigte, zeigen wollte, während er die Ausführungen sonst großzügig illustrierte.[10] Es könnte sein, daß im imaginären Album der Erinnerungsbilder das eine Bild nicht auftaucht, daß es im Museum der Gedächtnisinhalte nicht ausfindig zu machen oder aber ausfindig zu machen und dennoch nicht zu veräußern ist.

VI. DAS MUSEUM

Album oder Museum? Als Dispositiv der Bildbewahrung zieht *La Jetée* offensichtlich das zweite vor. Der Zeitreisende wird ein Museum besuchen, auf seinem vorletzten Ausflug in die Szenarien der Vergangenheit, und er wird, lange vor dieser Exkursion, über das Museum ein paar Mutmaßungen anstellen.

Other images appear, merge, in that museum, which is perhaps that of his memory.

Vielleicht, heißt es. Es könnte sein, daß dieser aufgelassene, nach wie vor zugängliche Ort als sein Gedächtnis betrachtet werden kann. In jedem Fall findet er dort noch ein paar Bilder vor, Restbestände einer Sammlung, die einmal umfassender gewesen sein könnte, vor allem aber zugänglich, verfügbar und geordnet, was für die Erinnerungsbilder der filmischen Erzählung kaum mehr zutrifft. Der Raum sei unbetretbar geworden, *space was off-limits*, heißt es gleich zu Beginn und meint zuallererst das, was unter anderen Voraussetzungen (in einer anderen Zeit) als Lebensraum bezeichnet würde. Affiziert ist aber auch der Raum des Gedächtnisses, der nur mehr als Ruine zugänglich scheint und sich entsprechend verwandelt präsentiert, i. e. als Ort der unauffindbaren und plötzlich eröffneten Zugänge, unbegehbaren Areale, verschobenen Anordnungen und Plateaus, verstreuten Bruchstücke etc.

Zugleich evozieren die Rede vom Museum, die Idee einer memorialen Sphäre und räumlich geordneter Bilder jene Gedächtnisarchitektur, die aus den antiken Konzepten zur *memoria* bekannt ist. Sowohl in den Schriften Quintilians als auch in der *Rhetorica ad Herennium* begegnet man dem Entwurf der *memoria* als einer proto-musealen Sphäre, in der Inhalte in Bilder gefaßt und dann an bestimmten Orten installiert werden, von denen man sie später abrufen kann.[11] Die Anordnungen, die dabei entstehen, sind Musterbeispiele festgelegter Abfolgen und anschaulich gemachter Verfügbarkeit; ebenso wären sie aber auch geeignet, die absolute Metaphorizität der räumlichen Konzeption zu illustrieren.

La Jetée hält an der Konzeption des Gedächtnisraumes fest und macht diesen zum Raum einer Reise oder immerhin gelegentlicher Besuche. Die Metapher bleibt, wenn man so will, intakt, auch und gerade dort, wo der Raum als versehrter vorgestellt wird.

VII. ANAGNORISIS

Antike zum zweiten: Neben den Szenarien der Rhetorik evoziert *La Jetée* gelegentlich auch die des Theaters.

Mit der analytischen Tragödie, so wie Sophokles sie in *Oedipus Rex* gestaltete, teilt dieser Film einen sehr spezifischen Moment der Erkenntnis: die Entdeckung des Protagonisten, daß jener Unbekannte kein anderer ist als er selbst. Der, nach dem die ganze Stadt sucht (Sophokles), der, der damals am Rande des Rollfelds starb (Marker), ist er, niemand anders als er; aber das wird erst ganz zuletzt begriffen und in jedem Fall zu spät, um etwa in den Ablauf der Ereignisse einzugreifen, das Ende abzuwenden, ein Unglück zu verhindern etc. Die unausweichliche Abfolge, die Entdeckung, nicht entkommen zu können, gehören bekanntlich zu den Grundmustern tragischer Erfahrung. Am Ende von *La Jetée* steht eine Einsicht, die zumindest vergleichbar formuliert ist:

> (H)e understood there was no way to escape Time …

Die Geschichte des Reisenden von Orly ließe sich also auch beschreiben als ein Erkenntnisprozeß mit tödlichem Ausgang. Der Terminus technicus dazu lautet: *anagnorisis*, das heißt: Wiedererkennen. In der antiken Tragödie kommt die *anagnorisis* in vielen Spielarten vor, aber kaum mehr als einmal so strukturiert, daß der, der zu Beginn als Beobachter auftritt (das Kind, das am Rande des Rollfelds den Tod eines Mannes mitansieht; der König, der in Theben die Nachforschungen überwacht), sich schließlich in demjenigen erkennen muß, auf den der Blick gerichtet war. In bestimmtem Sinne war er das sogar die ganze Zeit, denn auch wenn die Szene auf dem Flughafen viel kürzer ist als das investigative Drama in *Oedipus Rex*, wird dem, der sie angesehen hat, ein dauerhaftes Bild davon bleiben.
Mit dem Moment der *anagnorisis* sind die beiden Erkenntnisprozesse beendet, *La Jetée* auf der Stelle, *Oedipus Rex* ein paar Seiten später, nachdem sich der König, der die ganze Zeit auf keinen anderen blickte als sich selbst, die Augen ausgestochen hat, auch eine Form von Schwarzblende.

ANMERKUNGEN

[1] Alle Zitate aus dem Filmskript nach: »La Jetée's Script«; Chris Marker Website, http://cs.art.rmit.edu.au/projects/media/marker/Script-_La_ Jetee_354.html.

[2] vgl. Louis Marin, The ›I‹ as Autobiographical Eye, in: October, No. 9 (1979), S. 65-79, S. 66: »The writing of the cogito of birth as *my birth* as well as that of death as *my death* are both impossible.«

[3] Ambrose Bierce, Die Brücke über den Eulenfluss, in: Ders., Mein Lieblingsmord, FfM 1996, S. 22-35.

[4] Maurice Blanchot, Der Wahnsinn des Tages, Köln 2000.

[5] Jorge Louis Borges, »Das geheime Wunder«, in: Ausgewählte Werke, Band 1: Die Bibliothek von Babel. Erzählungen, Berlin 1987, S. 205-213.

[6] William Golding, Pincher Martin, Leipzig 1993.

[7] Eine kleine Auswahl von Muybridges Bewegungsstudien am Menschen findet sich in: Eadweard Muybridge, The Male and Female Figure in Motion, New York 1984.

[8] Roland Barthes, Die helle Kammer, FfM 1989, S. 86.

[9] vgl. Barthes 1989, S. 86f.: »Die Malerei kann wohl eine Realität fingieren, ohne sie gesehen zu haben. Der Diskurs fügt Zeichen aneinander, die gewiß Referenten haben, aber diese Referenten können »Chimären« sein, und meist sind sie es auch. Anders als bei diesen Imitationen läßt sich in der PHOTOGRAPHIE nicht leugnen, *daß die Sache dagewesen ist*. Hier gibt es eine Verbindung aus zweierlei: aus Realität und Vergangenheit. Und da diese Einschränkung nur hier existiert, muß man sie als das Wesen, den Sinngehalt (*noema*) der PHOTOGRAPHIE ansehen. Worauf ich mich in einer Photographie intentional richte (...) ist weder die KUNST noch die KOMMUNIKATION, sondern die REFERENZ, die das Grundprinzip der PHOTOGRAPHIE darstellt.«

[10] Barthes 1989, S. 83: »Ich kann das Photo aus dem Wintergarten nicht zeigen. Es existiert ausschließlich für mich.«

[11] vgl. Quintilian, Ausbildung des Redners, Darmstadt 1995, S. 593f. sowie Rhetorica ad Herennium, Buch 4, Zürich 1994, S. 167f.

BIBLIOGRAPHIE

Barthes, Roland, Die helle Kammer, FfM 1989.
Bierce, Ambrose, Die Brücke über den Eulenfluss, in: Ders., Mein Lieblingsmord, FfM 1996, S. 22-35.
Blanchot, Maurice, Der Wahnsinn des Tages, Köln 2000.
Borges, Jorge Louis, Das geheime Wunder, in: Ders., Ausgewählte Werke, Band 1: Die Bibliothek von Babel. Erzählungen, Berlin 1987, S. 205-213.
Golding, William, Pincher Martin, Leipzig 1993.
Marin, Louis, The ›I‹ as Autobiographical Eye, in: October, No. 9 (1979), S. 65-79.
Chris Marker Site, http://cs.art.rmit.edu.au/projects/media/marker/Script-_La_Jetee_354.html.
Muybridge, Eadweard, The Male and Female Figure in Motion, New York 1984.
Quintilian, Ausbildung des Redners, Darmstadt 1995.
Rhetorica ad Herennium, Zürich 1994.

Wissen erzählen. Die Enzyklopädie im literarischen Text

HILDEGARD HABERL

Im August 2001 wurde unter der Leitung von Nicolas Witkowski ein »kulturwissenschaftliches« Wörterbuch der Wissenschaften, ein *Dictionnaire culturel des sciences* publiziert. Es stehen darin nicht die (Natur-)Wissenschaften für sich allein im Blickfeld, sondern ihre Beziehungen zu Kunst, Literatur, Wirtschaft, Politik und Religion. Die Autoren und Autorinnen kommen aus den unterschiedlichsten Wissensbereichen und überschreiten bewusst ihre Disziplingrenzen. Der Kunstkritiker und Wissenschaftsjournalist Michel Ellenberger zum Beispiel, verfasst die Eintragungen *archétype, Bauhaus, Klee, Malevitch*. Jean Starobinski, der bekannte Literaturwissenschaftler, schreibt den Artikel *réaction*. Der Soziologe Bruno Latour zeichnet für die Artikel *épistémologie* und *Pasteur* verantwortlich. Die Wissenschaftshistorikerin Claudine Cohen verfasst u. a. die Eintragungen: *Australopithèque, Balzac, Boucher de Perthes, Bouvard et Pécuchet, dinosaure, Neandertal, paléontologie, phrénologie, preuve, Zadig*. Im Vorwort dieses Wörterbuches wird ausdrücklich auf die Interdependenz von Wissenschaft und Kultur verwiesen und betont, dass auch wenn die Vernunft wissenschaftlich ist, sie nicht ohne das Imaginäre auskommen kann, genauso wenig wie die Wissenschaft ohne ihre Fiktion: »[...] la raison, fut-elle scientifique, ne peut se passer de l'imaginaire, ni la science de sa fiction.«[1]
Ich möchte in diesem Artikel aus dem Blickwinkel der Literatur Enzyklopädien betrachten und der Frage nachgehen, wie die Enzyklopädie in ihrer Rolle als Medium der Wissenssammlung und Wissensordnung in literarischen Texten dargestellt wird, wie sich über das Motiv und die Idee der Enzyklopädie eine Auseinandersetzung der Literatur mit diesen Wissensordnungen gestaltet. Methodisch werde ich meine Argumente aus zwei Texten heraus entwickeln und mittels Textanalyse untersuchen, auf welche Art und Weise Enzyklopädien in den literarischen Text eingewoben werden bzw. in welcher Form die Enzyklopädie die bzw. das Enzyklopädische die Textstruktur selbst mitgestaltet. Mit anderen Worten: es soll gezeigt werden, wo sich die Textsorten Roman und Enzyklopädie ähneln bzw. wo Gat-

tungsgrenzen überschritten werden. Mit Mieke Bal teile ich das Interesse am Narrativen als »a mode of cultural self-expression« und interessiere mich für die Erzähltheorie in ihrer Rolle als heuristisches Werkzeug der Kulturanalyse, die sich in diesem vorliegenden Text auf literarische Erzählungen konzentriert.[2] Die ausgewählten Texte sind *Bouvard et Pécuchet* von Gustave Flaubert, 1881 als Fragment erschienen, sowie der 1984 publizierte Roman *Alizés* von Michel Rio.[3] Die Fragestellung nach dem Zusammenhang von Enzyklopädie und Roman dient mir als Verknüpfungspunkt und Vergleichsparameter bei der Analyse dieser beiden an sich sehr unterschiedlichen Texte.

Das Motiv »Enzyklopädie« soll auf zwei Ebenen thematisiert werden: zum einen auf der Inhaltsebene, zum anderen auf der Darstellungsebene. Ich werde in einem ersten Schritt die explizite Bezugnahme auf Enzyklopädien in den beiden Texten darstellen, um danach am Beispiel der Schlagwörter Klassifikation/Wissensordnung, Dokument/Nomenklatur und Visualisierung/Illustration zu zeigen, wie die Auseinandersetzung mit Enzyklopädien auch implizit die Erzählung prägt. In der jeweiligen literarischen Auseinandersetzung wird eine sich verändernde Konzeption von Enzyklopädie sichtbar, die den Anspruch auf fixierte und absolute Wissenssysteme in Frage stellt, sowie die kultur- und diskursraumspezifische Abhängigkeit von Wissen zum Thema macht.

AUSGANGSPUNKT

Gustave Flaubert beschreibt seinen letzten Roman als »l'histoire de ces deux bonshommes qui copient une espèce d'encyclopédie critique en farce«[4], also die Geschichte zweier Männer, die eine Art kritische Enzyklopädie in Form einer Farce abschreiben. Er überlegte auch, dem Text den Untertitel einer »Enzyklopädie der menschlichen Dummheit« zu geben.[5] Er konnte den Roman nicht fertigstellen; der Text endet mit einem unabgeschlossenen 10. Kapitel. Aus dem hinterlassenen Material, den Skizzen und Plänen geht hervor, dass dem erzählenden Teil der sogenannte »sottisier« bzw. die »copie« hätte folgen sollen. Diese »copie« setzt sich u. a. aus einem »Wörterbuch der Gemeinplätze« (*Dictionnaire des idées reçues*), einem »Album der Marquise« (*L'Album de la Marquise*) und einem »Katalog der schicken Meinungen« (*Catalogue des idées chic*) zusammen. Die im ersten Teil, d. h. dem Roman-Teil, von Bouvard und Pécuchet gemachten (Diskurs)Erfahrungen sollten in den erwähnten »Archiven«, also Wörterbuch, Album und Katalog, gesammelt und aufbewahrt werden. Es ist mir wichtig, die beabsichtigte Kombination der Textsorten Roman und Wörterbuch zu betonen, obwohl ich mich in der Folge in erster Linie auf den Roman-Teil des Textes beziehen werde. Mehrfach wurde vorgeschlagen, in

Bezug auf *Bouvard et Pécuchet* von einem »roman encyclopédique« bzw. einer »narrativen Enzyklopädie«[6] zu sprechen. Es wird zu zeigen sein, wie sich Flaubert in seinem Text der enzyklopädischen Idee bedient, diese gleichzeitig aber auch hinterfragt, kritisiert und ironisiert. Er wählt dafür den Stil einer Ideenkomik, die beispielsweise darin besteht, dass er zwei ältere, etwas einfältige und gutgläubige Herren auf die Reise ins Reich des Wissens schickt.

Die Thematisierung der Beziehung von Literatur und Wissen/Wissenschaften verbindet den Text Flauberts mit jenem Michel Rios. In dessen Romanen wie auch in seinen theoretischen Schriften spielt die Verknüpfung von Wissen und Imaginärem eine wichtige Rolle. Er nimmt dabei immer wieder Bezug auf Enzyklopädien und Enzyklopädisten, zu denen er auch Flaubert zählt. Die Bedeutung Flauberts für Rio zeigt sich in *Alizés* u. a. durch den intertextuellen Verweis auf dessen Roman *Salammbô*, der neben einer fiktiven Enzyklopädie als einziger literarischer Text erwähnt wird.

Im Gegensatz zu Bouvard und Pécuchet gibt der Ich-Erzähler und gleichzeitig Hauptfigur des Romans keine komische Figur ab, sondern er ist umfassend gebildet und erzählt zudem seine Geschichte in einem sehr gehobenen Sprachstil.

1. DIE ENZYKLOPÄDIE IM TEXT

ENCYCLOPÉDIE (l') Tonner contre.
En rire de pitié, comme étant un ouvrage rococo[7]

In beiden Texten kommen Enzyklopädien vor, sind mehr oder weniger wichtige Elemente der Erzählung. In *Bouvard et Pécuchet* handelt es sich dabei um die Nennung real existierender Enzyklopädien. Die im Text erwähnte *Enyclopédie Roret* – eine berühmte Sammlung allgemeinverständlicher Handbücher – erscheint ab dem Jahr 1822.[8] Sie wird bezeichnenderweise als erstes der zahlreich zitierten Bücher angeführt. Was die Handlung anbelangt, so ist diese Enzyklopädie nur ein Detail und nicht wirklich relevant für deren Verlauf. Die Idee der Enzyklopädie gestaltet sich vielmehr im übertragenen Sinn, indem sie auf die Lebensführung der beiden Hauptfiguren umgelegt wird. Ihre Geschichte entwickelt sich – wie Dietrich Scholler zeigt – entlang enzyklopädischer Topoi: Wissensaneignung (Rezeption), System (Klassifikation), Erziehung (Applikation) und Wörterbuch (Dokumentation).[9]

Bouvard und Pécuchet, beide von Beruf Kopisten, lernen sich im Juli oder August des Jahres 1838 in Paris kennen und entschließen sich, ihr Leben gemeinsam fortzusetzen. Eine Erbschaft erlaubt es ihnen, ihre Berufe aufzugeben und aufs Land zu ziehen, wo sie sich »endlich« den Wissenschaften widmen können. Sie befassen sich in der Folge mit sämtlichen Wissensbereichen: u. a. mit Landwirtschaft und Gartenbau, Chemie, Anatomie, Physiologie und Medizin, Geologie und Astronomie, Archäologie, Historiographie, Geschichtsphilosophie, Literatur, Grammatik, Ästhetik, Politik, Liebe, Gymnastik, Okkultismus, Philosophie, Psychologie, Logik, Mystik, Religion und Pädagogik. Die einzelnen Handlungssequenzen sind paradigmatisch durch den Beginn, die Ausführung und das »Scheitern« der wissenschaftlichen Tätigkeit gekennzeichnet. Auch ihre Versuche als Erzieher und Dozenten bleiben erfolglos. Die Zerstörung ihrer Wissensideale, ihres Glaubens an die Wissenschaften lässt sie schließlich wieder zu ihrer Tätigkeit als Kopisten zurückkehren, wobei sie u. a. das *Dictionnaire des idées reçues* hervorbringen.

In *Alizés* bildet eine fiktive Enzyklopädie den Ausgangspunkt und ein zentrales Element der Erzählung. Der Ich-Erzähler erbt eine zweisprachige (englisch-französische) Enzyklopädie gemeinsam mit einem Segelschiff. Auf den ersten Seiten des Romans wird nun die Entstehungsgeschichte dieser außergewöhnlichen Enzyklopädie beschrieben, die auf den reichen Großonkel des Ich-Erzählers zurückgeht. Dieser engagierte für teures Geld die besten Wissenschaftler, Schriftsteller und Künstler des jeweiligen Sprachraumes, die, ohne voneinander zu wissen, an dem Projekt arbeiteten, das am Ende aus hundert Exemplaren zu je zwanzig Quartbänden bestand. Der Verkaufspreis eines zwanzigbändigen Exemplars wurde auf fünfundzwanzig Millionen Francs geschätzt. Der Ich-Erzähler überlegt nun, wie er sein Erbe, d. h. Enzyklopädie und Segelschiff vernünftig kombinieren könnte und entscheidet sich, nachdem er je ein Exemplar der Enzyklopädie an der Französischen Nationalbibliothek, im British Museum und in der Kongressbibliothek in Washington hinterlegt hat, für eine Reise in den Indischen Ozean, mit dem Ziel, die restlichen Enzyklopädien dort zu verkaufen. Das Reiseziel ergab sich u. a. durch die Rolle der englischen und französischen Sprache, die diese in dieser Region spiel(t)en. Der Ich-Erzähler erleidet Schiffbruch und landet auf einer vom Rest der Welt abgeschiedenen Insel, wo er die Eingeborene Suzanne kennenlernt. Ihr Zusammentreffen, ihre Liebesbeziehung und ihr intellektueller Austausch repräsentieren die Auseinandersetzung des europäischen Wissens mit einer mythisch-legendären Weltsicht; den Konflikt zwischen Geschichte und Legende/Mythos.[10] Suzanne wie auch die übrigen Inselbewohner sind Mestizen. Französische Matrosen landeten im Jahr 1765 nach einem Schiffbruch auf der Insel und vermischten sich mit dem Inselvolk. Die Aufzeichnungen eines dieser Schiffbrüchigen wurden aufbewahrt, konnten aber von den nachfolgenden Generationen nicht mehr entziffert werden. Im Laufe der Zeit veränderte sich also das historische Ereignis der Landung der Europäer zu einer Legende bzw. einem Ursprungsmythos, der besagte, dass weiße Männer die Gründerväter des Inselvolkes seien. Aufgrund seiner Lesekenntnisse sowie der logischen Kombination gewisser (historischer) »Tatsachen«, wie z. B. die europäische Architektur der Häuser auf der Insel, die blauen Augen Suzannes oder das Vorkommen europäischer Lehnwörter in der Inselsprache, stellt der Ich-Erzähler die Ursprungserzählung in Frage und erklärt Suzanne, dass die weißen Ahnen ihr Volk nicht hervorgebracht hätten.

Sie hatten sich nur mit ihm vermischt und hatten seine Geschichte belastet. Sie waren nicht Ursprung, sondern zufällige Erscheinung, keine Halbgötter oder staatengründende Helden, sondern schiffbrüchige Seeleute, arm und unwissend, Entrechtete aus Europa. (dt. 76)

Nach dreijährigem Aufenthalt auf der Insel (1977-1980) baut sich der Ich-Erzähler ein neues Schiff, das er *Le Rêve de Suzanne* nennt und kehrt in die westliche Welt zurück.

Auch dieser Text orientiert sich inhaltlich an enzyklopädischen Topoi. Auffällig ist hier – im Unterschied zu Flauberts Text – die stark selbstreflexive Komponente des Textes, mit anderen Worten, die Reflexion über die Enzyklopädie erfolgt mittels einer Enzyklopädie. Der Ich-Erzähler wird als Erzieher tätig und versucht, sein (europäisches) Wissen an Suzanne weiterzugeben und gleichzeitig ihre Weltsicht zu verstehen (Applikation und Rezeption). Er bedient sich dabei seiner Enzyklopädie. Sowohl der Ich-Erzähler als auch Suzanne dokumentieren ihre Lernerfahrungen. Der Ich-Erzähler hinterlegt seine Notizen in Suzannes Truhe, in der sich bereits das Tagebuch ihrer europäischen Vorfahren aus dem 18. Jahrhundert befindet. Suzanne wiederum hinterlässt dem Ich-Erzähler einen Brief in Form einer Legende, den sie mit einem an den Ich-Erzähler gerichteten Kommentar abschließt:

Die Seiten, die Sie in die Truhe in meiner Hütte gelegt haben, werden nach mir ebenso rätselhaft sein, wie das Tagebuch des Offiziers. Auf die Art werden Sie, ganz gegen Ihren Willen, in unsere Legende eingehen. Ist das nicht ein äußerstes Paradoxon? (dt. 139)

Nicht die Geschichte, sondern die Legende wird in diesem Fall das letzte Wort behalten.

2. DIE ENZYKLOPÄDIE ALS TEXT

Klassifikation/Wissensordnung

In *Bouvard et Pécuchet* ist es vor allem die episodische Struktur, die serielle Abfolge der von den beiden Helden eroberten Wissensgebiete, die an die Form einer Enzyklopädie erinnern. Um auf die Frage der Wissensordnung in Flauberts Text eine Antwort zu finden, verweist Yvan Leclerc auf die geläufige Feststellung, dass den exakten Wissenschaften die Humanwissenschaften folgen. Neben dieser Grobeinteilung Physik – Metaphysik (»harte« – »weiche« Wissenschaften), erkennt er eine, wenn auch nur in Spuren vorhandene, so doch alphabetische Ordnung im Text: agriculture, arboriculture, chimie, diététique, géologie, histoire, littérature, magnétisme, métaphysique, philosophie, religion.[11] Leclerc betont außerdem die Dominanz einer vertikalen Schreibachse und bezieht sich dabei auf die erhaltenen, von Flaubert in langer Vorarbeit angefertigten Pläne und Skizzen, auf denen Eigennamen und Bücher häufig in Listen und Spalten angeführt werden. Um diese Bücher- und Namenlisten rankt sich nun die Idee der Enzyklopädie in Form eines ungewöhnlichen Romans, der die Handlung extrem zurücknimmt und »das Erzählen in Richtung Aufzählen sprengt«[12], wie das folgende Zitat aus dem 2. Kapitel (Agronomiekapitel) leider nur andeuten kann.

Aber auch Bouvard stieß auf Hindernisse. Der eine holte sich Rat beim anderen. Dann schlugen sie ein Buch auf und noch eins, und da diese jedesmal gegenteilige Ansichten vertraten, wußten sie nie, wozu sie sich entschließen sollten.
Puvis zum Beispiel empfahl den Mergel, Manuel Roret lehnte ihn ab.
Was den Gips betraf, so schienen trotz Franklins Beispiel Riéfel und Rigaud von ihm nicht begeistert zu sein.
Nach Bouvards Ansicht waren die Brachfelder ein altes Vorurteil. Leclerc jedoch verzeichnet die Fälle, wo sie fast unentbehrlich sind. Gasparin erwähnt einen Mann aus Lyon, der ein halbes Jahrhundert lang auf demselben Feld Getreide zog. Das aber wirft die Theorien der Koppelwirtschaft über den Haufen. Tull lobt über die Maßen das Pflügen der Felder auf Kosten der Düngung, und Major Beatson verwirft sogar die Düngung und das Pflügen. (dt. 72)

Zwar kann, wie gesagt, eine grobe Struktur in der Wissensanordnung festgestellt werden, im Detail aber folgt diese keiner Hierarchie, sondern scheint von gegebenen Notwendigkeiten oder dem Zufall abhängig zu sein. Bouvard und Pecuchet beginnen mit dem Gartenbau, denn »le plus pressé, c'était le jardin«, was natürlich auch als Anspielung auf oder Fortsetzung von Voltaires *Candide* gelesen werden kann. Was eine klare Abgrenzung der Wissensbereiche bzw. eine Einteilung in Disziplinen schwierig macht, ist weiters die Tatsache, dass Bouvard und Pécuchet sich auch für Dinge interessieren, die in offiziellen Wissensbereichen ausgeschlossen oder tabuisiert werden. Der Text lässt Platz für das »non-savoir«, d. h. für das nicht-kanonisierte oder in Disziplinen sich ordnende Wissen.[13] Sämtliche Lebensbereiche werden zu Wissensbereichen. Hinzu kommt, dass *Bouvard et Pécuchet* nicht nur eine Enzyklopädie des sowohl offiziellen als auch »alternativen« Wissens ist, sondern außerdem eine der kursierenden Meinungen und Gemeinplätze. Damit sind Ideen gemeint, die unhinterfragt nachgesprochen werden und somit gesellschaftliche Konventionen und Machtgefüge mittragen. Bouvard und Pécuchet erkennen in den Auseinandersetzungen

mit den Notabeln von Chavignolles (u. a. Arzt, Pfarrer, Bürgermeister), dass Wissen nicht unabhängig und eindeutig im Raum steht, sondern mit Positionskämpfen, Machtspielen und Ausschließungsmechanismen verbunden ist. Ulrich Schulz-Buschhaus verweist diesbezüglich zu Recht auf die Nähe der Flaubert'schen Sprachkritik zu Foucaults Diskursordnung. Für ihn gilt Flaubert als der Entdecker der »Abhängigkeit auch der intimsten und persönlichsten Rede von gesellschaftlichen Sprachregelungen.«[14]
In Rios Text wird die Wissensordnung der fiktiven Enzyklopädie als eine traditionell alphabetische beschrieben. Wenn aber John Steinbeck »einen Artikel über die amerikanische Literatur des zwanzigsten Jahrhunderts und sein persönliches Rezept für eine Bloody Mary« einbringt, oder Noam Chomsky »einen historisch-theoretischen Überblick über die Sprachwissenschaft seit Saussure und ein Kürbistortenrezept« (dt. 15) verfasst, so werden auch hier traditionelle Enzyklopädiegrenzen gesprengt und Wissenshierarchien destabilisiert.
Die bereits von Bouvard und Pécuchet erlebten und häufig in Dialogform abgehandelten Widersprüchlichkeiten innerhalb der Wissenschaften sind auch ein Thema in Rios Roman, was sich in diesem Text in erster Linie in den Kommentaren des Ich-Erzählers ausdrückt. Er stellt dem Wunsch seines Großonkels, das »von aller Welt geteilte und anerkannte Wissen« (»savoir universellement partagé et admis«) zu sammeln und zu überprüfen, nicht nur den Einfluss der Kulturen gegenüber, sondern auch die persönlichen Besonderheiten der Autoren, ihre Lebensgeschichten und Charaktere sowie die Abhängigkeit der Disziplinen und glaubt nur an einen »bedingten Aussagewert« eines solchen Unternehmens. Dieser bedingte Aussagewert der Enzyklopädie besteht z. B. darin, dass sich der Ich-Erzähler trotz seiner Vorbehalte der Enzyklopädie bedient, um sich einen Überblick über die Insel zu verschaffen. Er greift außerdem vermehrt auf die Enzyklopädie zurück, um Suzanne »systematisch« seine europäische Kultur zu erklären. Diese Erklärung wird im Text in Form einer Aufzählung wiedergegeben, eingebaut in einen deskriptiven Part, der sich über mehrere Seiten hin fortsetzt. Das europäische Wissen wird dabei an folgende Männernamen gekoppelt: Demokrit, Lukrez, Ptolemäus, Kopernikus, Galilei, Kepler, Einstein, Newton, Planck, Dyson.
An einer anderen Stelle antwortet der Ich-Erzähler auf die Frage Suzannes, ob es besser sei zu glauben oder zu wissen bzw. ob Wissen nützlich sei:

> – Ja und nein. Das Wissen hat einen Vorteil. Es erlaubt, besser auf die Dinge einzuwirken. Und einen Nachteil. Es läuft nur auf sich selbst hinaus, auf seine eigene Fortdauer, bis zum Tode dessen, der weiß, dann aller derer, die wissen. Der Glaube, die Legende, wenn Ihnen das lieber ist, hat nur ein Ziel: den Sieg des Lebens über den Tod. (dt. 81)

Dieses Zitat beschreibt sehr deutlich, dass auch in diesem Text unterschiedliche Wissenskonzeptionen dargestellt werden: das rationale (wissenschaftliche) europäische Wissen und das mythisch-legendäre Wissen. Suzanne selbst eignet sich die ihr fremde »Weltsicht« an, entscheidet sich jedoch in der Folge für das »primitive« Denken und distanziert sich vom Ich-Erzähler, dessen »enzyklopädisches«, ständig sammelndes und ordnendes Denken Unsicherheit und Angst in ihr Leben bringt.[15]

Dokument und Nomenklatur

Enzyklopädien zeichnen sich, wie deutlich wurde, durch eine Sammlung von Wissen und Material aus. Flaubert las für die Konzeption seines Romans über 1500 Bücher. Auch Bouvard und Pécuchet verwenden für ihre Forschungen eine Unmenge an Büchern, die im Text angeführt werden und mit wenigen Ausnahmen aus real existierenden Texten bestehen. Es handelt sich dabei in zahlreichen Fällen um populärwissenschaftliche Literatur.[16] Der Literaturwissenschaftler Jacques Neefs spricht hinsichtlich des Zitats realer Texte von einem ganz speziellen Intertextualitätsprozess, bei dem das, was gelesen wird, auch sofort im Text verarbeitet wird.[17] Das Gelesene, die Dokumente werden Teil der fiktiven Welt, sie werden in den Text montiert. Im 3. Kapitel (Chemie, Anatomie, Physiologie, Geologie) werden z. B. folgende Texte erwähnt: le cours de Regnault (116), l'ouvrage de Girardin (116), le manuel d'Alexandre Lauth (118), le *Dictionnaire des Sciences médicales* (121), les traités de Richerand et d'Adelon (122), le *Manuel de la Santé* (128) etc. Diese Dokumente werden folgendermaßen in den Text integriert:

> Sie schafften sich das Lehrbuch von Regnault an, nach dem sie die Chemie studieren wollten, und erfuhren als erstes, »daß die einfachen Körper wahrscheinlich zusammengesetzt sind«. (dt. 99)

> Sie gingen wieder zu Vaucorbeil und lernten aus dem Handbuch von Alexandre Lauth die Einteilung des Knochengerüstes kennen; sie staunten besonders über das Rückgrat, von dem es heißt, es sei sechzehnmal stärker, als wenn es der Herrgott gerade gemacht hätte. – Warum genau sechzehnmal? (dt. 101)

> Vor allem fehlte ihnen die Bekanntschaft mit der Physiologie; ein Buchhändler beschaffte ihnen die damals berühmten Abhandlungen von Richerand et Adelon. (dt. 104)

Diese »neue Notwendigkeit« sich aus Quellen zu speisen, seien es Dokumente oder die Vielfalt der Diskurse, ist nach Neefs eine Eigenheit der Literatur des 19. u. 20 Jahrhunderts, für die die Frage des Dokuments, der Referentialität, der Exaktheit und der Authentizität einen vorrangigen Platz in der ästhetischen Konstruktion einnimmt. Was die Authentizität anbelangt, so ist auf eine weitere Besonderheit in Flauberts Text hinzuweisen.

Die Dokumente werden nämlich nicht nur zitiert, sondern durch ein Spiel mit wechselnden Perspektivsetzungen und ironischen Distanzierungen wird ihnen an manchen Stellen selbst das Wort überlassen, d. h. wenn Bouvard und Pécuchet sich mit einem Thema beschäftigen, sich dafür bestimmter Quellen bedienen und im Text darüber sprechen, wird die Grenze zwischen Erzähler, Figuren- und Quellenrede so undeutlich, dass es nicht mehr ganz eindeutig ist, wer zitiert wird. Dieses Spiel mit dem Zitat ergibt sich aus der Spezifizität Flauberts, nicht nur schriftliche Dokumente, sondern, wie bereits erwähnt, auch kursierende Meinungen und Gemeinplätze in den Text zu integrieren. Alles Mögliche wird im Text zum Dokument bzw. Zitat. Der geplante zweite Teil des Romans sollte ausschließlich aus diesen Dokument- und Zitatsammlungen der beiden Protagonisten bestehen: aus Gemeinplätzen, schicken Meinungen sowie ihren Lektürenotizen. In Rios Text findet sich kein vergleichbarer Dokumentbezug. Flaubert sehr ähnlich jedoch sind die Präsenz, Verwendung und Anhäufung exakten fachspezifischen Vokabulars, die literarische Auseinandersetzung mit wissenschaftlicher Nomenklatur. Christian Metz – Filmsemiotiker und Dissertationsbetreuer Rios – spricht von »rafales terminologiques« (terminologischen Windstößen) und betont dessen »exactitude matérielle«.[18] Rio beschreibt in *Alizés* zum Beispiel äußerst genau die Konstruktion des Segelbootes, die Architektur von Suzannes Haus oder auch die Flora und Fauna der Insel, wie das folgende Zitat zeigt:

> Zahlreiche Tierarten bevölkerten das Unterholz, worunter die außerordentliche Mannigfaltigkeit der Affen und Stelzvögel auffiel. Ein Gewimmel von kurzschwänzigen Hundsaffen, Stummelaffen, Mandrillen, afrikanischen Nachtaffen, Rhesus- und Hutaffen, schwarzen Gibbons, braunen Kapuzineraffen, roten Brüllaffen, Seidenäffchen, Siamangs führte in den Bäumen ein lärmendes und vulgäres Dasein; dabei kamen sie bis auf die Erde herunter, um einen aus nächster Nähe in Augenschein zu nehmen, eine Dreistigkeit, die auf das fast gänzliche Fehlen von Raubtieren hinwies [...]. (dt. 83)

Das Übermaß an technischem Vokabular und die Bedeutung der Konstruktion selbst zeigt sich besonders auffällig in der Baubeschreibung des Ersatzsegelschiffes – *Le Rêve de Suzanne* – das der Ich-Erzähler auf der Insel konstruiert. Der Fabrikationsprozess wird außergewöhnlich genau beschrieben und dafür sehr spezifisches Vokabular aus dem Schiffsbau und der Seemannssprache verwendet.

Diese auffällige Verwendung bzw. listenartige Anhäufung von spezifischem Vokabular erinnert einerseits an die Sammeltätigkeit der Lexikographen, andererseits werden dem literarischen Text durch die exakten Beschreibungen und Benennungen spezifische Wissensbereiche (Architektur, Schiffsbau, exotische Pflanzen- und Tierwelt) erschlossen.

Visualisierung und Illustration

Enzyklopädien kennzeichnen sich spätestens seit der Enzyklopädie von Diderot und d'Alembert durch die wichtige Rolle, die der Illustration zukommt. Wissen (Gegenstände, Maschinen, Produktionsprozesse) wird in Wort und Bild vermittelt, anschaulich gemacht. Gemäß Roland Barthes praktiziert die Enzyklopädie lange vor der Literatur eine gewisse »Philosophie der Gegenstände« (Objekte), sie reflektiert über das Dasein der Dinge, zählt und definiert diese.[19] Für Flaubert ist das Thema der Visualisierung, der »bildlichen« Darstellung und Beschreibung von »Dingen« im Text von großer Bedeutung. Bereits im Jahre 1853 schreibt er in einem Brief an Louise Colet:[20]

> Die Literatur wird mehr und mehr das Gebaren der Wissenschaft annehmen; sie wird insbesondere *darlegend* sein, was nicht heißen will didaktisch. Man muß Gemälde schaffen, die Natur zeigen wie sie ist, aber vollständige Gemälde, man muß das Oben und Unten schildern.

In der Exaktheit der Bilder also wird sich laut Flaubert die Literatur den Wissenschaften annähern. Der Beginn des 4. Kapitels ist ein sehr schönes Beispiel für Flauberts »Dingpoesie« und sein Bemühen der genauen Abbildung. Es wird das zu einem eigenartigen Museum sich gewandelte Haus der beiden Helden beschrieben bzw. inventarisiert:

> Ein halbes Jahr später waren sie Archäologen geworden, und ihr Haus glich einem Museum.
>
> Ein alter Holzbalken stand in der Vorhalle. Die Gesteinsproben lagen haufenweise auf der Treppe, und eine riesige Kette zog sich über den Boden des ganzen Korridors. [...]
>
> Kaum hatte man die Schwelle betreten, stieß man sich an einem Steintrog (einem gallo-romanischen Sarkophag), man war frappiert von einer Menge Gegenstände aus Metall.
>
> An der gegenüberliegenden Wand überragte eine Wärmpfanne zwei Feuerböcke und ein Herdblech, auf dem ein Mönch mit einer Hirtin schäkerte. Auf kleinen Wandbrettern sah man Leuchter, Schlösser, Bolzen, Schrauben. Der Boden verschwand unter roten Ziegelscherben. Auf einem Tisch in der Mitte lagen die größten Seltenheiten: das Gestell einer Mütze, wie sie die Frauen in Caux tragen, zwei tönerne Urnen, Denkmünzen und eine Phiole aus Opalglas. Auf der Rückenlehne eines gestickten Sessels lag eine dreieckige Seidenspitze. Die rechte Wand zierte das Stück eines Panzerhemdes; eine Hellebarde, ein ganz besonders gut erhaltenes Stück, war horizontal darunter angenagelt. Das zweite Zimmer, in das zwei Stufen führten, enthielt sowohl die alten aus Paris mitgebrachten Bücher, als auch die, die sie bei ihrer Ankunft in einem Schrank vorgefunden hatten. Die Türen des Schranks hatten sie ausgehängt. Hier war jetzt ihre Bibliothek. (dt. 142)

Dietrich Scholler stellt zu Recht fest, dass sich hinter dem bunten Sammelsurium nicht aufeinander beziehbarer Gegenstände nirgends eine ordnende Hand ausmachen lässt.[21] Die genaue Abbildung einer eigentlichen

»Unordnung« spiegelt außerdem sehr deutlich die Ambivalenz in Flauberts Text, der einerseits Wissenschaftlichkeit in der Literatur durch exakte Darstellung zu suchen scheint und gleichzeitig in der Unordnung und Bizarrerie der Gegenstände die Aporie des Wissens- und Systematisierungsdranges aufzeigt.

Der im Zitat durch das neutrale »on/man« sich gestaltende, wissenschaftliche Blick auf das Museum wird nachträglich Pécuchet zugedacht, wenn dem Beschreibungsteil wieder ein Erzählteil folgt, in dem es heißt:

> Pécuchet sah das alles, wie aufgefädelt, von seinem Bett aus und manchmal ging er sogar in Bouvards Zimmer, um sein Blickfeld zu erweitern. (Übersetzung H.H.)

Ein zuerst »neutraler« Blick wird einer bestimmten »personalen« Perspektive zugeteilt. Der »objektive« Blick wird ein subjektiver. Pécuchet sieht das alles, wie aufgefädelt von seinem Bett aus. Die Anordnung der Dinge konstruiert sich in Abhängigkeit von der Perspektive bzw. vom Standpunkt. Die ständige Verundeutlichung des Orientierungszentrums im Text (Figuren- oder Erzählerperspektive) ist, wie bereits erwähnt, eine für Flaubert typische Erzählstrategie und im Zusammenhang mit dem Motiv der Enzyklopädie als Infragestellung einseitiger, nach Absolutheit und Autorität strebender Sichtweisen interpretierbar.

In Rios Text wird über das Thema der Illustrierung der Enzyklopädie das Verhältnis von Kunst und photographischer Reproduktion thematisiert. Der Ich-Erzähler beschreibt ausführlich die ungewöhnliche Art der Illustrierung seiner Erbschaft. Es wurde dafür bewusst nicht auf die Photographie zurückgegriffen, sondern einzig und allein auf Stiche, Zeichnungen und Gemälde.

> Nie wurde der wirkliche Raum als solcher gezeigt. Das Schauspiel der Welt, ob es sich dabei um Menschen handelte oder um Dinge, um Natur oder Manufaktur, um Technik oder Traumbild, ging durch die Hand des Künstlers. (dt. 11)

Die Hand des Künstlers wird der industriellen Reproduktion gegenübergestellt bzw. vorgezogen. Es werden weiters die »größten zeitgenössischen Maler und Zeichner« vom Herausgeber ersucht:

> [...] sämtliche Bildtafeln und Vignetten des Werkes anzufertigen, sei es mit einigen vertretbaren Zugeständnissen an ihre Manier – sofern eine Interpretation möglich war, zum Beispiel bei Porträts oder Landschaften – oder sei es im Gegenteil durch eine radikale Verfremdung des Schöpferischen, das heißt durch die präzise naturalistische Wiedergabe der gigantischen Anhäufung von Gegebenem und Konstruiertem, der Gegenstände und Materialien des Wissens. (dt. 11)

Diese Beschreibungen lese ich als eine Anspielung auf das Enzyklopädieprojekt von Diderot und d'Alembert, auf die Kunst, die sich in den *planches* (Kupferstichen) darstellt, wo die eben erwähnten Gegenstände und Materialien des Wissens auf eindrucksvolle Weise abgebildet sind. Wie bereits gezeigt wurde, werden auch in Rios Texten bestimmte Gegenstände, wie Suzannes Haus oder das Segelboot, aber auch die Fauna und Flora der Insel auf enzyklopädische Art und Weise, d. h. äußerst genau und umfassend beschrieben.

In Rios Text fertigt Salvador Dalí für die Enzyklopädie Pastelle von Boretschgewächsen an sowie Tuschzeichnungen von einem Beschleuniger schwerer Elementarteilchen. Pollock, Soulages, Kline und Poliakoff, bekannt für ihre abstrakte Kunst, zeichnen mit vollendeter Genauigkeit Kopulationen von Hautflüglern, Geschwindigkeitsmesser, Fichtennadeln oder Schleusengrundrisse. Diese genauen Bilder erfüllen eine der Zielvorstellungen von Enzyklopädien: Verständlichkeit und Anschaulichkeit. Gleichzeitig aber erhält die beschriebene Enzyklopädie durch die besondere Autorschaft eine ironisch-absurde Note.

Literatur und Wissen

Das 19. Jahrhundert gilt als das »Goldene Zeitalter« der Enzyklopädien, einerseits verbunden mit zunehmender Buchproduktion und Leserschaft, andererseits mit den Entwicklungen von Positivismus und Szientismus. Inmitten der Geschichte der Enzyklopädie – so Roland Barthes – gibt es das Moment Flaubert, ein »moment-farce«.[22] Flaubert macht sich über den Enzyklopädiediskurs seiner Zeit lustig. Gleichzeitig aber ist Uwe Japp zuzustimmen, wenn dieser betont, dass Flaubert mittels Komik die Wissenschaft an die Literatur annähert und somit eine eminent ästhetische Perspektive ins Spiel bringt: »Verwissenschaftlichung der Literatur einerseits, Literarisierung der Wissenschaft andererseits: in dieser prekären Balance gipfelt das Spätwerk Flauberts.«[23]

Für Rio hat die Enzyklopädie weniger Diskurs- denn vielmehr Monumentcharakter: sie repräsentiert das europäische Wissen, dem eine Orientierungs- und Systematisierungsfunktion zugestanden wird. Gleichzeitig werden aber auch die Zweifel an diesem Wissen und die Defizite dieses Wissens dargestellt. Wissen – wie bereits in einem Zitat erwähnt – läuft immer nur auf sich selbst hinaus. Die Legende (das Imaginäre) hingegen kann der »condition humaine« eher gerecht werden und durch die ihr eigene Vorstellungskraft Utopien und Träume hervorbringen. Die Literatur bzw. der Roman stellt für Rio den Ort dar, an dem die beiden Pole Wissen (Logik) und Imagination (Traum) idealerweise verknüpft werden können. In diesem Sinn ist die Enzyklopädie Metapher für Rios Forderung an Literaturschaffende, sich mit dem zeitgenössischen Wissen auseinander zu setzen und es in den Text einfließen zu lassen. In beiden Texten wird anhand des Motivs der Enzyklopädie über die heuristische Funktion von Literatur nachgedacht; dem Roman die mögliche Annäherung von Literatur und Wissenschaft zugestanden.

ANMERKUNGEN

[1] *Dictionnaire culturel des sciences*, hg. v. Nicolas Witkowski, Paris 2001, S. 13.
[2] Mieke Bal, *Narratology. Introduction to the theory of narrative*, Toronto/Buffalo/London 1997, S. xi.
[3] Ich habe folgende Ausgaben verwendet: Gustave Flaubert, *Bouvard et Pécuchet*, hg. v. Claudine Gothot Mersch, Paris 1979. Michel Rio, *Alizés*, Paris 1984. Wenn nicht anders angegeben, sind die Übersetzungen folgenden deutschsprachigen Ausgaben entnommen: Gustave Flaubert, *Bouvard und Pécuchet*, übers. v. Georg Goyert, Frankfurt/Main 1979. Michel Rio, *Passatwinde*, übers. v. Thorgerd Schücker, Berlin 1991.
[4] Gustave Flaubert, *Correspondance*, Bd. 4, Paris 1998 (Pléiade), S. 558-559 (Brief an Edma Roger des Genettes vom 19. August 1872).
[5] »Vous me parlez de la bêtise générale, mon cher ami, ah! je la connais, je l'étudie. C'est là l'ennemi, et même il n'y a pas d'autre ennemi. Je m'acharne dessus dans la mesure de mes moyens. L'ouvrage que je fais pourrait avoir comme sous-titre ›encyclopédie de la bêtise humaine‹. L'entreprise m'accable et mon sujet me pénètre.«; Brief an Raoul-Duval (Mitte Februar 1879) in: Gustave Flaubert, *Œuvres complètes: Correspondance 1877-1880*, Bd. 16, Paris 1975 (Club de l'Honnête Homme), S. 150.
[6] Diese Typisierung entnehme ich einem Text Dietrich Schollers, der neben drei klassischen Grundtypen von Enzyklopädien (Darstellung des Zusammenhangs aller Wissenschaften, Sammlung und Darstellung alles Wissens in alphabetisch geordneten Lexika, systematisierende Darstellung einer Wissenschaft in einschlägigen Handbüchern oder Reallexika) narrative und visuelle Enzyklopädien unterscheidet. Vgl. Dietrich Scholler, »›Mais on ne voit chez vous que des choses lugubres!‹ – Enzyklopädische Sichtbarkeit in Flauberts *Bouvard et Pécuchet*«, in: *PhiN (Philologie im Netz)* 1 (1997), S. 44-45.
[7] Aus dem *Dictionnaire des idées reçues* (Wörterbuch der Gemeinplätze): »Gegen sie wettern. Mitleidig über sie lachen, wie über ein Werk des Rokoko.« (Übersetzung H.H.)
[8] Der Name geht zurück auf den ursprünglichen Verleger Nicolas-Edme Roret. Berühmt wurde sein Verlagshaus v.a. durch die Publikation einer Serie von technischen Handbüchern wie z. B. das »Manuel du distillateur«, die unter dem Namen *Encyclopédie Roret* oder *Collection des Manuels Roret* erschienen (1822-1939). Vgl. Alfred Fierro, »Les manuels Roret«, in: Roger Chartier und Henri-Jean Martin (Hg), *Histoire de l'édition française*, Bd. 3, Paris 1990, S. 443-444.
[9] Dietrich Scholler, *Die Idee der Enzyklopädie in Flauberts Bouvard et Pécuchet*, Freie Universität Berlin: Staatsexamensarbeit, 1991, S. 40.
[10] Vgl. Wolfgang Asholt, »Aufklärung nach der Postmoderne? Die Segel-Tetralogie von Michel Rio«, in: Anja Bandau et al. (Hg), *Korrespondenzen. Literarische Imagination und kultureller Dialog in der Romania*, Festschrift für Helene Harth zum 60. Geburtstag, Tübingen 2000, S. 237-251. Ich kann hier nur darauf hinweisen, dass das europäische, auf Rationalität begründete Wissen bezeichnenderweise mit einem Mann und das mythisch-legendäre Wissen mit einer Frau verbunden ist, werde aber nicht weiter darauf eingehen.

[11] Vgl. Yvan Leclerc, *La spirale et le monument. Essai sur Bouvard et Pécuchet de Gustave Flaubert*, Paris 1988, S. 68-69.
[12] Ulrike Sprenger, »Die Früchte des Wissens – Agronomie und Imagination in *Bouvard et Pécuchet*«, in: *Romanistisches Jahrbuch* 48 (1997), S. 115.
[13] Vgl. Laurent Adert, *Les mots des autres. Lieu commun et création romanesque dans les œuvres de Gustave Flaubert, Nathalie Sarraute et Robert Pinget*, Villeneuve d'Ascq (Nord) 1996, S. 126.
[14] Ulrich Schulz-Buschhaus, »Statt eines Nachworts: Die moderne Rhetorik des Schweigens und die postmoderne Poetik des Zitats«, in: Ders., *Flaubert – Die Rhetorik des Schweigens und die Poetik des Zitats*, Münster 1995, S. 135.
[15] Vgl. Ursula Bähler, »Lettre de Suzanne. Le dialogisme à l'œuvre dans *Alizés* de Michel Rio«, in: *Versant* 31 (1997), S. 5-34. Bähler verweist in ihrem Artikel auf die Nähe Rios zu den Arbeiten Claude Lévi-Strauss' u. a. in der Dichotomie »scientific/primitive thinking«.
[16] Vgl. Claudine Cohen, »Bouvard et Pécuchet réécrivent les sciences«, in: *Alliage* 37-38 (1998-1999), S. 113. Vgl. auch Alberto Cento, *Commentaire de »Bouvard et Pécuchet«*, hg. von Lea Caminiti Pennarola, Napoli 1973. In diesem Kommentar ist ein Großteil der Werke gesammelt, die Flaubert für seinen letzten Roman verwendet hat.
[17] Jacques Neefs, »L'imaginaire des documents«, in: Raymonde Debray-Genette et Jacques Neefs (Hg), *Romans d'archives*, Presses Universitaires de Lille, 1987, S. 175-190 (hier 176).
[18] Christian Metz, »Le Je et le jeu«, in: Margery Arent Safir (Hg), *Mélancolies du savoir. Essais sur l'œuvre de Michel Rio*, Paris 1995, S. 181-199.
[19] Roland Barthes, *Les planches de l'»Encyclopédie«*, in: *Œuvres complètes*, Bd. 2, Paris 1994, S. 1348-1358.
[20] 6. April 1853 an Louise Colet (*Correspondance*, juillet 1851 – décembre 1858, Bd. 2, Paris 1980, S. 298): La littérature prendra de plus en plus les allures de la science; elle sera surtout *exposante*, ce qui ne veut pas dire didactique. Il faut faire des tableaux, montrer la nature telle qu'elle est, mais des tableaux complets, peindre le dessous et le dessus. (Hervorhebung Flaubert; dt. Übersetzung Helmut Scheffel, in: Gustave Flaubert, *Briefe*, hg. u. übers. v. Helmut Scheffel, Zürich 1977, S. 248)
[21] Vgl. Dietrich Scholler, »Mais on ne voit chez vous que des choses lugubres!«, a.a.O., S. 49.
[22] Roland Barthes, »La crise de la vérité«, in *Œuvres complètes*, Bd. 3, Paris 1995, S. 434.
[23] Uwe Japp, »Die Komik des Wissens«, in: Bouvard et Pécuchet, a. a. O., S. 399-431 (hier S. 402).

BIBLIOGRAPHIE

Adert, Laurent, Les mots des autres. Lieu commun et création romanesque dans les œuvres de Gustave Flaubert, Nathalie Sarraute et Robert Pinget, Villeneuve d'Ascq (Nord) 1996

Asholt, Wolfgang, Aufklärung nach der Postmoderne? Die Segel-Tetralogie von Michel Rio, in: Anja Bandau et al. (Hg), Korrespondenzen. Literarische Imagination und kultureller Dialog in der Romania, Festschrift für Helene Harth zum 60. Geburtstag, Tübingen 2000, S.237-251

Bähler, Ursula, Lettre de Suzanne. Le dialogisme à l'œuvre dans *Alizés* de Michel Rio, in: Versant 31 (1997), S.5-34

Bal, Mieke, Narratology. Introduction to the theory of narrative, Toronto/Buffalo/London 1997

Barthes, Roland, La crise de la vérité, in: Ders., Œuvres complètes, Bd. 3, Paris 1995, S.434-437

Barthes, Roland, Les planches de l'»Encyclopédie«, in: Ders., Œuvres complètes, Bd. 2, Paris 1994, S.1348-1358

Cento, Alberto, Commentaire de »Bouvard et Pécuchet«, hg. v. Lea Caminiti Pennarola, Napoli 1973

Cohen, Claudine, Bouvard et Pécuchet réécrivent les sciences, in: Alliage 37-38 (1998-1999), S.110-122

Dictionnaire culturel des sciences, hg. v. Nicolas Witkowski, Paris 2001

Fierro, Alfred, »Les manuels Roret«, in: Roger Chartier und Henri-Jean Martin (Hg), Histoire de l'édition française, Bd. 3, Paris 1990, S.443-444

Flaubert, Gustave, Bouvard et Pécuchet, hg. von Claudine Gothot Mersch, Paris 1979

Flaubert, Gustave, Bouvard und Pécuchet, übers. von Georg Goyert, Frankfurt/Main 1979

Flaubert, Gustave, Correspondance, Bd. 1, Paris 1973

Flaubert, Gustave, Correspondance, Bd. 2, Paris 1980

Flaubert, Gustave, Correspondance, Bd. 4, Paris 1998

Flaubert, Gustave, Œuvres complètes: Correspondance 1877-1880, Bd.16, Paris 1975

Flaubert, Gustave, Briefe, hg. u. übers. v. Helmut Scheffel, Zürich 1977

Koppe, Franz, Literarische Versachlichung: zum Dilemma der neueren Literatur zwischen Mythos und Szientismus. Paradigmen: Voltaire, Flaubert, Robbe-Grillet. München 1977

Leclerc, Yvan, La spirale et le monument. Essai sur *Bouvard et Pécuchet* de Gustave Flaubert, Paris 1988

Metz, Christian, Le Je et le jeu, in: Margery Arent Safir (Hg), Mélancolies du savoir. Essais sur l'œuvre de Michel Rio, Paris 1995, S.181-199

Neefs, Jacques, L'imaginaire des documents, in: Raymonde Debray-Genette et Jacques Neefs (Hg), Romans d'archives, Presses Universitaires de Lille, 1987, S.175-190

Rio, Michel, Alizés, Paris 1984

Rio, Michel, Passatwinde, übers. v. Thorgerd Schücker, Berlin 1991

Rio, Michel, Rêve de logique. Essais critiques, Paris 1992

Scholler, Dietrich, »Mais on ne voit chez vous que des choses lugubres!« – Enzyklopädische Sichtbarkeit in Flauberts *Bouvard et Pécuchet*, in: PhiN (Philologie im Netz) 1 (1997), S.43-62

Scholler, Dietrich, Die Idee der Enzyklopädie in Flauberts *Bouvard et Pécuchet*, Freie Universität Berlin, Staatsexamensarbeit, 1991

Schulz-Buschhaus, Ulrich, Flaubert – Die Rhetorik des Schweigens und die Poetik des Zitats, Münster 1995

Sprenger, Ulrike, Die Früchte des Wissens – Agronomie und Imagination in *Bouvard et Pécuchet*, in: Romanistisches Jahrbuch 48 (1997), S.84-119

Narrating Communities/Media

Narratives and Media Change: Making ›National‹ Documentaries in a Global Television Era

TAMAR ASHURI

Recent discussions of globalization contain frequent reference to the media as one of the main constituents of contemporary society, reflecting and fostering globalization. This paper adopts this point of view and focuses on broadcasting, and specifically, on television. It concentrates on television production practices especially in the making of historical documentaries. Its aim is to observe the ways in which the changes now taking place within the documentary sector, notably the shift of the industry from being national to being global, lead to new forms of representations.

The paper argues that although the television industry is becoming increasingly global, the production of television documentaries is still influenced strongly by ideas of national belonging. Films are made to reflect a particular national narrative.

CHANGED LANDSCAPE

It is a point very widely discussed in media studies that television has been very central to the development of national societies within the Western world. Radio and then television have been implicated in producing and reproducing the national imaginary. This kind of topic often gets linked to Benedict Anderson's *Imagined Community* (1983) and it is often said that earlier media (such as newspapers) were linked to the creation of an imagined community, and broadcasting in the 20th century have been central in the creation of modern imagined communities. Television for example, has made visible to all of us those people who feel that they are part of the same national community but whom we would never otherwise generally have seen.

It becomes apparent that since the mid 1980s this symbiosis between the nation and the television industry has increasingly come to be undermined (e.g. Barker 1997; Morley and Robins 1995; Thussu, 2000; Wang *et al* 2000; Wieten, *et al* 2000). The television industry in general and the documentary sector in particular has been shifting from being a national and mostly monopolised sector to being an international and even a global enterprise. This trend accelerated as a result of the rapid developments in digital, satellite and cable technologies, and were reinforced by the triumph of free market economics. As David Morley and Kevin Robins (1995) observed:

> Audiovisual geographies ... becoming detached from the symbolic spaces of national culture, and realigned on the basis of the more universal principle of international consumer culture (Morley and Robins 1995:11)

This ›globalization-commercialization‹ trend (Herman & McChesney 1997) has led to the emergence of more channels available to the viewing public, resulting in turn in a growing competition among different television providers. But by the same token, for the typical television network, intensifying competition has meant smaller television audiences and higher cost of programming. This development forces television producers to re-think the essential questions regarding the funding of television programmes. In order to lower the cost of production the creators of programmes find themselves increasingly involved in international collaborations with other foreign television networks (e.g. Hoskins *et al* 1997).

In what follows I shall describe the manner in which these economic collaborations reflect themselves in the *contents* of the documentaries being produced, thus affecting the ways in which »reality« is being conveyed.

The form of collaboration known as International Co-Production provides a particularly appropriate setting for looking at this issue. International co-production is one of the significant forms of economic and creative interaction among broadcasters from different countries, and is consequently an arena where the interplay between the global and the national and between funding and content is particularly apparent.

INTERNATIONAL CO-PRODUCTIONS

The term international co-production is used to characterise a situation where broadcasters in more than one country are involved, *creatively* and *financially*, in the production of a particular film. This form permits partners to pool resources, in order to raise the substantial budgets required to produce the ›master copies‹, which can be produced and then made, at minimal cost, to accommodate additional markets (Hoskins *et al* 1997). The goal of this strategy is to produce cultural programmes that are nationally relevant in all countries involved which allows producers access to funding mechanisms such as tax incentives, grants and investments.

Steven Seidenberg, a leading independent producer, has characterized international co-production as follows:

> ...The broadcaster puts up funds but simultaneously expects to have editorial in-put into the project. (In return for putting up the cash to make the film the broadcaster wants to be able to say »This works for my audience« or »That doesn't work for my audience, change it«) (Steven Seidenberg 2000)[1]

This observation highlights the distinctive features of this mode of production. Unlike other forms of international co-ventures (›Acquisition‹ and ›Programme Sales‹) the final product of an international co-production is being split into different versions, where each of the broadcasters who had participated in financing it is given the right to produce its own national version of the product. The result is a situation where a co-produced programme exists in different national versions.
Interestingly, despite the fact that co-productions usually arise in response to the need to lower costs of production, broadcasters are willing to incur additional costs by creating the same programme in different national versions. Examining this apparent paradox, I argue that although the television industry is becoming global, the production of programmes is still influenced strongly by factors of national belonging.
In the case of television dramas this paradox could be explained simply in terms of the need to respond to consumer demand, i.e., producers gain extra revenues by producing different national versions of what is basically the same programme. This is not, however, a sufficient explanation in the case of the production of documentaries, since programmes of this type are not normally perceived in terms of their financial revenue potential. As Tom Kock, director of WGBH International, explained:

> Remember, one of the underlying assumption of co-production of documentaries (unlike dramas) in which I could be technically a co-producer but I have a financial investment which I can recruit. The investment which I can recruit from documentaries is very very small it is probably insignificant, so that the only capital that one really looks for is editorial capital. That's my investment. I put up money and I expect something in return. With features film I expect a profit with documentaries I expect something else, I want to serve my audience, I want to get an involvement. I want to get a project that will work for my country, or my cultural ... my audiences' taste, or my perceived assumption of what my audiences' taste is (Interview Tom Kock, October 2001).

This phenomenon, where broadcasters initiate a co-production of a single product, which is then split into different national versions, is not novel. However, in recent years this pattern is becoming more and more popular. Several studies have recently been carried out to explore this growing trend of international co-productions. The findings indicate that the main motivation for broadcasters' involvement in this production mode is a growing need to lower the costs of production by poling financial resources (e.g. Hoskins *et al* 1998).

These findings may now be investigated further through the manner in which economic considerations reflect themselves in the *contents* of the programmes being co-produced, thus affecting the ways in which ›reality‹ is being conveyed.

MONEY AND CONTENT

The interplay between money and content has been explored in recent studies of international co-production. A good example for this type of research is Sharon Strover's article *Recent Trends in Coproductions: The Demise of the National* (1995). In this study the author claims that:

> ... the coproduction, among other forms of media ventures such as format licensing, makes economic sense but chips away at the notion of media that can build national collectivities or represent single countries. In the face of calls for revitalised »national media«, impulses toward transnational products and media content that easily cross borders may portend a demise of the national. (Strover 1995:98)

Similarly, Doris Baltuschart (2002) argues that:

> ... co-productions are predominantly used as a mean to access funding in an international marketplace—-a market dominated by commercial productions which fail to address audience as nationally and locally differentiated and unique (Baltruschat 2002)[2].

Looking specifically at international co-production in the making on documentaries, the author argues that: ›Co-productions focus less on stories relevant for local communities....‹ (Baltruschat 2002).

Other commentators offer a different view, pointing to the reverse phenomenon. In her study *The Search for National in Canadian Multilateral Cinematographic Co-productions* (2001) Anne Jäckel argued that:

> co-productions, not only helped the emergence and guarantees the very existence of national film industries, but in some countries, they have also been seen as ›a mechanism for nation building‹ (Jäckel 2001:155).

Similarly, Paul W. Taylor (1995), in exploring the usage of international co-productions in Canada showed how this mode of production was used by Canada to help find its own national identity in the midst of a popular culture dominated by its neighbour, the USA (Taylor 1995). The employment of the international co-production strategy by the Canadian film industry was explored also by Finn, Hoskines and McFadyen (1996). In their study of the production of feature films in the 1980s and early 1990s, the authors argue that ›international co-productions are neither less likely to be identifiably Canadian‹ nor ›less likely to have artistic merit then purely domestic production‹ (cited in Jäckel 2001:156). This line of thinking was also present in studies conducted in other parts of the Western world. For example

Bergfelder (2000) demonstrated how this strategy helped re-establish the German post war film industry.

As we have seen, the literature on international co-production in the making of films is divided into two distinct strands. One approach suggests that co-productions have led to standardized commodities, with national symbols gradually withering away (Baltruschat 2002; Strover 1995). The other approach sees co-production as a tool for resisting globalization, and pays special attention to the manner in which this strategy actually contributes to the building of a national culture (e.g. Bergfelder 2000; Jäckel 2001). However, neither strand pays much attention to the *interplay* between these two processes, thereby failing to capture a fundamental aspect of international co-production, namely the interaction of the global and the national as expressed in the contents of audio-visual products. This paper tries to fill this gap. In contrast to existing studies, which offer mainly a macro perspective of the co-production practice, I shall try to explore in detail the actual end product of a co-production. I believe that an analysis of the similarities and differences among the separate end products of an international co-production may well reveal the fundamental tension between the global and the national.

I shall restrict myself to an examination of one specific co-production, which, in my opinion, provides an especially vivid view of the underlying issues.

I focus on a documentary film which was produced in the connection with the 50th anniversary of the State of Israel by three networks, BBC2, PBS and MBC, under the title: *The Fifty Years War: Israel and the Arabs.* Its topic is the ongoing conflict between the Israelis and their the Palestinians.

To make this series possible, funding from three separate sources was secured, with each funding source given the right to use the produced footage to construct its own version of the final product. The completed series thus exists in three distinct versions, British (BBC2), American (PBS) and Middle-Eastern (MBC), respectively. To put it in other words, each broadcaster brought the right to re-create the event in his version of the film.

In order to see how the above-mentioned phenomenon manifests itself, it is necessary to start at the beginning, i.e., at the early stages of the film's production.

Israel and the Arabs was initiated by the former executive producer of BBC Michael Jackson. Brian Lapping and Associates, a London-based independent production company, was approached to produce it. However, Jackson was reluctant to commission such an expensive project, forcing the independent production company to formulate a film proposal with a potential to be of interest to different foreign broadcasters. The Arab-Israeli conflict seemed to be a promising topic in this respect. Firstly, Pa-

lestine carries strong religious connotations which could help the film to attract Christian viewers. Secondly, the political dispute between the Jews and the Arabs is constantly being covered in Western media, so Western audiences are familiar with its context. Finally, much of the film concerns human suffering, thus evoking emotions, which are shared by all. It was therefore possible for Brian Lapping, on the basis of this initial proposal, to secure funding from three different networks, BBC, PBS and MBC. Each funding source ›bought‹ the right to re-edit its own version of the film. The completed documentary series thus exists in three distinct national versions, British, American and Middle-Eastern (Norma Percy, Series Producer, personal communication, August 1999).
In the following pages I shall show how each of these national versions provides a different historical narrative concerning the conflict between Israel and the Arabs. I will pay special attention to the way in which national consciousness became a key ideological component in these audio-visual narratives. I turn, first of all, to a brief discussion of the media's role in constituting national consciousness through the use of national narratives.

MEDIA AND NATIONAL NARRATIVES

Building on Benedict Anderson's (1983) concepts, one can charecterize the mass media as one of the main realms in which the national community is ›imagined‹. One of the more fruitful ways to understand this function is derived from the role of the media in the construction of reality, namely the ›framing‹ of experiential fragments into coherent narrative-interpretive patterns, each with its own internal logic and structure.
Thus, media practitioners, notably journalists and filmmakers, join the rather short list of social agents that fulfil the role of interpreting and presenting reality as a coherent and meaningful construct. These interpreters of reality provide relevant frameworks for political, cultural and social discourse. The primary instruments they use to fulfil this function are symbols and memories (see Yadgar 2002). These are the tools used in the interpretation of reality: they facilitate a narrative representation of events, based on specific system of values. Symbols associate events with values, introducing, ›updating‹ and reinforcing them. Their function in the representation of reality can be described as a placing of events into meaningful narrative frameworks, based on shared symbolic systems that are reinforced as they are used (see Kane 2000; Yadgar 2002).
It is apparent that media's messages are expressions of interpretive narratives. These messages are used, in turn, for disseminating the narratives, reaffirming and rewriting them. The national narrative is one of the most salient of the symbolic tools used for this purpose. This narrative is the ex-

pression of sets of symbols and values, which relate to the national collective as a distinct unit. It is a story that a (national) community tells about itself. It tells the individuals constituting the nation who they are, what comprises their past, the structure of their characteristics as a collective and what is their destiny. Focusing on cinematic construction of national narratives Anthony Smith (2000) writes:

> ...in all historical film, as well as in the texts from which they stem, the sequence of events provides the essential framework, not for detached and ›truthful‹ account of *wie es eigentlich war*, but to convince the viewer of the epic grandeur of the nation, that is to say, in the first place, his or her nation. ... such works aim to provide a ›historical map‹ of the nation past in order to bind the spectator more firmly to present national identity (Smith: 2000:52).

These selective and sometimes exclusionary representations of the past, in turn have implications for how a nation is imagined (Lo 2001:111).

AN EXAMPLE – *THE FIFTY YEAR WAR: ISRAEL AND THE ARABS* (1998)

Recall that the question being explored is how three different national narratives (American, British and Arab) regarding the conflict between Israel and the Arabs had emerged in a television documentary commissioned by broadcasters coming from these three nations. My aim was to answer this question by exploring the ways in which elements of the national past were reflected and presented in each version of this film.

Due to the limitations in scope of this paper, I shall approach this task by looking only at the first sequence of the film *The FiftyYear War: Israel and the Arabs.*

Drawing on Michael Billig's notion of ›Banal Nationalism‹ (1995), one can identify two main messages in each of the three versions of the films. The first message tells each national target audience something about the Others, ›them‹, the nations being portrayed in the films. The second message tells each national audience something about ›us‹: what is ›our‹ role in the event and what are ›we‹ expected to know about it.

Given this dichotomy, one can proceed to analyse the three versions along three key dimensions which have significance in the development of national consciousness: the temporal, the spatial, and the heroes.

THE TEMPORAL DIMENSION

The British version of the film *Israel and the Arabs* begins with the caption – ›1947‹, thus directing its viewers to a specific point in time. This suggests the conflict between Israel and its Arab neighbours started 50 years before[3]

(fig. 1)

(fig. 2)

(fig. 3)

(fig. 4)

only when the British left Palestine. The second scene reinforces this notion. We see a tree (fig. 1) in the desert and hear the narrator's commentary[4]:

Palestine-One land two peoples.
50 years ago the British rulers washed their hands of Palestine.
The Jews saw their chance to declare their own state.
The Arabs were determined to stop them.

The American producer opted for a somewhat different beginning. Using the same image (fig. 2) of the tree in the desert, the producer made no mention to the year 1947 (the year when the British left Palestine). The American version did not find it necessary to make reference to a specific point in time. In this version the commentary[5] presents the conflict between Israel and the Arabs as ›timeless‹:

Palestine-A land divided.
A Holy land. A battle-ground.
A homeland claimed by Arabs and Jews.

In contrast to both the British and the American versions, the Arabic version (MBC) of the film offers a different visual image, namely the image of the »Dome of the Rock« – a mosque, built in the 7th century in Jerusalem, which has become a symbol of Islam and of the Muslim presence in Palestine. The commentary that accompanied this visual image – a *current* photo of the »Dome of the Rock« in colour (fig. 3), gradually dissolving into a black-and-white, *old* rendering of the same mosque (fig. 4) serves to reinforce this notion by concentrating on Muslims' long presence in the Holy Land – mentioning the Ottoman Empire and its collapse at the beginning of the 20th century[6].

Palestine: A land in dispute, between Arabs and Jews, a dispute
which has been going on for more then 50 years.
In 1917 Britain was granted the mandate over Palestine,
following the collapse of the Ottoman regime after World War One

It should be noted, furthermore, that all three producers largely ignored the wider historical context within which the conflict took place. The British producer did not inform his audience of the situation in Palestine before the British left, nor was it made known why the British were in Palestine in the first place.
Neither did the American producer familiarize his viewers with the history of this conflict. The dispute between the Arabs and Jews was represented as religious (holy) and therefore timeless.

The Arab producer did not bring to light the origins of the dispute, nor did he explain the context of the claiming by the Jews of political rights in Palestine.

SPATIAL DIMENSION

Theorists frequently refer to the notion of ›territory‹ as a significant factor in the development of national identity and historical awareness (e.g. Hall 1992; Kane 2000; Zamponi 1998).

Reference to geographic elements, which include images of distinctive landscapes and places, were made in all three versions of the film. In both the British and the American versions the conflict takes place in an unspecified landscape (e.g. the lone tree in the desert). This image being evoked is largely the 19th century representation of the Holy Land – the biblical land, as seen by the Christian pilgrims of the period. It is quite apparent that the two producers (the British and the American) targeted Christian viewers and therefore made reference to the Christians' sentiment of the ›holy region‹. There is an implicit message here regarding the significance of a conflict that takes place in a far away region whose holiness renders it familiar and relevant nevertheless.

The Arab producer, on the other hand, chose a completely different image, symbolized by the showing of the »Dome of the Rock«. This mosque, which is situated in the heart of Jerusalem, resonates well with contemporary Arab sensibilities regarding the struggle between the Arabs and the Israelis. The mosque represents ancient Arab presence in the city, symbolizing the Arabs' rights in Palestine, in the Holy Land.

HEROES

Audio-visual narrative insist on history of humans (e.g. Hesling 2001; Toplin 2000). Consequently, Audio-visual narratives concentrate on key people and/or peoples. In each version of the film the producers chose different key heroes to lead the cinematic story.

Despite the fact that the film is about the conflict between the Jews and the Arabs, the British producers (and only they) made sure that the British are mentioned first. The Arabs and the Jews came up only in the second sentence.

Yet, no one is informed as to why the British left, nor is it made known why they where in Palestine in the first place. The Ottomans are mentioned only in the Arab version. There is also no mention of any direct ›national link‹ between the Turks and the Arabs.

In contrast to both the British and the Arab producers, the American broadcaster ignored the British and the Turks altogether. No information is given regarding the role of these two colonial powers in the region.

CONCLUSIONS

The analysis presented in this paper largely scratches the surface. The cinematic construction of national narratives, on which I have focused clearly requires a more detailed analysis. My aim has been only to demonstrate how in each national version of this trans-national product, the conflict between Israel and the Arabs was represented differently. By analysing the similarities and differences among the separate end products, I hoped to shed some light on the relationship between the global and the national, between the universal and the particular, between the »we« and the »they«. The study seems to indicate that despite the considerable loosening of the symbiotic ties between nation-states and the national broadcasters operating in them, the creators of films are still committed to adjusting the contents of their products to what they see as the sensibilities of their national target audience. In the final analysis, films are embedded in a definite ›national narrative‹ even where they are made through a global or international production.

NOTES

[1] Cited from a communication sent to the ›Israeli Forum of Co-Productions‹ (March 2000).
[2] A paper delivered at a conference: Media in Transition: Globalization and Convergence, May 10-12, 2002, MIT Cambridge Massachusetts, USA.
[3] The film was transmitted on BBC2 in 1997.
[4] The commentary was narrated by a native English speaker.
[5] The commentary was narrated in English by an American narrator.
[6] The commentary was narrated in Arabic by a native Arabic speaker. The text used here is a translated version of it.

BIBLIOGRAPHY

Anderson, B. (1983). Imagined Communities: Reflections on the Origin and Spread of Nationalism . London, Verso.

Baker, C. (1997). Global Television, An Introduction. Oxford, Blackwell.

Baltruschat, D. (2002). Globalization and International TV and Film Co-productions: In Search of New Narratives. Media in Transition: Globalization and Convergence, MIT Cambridge Massachusetts, USA.

Bergfelder, T. (2000). The Nation Vanishes: European Co-Productions and Popular Genre Formulae in the 1950s and 1960s. Cinema and Nation. Hjort M., Mackenzie S., London, Routledge.

Billig, M. (1995). Banal Nationalism. London, Sage.

Herman E. S., McChesney R. (1997). The Global Media: the new missionaries of corporate capitalism. London, Cassell.

Hesling, W. (2001). »The Past as History.« European Journal of Cultural Studies 4(2): 189-205.

Hoskins C., Finn, A., McFadyen S., (1996). Telefilm Canada Investment in Feature Films: Empirical Foundations for Public Policy, Canadian Public Policy-Analyses de Politiques XX11/2: 151-161.

Hoskins, C., Finn, A., McFadyen S., et al. (1997). Global Television and Film: An Introduction to the Economics of the Business, Oxford University Press.

Hoskins C., Finn, A., McFadyen S., et al. (1998). »The Effect of Cultural Differences on the International Co-Production of Television Programs and Feature Films.« Canadian Journal of Communication 23: 523-538.

Jäckel, A. (2001). »The Search for the National in Canadian Multilateral Cinematographic Co-Productions.« National Identities 3(2): 156-167.

Kane, A. (2000). »Narratives of Nationalism: Constructing Irish National Identity During the Land War, 1879-82.« National Identity 2(3).

Lo, S. H. (2001). Mediating National Identity: Television, Politics and Audience in Taiwan. Media@LSE, Social Psychology. London, London School of Economics and Political Science, University of London.

Morley, D. and Robins, K. (1995). Spaces of Identity: global media, electronic landscapes and cultural boundaries. London ; New York, Routledge.

Smith, A. D. (2000). Images of the Nation: Cinema Art and National Identity. Cinema and Nation. Hjort M., Mackenzie S., London, Routledge.

Strover, S. (1995). Recent Trends in Coproductions: The Demise of the National. Democracy and Communication in the New Europe. C. a. Preston. New Jersey, Hampton Press, Ins: 97-123.

Taylor, P. W. (1995). »Co-productions—Content and Change: International Television in the Americas.« Canadian Journal of Communication 20: 411- 416.

Thussu, D. K. (2000). International Communication: continuity and change. London, Arnold.

Toplin, R., Ed. (2000). Stone's USA. USA, University Press of Kansas.

Wang, G., Goonasekera A., et al. (2000). The New Communications Landscape: demystifying media globalization. London ; New York, Routledge.

Wieten, J., Murdock G., et al. (2000). Television Across Europe: a comparative introduction. London, Sage.

Yadgar, Y. (2002). »From the Particularistic to the Universalistic: national narratives in Israel's mainstream press, 1967-97.« Nations and Nationalism 8(1): 55-72.

Zamponi, S. F. (1998). »Of Storytellers and Master Narratives: modernity, memory and history in Fascist Italy.« Social Science History 22:4 (Winter).

Denk-Orte: ein Dorf erzählt sein Gedächtnis

ERNST LANGTHALER

Gedächtnis ist in aller Munde: »The notion of ›memory‹ has taken its place now as a leading term, recently perhaps *the* leading term, in cultural history«.[1] Wie bei vielen anderen Leitbegriffen, so scheint es, nimmt die Genauigkeit, mit der das theoretische Konzept Gedächtnis auf empirische Phänomene bezogen wird, mit zunehmendem Gebrauch ab. Vielfach werden Gedächtnisse über große Spannen an Raum und Zeit gebreitet – das Gedächtnis des antiken Ägypten ebenso wie das Gedächtnis Nachkriegsösterreichs. Dagegen lässt sich einwenden: Gedächtnis ist weniger ein raum- und zeitumspannendes *Sein*, als ein auf das Hier und Jetzt bezogenes *Tun*. Unterstützung findet diese Annahme bei Maurice Halbwachs, der in den zwanziger Jahren des 20. Jahrhundert den Begriff Kollektivgedächtnis (*mémoire collective*) geprägt hat: »Man kann ebensogut sagen, daß das Individuum sich erinnert, indem es sich auf den Standpunkt der Gruppe stellt, und daß das Gedächtnis der Gruppe sich verwirklicht und offenbart in den individuellen Gedächtnissen.«[2] Individuen *identifizieren sich* und *werden identifiziert* mit Kollektiven – eine solche (sozial-)konstruktivistische Perspektive könnte, so meine ich, essenzialistischen Tendenzen in der historisch-kulturwissenschaftlichen Gedächtnisforschung entgegenwirken. Dieses Wechselspiel von Sich-Identifizieren und Identifiziert-Werden in Raum und Zeit lässt sich als *doing memory* fassen.[3]

Einer von mehreren Zugängen zu einer (sozial-)konstruktivistischen Gedächtnisforschung führt über die Erzähltheorie: »Eine Erzählung stellt eine Form der Rede dar, dank derer jemand jemandem ein Geschehen vergegenwärtigt.«[4] Von dieser knappen Begriffsklärung ausgehend können wir wichtige Dimensionen von *doing memory* ausführlicher benennen: Erstens werden Gedächtnisse *narrativ*, in Form mündlich, schriftlich, bildlich, gestisch oder anders gestalteter Erzählungen konstruiert. Zweitens werden Gedächtnisse *interaktiv*, zwischen ErzählerInnen und deren Publikum konstruiert. Drittens werden Gedächtnisse *retrospektiv* (und prospektiv), im gegenwartsgebundenen Blick auf Vergangenheit (und Zukunft) konstruiert. Die Betonung von Narration, Interaktion und Retrospektive setzt voraus, dass Menschen deutend und handelnd die vorgefundene Welt zu *ihrer* Welt machen. In diesem Sinn erzeugt die Konstruktion von Gedächtnissen nicht etwas Irreales, sondern eine Realität *sui generis*. Erzählen in diesem komplexen Verständnis bezeichnet jedoch nur eine Seite der Konstruktion von Gedächtnissen; die andere Seite umfasst das Nicht-Erzählen: Über etwas zu sprechen heißt zwangsläufig, über anderes zu schweigen. Gerade solche latenten, unausgesprochenen Erzählungen sind auf Grund ihres hohen Maßes an Selbstverständlichkeit vielfach wirksamer als manifeste, ausgesprochene Erzählungen.[5]

Im Jahr 2000 hatte ich gemeinsam mit Bernhard Ecker und Martin Neubauer die Möglichkeit, ein solches Konzept von *doing memory* in einer historisch-kulturwissenschaftlichen Feldforschung in einer etwa 2.000 Einwohner zählenden Marktgemeinde in den niederösterreichischen Voralpen zu erproben: Wie kommt es, dass Individuen beim lebensgeschichtlichen Erzählen sich mit Kollektiven identifizieren beziehungsweise damit identifiziert werden – und darüber Einverständnis erzielen oder in Streit um das Geschichtsbild geraten?[6] Um Antworten auf diese Frage zu finden, arrangierten wir im Lauf des Projektes unterschiedliche Kontexte, die jeweils eigene Erzählspielräume absteckten. Zwar begrenzten diese Kontexte die erzählerische Vielfalt; doch das Zusammentreffen von konkreten Menschen an konkreten Orten zu konkreten Zeiten machte das Erzählen erst möglich. Auf diese Weise intervenierten wir, in höherem oder geringerem Maß, in unseren Forschungsgegenstand. Kurz, wir wurden zu Teilnehmern jenes Geschehens, das wir beobachteten – ein Faktum, das wir in der Interpretation der Erzählungen zu reflektieren hatten.[7]

Im ersten Drittel der Projektlaufzeit führten wir biografisch-narrative Einzelinterviews mit elf Frauen und Männern aus dem Dorf in deren Privatwohnungen durch. Unsere Intervention beschränkte sich darauf, lebensgeschichtliche Erzählungen in Gang zu setzen. Die Erzählungen sollten durch ein hohes Maß an Offenheit gekennzeichnet sein; demgemäß lautete unsere Erzähleinladung: »Wir interessieren uns für die Erlebnisse, die Menschen in der Zeit zwischen den dreißiger und sechziger Jahren an verschiedenen Orten erfahren haben. Ich bitte Sie daher, mir über Ihr Leben zu erzählen.«[8] Das zweite Drittel der Projektlaufzeit war der Herstellung einer Audio-CD gewidmet, die wir der dörflichen Öffentlichkeit im Rahmen eines »Heimatabends«, einer Folkloreveranstaltung in einem Dorfwirtshaus, vorstellten. In die Erzählung, die sich den HörerInnen darbot, flossen mehrere Interventionen von unserer Seite ein: Wir wählten ereignisreiche, eindringliche Interviewpassagen aus; wir verfassten Kommentartexte, die auf den manifesten und latenten Sinn des Gesagten Bezug nahmen; wir orientierten uns bei der Gestaltung der CD an einem essayistischen Stil, und so fort.[9]

Beide Kontexte, jener der Einzelinterviews in der Privatsphäre und jener der öffentlichen Präsentation, waren wenig geeignet, die narrative, interaktive und retrospektive Konstruktion von Gedächtnissen zu erfassen. Im ersteren Fall fehlten die dafür nötigen Interaktionspartner, im letzteren Fall entzog sich die Interaktion unserer Wahrnehmung. Aus diesem Grund arrangierten wir im letzten Drittel der Projektlaufzeit einen neuen Kontext. Wir luden eine aus acht DorfbewohnerInnen bestehende Fokusgruppe zu einer Diskussion ein, in der wir Sinn und Zweck der CD zur Debatte stellen wollten. Obwohl ein Projektmitarbeiter die Rolle eines Moderators übernahm, waren Form und Inhalt der Diskussion weitgehend offen. Die Fokusgruppe setzte sich nach Geschlechtern, Generationen, Klassen, politischen Lagern und Milieus vielfältig zusammen: Sophie, geboren 1955, Sozialarbeiterin; Georg, geboren 1956, Vollerwerbsbauer und ehrenamtlicher Mitarbeiter im Arbeiter-Samariterbund; Margarete, geboren 1930, Hausfrau; Theresia, geboren 1925, pensionierte Fabriksarbeiterin und ehrenamtliche Mitarbeiterin in der Pfarrgemeinde; Friedrich, geboren 1926, pensionierter Angestellter der Österreichischen Bundesbahnen und ehrenamtlicher Tourismusbeauftragter der Gemeinde, Rudolf, geboren 1943, pensionierter Arbeiter der Österreichischen Bundesbahnen, Nebenerwerbsbauer und Obmann des Trachtenvereins; Karl, geboren 1939, pensionierter Installateurmeister und ehemaliger Gemeinderat der Österreichischen Volkspartei; Irene, geboren 1976, Absolventin des Studiums der Landschaftsplanung und ehrenamtliche Mitarbeiterin in der Landjugend.[10] Die Interpretation dieser Gruppendiskussion erforderte, unser Konzept von *doing memory* zu verfeinern. Anknüpfend an Maurice Halbwachs' Vorstellung des Individuums, das sich auf den Standpunkt einer Gruppe stellt und dorthin gestellt wird, begreifen wir die Konstruktion von Gedächtnissen als Bewegung im symbolischen und sozialen Raum. Dahinter steht die Annahme, dass symbolische und soziale Praktiken wechselseitig aufeinander Bezug nehmen. *Wer* man ist, beeinflusst, *was* man sagt; umgekehrt wirkt sich der *Standpunkt* im symbolischen Raum auf den *Standort* im sozialen Raum aus. Der *soziale Raum der Handlungen* und der *symbolische Raum der Deutungen* konstituieren sich aus Beziehungen zwischen einzelnen Positionen. Im einen Fall sind es unterschiedlich mächtige Akteure, die Positionen im sozialen Raum besetzen. Im anderen Fall sind es unterschiedlich mächtige Diskurse, die Positionen im symbolischen Raum bezeichnen. In Sprechsituationen treten diese beiden Räume miteinander in Beziehung: Akteure mit einer bestimmten Sprecherposition im sozialen Raum bringen eine bestimmte Sprechposition im symbolischen Raum zum Ausdruck. Wir bezeichnen solche symbolischen Positionen, die Einzelne oder Gruppen einnehmen können, als *Denk-Orte*.[11]

Diese Beziehung zwischen Handeln und Sprechen ist keineswegs beliebig; sie folgt einer »Ökonomie des sprachlichen Tausches« (Pierre Bourdieu): Die sozialen Positionen von Akteuren *strukturieren* und *sind strukturiert durch* die symbolischen Positionen, die sie sprachlich zum Ausdruck bringen. Sprechen erscheint unter dieser Sichtweise als Tauschvorgang, der durch Nachfrage und Angebot auf einem sprachlichen Markt bestimmt ist. Das Angebot, die Neigung eines Akteurs zu bestimmten Aussagen, erwächst aus den verinnerlichten Strukturen des *Habitus*, den im Lauf der Lebensgeschichte einverleibten Wahrnehmungs-, Denk- und Handlungsschemata. Die Nachfrage, die Unterscheidung zulässiger und unzulässiger Aussagen, wird durch die äußerlichen Strukturen des sprachlichen Marktes in Form machtvoller *Diskurse* bereitgestellt, die über Medien und Mediatoren Dauerhaftigkeit erlangen. Im Wechselspiel von Habitus und Diskurs entwickeln Akteure bewusste und unbewusste *Deutungs- und Handlungsstrategien*, um Profit auf dem sprachlichen Markt zu erzielen.[12]
Der erste mögliche Denk-Ort war durch die CD vorgegeben. Wo werden sich nun die TeilnehmerInnen der Gruppendiskussion in Bezug auf das veröffentlichte Dorfgedächtnis verorten? Ich kann die Bewegungen der einzelnen SprecherInnen hier nicht im Detail nachzeichnen; dennoch möchte ich den Ablauf der Diskussion grob skizzieren.[13] Die SprecherInnen nützen in den ersten Etappen der Diskussion das affirmative Potenzial der CD; sie gruppieren sich im Zentrum, im Nahbereich oder am Rand einer imaginierten Dorfgemeinschaft. Dabei erscheinen die Topoi von *Fleiß und Genügsamkeit*, *Gemütlichkeit* und *Bodenständigkeit*, um die sich die Individuen scharen, als Gravitationszentren eines kollektiven Gedächtnisses. Vermutlich bezeichnen diese drei Denk-Orte das, was man das »Ethos des Dorfes« nennen könnte: die Neigung *zu* wie der Ausdruck *von* einer dörflichen Lebensform. *Fleiß und Genügsamkeit*, *Gemütlichkeit* und *Bodenständigkeit* erscheinen als jene unhinterfragten Gewissheiten, in deren Gestalt kulturelle Repräsentationen von bäuerlich-handwerklichen Gruppen bestimmend für einen Großteil der Dorfgesellschaft geworden sind. Das dörfliche Ethos konturiert durch räumliche Differenzen nach außen hin eine Lokalidentität, die klassen-, geschlechter- und generationenspezifische Differenzen im Inneren verblassen lässt.[14] Fleißig und genügsam, gemütlich und bodenständig – so sieht sich die typische Gemeindebewohnerin und der typische Gemeindebewohner, und so möchten sie und er von anderen gesehen werden.
Die weitere Diskussion nimmt einen ambivalenten Verlauf. Einerseits zeigt sich das Dorfgedächtnis über weite Strecken als zähe, reproduktive Struktur. Die Topoi *Fleiß und Genügsamkeit* sowie *Bodenständigkeit* werden von niemand auch nur ansatzweise hinterfragt. Andererseits wird das Dorfgedächtnis in gewisser Weise auch als flüssige, transformative Struktur fass-

bar. Indem einige SprecherInnen das kritische Potenzial der CD entfalten, stellen sie den Denk-Ort der *Gemütlichkeit* in Frage. Es sind die VertreterInnen der mittleren Generation, die in den vierziger und fünfziger Jahren Geborenen (Karl, Sophie und Georg), die das unausgesprochene Schweigegebot der älteren SprecherInnen brechen, die sich im Kernbereich des Dorfgedächtnisses eingefunden haben (Friedrich, Theresia, Margarete und Rudolf). Sie betreten ein vermintes Gelände: »das Politische« im allgemeinen, die nationalsozialistische Ära im besonderen; darüber zwingen sie die »ZeitzeugInnen«, klarer Position zu beziehen.

Zunächst können die Älteren konfliktträchtige Topoi umgehen, indem sie das Handeln der dörflichen Elite – Bürgermeister, Pfarrer, Lehrer – erörtern. Doch bald betritt Theresia das gefährliche Terrain des alltäglichen Handelns der Dorfbevölkerung. Sie schildert das aufmüpfige »Heil Hitler«-Schreien vor den Ohren der Eltern nach dem »Anschluss« im Jahr 1938. Dies wird vor allem gegenüber den jüngeren ZuhörerInnen erklärungsbedürftig; Externalisierung und Infantilisierung bieten sich als Auswege an: Den ohnmächtigen Kindern wird das Politische von mächtigen Erwachsenen »eingeimpft«, wie sie sagt. Auf diese Weise besetzt sie den Denk-Ort des Opfer-Seins. Dieser Rückzug auf den außerdörflichen Opfer-Täter-Diskurs veranlasst Karl, den Weg zurück ins Dorf zu gehen. Er lokalisiert die ehemaligen Soldaten der Deutschen Wehrmacht, denen er zumindest Mitwisserschaft unterstellt, im Denk-Ort des Täter-Seins. Friedrich, der einzige ehemalige Wehrmachtssoldat in der Diskussionsrunde, gerät nun unter Druck, das Soldaten-Kollektiv zu verteidigen. Die Mangelgesellschaft der dreißiger Jahre, so die Argumentation, habe die Verführbarkeit durch die Nationalsozialisten erst ermöglicht. Noch einmal kommt ihm Karl entgegen, indem er Verständnis für die Verführungskraft des Nationalsozialismus bekundet; doch dann lokalisiert er die Diskussion endgültig im Dorf. Er prangert diejenigen Stammtischbesucher an, die von der NS-Zeit nicht nur keinen Abstand genommen haben, sondern die Jahre 1938 bis 1945 sogar noch verherrlichen. Noch werden keine Namen genannt, aber unmissverständlich hat die imaginierte Dorfgemeinschaft Risse bekommen. Es leben auch Täter im Ort – ehemalige Wehrmachtssoldaten, die Partisaninnen getötet haben und ihre damaligen Taten noch heute glorifizieren.[15]

Nun ist das Kampffeld abgesteckt; es entsteht ein offener Schlagabtausch zwischen VertreterInnen der älteren und der jüngeren Generationen. Auch die Forscher geraten nun zwischen die Fronten, weil manche ihrer Fragen als Regelverletzungen empfunden werden. Im Zuge dieses Wortgefechts pendeln die SprecherInnen mehrmals zwischen dem veröffentlichten Dorfgedächtnis und den beiden Sphären des Politischen. Die Leitfiguren dieser Konfrontation sind Friedrich als Verteidiger der dörflichen *Gemütlichkeit* und Karl als deren Ankläger. An beiden Kontrahenten lassen sich die

Wechselwirkungen von Habitus und Diskurs exemplarisch zeigen. Friedrich wie Karl werden durch Wahrnehmungs-, Denk- und Handlungsmuster, die sie sich im Lauf ihrer jeweiligen Lebensgeschichten einverleibt haben, zu bestimmten Denk-Orten hingezogen: der eine als ehemals vom NS-Regime faszinierter Hitlerjunge und Wehrmachtssoldat, der sich mit dem Vorwurf des Mitmachens und -wissens konfrontiert sieht; der andere als Sohn einer Betroffenen und eines Augenzeugen des NS-Terrors, der die Hitlerjugend- und Soldatengeneration mit dem Vorwurf des Mitmachens und -wissens konfrontiert. Machtvolle Diskurse, die mögliche Denk-Orte markieren, üben Anziehungskraft auf Friedrich und Karl aus: im Fall des ersteren Spielarten des Opfer-Diskurses, etwa Guido Knopps Fernsehdokumentation »Holokaust«, welche die Verantwortung der wenigen Mächtigen für Krieg und Genozid betonen;[16] im Fall des letzteren Varianten des Täter-Diskurses, etwa die sogenannte »Wehrmachtsausstellung«, die den Vielen eine direkte oder indirekte Mitverantwortung an den NS-Verbrechen zuschreiben.[17]

Die Schärfe der Auseinandersetzung erklärt sich nicht allein aus dem Spannungsverhältnis von Verteidigern und Anklägern, die zeitlich befristete Bündnisse mit anderen DiskutantInnen eingingen. Die Diskussion über Mitwisser- und Mittäterschaft in der NS-Zeit war wohl auch darum so heftig, weil so unterschiedliche Auffassungen über die private und öffentliche Tradierung dieses Wissens an die jüngere Generation bestanden. Vor diesem Hintergrund wurden wir Forscher weniger über Beruf, Geschlecht oder Herkunft, sondern vor allem über unser Alter wahrgenommen. Unser Interesse an einer Zeit, die wir selbst nicht erlebt hatten, ließ uns, je nach sozialer und symbolischer Position des jeweiligen Sprechers, als potenzielle Verbündete oder Gegner im Tauziehen um Anerkennung erscheinen. Zusammen mit jüngeren DiskutantInnen repräsentierten wir die Generation der »Nachgeborenen«, gegenüber der die Generation der »ZeitzeugInnen« ihre Deutungen und Handlungen zu rechtfertigten versuchte. Vielleicht war aber gerade Irene, die jüngste und schweigsamste Teilnehmerin, diejenige, um deren Anerkennung die Kontrahenten am heftigsten rangen. Sie erhielt, ohne dass dies jemand beabsichtigt hätte, zusehends die Rolle einer über den Streitparteien stehenden Richterin zugesprochen – eine Rolle, die sie schließlich auch wahrnahm. Am Ende der heftigen Kontroverse stand Irenes salomonischer Vorschlag eines Denkmals für die Opfer des kurz vor Kriegsende durch das Dorf ziehenden »Todesmarsches« jüdischer Häftlinge am Friedhof und ihr Plädoyer gegen die Verurteilung einer Zeit, in der man nicht selbst gelebt hat. Damit war gewissermaßen das versöhnliche Schlusswort einer konfliktreichen Debatte gesprochen. Auf diese Weise wurde am Ende der Diskussion die Dorfgemeinschaft in der Imagination wiederhergestellt.

Die genaue Lektüre der Gruppendiskussion widerspricht allen Vorstellungen von raum- und zeitübergreifenden Gedächtnissen; vielmehr erscheint das Kollektivgedächtnis des Dorfes in synchroner Perspektive als *heterogen* und in diachroner Perspektive als *dynamisch*. Die Heterogenität und Dynamik des dörflichen Kollektivgedächtnisses speisen sich, so unsere These, aus dem Wechselspiel zweier grundlegender Gedächtnispraktiken: Gedenken und Erinnern. Aleida Assmann fasst diese unterschiedlichen Strategien in die Begriffe von *ars* (»Kunst«) und *vis* (»Kraft«). Das Gedächtnis als *ars*, wie es in der rhetorischen Gedächtniskunst seit der Antike geübt wird, bezieht sich auf Verfahren des reproduzierenden Gedenkens nach räumlichen Vorbildern. Dagegen wendet sich seit der Aufklärung immer deutlicher das Gedächtnis als *vis*, die Kraft der transformierenden Erinnerung in der Zeit. Daraus leitet Assmann die Unterscheidung von *Funktions-* und *Speichergedächtnis* ab. Das »bewohnte Funktionsgedächtnis« umfasst jene lebendigen Erinnerungen, die in der jeweiligen Gegenwart Sinn generieren. Das »unbewohnte Speichergedächtnis« hingegen versammelt tote, sinnentleerte Fakten. Zwischen Funktions- und Speichergedächtnis bestehe keine Trennung, sondern eine Übergangszone für den »Binnenverkehr zwischen aktualisierten und nichtaktualisierten Elementen«, der die Dynamik des Gedächtnisses ermögliche.[18]

Die Spannung von Gedenken und Erinnern durchzieht auch das Werk Pierre Noras. In seinem enzyklopädischen Projekt *Les lieux de mémoire* zieht er eine klare Trennung zwischen Gedächtnis und Geschichte: Während Ersteres sakralisierend, gruppenbezogen und punktuell ausgerichtet sei, arbeite Letztere entzaubernd, verallgemeinernd und kontinuierlich. Kurz, »das Gedächtnis ist ein Absolutes, die Geschichte kennt nur das Relative«. Nora sieht diese Trennung als spezifischen Zug der Moderne und deutet diesen, versetzt mit einem Schuss Kulturpessimismus, als Herrschaft der Geschichte über das Gedächtnis – als »Entlegitimierung der gelebten Vergangenheit«. Dort, wo sich die Geschichte der *milieux de mémoire*, der gelebten Gedächtnisse, bemächtigt, sieht Nora die *lieux de mémoire*, die Gedächtnisorte, im Entstehen. Die Gedächtnisorte liegen zwischen Gedächtnis und Geschichte – dem Gedächtnis nicht mehr, der Geschichte noch nicht zugehörig. Die Gedächtnisorte, die als Museen, Archive, Denkmäler, Feste oder Wallfahrtsstätten fassbar werden, schützen das Gedächtnis vor dem Zugriff der Geschichte: »Das Gedächtnis klammert sich an Orte wie die Geschichte an Ereignisse.«[19]

Unser spezieller Fall zeigt, dass sich weder Aleida Assmanns Komplementaritätsmodell noch Pierre Noras Konfrontationsmodell generalisieren lassen. Zu Beginn der Diskussion überwiegt die Komplementarität zwischen den Denk-Orten erster Ordnung und der CD als Denk-Ort zweiter Ordnung. Doch bald zeichnet sich – zunächst unbemerkt und erst in der nachfolgenden Interpretation erkennbar – die kommende Konfrontation ab. Ab nun werden Verschärfung, Höhepunkt und Abklingen der Konfrontation zwischen Denk-Orten erster Ordnung und massenmedialen Diskursen als Denk-Orten zweiter Ordnung fassbar. In der Auseinandersetzung um Mitwisser- und Mittäterschaft in der NS-Zeit manifestiert sich nun besonders deutlich das Wechselspiel von Gedächtnis und Geschichte (im Sinn Noras), von Funktions- und Speichergedächtnis (im Sinn Assmanns). Einerseits *zwingen* machtvolle Gedächtnisdiskurse die Subjekte in vorgegebene Positionen. Die Vehemenz, mit der Friedrich gegen die von Karl vertretene Täter-Position der »Wehrmachtsausstellung« seine Opfer-Position verteidigen muss, verdeutlicht die Dominanz der Geschichte beziehungsweise des Speichergedächtnisses. Die CD dient ihm in diesem symbolischen Abwehrkampf, gleich einer Bastion, als *lieu de mémoire*. Andererseits *ermöglichen* machtvolle Gedächtnisdiskurse den Subjekten, sich vorgegebene Positionen zu Eigen zu machen. Die Vehemenz, mit der sich Friedrich als Opfer darstellt, speist sich auch aus der selektiven Aneignung der Fernsehdokumentation »Holokaust«; diese steht gewissermaßen für die Dominanz des Gedächtnisses beziehungsweise des Funktionsgedächtnisses. Populäre und elitäre Gedächtnisdiskurse stecken *Erzählspielräume* ab, indem sie Äußerungen von SprecherInnen erzwingen *und* ermöglichen. Diese Zwänge und Möglichkeiten werden *in praxi* erst dann wirksam, wenn SprecherInnen in Interaktion mit anderen solche Diskurse in *Erzählungen* umformen. Kurz, Positionen *für* Subjekte und Positionierungen *durch* Subjekte sind wechselseitig aufeinander bezogen. Einmal gehen sie ein konfrontatives Verhältnis ein, ein andermal ein komplementäres. Wie unser Projekt gezeigt hat, ist in solchen Sprachspielen auch die Dynamisierung statischer Geschichtsbilder angelegt.

ANMERKUNGEN

1 Confino, Alon, Collective Memory and Cultural History: Problems of Method, in: American Historical Review 102 (1997), S. 1386-1403, hier S. 1386

2 Halbwachs, Maurice, Das Gedächtnis und seine sozialen Bedingungen, Frankfurt a. M. 1985, S. 23

3 Vgl. Langthaler, Ernst, Gedächtnisgeschichte: Positionen, Probleme, Perspektiven, in: Beiträge zur Historischen Sozialkunde 29 (1999), Sondernummer Kulturwissenschaften, S. 30-46

4 Martinez, Matias, Michael Scheffel, Einführung in die Erzähltheorie, 3. Aufl., München 2002, S. 17

5 Vgl. Müller-Funk, Wolfgang, Die Kultur und ihre Narrative. Eine Einführung, Wien/New York 2002, S. 87 ff.

6 Das Forschungsprojekt *Denk-Orte. Erinnern und Vergessen in der ländlichen Kultur* wurde im Auftrag des Bundesministeriums für Bildung, Wissenschaft und Kultur im

Rahmen des Forschungsschwerpunkts »Kulturwissenschaften/Cultural Studies« (http://www.culturalstudies.at) durchgeführt. Eine Online-Publikation des Projektberichtes ist unter http://www.eforum-zeitgeschichte.at verfügbar.

[7] Zur reflexiven Feldforschung in ländlichen Kontexten vgl. Langthaler, Ernst, Dorfgeschichte als reflexiver Prozeß, in: Historische Anthropologie 10 (2002), S. 125-133.

[8] Die elf InterviewpartnerInnen, sechs Frauen und fünf Männer, gehören den Geburtsjahrgängen zwischen etwa 1910 und 1930 an und stammen aus dem Bauern-, Handwerker- und Lohnarbeitermilieu. In der Interviewführung orientierten wir uns am »narrativ-biographischen Interview« nach Sieder, Reinhard, Erzählungen analysieren – Analysen erzählen. Narrativ-biographisches Interview, Textanalyse und Falldarstellung, in: Karl R. Wernhart, Werner Zips (Hg.), Ethnohistorie: Rekonstruktion und Kulturkritik. Eine Einführung, Wien 1998, S. 145-172: Haupterzählung, immanentes und exmanentes Nachfragen. Die zwei- bis vierstündigen Interviews wurden mittels MiniDisc-Recorder aufgezeichnet und anschließend in zwei- bis dreiminütige Spuren gegliedert, die jeweils eine Sinneinheit bilden. Jede Sinneinheit wurde nach Form (Geschichte, Bericht, Beschreibung, Argumentation, Evaluation) und Inhalt mit Hilfe eines Datenbankprogramms verschlagwortet.

[9] Vgl. Ecker, Bernhard, Ernst Langthaler, Martin Neubauer, Denk-Orte. Aus dem Gedächtnis eines Dorfes, Audio-CD, Frankenfels 2000. In mehreren Abfragedurchgängen wurden aus dem rund 25 Stunden umfassenden Interviewmaterial jene Passagen ausgewählt, die auf der CD veröffentlicht werden sollten. Diese etwa 50 Minuten umfassenden Passagen wurden für die Textanalyse transkribiert, die nach manifester Bedeutung und latentem Sinn des Erzählten fragte. Aus dem Analysematerial entstanden schließlich die etwa 30 Minuten umfassenden Kommentare, die die Interviewpassagen verbinden.

[10] In der Planung, Durchführung und Analyse der Gruppendiskussion folgten wir methodischen Anregungen von Flick, Uwe, Qualitative Forschung. Theorie, Methoden, Anwendung in Psychologie und Sozialwissenschaften, Reinbek 1995, S. 131 ff. Unsere interne Rollenverteilung sah vor, dass Bernhard Ecker, der als einziger nicht im Ort wohnhaft war, die Diskussionsleitung übernahm; Ernst Langthaler vertrat die Position des Forschers; Martin Neubauer achtete als stiller Beobachter auf nonverbale Äußerungen der TeilnehmerInnen. Wir hatten mehrere Impulse vorbereitet, die eine offene Diskussion in Gang setzen sollten. Die Diskussion wurde mit einer Vorstellungsrunde eröffnet; daran schloss eine Schilderung der Hörsituationen an; danach fragten wir nach dem Lokalspezifischen, das auf der CD zu hören war oder darauf fehlte. Den weiteren Verlauf ließen wir offen und streuten je nach Bedarf zusätzliche Impulse ein. Die etwa zweieinhalbstündige Diskussion, die wir auf MiniDisc aufzeichneten, wurde vollständig transkribiert, in Sinneinheiten gegliedert und auf fünf Ebenen analysiert: Kontext der Gesprächssituation, Paraphrase des Gesprächsinhaltes, Assoziationen zu vorangegangenen Sinneinheiten, manifeste Bedeutung und latenter Sinn der Äußerungen. Nach einer Grobanalyse des gesamten Transkripts, die wir einzeln durchführten, erfolgten Feinanalysen einzelner Sinneinheiten und die Theoriebildung in der Gruppe.

[11] Vgl. Bourdieu, Pierre, Loïc J. D. Wacquant, Reflexive Anthropologie, Frankfurt a. M. 1996; Sperber, Dan, Explaining Culture. A Naturalistic Approach, Oxford/Malden 1998, S. 106 ff; Hall, Stuart, Encoding, Decoding, in: Simon During (Hg.), The Cultural Studies Reader, London/New York 1999, S. 507-517; Johnson, Richard, What Is Cultural Studies Anyway?, in: John Storey (Hg.), What Is Cultural Studies? A Rea-

der, London u. a.1996, S. 75-114; Woodward, Kathryn, Concepts Of Identity and Difference, in: Dies. (Hg.), Identity and Difference, London u. a. 1997, S. 7-61.
[12] Vgl. Bourdieu, Pierre, Was heißt sprechen? Die Ökonomie des sprachlichen Tausches, Wien 1990.
[13] Zu einer ausführlichen Interpretation der Gruppendiskussion vgl. Ecker, Bernhard, Ernst Langthaler, Martin Neubauer, Denk-Orte. Ein Dorf reflektiert sein Gedächtnis, in: Österreichische Zeitschrift für Geschichtswissenschaften 13 (2002) H. 2 (im Druck)
[14] Vgl. Lindner, Rolf, Das Ethos der Region, in: Ders. (Hg.), Die Wiederkehr des Regionalen. Über neue Formen kultureller Identität, Frankfurt a. M./New York 1994, S. 201-231
[15] Zu Opfer-Täter-Diskursen in Bezug auf die NS-Zeit nach 1945 vgl. Uhl, Heidemarie, Das »erste Opfer«. Der österreichische Opfermythos und seine Transformationen in der Zweiten Republik, in: Österreichische Zeitschrift für Politikwissenschaft 30 (2001), S. 19-34.
[16] Diese dreiteilige Fernsehdokumentation des ZDF-»Fernsehhistorikers« Guido Knopp über den nationalsozialistischen Genozid wurde im Jahr 2000 von deutschen und österreichischen Sendern ausgestraht. Als Begleitbuch vgl. Knopp, Guido, Holokaust, München 2000.
[17] Die Ausstellung »Vernichtungskrieg. Verbrechen der Wehrmacht 1941 bis 1944« wurde in den 1990er Jahren in Wien und einigen österreichischen Landeshauptstädten gezeigt. Als Begleitbuch vgl. Hamburger Institut für Sozialforschung (Hg.), Vernichtungskrieg. Verbrechen der Wehrmacht 1941 bis 1944, Hamburg 1996.
[18] Vgl. Assmann, Aleida, Erinnerungsräume. Formen und Wandlungen des kulturellen Gedächtnisses, München 1999, S. 130 ff.
[19] Vgl. Nora, Pierre, Zwischen Geschichte und Gedächtnis, Frankfurt a. M. 1998, S. 32 ff.

BIBLIOGRAPHIE

Assmann, Aleida, Erinnerungsräume. Formen und Wandlungen des kulturellen Gedächtnisses, München 1999

Bourdieu, Pierre, Loïc J. D. Wacquant, Reflexive Anthropologie, Frankfurt a. M. 1996

Bourdieu, Pierre, Was heißt sprechen? Die Ökonomie des sprachlichen Tausches, Wien 1990

Confino, Alon, Collective Memory and Cultural History: Problems of Method, in: American Historical Review 102 (1997), S. 1386-1403, hier S. 1386

Ecker, Bernhard, Ernst Langthaler, Martin Neubauer, Denk-Orte. Aus dem Gedächtnis eines Dorfes, Audio-CD, Frankenfels 2000

Ecker, Bernhard, Ernst Langthaler, Martin Neubauer, Denk-Orte. Ein Dorf reflektiert sein Gedächtnis, in: Österreichische Zeitschrift für Geschichtswissenschaften 13 (2002) H. 2 (im Druck)

Flick, Uwe, Qualitative Forschung. Theorie, Methoden, Anwendung in Psychologie und Sozialwissenschaften, Reinbek 1995

Halbwachs, Maurice, Das Gedächtnis und seine sozialen Bedingungen, Frankfurt a. M. 1985

Hall, Stuart, Encoding, Decoding, in: Simon During (Hg.), The Cultural Studies Reader, London/New York 1999, S. 507-517

Hamburger Institut für Sozialforschung (Hg.), Vernichtungskrieg. Verbrechen der Wehrmacht 1941 bis 1944, Hamburg 1996

Johnson, Richard, What Is Cultural Studies Anyway?, in: John Storey (Hg.), What Is Cultural Studies? A Reader, London u. a.1996, S. 75-114

Knopp, Guido, Holokaust, München 2000

Langthaler, Ernst, Dorfgeschichte als reflexiver Prozeß, in: Historische Anthropologie 10 (2002), S. 125-133

Langthaler, Ernst, Gedächtnisgeschichte: Positionen, Probleme, Perspektiven, in: Beiträge zur Historischen Sozialkunde 29 (1999), Sondernummer Kulturwissenschaften, S. 30-46

Lindner, Rolf, Das Ethos der Region, in: Ders. (Hg.), Die Wiederkehr des Regionalen. Über neue Formen kultureller Identität, Frankfurt a. M./New York 1994, S. 201-231

Martinez, Matias, Michael Scheffel, Einführung in die Erzähltheorie, 3. Aufl., München 2002

Müller-Funk, Wolfgang, Die Kultur und ihre Narrative. Eine Einführung, Wien/New York 2002

Nora, Pierre, Zwischen Geschichte und Gedächtnis, Frankfurt a. M. 1998

Sieder, Reinhard, Erzählungen analysieren – Analysen erzählen. Narrativ-biographisches Interview, Textanalyse und Falldarstellung, in: Karl R. Wernhart, Werner Zips (Hg.), Ethnohistorie: Rekonstruktion und Kulturkritik. Eine Einführung, Wien 1998, S. 145-172

Sperber, Dan, Explaining Culture. A Naturalistic Approach, Oxford/Malden 1998

Uhl, Heidemarie, Das »erste Opfer«. Der österreichische Opfermythos und seine Transformationen in der Zweiten Republik, in: Österreichische Zeitschrift für Politikwissenschaft 30 (2001), S. 19-34

Woodward, Kathryn, Concepts Of Identity and Difference, in: Dies. (Hg.), Identity and Difference, London u. a. 1997, S. 7-61

Leidkultur or Leitverantwortung? The Legacy of the Third Reich in the National Memory Narratives of the ›Berlin Republic‹

CAROLINE GAY

INTRODUCTION

In November 1998, Jan Ross wrote:

> Was die Menschheitsverbrechen des 21. Jahrhunderts sein werden, wissen wir nicht, aber es ist gut möglich, daß sie Auschwitz gar nicht ähnlich sehen und daß wir sie nicht bemerken, wenn wir wie gebannt nur auf Auschwitz starren.[1]

The events of 11 September 2001 revealed a new form of human rights violation. Whether or not they also represented a new *Zivilisationsbruch*, as Josef Joffe termed it,[2] comparisons with the atrocities of the Third Reich became redundant; the terrorist attacks revealed a different sort of enemy with a different target. Germany's reaction was further indication that recollection of ›Auschwitz‹ is inevitably losing its force in political decision-making as the country assumes European and global responsibilities in the present. For Bernd Ulrich, ›Niemand interessiert jetzt, was gegen Hitler das Richtige gewesen wäre, sondern nur, was heute das Richtige ist. Und das Falsche.‹[3] However, this does not mean that national memory of the atrocities of the Third Reich is fading in Germany. On the contrary, media attention together with ritual commemoration and educational initiatives keep it very much alive. This paper will examine continuity and change in the national memory narratives of the so-called ›Berlin Republic‹ relating to Germany's Third Reich past. It will aim to show how many complex layers of ritual and active memory co-exist with regard to this period, concerning not only the history itself but also increasingly its legacy in German political culture.

NATIONAL MEMORY NARRATIVES IN POST-WAR GERMANY

With the growing distance from the National Socialist past the term ›memory‹ nowadays more often than not means ›interpretation‹. Memory of this period, and of any other for that matter, has never been a mirror image of the past but rather a reconstruction viewed and modified through the prism of present circumstances. Memory will be considered here as a narrative in that it is always manipulated or selected to give a certain interpretation of events, with some parts embellished or wilfully obliterated depending on narrator and audience. A narrative of memory should not be confused with historiography; it is not a fixed account, just as memory is not a fixed phenomenon. Narratives of memory can be individual, collective or national. The focus here will be national memory narratives, which can be defined as a public or official version of the past anchoring what Jan Assmann refers to as the ›konnektive Struktur‹[4] of a society. National memory narratives go some way to providing a sense of identity whether or not individuals have actual experience of the events recalled. They are also intended to portray the nation in a certain way at a certain time. Hence, in the Bundesrepublik memory narratives on the Nazi past have continued to change in line with political and social developments. It is important here to distinguish between political and historical memory narratives. A political narrative based on achievements in the present (in West Germany the *Wirtschaftswunder*, (re)integration into Europe, democracy and anti-communism) succeeded in establishing some sense of positive identity in post-war Germany. Yet the dominant *historical* memory narrative has been that of the Third Reich, with events pre- and post 1933 inevitably filtered through the prism of Auschwitz. In the immediate post-war years this historical narrative, to the extent that it was not repressed, dealt largely with the direct experience of defeat and destruction. By the 1960s, Nazi war crimes trials, increased information and generational change led the so-called ›vaterlose Gesellschaft‹[5] to refashion the narrative into one of guilt and demonisation. A dominant feature of national memory has since remained the assumed need for *Vergangenheitsbewältigung*. Time has not made the negative historical narrative any less painful. As chronological distance increases from the period so do the number of debates on how best to ›remember‹ it and the number of memory narratives, particularly on the Holocaust. The result is many layers of recollection: one page of a newspaper may, for example, contain articles about payments to former forced labourers, the Holocaust monument, some new historical research into National Socialism and a political debate on national pride. The paradox is that it is easy to read a number of co-existing narratives on one page of the newspaper as if they belonged to different histories.

GLOBAL MEMORY NARRATIVES OF THE HOLOCAUST

It is not just in Germany that the number of memory narratives based on the National Socialist period has increased. The appropriation of the Holocaust as an ersatz national memory narrative in America is a well-known phenomenon that has been documented by those such as Tim Cole, Peter Novick and Edward Linenthal and polemicised by Norman Finkelstein.[6] What is interesting is that the Holocaust has also started to feature increasingly at *European* level. Over the past decade in particular the revelation of the sometimes murky past of countries that formerly proclaimed themselves victim or victorious has led to a gradual turnaround in the respective national memory narratives.[7] Michael Jeismann sees the Holocaust as part of a new *European* memory narrative. In his view, the National Socialist past has latterly been functionalised in the framework of the European Union as a means of promoting eastward enlargement, enhanced integration or intervention in Kosovo. Jeismann goes as far as to suggest that ›Die neue Geschichtspolitik könnte [...] ein bedeutender Teil einer künftigen Geschäftsgrundlage der Europäischen Union sein.‹[8] This rather bold theory does contain a grain of truth if one considers the reasons for the establishment of the EU, i.e., to prevent another war such as that unleashed by the Nazis.

The internationalisation and increased medialisation of memory of the Third Reich or, more specifically, the Holocaust, has made it into ›everyone's history‹. In what Michael Berenbaum has termed the nativization of memory[9] a variety of at times conflicting national memories and representations of the period have thus emerged, reflecting multiple agendas. The UK, for example, introduced an annual Holocaust Remembrance Day in January 2001, which aims to promote tolerance and good citizenship and oppose racism.[10] It is unclear why evocation of the Holocaust is needed as a tag to promote values that should surely be self-evident in any civil society. It could however be the case that memory narratives no longer operate on a purely national level. Natan Sznaider sees the Holocaust as part of a global narrative that can be put to positive use:

> Gerade Erinnerungen an den Holocaust werden in einer Epoche ideologischer Ungewissheiten zu einem Maßstab für humanistische und universalistische Identifikationen. Die Erinnerungen an den Holocaust erlauben zu Beginn des dritten Jahrtausends die Formierung Nationen übergreifender Gedächtniskulturen, die wiederum zur Grundlage für globale Menschenrechtspolitik werden... Der Holocaust wird so zum Allgemeingut und erlaubt es Menschen in den verschiedensten Ländern, sich mit ihm auf unterschiedlichste Weise auseinander zu setzen.[11]

A good example of such universalisation of Holocaust recollection was the international Holocaust conference held in Stockholm in January 2000. Leading politicians and academics discussed how memory of the Holocaust could be kept alive and how it could contribute to the campaign against racism, anti-semitism and ethnic conflict.[12] Solemn statements were made about the importance of remembering and never letting ›it‹ happen again, whereby the past was used to shape a specific narrative in the present. This in turn somewhat overshadowed the authentic memory of the survivors present at the conference.
A global narrative of the Holocaust may indeed be a productive response to the fear of a constant threat to democracy and civil society, for example by begging common solutions to human rights violations. However, to use Peter Novick's argument, it can also be instrumentalised as the ›absolute evil‹ in order to paper over a nation's own shortcomings.[13]

AN END TO THE NEGATIVE NATIONAL MEMORY NARRATIVE IN GERMANY?

The Stockholm conference did not then focus on *German guilt* but rather *international responsibility*.[14] Ironically, it seems as if Germany has become part of an international Holocaust narrative, which concentrates on the victims rather than the perpetrators of genocide. Yet at the same time, the German narrative remains influenced by the country's ethnic ties to the perpetrator regime of National Socialism and the continuing need to reconcile present identity with past guilt. These ties were seen to loosen somewhat with the arrival into power of the Schröder government in autumn 1998. This government represents a generation whose founding historical moment is 1968 – or even 1989 – and for whom the Nazi past is perhaps more of an alien baggage than a moral concern. As such it is also representative of the definitive shift, to use Assmann's terms, from *communicative* to *cultural* memory of the period.[15] According to this theory, communicative memory is the exchange of direct, biographical experience in the framework of the collective. After a period of around eighty years, it fades into cultural – that is non-direct – memory, which is formal and structured, requiring ›props‹ to keep it alive, such as monuments, speeches, books and films. Cultural memory narratives are shaped by elite groups in society such as politicians, intellectuals and, increasingly, the media. They are of course also subject to instrumentalisation, manipulation and ritualisation. The national memory narratives of the Third Reich in the Berlin Republic are thus interpretations based on cultural rather than communicative memory. These interpretations can be both positive in the sense of a focus on responsibility rather than guilt, and negative in terms of excessive instrumentalisation of ›Auschwitz‹. They will be defined here as *Leitverantwortung* and *Leidkultur* respectively.

RESPONSIBILITY OVER GUILT: LEITVERANTWORTUNG

Schröder is not known for his historical pathos and has come under fire for some apparently flippant remarks relating to the legacy of the German past in the new capital.[16] And yet the call for a ›neue Unbefangenheit‹[17] should not be read as an attempt to draw a line under the memory of the National Socialist past. Rather it stands for an approach that whilst openly acknowledging German atrocities under the Third Reich emphasises present responsibility for maintaining human rights and democracy rather than past guilt. The notion could be defined as *Leitverantwortung*. Its parameters were laid down by Schröder in his *Regierungserklärung* just after the move of the government from Bonn to Berlin in April 1999 when he referred to German intervention in Kosovo:

> ...die Ereignisse der letzten Wochen und Monate [haben] uns dramatisch vor Augen geführt, daß sich Deutschlands Rolle in der Welt verändert hat. Daß wir heute anders und intensiver in der Verantwortung für das Schicksal anderer Völker stehen, als dies in den Jahren der Teilung und unmittelbar danach der Fall war.[18]

The debate and decision to deploy German troops marked a caesura in Germany's post-war foreign policy. Germany entered this war not ›gegen‹ but rather ›wegen‹ Auschwitz, as an apparently ›normal‹ nation that however remembers the abnormality of its past, has learnt from it and is now committed to the ensuing responsibility. The national memory narrative can then be said to have translated into a *moral duty* or vocation to intervene on the world stage and prevent another ›Auschwitz‹, defined as a violation of human rights. The notion of *Leitverantwortung* is partly to do with necessity, that is unified Germany accepting increased responsibility as part of Nato and the EU. Yet it can also be used in Germany's interests. Schröder and his Foreign Minister Joschka Fischer are skilled at linking responsibility for the past with German political interests in the present, for example eastward enlargement.[19] A good example of the way that an assumed *Leitverantwortung* can enhance Germany's image was the opening of the Jewish Museum in Berlin in September 2001. This museum, which significantly is about 2,000 years of German-Jewish history rather than the Holocaust alone,[20] was heralded a ›Weltkulturereignis‹[21] reflecting the new German responsibility. After decades of political ›Erinnerungsarbeit‹,[22] Michael Blumenthal, the American Director of the Museum, said the words everyone wanted to hear in front of assembled VIP guests from all over the world:

> Die wiedervereinigte Bundesrepublik Deutschland ist die größte und stärkste Wirtschaftsmacht in Europa und eine der wichtigsten Nationen der Welt. Dadurch, daß Sie sich der Vergangenheit stellen, Wiedergutmachung versuchen, dieses Museum und andere vergleichbare Institutionen in Ihrer Hauptstadt fördern, haben Sie ein Zeichen gesetzt und ein moralisches Recht erworben, zu den Wortführern im weltweiten Kampf gegen Rassismus und für religiöse Toleranz, für die Rechte aller Minderheiten und für die Menschenrechte im allgemeinen zu gehören.[23]

His words came just a few days before the September 11 attacks. In a speech in support of America delivered at the Brandenburg Gate, President Rau used phrases that could well have come from the campaign against Nazi Germany just 50 years ago, such as ›Fanatismus zerstört jede Kultur‹ or ›Alle Menschen haben das Recht auf Anerkennung und auf Würde.‹[24] This suggests a seeming metamorphosis in political culture, whereby Germany prescribes rather than struggles with values such as democracy and tolerance.

THE CONTINUED IMPACT OF THE NEGATIVE NARRATIVE: LEIDKULTUR

Leitverantwortung ensues from a narrative based on the values enshrined in the Bundesrepublik, themselves a response to the negative experience of Nazism. It has not however replaced the negative historical memory narrative, which remains apparent – especially in the media. In the book *www.Deutsche-Leidkultur.de*, Henryk M. Broder uses the term *Leidkultur* to criticise excessive reference to and instrumentalisation of the Holocaust and German guilt together with pseudo-identification with the victim narrative.[25] The so-called ›Leitkultur‹ and ›Nationalstolz‹ debates on German identity and patriotism in October 2000 and March 2001 respectively bore traits of *Leidkultur* through instrumentalisation and manipulation of the national memory narrative at political level. They continued the schema of *Vergangenheitsbewältigung* debates in addressing the problem of how to reconcile a national memory narrative overshadowed by Auschwitz with the positive achievements of the Bundesrepublik. Yet they were also different in having less to do with the direct memory, history and consequences of National Socialism than with its legacy in present-day political culture; that is they are debates of cultural rather than communicative memory. Moreover, they involved the stated – rather than implied – desire from some quarters to start identifying with the country again after decades where patriotism could stretch to the constitution but no further.

THE ›LEITKULTUR‹ DEBATE

The ›Leitkultur‹ debate was triggered by the CDU politician Friedrich Merz. During the Union's debate on immigration and asylum he said that those wishing to stay permanently in Germany should adapt to a ›freiheitliche deutsche Leitkultur‹.[26] The term was from the start ambiguous; it could refer to German culture as the dominant culture or the dominant culture within Germany. This was evident in the definitions given, which ranged from language to landscape to ›Kartoffelsuppe‹.[27] The term in fact comes from Bassam Tibi, a political scientist of Syrian origin. In his 1998 book *Europa ohne Identität?*[28] Tibi states that heterogeneous immigrant societies such as Germany do need a ›Leitkultur‹ to allow integration. This does not imply specifically German characteristics or symbols but rather the ideas of the European enlightenment. This definition could have sparked a productive discussion on the integration of foreigners in multi-ethnic Germany. However, it was taken out of context to become a purely national and largely media-fuelled debate on what it means to be German and the aspects of ›German-ness‹ that foreigners in the country should be expected to take on.

The CDU eventually pared the term down to the innocuous – and surely self-evident – notion of following the constitution and democratic standards, learning the German language and adapting to social and cultural life in Germany and western Christian values.[29] These are all ingredients of a national narrative that only seems to stretch back as far as 1949 and the notion of *Verfassungspatriotismus*. By this stage however the meaning and context of ›Leitkultur‹ mattered less than its emergence as a tool for the CDU to attack the opposition with, this time not based on Auschwitz but rather the way that the left liberals had dealt with it in the post-war period. Hence, the Union could claim itself the party of patriotic national identity whilst accusing the former 68ers for having, as Angela Merkel put it, ›ein gestörtes Verhältnis zu ihrem Vaterland.‹[30]

THE ›NATIONALSTOLZ‹ DEBATE

This tactic became apparent in the more aggressive follow-up to the ›Leitkultur‹ debate a few months later. The so-called ›Nationalstolz‹ debate was triggered by the Green Environment Minister Jürgen Trittin, who declared that Laurenz Meyer, General Secretary of the CDU, not only had the looks but also the mentality of a skinhead in response to Meyer's assertion that he was proud to be German.[31] The Union called for Trittin's resignation, not least because he had associated it with the far right. After initially receiving scant column inches, the affair was soon blown out of proportion and context, the media gleefully asking stars ranging from Peter Maffay to Michael Schumacher whether they were proud to be German, hoping for a good – or controversial – quote. Yet this debate was not just driven by the media; it turned into a political affair. Those politicians who did not play the pride game courted criticism: the CSU and FDP even called for President Rau's resignation after he said that one could be ›froh oder dankbar‹ to be German but added ›Man kann nicht stolz sein auf etwas, was man gar nicht zu Stande gebracht hat.‹[32] A Bundestag debate on patriotism was held on the instigation of the CDU. Although ostensibly about whether or not Trittin should resign, in the end it was not about him at all. Instead delegates scrambled to outdo each other on declaring how proud they were of their nation. Friedrich Merz, for example, stated that 50 years after the war Germans had the right to be a bit proud of their country and those (i.e. Trittin and his government) that thought otherwise had a hate relationship with it. The ›Nationalstolz‹ debate was a clear case of political instrumentalisation for present aims. Trittin's remark had been made less than two weeks before Land elections were due to take place in Baden-Württemberg and Rheinland-Pfalz, the latter being particularly difficult territory for the Greens. The conservatives hoped to turn it to their advantage by playing the fatherland card. It is of course uncertain whether the public at large feels the need to reclaim far right slogans for themselves. However, it is worth reflecting on a point made by Herbert Riehl-Heyse in the *Süddeutsche Zeitung*. He saw the ›Nationalstolz‹ debate as a backlash against what he terms ›Inländerfeindlichkeit‹:

> In manchen gebildeten Kreisen gehört es seit langem zum guten Ton eines Satzes den deutschen Hang zum Vorurteil zu geißeln, um dann im zweiten Teil das Deutsche als solches grässlich zu finden. Eine ganze Generation ist mit diesen Vorgaben aufgewachsen und hat fälschlich gedacht, es würde ihr die Sünden der deutschen Geschichte vergeben, wenn sie nur auch davon ausgingen, es gebe ein geheimnisvolles Gen, das die Deutschen besonders widerlich-reaktionär mache.[33]

As strong as the call to adopt a more positive stance towards Germany is an increasingly critical tone with regard to the attitude to the National Socialist past in the Berlin Republic, which recalls the bitter narrative of *Vergangenheitsbewältigung* in the 1960s. Concern over a ›Schlussstrichmentalität‹ or Vergangenheits-›Bewältigung‹[34] is coupled with fear of an intellectual and political shift to the right and secondary anti-Semitism.[35] The authors of the book *Umkämpftes Vergessen* note:

> Tendenzen einer deutschen Vergangenheitspolitik ..., die in »unbekümmerten«, zukunftsorientierten und selbstbewußten Formen auf die Abwehr der Erinnerung an die deutsche Verbrechen und die kollektive Selbstversöhnung der Nation mit der Geschichte zielen.[36]

The perceived aim is to draw a line under the National Socialist past as it poses an obstacle to the desired ›normality‹ in the present – a normality that is however marred by the spectre of far right extremism. For Johannes Klotz and Gerd Wiegel:

> Die NS-Vergangenheit ist nicht »bewältigt«, im Gegenteil, Rassismus und Antisemitismus wirken in der ›Moderne‹ fort bzw. scheinen mit den gesellschaftlichen Problemlagen zu wachsen. Es handelt sich um Kontinuitäten, die Vergangenheit und Gegenwart miteinander verknüpfen.[37]

A SHIFT IN THE ROLE AND APPLICATION OF MEMORY NARRATIVES

The ›Leitkultur‹ and ›Nationalstolz‹ debates continued the narratives of two identifiable political communities of memory with regard to the Third Reich in the post-war period, one seeking to assert an unbroken sense of identity and one that ensures that this stays broken. They also indicated a shift in the priorities and role attached to the narratives on this past as it becomes cultural memory. Whilst the debates on the legacy of National Socialism continue apace, to a certain extent they are now overshadowed by contemporary concerns. A key example of this was the 9 November 2000 demonstration ›Wir stehen auf für Menschlichkeit und Toleranz‹ which brought some 200,000 people out onto the streets of Berlin to take a stand against intolerance and racism. The annual commemoration of the *Kristallnacht* of 9 November 1938 (as well as the fall of the Berlin wall in 1989) remained very much in the background. The demonstration was largely a response to the increase in right-wing violence in Germany, which had been a major topic of political and media debate that summer, and to Gerhard Schröder's call for an ›Aufstand der Anständigen‹. In other words, this was a plea to uphold the values that had gone astray under National Socialism and that had subsequently been re-anchored in the *Grundgesetz*. However, the emphasis of this demonstration was very much on the present. As both President Rau and Paul Spiegel, Chairman of the Central Council of Jews in Germany, pointed out in their speeches, it was also about the image Germany wished to project to the outside world.[38] An advert for the *Berliner Morgenpost* at the time quoted Michael Friedman as saying that Germany had to ›show it's face‹ (*Gesicht zeigen*) or else lose face.

The above would suggest that memory of the National Socialist past is now working on two levels. On the one hand there is the ritualised form of cultural memory through speeches, commemorations and so on which remains necessary for formal remembrance as well as to show respect for the victims. Running parallel to this is a kind of ›active‹ memory based on the National Socialist legacy and focusing on political and democratic education, applying the ›lessons‹ of this past to challenges in the present. The ›active‹ uses of the past would seem to be increasingly dominant. This development is reflected in the work of a growing number of organisations campaigning against racism and for tolerance. These include *Gesichtzeigen: Aktion weltoffenes Deutschland e.V.*; the ›Noteingang‹ scheme offering refuge to victims of the far right; the youth initiative *Step21*; and the ›Exit‹ scheme for those seeking to quit the far right scene.[39] Moreover, those organisations that aim to keep memory of the National Socialist past alive now frequently place this past into the context of the present as well as providing historical information. This can be seen, for example, in the education programmes of the House of the Wannsee Conference, which invite participants to consider issues relating to the Holocaust through the perspective of their own occupation.[40] There is of course the risk of the past being relativised or distorted by aligning it too much with the present: the debates on the far right and National Socialism should not be fused into one. This is however to a certain extent inevitable, particularly with generational change and increased distance from the past.

CONCLUSION: A NARRATIVE FREE OF ALL TABOOS?

It is uncertain how the German narrative on the Third Reich will develop in the future. The tendency does however seem to be towards a ›neue Unbefangenheit‹ with regard to the terms if not the themes of the narrative. A recent example was the so-called ›Antisemitismus-Streit‹ provoked by Jürgen Möllemann, then FDP vice-chairman, who stated that hardly anyone encouraged the anti-semitism that unfortunately existed in Germany more than Ariel Sharon and, in Germany, Michael Friedman.[41] The ensuing political squabble was extended into the cultural sphere with the controversy surrounding Martin Walser's new novel *Tod eines Kritikers*, which was deemed to contain anti-semitic passages.[42] These debates touched on one of the final taboos in Germany's post-war narrative – that is criticism of Israel and Jews – and touched the moral parameters of the narrative to the limit. National memory narratives will continue to have a role and responsibility in providing a connecting thread to place the increasing layers of memory into their correct historical context. Unfortunately, the many laudable efforts to keep knowledge of the National Socialist past alive are often overshadowed by inappropriate instrumentalisation of this past in unproductive, though headline-grabbing, debates instigated for political gain or publicity. Such distortion of the narrative can have a negative effect on the audience in that, to cite Eva Hoffmann, ›Memory not accompanied by knowledge and thought can too easily become the vehicle of sentimental subjectivism – or of a collective narcissism.‹[43] They are equally bad for the narrator. As Michael Naumann has written in *Die Zeit,* one should curb the temptation to open the lid on the German past when trying to make a political point; it always slams shut on one's fingers.[44]

NOTES

[1] Jan Ross, ›Aus Auschwitz lernen? Das Gedenken ist nicht deshalb wichtig, weil es für die politische Moral nützlich wäre‹, Die Zeit, Nr. 49, 26/11/98.
[2] See Josef Joffe, ›Krieg gegen die USA‹, Die Zeit, Nr. 38, 13/9/00.
[3] Bernd Ulrich, ›Diesmal bitte ohne Hitler‹, Der Tagesspiegel, Nr. 17 533, 19/9/01.
[4] Jan Assmann, Das kulturelle Gedächtnis. Schrift, Erinnerung und politische Identität in frühen Hochkulturen, München 1999, p.16.
[5] The term comes from Alexander and Margarete Mitscherlich. See Alexander Mitscherlich, Margarete Mitscherlich, Die Unfähigkeit zu trauern, München 1977 [1967].
[6] See Tim Cole, Images of the Holocaust. The Myth of the »Shoah Business«, London 1999; Peter Novick, The Holocaust and Collective Memory, London 2001; Edward Linenthal, Preserving Memory: The Struggle to Create America's Holocaust Museum, New York 1995; and Norman Finkelstein, The Holocaust Industry: Reflections on the Exploitation of Jewish Suffering, London/New York July 2000.
[7] For an interesting perspective on the heroic narratives established in the early postwar period – ignoring both the victims and any collaboration with the Nazi regime – see Pieter Lagrou, Victims of Genocide and National Memory: Belgium, France and the Netherlands 1945-1965, in: Past and Present, No. 154 (1997), pp. 181-223.
[8] Michael Jeismann, Auf Wiedersehen Gestern. Die deutsche Vergangenheit und die Politik von morgen, Stuttgart/München 2001, p.163
[9] The term is used in Isobel Wollaston, ›A War Against Memory? Nativizing the Holocaust‹, in John K. Roth and Elisabeth Maxwell, (eds.). Remembering for the Future: The Holocaust in an Age of Genocide. Vol. 3 ›Memory‹, Basingstoke/New York, 2001, pp. 501-13.
[10] For a somewhat critical view, see Geoffrey Wheatcroft, ›Holocaust chic‹, The Guardian, 27/1/00.
[11] Natan Sznaider, ›Wem gehört das Jüdische Museum?‹, die tageszeitung, Nr. 6544, 8/9/01. Also see Natan Sznaider and Daniel Levy, Erinnerungen im globalen Zeitalter, Frankfurt a. M. 2001.
[12] The conference produced an eight-point declaration, stating that the Holocaust would always hold universal meaning and should be seared in collective memory to help understand good and evil. The international community held the responsibility to fight racism and xenophobia and moral and political commitment should be strengthened so that future generations would understand the causes of the Holocaust and reflect upon the consequences. There was a pledge to promote education, remembrance and research regarding all aspects of the Holocaust and to commemorate the victims and the resistance. An international task force on Holocaust remembrance was also established. The declaration ends with the stated desire to plant the seeds of a better future in the soil of a bitter past. See ›Declaration of the Stockholm International Forum on the Holocaust‹, http://www.holocaustforum.gov.se/conference/official_documents/declaration/index.htm.
[13] Focussing specifically on the situation in America, Novick says the ›talk of uni-

queness and incomparability surrounding the Holocaust...promotes evasion of moral and historical responsibility. The repeated assertion that whatever the United States has done to blacks, Native Americans, Vietnamese, or others pales in comparison to the Holocaust is true – and evasive. And whereas serious and sustained encounter with the history of hundreds of years of enslavement and oppression of blacks might imply costly demands on Americans to redress the wrongs of the past, contemplating the Holocaust is virtually cost-free: a few cheap tears.‹ See Novick, p. 15.

[14] At this conference, it was indeed Jörg Haider and his far right-wing Freedom party in Austria that were seen as the embodiment of evil rather than Adolf Hitler.

[15] See Assmann, Das kulturelle Gedächtnis.

[16] One example was his comment that the Holocaust monument should be ›ein Ort, wo man gerne hingeht‹. See Reinhard Mohr, ›Total normal?‹, *Der Spiegel*, Nr. 49/98.

[17] Gerhard Schröder quoted in Mohr, ›Total normal?‹

[18] Regierungserklärung abgegeben vom Bundeskanzler Gerhard Schröder zum Stand der deutschen Einheit vor dem deutschen Bundestag (Reichstagsgebäude Berlin) am 19. April 1999, Presse- und Informationsamt der Bundesregierung, Pressemitteilung vom 19.04.1999.

[19] See, for example, ›Vom Staatenverbund zur Föderation – Gedanken über die Finalität der europäischen Integration‹, Rede von Joschka Fischer in der Humboldt-Universität in Berlin am 12. Mai 2000, http://www.gruene-fraktion.de/rsvgn/rs_dok/0,,616,00.htm.

[20] In his speech at the opening ceremony, Johannes Rau stressed that whilst it was important to remember the Holocaust this was not the sum of German-Jewish history. See Grußwort von Bundespräsident Johannes Rau bei der Eröffnung der ständigen Ausstellung des Jüdischen Museums Berlin am 9. September 2001 in Berlin, Presse- und Informationsamt der Bundesregierung, Pressemitteilung vom 10.09.01.

[21] See Volker Müller, ›Das möblierte Symbol‹, Berliner Zeitung, 10/9/01.

[22] ›Nirgends ist so ein Haus richtiger als in Berlin‹, Berliner Zeitung, 10/9/01.

[23] Quoted in Alexander Reich, ›Mächtig erinnert. Die Berliner Republik im Glanz ihres Jüdischen Museums – und ein kleiner Nachtrag zu den Eröffnungsfeiern‹, Junge Welt, 10/9/01.

[24] See Johannes Rau, ›Wir müssen den Terrorismus bekämpfen‹, Die Welt, 14/9/01.

[25] Broder for example criticises the ›Post-Shoah Business der Hobby Judologen‹ and the ›Rent a Jew‹ trend whereby Jewish rather than German representatives are invited to speak every time there is a spate of far right violence. With regard to instrumentalisation, he mentions an anti-abortion demonstration in Augsburg which used the slogan ›Gestern Holocaust – heute: Babycaust‹. See Henryk M. Broder, www.Deutsche-Leidkultur.de, Augsburg 2001., p. 45.

[26] Quoted in Guido Heinen, ›Ein Begriff macht Karriere‹, Die Welt, 1/11/00.

[27] The latter was Angela Merkel's definition of the term.

[28] Bassam Tibi, Europa ohne Identität? Die Krise der multikulturellen Gesellschaft, München 1998.

[29] See ›Die Wertegemeinschaft des christlichen Abendlandes‹, Frankfurter Rundschau, Nr. 260, 8/11/00.

[30] See ›»Leitkultur ist eine Chance in einer offenen Gesellschaft«. CDU-Chefin Merkel: SPD und Grüne offenbaren gestörtes Verhältnis zum Vaterland, Interview mit Roland Nelles‹, Die Welt, 2/11/00.

[31] Trittin said ›Laurenz Meyer hat die Mentalität eines Skinhead und nicht nur das

Aussehen. Laurenz Meyer hat selber bekundet, daß er stolz darauf sei, daß er Deutscher ist. Das ist so eine Flachheit, der geistige Tiefflug, der jeden rassistischen Schläger in dieser Republik auszeichnet.‹ Quoted in Günter Bannas, ›»Trittin muß endlich den AStA verlassen«. Im Bundestag wird die Verrohung der Sitten beklagt‹, Frankfurter Allgemeine Zeitung, Nr. 65, 17/3/01.

[32] Susanne Höll, ›Union fordert Debatte über Trittin‹, Süddeutsche Zeitung, Nr. 64, 17-18/3/01.

[33] Herbert Riehl-Heyse, ›Stolz und Vorurteil‹, Süddeutsche Zeitung, Nr. 70, 24-25/3/01.

[34] See Norbert Klotz, ›Vergangenheitspolitik. Deutsche Geschichtsdebatten zwischen Schlussstrich und Normalisierung‹, in: Tribüne. Zeitschrift zum Verständnis des Judentums, 39. Jahrgang, Heft 154, 2. Quartal (2000), pp. 166-191, here p. 166.

[35] The latter was first defined by Adorno as anti-Jewish feeling arising because Jews represent unwanted memory of the Holocaust.

[36] See Micha Brumlik, Hajo Funke, Lars Rensmann, Umkämpftes Vergessen. Walser-Debatte, Holocaust-Mahnmal und neuere deutsche Geschichtspolitik, Berlin 2000, p. 6.

[37] Johannes Klotz, Gerd Wiegel (eds.), Geistige Brandstiftung. Die neue Sprache der Berliner Republik, Berlin 2001, p. 18.

[38] See ›»Gebt dem Hass und der Gewalt keine Chance!« Rede von Bundespräsident Johannes Rau‹, http://www.welt.de/daten/2000/11/10/1110pod201608.htx?search=gebt+dem+hass+und+der+gewalt+keine+chance; and ›»Hören Sie damit auf, verbal zu zündeln«, Rede des Präsidenten des Zentralrats der Juden in Deutschland Paul Spiegel anlässlich der Veranstaltung zum Gedenken an die Reichspogromnacht am 9. November 1938‹, http://www.welt.de/daten/2000/11/10/1110pod201606.htx?search=Paul+Spiegel+november+2000&searchHILI=1.

[39] ›Gesichtzeigen‹: http://www.gesichtzeigen.de; ›Noteingang‹: http://www.aktion-noteingang-berlin.de; ›Step21‹: http://www.step21.de; ›Exit‹: http://www.exit-deutschland.de.

[40] For further information, see Gedenk-und Bildungsstätte Haus der Wannsee-Konferenz, Das Bildungsangebot, Berlin 2000, and Elke Gryglewski, Christoph Kreutzmüller, führeinander. Pädagogisches Arbeitsmittel und Kopiervorlagen zur Geschichte des Nationalsozialismus, Berlin 2000.

[41] Möllemann said: ›Ich fürchte, dass kaum jemand den Antisemiten, die es in Deutschland gibt, die es leider gibt, die wir bekämpfen müssen, mehr Zulauf verschafft hat, als Herr Scharon und in Deutschland Herr Friedman.‹ Quoted in ›Möllemann: »Ich möchte mich entschuldigen«‹, Die Welt, 7/6/02.

[42] Martin Walser, Tod eines Kritikers, Frankfurt a. M., 2002. For the context to these debates, see ›Inszenierter Tabubruch‹, Der Spiegel, Nr. 23, 3/6/02.

[43] See Eva Hoffman, ›The Uses of Hell‹, The New York Review, 9/3/00.

[44] See Michael Naumann, ›Ein Land im Rückwartsgang‹, Die Zeit, Nr. 9, 21/2/02.

BIBLIOGRAPHY

Assman, Jan, Das kulturelle Gedächtnis. Schrift, Erinnerung und politische Identität in frühen Hochkulturen, München 1999

Bannas, Günter ›»Trittin muß endlich den AStA verlassen«. Im Bundestag wird die Verrohung der Sitten beklagt‹, Frankfurter Allgemeine Zeitung, Nr. 65, 17/3/01

›Nirgends ist so ein Haus richtiger als in Berlin‹, Berliner Zeitung, 10/9/01

Broder, Henryk M., www.Deutsche-Leidkultur.de, Augsburg 2001

Brumlik, Micha, Hajo Funke, Lars Rensmann, Umkämpftes Vergessen. Walser-Debatte, Holocaust-Mahnmal und neuere deutsche Geschichtspolitik, Berlin 2000

Cole, Tim, Images of the Holocaust. The Myth of the »Shoah Business«, London 1999

Finkelstein, Norman, The Holocaust Industry: Reflections on the Exploitation of Jewish Suffering, London/New York, July 2000

›Die Wertegemeinschaft des christlichen Abendlandes‹, Frankfurter Rundschau, Nr. 260, 8/11/00

Fuhr, Eckhard, ›Kein Mahnmal‹, Die Welt, 10/09/01

Gedenk-und Bildungsstätte Haus der Wannsee-Konferenz, Das Bildungsangebot, Berlin 2000

Grußwort von Bundespräsident Johannes Rau bei der Eröffnung der ständigen Ausstellung des Jüdischen Museums Berlin am 9. September 2001 in Berlin, Presse- und Informationsamt der Bundesregierung, Pressemitteilung vom 10.09.01

Gryglewski, Elke, Christoph Kreutzmüller, führeinander. Pädagogisches Arbeitsmittel und Kopiervorlagen zur Geschichte des Nationalsozialismus, Edition Hentrich, Berlin 2000

Heinen, Guido, ›Ein Begriff macht Karriere‹, Die Welt, 1/11/00

Hoffman, Eva, ›The Uses of Hell‹, The New York Review, 9/3/00

Höll, Susanne, ›Union fordert Debatte über Trittin‹, Süddeutsche Zeitung, Nr. 64, 17-18/3/01

Jeismann, Michael, Auf Wiedersehen Gestern. Die deutsche Vergangenheit und die Politik von morgen, Stuttgart/München 2001

Joffe, Josef, ›Krieg gegen die USA‹, Die Zeit, Nr. 38, 13/9/00

Klotz, Norbert, Vergangenheitspolitik. Deutsche Geschichtsdebatten zwischen Schlussstrich und Normalisierung, in: Tribüne. Zeitschrift zum Verständnis des Judentums, 39. Jahrgang, Heft 154, 2. Quartal (2000), S. 166-191

Klotz, Johannes, Gerd Wiegel (Hg), Geistige Brandstiftung. Die neue Sprache der Berliner Republik, Berlin 2001

Lagrou, Pieter, Victims of Genocide and National Memory: Belgium, France and the Netherlands 1945-1965, in: Past and Present, No. 154, (1997), S. 181-223

Levy, Daniel, Natan Sznaider, Erinnerungen im globalen Zeitalter, Frankfurt a. M. 2001

Linenthal, Edward, Preserving Memory: The Struggle to Create America's Holocaust Museum, New York 1995

Roth, John K., Maxwell, Elisabeth (Hg). Remembering for the Future: The Holocaust in an Age of Genocide. Vol. 3 »Memory«, Basingstoke/New York, 2001

Mitscherlich, Alexander, Margarete Mitscherlich, Die Unfähigkeit zu trauern, München 1977 [1967]

Mohr, Reinhard, ›Total normal?‹, Der Spiegel, Nr. 49/98

Müller, Volker, ›Das möblierte Symbol‹, Berliner Zeitung, 10/9/01

Naumann, Michael, ›Ein Land im Rückwartsgang‹, Die Zeit, Nr. 9, 21/2/02

Novick, Peter, The Holocaust and Collective Memory, London 2001

Rau, Johannes, ›Wir müssen den Terrorismus bekämpfen‹, Die Welt, 14/9/01

Regierungserklärung abgegeben vom Bundeskanzler Gerhard Schröder zum Stand der deutschen Einheit vor dem deutschen Bundestag (Reichstagsgebäude Berlin) am 19. April 1999, Presse- und Informationsamt der Bundesregierung, Pressemittelung vom 19.04.1999

Reich, Alexander, ›Mächtig erinnert. Die Berliner Republik im Glanz ihres Jüdischen Museums – und ein kleiner Nachtrag zu den Eröffnungsfeiern‹, Junge Welt, 10/9/01

Riehl-Heyse, Herbert, ›Stolz und Vorurteil‹, Süddeutsche Zeitung, Nr. 70, 24-25/3/01

Ross, Jan, ›Aus Auschwitz Lernen? Das Gedenken ist nicht deshalb wichtig, weil es für die politische Moral nützlich wäre‹, Die Zeit, Nr. 49, 26/11/985

›Inszinierter Tabubruch‹, Der Spiegel, Nr. 23, 3/6/02

Sznaider, Natan, ›Wem gehört das Jüdische Museum?‹, die tageszeitung, Nr. 6544, 8/9/01

Tibi, Bassam, Europa ohne Identität? Die Krise der multikulturellen Gesellschaft, München 1998

Ulrich, Bernd, ›Diesmal bitte ohne Hitler‹, Der Tagesspiegel, Nr. 17 533, 19/9/01

›»Leitkultur ist eine Chance in einer offenen Gesellschaft«. CDU-Chefin Merkel: SPD und Grüne offenbaren gestörtes Verhältnis zum Vaterland. Interview with Roland Nelles‹, Die Welt, 2/11/00

›Möllemann: »Ich möchte mich entschuldigen«‹, Die Welt, 7/6/02

Walser, Martin, Tod eines Kritikers, Frankfurt a. M., 2002.

Wheatcroft, Geoffrey, ›Holocaust chic‹, The Guardian, 27/1/00

WEBSITES

Declaration of the Stockholm International Forum on the Holocaust

http://www.holocaustforum.gov.se/conference/official_documents/declaration/index.htm

Fischer, Joschka, ›Vom Staatenverbund zur Föderation – Gedanken über die Finalität der europäischen Integration‹, Rede von Joschka Fischer in der Humboldt-Universität in Berlin am 12. Mai 2000

http://www.gruene-fraktion.de/rsvgn/rs_dok/0,,616,00.htm

»Gebt dem Hass und der Gewalt keine Chance!«, Rede von Bundespräsident Johannes Rau

http://www.welt.de/daten/2000/11/10/1110pod201608.htx?search=gebt+dem+hass+und+der+gewalt+keine+chance

»Hören Sie damit auf, verbal zu zündeln«, Rede des Präsidenten des Zentralrats der Juden in Deutschland Paul Spiegel anlässlich der Veranstaltung zum Gedenken an die Reichspogromnacht am 9. November 1938

http://www.welt.de/daten/2000/11/10/1110pod201606.htx?search=Paul+Spiegel+november+2000&searchHILI=1

Gesichtzeigen:	http://www.gesichtzeigen.de
Step21:	http://www.step21.de
Noteingang:	http://www.aktion-noteingang-berlin.de
Exit:	http://www.exit-deutschland.de

Medialer Wandel

Narration und Fernsehkartographie

ROLF F. NOHR

> Sehe ich einen Menschen auf dem Eise gehen, so ist dies keine Wahrscheinlichkeit, sondern Gewissheit; erzählt mir aber Jemand, dass er in England an einem kalten Wintertage einen Menschen auf dem Eise habe gehen sehen, so stimmt dies so mit dem gewöhnlichen Lauf der Natur, dass ich es für wahr zu halten geneigt bin, wenn nicht ein Verdacht gegen die Erzählung vorhanden ist. Wird dasselbe aber Jemand innerhalb der Wendekreise erzählt, der bis dahin vom Eise nie etwas gehört hat, so ruht die Wahrscheinlichkeit nur auf dem Zeugniss, und die Sache findet mehr oder weniger Glauben, je nach der Zahl, der Glaubwürdigkeit und Uninteressirtheit der Zeugen; obgleich ein Mensch, dessen Erfahrungen ganz dagegen sprechen und der nie von dergleichen gehört hat, kaum dem ehrlichsten Zeugen hier Glauben schenken wird.
>
> *John Locke: Versuch über den menschlichen Verstand, 1872*

Kartographie im Fersehen scheint auf den ersten Blick nur schwer zusammen zu gehen mit einem konstatierten Wandel von Narrationen. In dem Sinne, wie aber John Locke in dem einführenden Zitat über die Grundlegung eines Wahrheitsbegiffes reflektiert, so kann auch über das Medium Fernsehen nachgedacht werden. Auch das televisuelle System arbeitet an der Herstellung von Erfahrbarkeit und Wahrheitsbeweisen, konstruiert und stabilisiert Glaubwürdigkeiten mithilfe von Zeugenschaften. Eine Nachrichtensendung zitiert einen ›Jemand des anderen Wendekreises‹ in objektiver Augenzeugenschaft; nur dass das Ereignis der Bezeugung meist weitaus komplexer ist als der Locke'sche Gang auf dem Eise. Idee meiner Ausführungen ist es in diesem Sinne, Strategien des Fernsehens anzudeuten, die komplexe Ereignisse ambivalenter Ortshaftigkeiten über Zeugenerzählungen und den Rückgriff auf ›natürliche‹ Sprechweisen ›glaubwürdig‹ und ›wahrscheinlich‹ machen. Im Zentrum sollen dabei Zeugen ganz besonderer Natur stehen – eben Karten. Dabei möchte ich – thesenhaft und verkürzt – darlegen, in welchem Verständnis Narrative von Kartographie interdependent mit erzählenden und kommonsensualen Praktiken sind. So gibt es in meinem Verständnis zwei Zugriffsmöglichkeiten auf narrative

Momente der Fernsehkartographie: zum einen eine offensichtliche Ebene ›formatierter‹ Erzählungen und eine tiefer liegende Ebene ›kommonsensualer‹ Erzählmuster.

Fragen wir uns nach auffälligen Formen von Kartographie im Fernsehen, so wird sicherlich den meisten von uns zunächst die allabendliche Wetterkarte vor Augen stehen. Werfen wir zunächst einen Blick auf die standardisierte Form von Wetterberichterstattung und Wetterkarten. Wetterkarten sind Teil der Nachrichten und stehen somit in einem Kontext der ›Informationsvermittlung‹. Nichts läge also näher, als Wetterkarten im Sinne einer weiteren Form der Ereignisberichterstattung zu werten und somit das Ereignis ›Wetter‹ als Teil der Nachrichten über die Welt zu verstehen. Hans-Jürgen Wulff (1998) stellt demgegenüber die Frage, ob Wetternachrichten als neutrale Informationen oder nicht doch vielmehr als ›formatierte‹ Ereignisgestaltungen zu verstehen seien. Dabei ist die Frage nach einer konkreten narrativen Kontur von Wetternachrichten obsolet: »Handlungen im engeren Sinne fehlen, da es keine belebenden Agenten gibt, die Objekte intentional verändern« (ebd., 34). Objekte des Wetters erhalten jedoch durch sprachliche Mittel zum Teil Individuenstatus (»Das Tief Markus«); sie sind auch als komplexe Situationen beschreibbar. In diesem erweiterten Verständnis können also Pseudoagenten und Handlungsfragmente benannt werden. Da eine (Wetter-) Karte per se (auch in ihrer knappsten Form) ein temporales Gefüge ist, ist im Gegenteil fast jedes Ereignis in ihr als zeitlich erstreckt anzunehmen. Ein Moment, das aber eben sehr viel mehr vom Rezipienten an die Karte herangetragen als von ihr selbst ›intendiert‹ wird. Eine Wetterkarte ist, so betrachtet, ein zeitlich-dynamisches und somit narrativ markiertes Rezeptionsfeld, innerhalb dessen die benannten Pseudoagenten fast zwangsläufig zu Handlungsträgern überformt werden. So kann die (an Rudolf Arnheim (1978, 373) angelehnte) Formel: ›raumzeitliche Dynamik generiert Narration‹ in ihrer Verkürzung dennoch geltend gemacht werden – und dies eben nicht nur im Hinblick auf Wetterflüge und -animationen.

Festzuhalten bleibt also, dass im speziellen Fall der Wetterkarten (und natürlich damit eingeschränkt auch für andere Kartenformen) Wetter als Ereignis zumindest durch den Rezipienten narrativisiert wird. Es werden aus dem Ausgangsmaterial Akteure synthetisiert (beispielsweise Hochdruckgebiete oder Wolkenfelder), welche als Flächenakteure mit Zentrum und (identitätsschwächerer) Peripherie wirksam handeln.

Diese Handlungen finden in einem – durch kartographisches Wissen – klar determinierten Handlungsraum statt (bspw. Deutschland oder Mitteleuropa) und zeichnen sich in ihrer Dramaturgie durch eine hohe Parallelität von *plot* und *story* im Sinne Hayden Whites (1987) aus. Entstehende Bedeutungsebenen können zunächst als schlicht polare, an ›instinktiven‹

Dramaturgien orientiert dargestellt werden: beispielsweise scheint die Konfliktmetapher bestimmend. ›Fronten‹ und ›Blöcke‹ prallen aufeinander, Pfeile symbolisieren das ›Vorrücken‹ und ›Durchdringen‹ von Antipoden, ›gute‹ Wolken sind weiß, ›schlechte‹ dunkel, die Sonne ›lacht‹ und die Wolken ›weinen‹.

Diese narrative Konstruktion steht erkennbar in einem Wirkungszusammenhang mit dem (Karten-) Kontext. Wulff (1998) verweist darauf, dass Wetterinformationen unter der Primärfunktion der Information und deren Präsentationsmodus stehen, und im Rahmen dieser Informationsaufgabe ihre Ereignishaftigkeit im wesentlichen durch kommunikative Akteure authentifizieren. Interessant ist die daraus resultierende Adressierungsdivergenz: schönes oder normales Wetter adressiert den privaten und individuellen Rezipienten – schlechtes und katastrophales Wetter die intersubjektive Gruppe; im Falle des Katastrophenwetters rückt die Wetternachricht sogar in den zentralen Block der Nachrichten. Insofern ließe sich, vor allem unter dem Aspekt des narrativen Gehaltes, die Privatheit der Kartenerzählung als Heraustreten aus dem Nachrichtenzusammenhang – im Sinne des Ereigniskontextes – bestimmen. Wetter würde dann auf das Subjekt selbst bezogen sein, seine Handlungsrelevanz vielleicht eher sekundär in den Bestimmungsvordergrund rücken, und gerade aus seiner basalen Dramaturgie auf eine urmythische Ebene der Bedeutungsproduktion verweisen: die Korrelation von Mensch und Natur(raum).

> One can easily argue, that the weather programm is only another rural ritual, whose aim is to establish the tribe's relations with his natural enviroment [...]. The participants in the ritual are [...] not seeking information, but are attempting to make their positions secure in a complex and erratic enviroment, exerting what seems to be control through ritual (Mohr 1971, 629).

Worauf diese einführenden Reflexionen abzielen, ist darzustellen, dass Karten im Fernsehen zwei miteinander verwobene, aber dennoch unterschiedliche Modi einnehmen. Zum einen den Präsentationsmodus, welcher sich vordergründig informativ generiert, indem er eine Koppelung an Nachrichten betont, und durch die Zitierung der Meteorologie auf eine distanzierende Expertensprache[1] rekurriert und auf Expertenwissen verweist. Auf dieser Ebene scheint es sehr einfach, Wetterkarten eine gesteigerte Narrativität vor allem in der subjektiven Rezeption nachzuweisen. Damit wird der Präsentationsmodus als eine Form der Narrativität erkennbar, die sich augenscheinlich nur auf dynamische und in die konkrete Erfahrung rückkoppelbare Karten bezieht. Dies liefert aber nur ein schwaches Argument für die hohe Attraktivität beziehungsweise offensichtliche ›Überfunktionalisierung‹ der Karten im Kontext der Nachrichtenberichterstattung. Diesem Präsentationsmodus gegenüber steht dementsprechend etwas, was sich als Handlungsmodus bezeichnen ließe. Es ist dies der Modus der Rezeption, in dem das kommunizierte Ereignis Wetter auf den Rezipienten – und entscheidender – auf einen intersubjektiven *common sense* bezogen wird. Nicht nur dass das Wetter (und das Sprechen über Wetter) ein ritualisiertes Moment kommonsensualer Diskursivität ist, auch im Sinne der Ereignisberichterstattung narrativisiert die Karte im Fernsehen kommonsensuale Formationen.

Um diesen Aspekt zu vertiefen, gilt es aber, einen Schnitt zurückzutreten, und die beteiligten Aufschreibesysteme (nämlich Karten und Fernsehen) kurz zu beleuchten.

Hierbei gilt es, einen mir sehr wichtigen Begriff zu etablieren. Ich möchte darstellen, dass Kartographie ein ›sprechendes Aufschreibesystem‹ ist, also ein Medium impliziter und diskursiver (im obigen Sinne kommonsensualer) Ideologeme[2]. Der amerikanische Karthographietheoretiker Brian Harley (1988) spricht darüber hinaus auch von einer interpretativen Methode der kartographischen Dekonstruktion, innerhalb derer es gilt, das Schweigen der Karte (*silence in the map*) zu analysieren – also genau die Werthaltigkeiten zum ›Klingen zu bringen‹, die in einer ersten Rezeption absent zu sein scheinen. Oder anders ausgedrückt: die Karte als Diskursmaterialisation zu begreifen und analytisch das diskursiv Artikulierte vom Nicht-Artikulierten zu trennen. Oder aber eben noch einmal anders ausgedrückt: Was erzählt und was verschweigt eine Karte?

Kartographie kann als Verfahren der Geographie verstanden werden. Geographie geht zurück auf das griechische *geo graphein*: ›die Erde schreiben‹. Hier formt sich ein sowohl analytisches wie auch normatives Verständnis des *Welt-Schreibens* als textuelles, diskursives oder metaphorisches Verfahren. Wir können somit Karten (unter Vorbehalten) zunächst als Texte verstehen. Ein erweiterter Textbegriff kann kulturelle Produktionen ebenso wie soziale, ökonomische oder politisch-institutionelle Organisationsformen (vor allem aber das soziale Feld insgesamt) umfassen. Dabei ist vor allem aber offensichtlich, dass im Zusammenhang mit der *postmodern geography* der Begriff des Raumes gegenläufig und uneindeutiger zu mathematisch-deskriptiven Modellen gesetzt wird.

> Not so many years ago, the word ›space‹ had a strictly geometrical meaning: the idea it evoked was simply that of an empty area. In scholarly use it was generally accompanied by some such epithet as ›Euclidean‹, ›isotropic‹, or ›infinite‹, and the general feeling was that the concept of space was ultimately a mathematical one. To speak of ›social space‹, therefore, would have sounded strange (Lefebvre 1991, 1).

Führen wir uns eine der bekanntesten mittelalterlichen Radkarten, die Ebsdorfer Weltkarte vor Augen. Diese Karte, sicherlich eine der eindrucksvollsten (und meistinterpretierten) mittelalterlichen Radkarten, weist eine Dichte von unterschiedlichen Kommunikationssystemen auf. Sie erscheint als Momentaufnahme ebenso des geographischen Wissens als auch der politischen Verhältnisse um 1239. Gleichzeitig kann sie als Verkünderin christlicher Heilslehre, als Bilderbuch der bekannten Flora und Fauna, aber auch als Vorläuferin des Satellitenbildes und Hypertextes gelesen werden.[3] Sie ist die archetypische *mappa mundi*, an der augenfällig die Frage nach ihrer bildlichen oder textuellen Form behandelt werden kann. Denn schon auf einer ersten Ebene der Reflexion wird deutlich, dass die Ebsdorfer Weltkarte mitnichten nur ›Ab-Bild‹ ist. Nicht nur die sie umgebenden 1400 Textpassagen, auch die Komplexität des in ihr zum Ausdruck gebrachten Wissens lässt sie zum Aufschreibesystem eines Ausdrucks des mittelalterlichen Weltbildes werden. Dieses Problem der Multidimensionalität des visuellen Ausdrucks ist selbstverständlich kein allein auf Kartographie bezogenes. Es ist vielmehr die Grundauseinandersetzung in der Beschäftigung mit dem Status des visuellen Ausdrucks von Wissen. Aber eben ein Ausdruck des Wissens nicht im Sinne der enzyklopädischen oder archivischen ›linearen‹ Aufschreibung, sondern viel eher die Verfestigung des eigentlich mäandernden oralen (oder eben: narrativen) Wissens über die Welt. Somit also ein *Erde-Schreiben* fast im Sinne eines *Erde-Erzählens*.

Deutlich wird somit aber auch, dass Karten nicht per se objektive Aufschreibungen von Raum sind, sondern – so die These – als Bedeutungssysteme in ihren jeweiligen Epistemen different verwendet und gelesen werden. Das Allegorische der Ebsdorfer Weltkarte scheint unserem heutigen Verständnis von Kartographie fremd. Aktuell begreifen wir Karten (naiv) als mathematisch-objektive Orientierungsanleitungen, als Raumabbilder mit Realitätseffekten. Diese vor allem im Schulunterricht eingeübte Lesweise der Kartographie begreift Karten als wissenschaftliches Deskriptionswerkzeug, als Modellation konkreter räumlicher Zusammenhänge oder als Simulation komplexer Kausalitäten. Darüber verschwindet aber ein Verständnis, Karten als generalisiertes und allegorisches Textsystem zu begreifen, welches mehr ›aufschreibt‹ als nur den Raum. Der Schulatlas als geographisches Lehrbuch steht somit zunächst im Kontext eines etablierten Regelwissens, eines konsensfähigen hegemonialen Wissens, das deutlich abgegrenzt ist von einem wie auch immer anzunehmenden ›objektiven‹ wissenschaftlichen Wissensbestand. Diese Funktion der Aushandlung von Wissensbeständen über einen öffentlichen Diskurs des Lernens und Erziehens ist dabei historisch von Anfang an an den Lehratlas gebunden (vgl. Zahn / Kleinschmidt 1995, 158ff.).[4]

So wird deutlich, dass die vorgeblich mathematisch-objektive Aufschreibung von Raum mittels eines Lehrbuches bei weitem über die rein faktische Vermittlung topographischer Daten hinausgeht, ja – per definitionem – hinausgehen muss. Die Schulkarte positioniert sich somit zumindest schon einmal im diskursiven Feld des hegemonial organisierten Regelwissens, steht aber auch im engeren Kontext mit beispielsweise geopolitischen

Argumentationen. Verkürzt versucht die Schulkarte also, einerseits Lesweisen von Raumrepräsentationen einzuüben und andererseits im Kontext der Atlanten als Ausdruckssystem im weitesten Sinne herstellungsgeprägte ›territorialpolitische‹ Setzungen einzuüben – in den Worten Jürgen Links (1998) »flexible Normalisierungen« herzustellen, oder weiter gefasst: einen *common sense* herzustellen beziehungsweise sich an ihm zu positionieren. Ebenso scheint es aber deutlich, dass ›Sprechen‹ an sich eine Praktik der Stabilisierung von Wertsystemen darstellt. Darüber hinaus muss ›Erzählen‹ als eine Formation von Sprechen gewertet werden, die – auch wenn an Bilder gekoppelt – Formen offener Wissensbestände instantiiert, reglementiert und immer neu bestätigt. Eine Narrativität der Karten muss in diesem Zusammenhang dann auch als eine Form der Herstellung kommonsensualer Tropen verstanden werden. Der *common sense* ist – in den Worten Wolfgang Müller-Funks (2002) – ein »symbolisch-narrativer Gemeinbestand einer Kultur«, der ihr

> ... Stabilität verleiht und ihr Härte gegen Devianz ermöglicht. Dabei kann man den *common sense* als ein Insgesamt der in einer Kultur verfügbaren, nicht-impliziten, in den Zustand der Selbstverständlichkeit versetzten Wissensbestände begreifen oder aber auch als ein eigenes Symbolsystem, das mit anderen (Wissenschaft, Religion) in Interaktion steht, aber durchaus eigenen Gesetzmäßigkeiten folgt (ebd., 155).

So gehen *common sense*, Diskurs und Zeichensystem eine Verbindung ein, die die ›Gemachtheit‹ des vorgeblich transparenten Symbolsystems analytisch erkennbar werden lässt. Ich gehe im Folgenden von der Annahme aus, dass die an sich beliebig zu setzende Abhängigkeit der Zeichenkategorien Signifikant und Signifikat, also deren arbiträres Verhältnis[5], durch diskursive Systeme bestimmt und determiniert wird. Somit besteht der Diskurs zwar aus Zeichen, ist aber – im Sinne Michel Foucaults (1974, 20) – irreduzibel auf den bloßen Zeichencharakter. Die Zeichenordnung als Basis der Repräsentationsordnung wird durch den Diskurs als Strukturmechanismus jenseits des Textes eingeschränkt (Hartley 1994, 94).

> Alles Ideologische hat Zeichencharakter. [...] Jedes ideologische Zeichen ist nicht nur die Widerspiegelung oder der Schatten der Wirklichkeit, sondern auch ein materieller Bestandteil dieser Wirklichkeit. Jedes ideologische Zeichenphänomen manifestiert sich in irgendeinem Material, einem Ton, einer physikalischen Masse, einer Farbe, einer Körperbewegung usw. (Vološinov 1975, 56).[6]

Der Diskurs verweist in dieser Auffassung vor allem auf den der Bedeutung innewohnenden Machtcharakter, macht aber auch deutlich, dass Bedeutung jenseits des Textes instantiiert wird. Der Diskurs selbst erfährt seine interne Strukturierung und Ordnung durch interdiskursive oder aber durch institutionelle Machtfaktoren. Dabei ist die diskursive Ordnung, ja der Diskurs selbst, sozial hervorgebracht und produziert (vgl. Fiske 1987,

15).[7] Soziale Realität wird in diesem Verständnis aber nicht durch einen einzigen, sondern durch eine Pluralität der Diskurse geprägt, die Gesellschaft wird als multidiskursiv geordnet angenommen. Jedwede Artikulation ist somit aber eingebunden in die Ordnung des Repräsentationszusammenhangs durch die ideologische und diskursive Setzung der (Foucault'schen) Mikrophysik der Macht. Diese Einbindung bildet den Ausgangspunkt von Institutionalisierungspraktiken, Machtkonstellationen und deren Artikulation. Diese Artikulationen kultureller und symbolischer Zusammenhänge prägen nicht zuletzt die Wissensbestände sozialer Subjekte, stiften somit (sozialen wie individualen) Sinn. Dabei stehen Diskurs und Wissen nicht nur empirisch, sondern auch kategorial in einem Wechselverhältnis:

> Das Wissen ist eine Voraussetzung für die Diskursivierung des Wissens, welches wiederum eine Voraussetzung bildet für die Entstehung und Veränderung von Wissen (Müller/Wulff 1997, 174).

Diese vorgebliche ›Tautologie‹ der gegenseitigen Bedingtheit von Wissen und Diskurs lässt sich noch am ehesten durch die historische Fundierung der beständigen Austausch- und Zirkulationsbewegungen auflösen, aber eben auch durch die Anerkennung der sozialen Praktik als Handeln im Wechselverhältnis von Diskurs *und* Wissen. Eine Konsequenz dieses Wechselverhältnisses wäre sicherlich die *Naturalisierung*[8] von diskursiven Zusammenhängen als ›innersubjektivem‹ Wissen. So wäre *Ideologie* als der Versuch des sozialen Subjekts zu werten, »Widersprüche der Existenz, die es zerreißen und es im Kern konstruieren, ›zusammenzunähen‹« (Eagleton 1993, 229). Diese pragmatische Form der Ideologiekonstitution verweist wiederum auf die konstitutive Kraft der ›widerständigen Handlung‹, des ›Wilderns‹ in Sinn- und Textzusammenhängen: Es wäre als ein kompensatives Handeln gegen ›selbst gemachte‹ Machtstrukturen zu verstehen, die sich letztlich auch als Verschleierung gesellschaftlich-hegemonialer Verhältnisse interpretieren ließen. Somit ist das angedeutete Schweigen jedweder Kartographie aber benennbar: die Machtbedingungen der Hervorbringung, die sich zeichenhaft in jede Aufschreibung von Raum eintragen, und die dann kompensativ naturalisiert und verselbstständigt werden – eben zu kommonsensualem ›natürlichem‹ Wissen umgeformt werden. Der – in unserem Falle im Aufschreibesystem Karte manifestierte – *common sense* kann auch als im weitesten Sinne hegemoniale Erzählung selbstdisziplinatorischer Effekte des *Wissens* und (im Sinne Harleys) des *Schweigens* verstanden werden. So gelangen wir explizit zu den Karten im Fernsehen zurück. Dass Wetterkarten tendenziell als narrativ gelten mögen, habe ich einführend angedeutet. Entscheidender ist für mich allerdings die Frage, inwieweit andere Formen der Kartographie in ebensolcherweise und vor allem im Kontext der Nachrichten narrative (eben im Sinne kommonsensualer Effekte) Funktionen entfalten.

Grundsätzlich zum Verständnis einer solchen visuellen Argumentation ist eine Konturierung des Phänomenfeldes Nachrichten innerhalb des Fernsehens. Es würde zu weit führen, hier die breite medientheoretische Debatte zu Nachrichten und Nachrichtenkommunikation zu entfalten. Es muss an dieser Stelle genügen, Nachrichten als ein ›kaleidoskopisches‹ Programmelement zu verstehen, welches unter dem Verdikt der vorgeblichen Objektivitätskonstruktion zu verstehen ist (vgl. Wulff 1995). Nachrichten sollen und wollen Ereignisse in Zeit und Raum positionieren und kommunizieren (eine Definition, die natürlich ad-hoc-Status hat und extrem auf das Untersuchungsobjekt Karte zugeschnitten ist). Somit ist aber auch die grundsätzliche Frage zum Verhältnis von Ereignis, Information und Kommunikation in den Nachrichten gestellt. Die postulierte Normativität und Normalisierungsfunktion der Nachrichten gibt eine erste Antwort. Grundsätzlich kann eine Nachricht verstanden werden als ein ausgewähltes, selektiertes und mit dem Kriterium der Relevanz aufgeladenes Ereignis, das in eine audiovisuelle Präsentationsdramaturgie umgearbeitet wird. Eine Nachricht zeichnet sich in diesem Verständnis als durch eine bestimmte und zugeschriebene Relevanz aus, die sich nicht zuletzt aus ihrem innewohnenden Potenzial der Thematisierungs- und Darstellungsfähigkeit ableitet, die von einer notwendigen ›Simplifizierbarkeit‹ und auch einer Tendenz zur Visualität gestützt wird. Verkürzt könnte gesagt werden, dass ein Ereignis nur dann zur Nachricht wird, wenn es im positiven wie negativen Sinne in seiner Komplexität reduziert werden kann: Die Nachricht will das Ereignis und damit die Welt via Fernsehen verständlich aber auch sendbar machen. Eine Nachrichtenwirklichkeit kann somit auch als eine konstruktive Wirklichkeitsfunktion verstanden werden. Damit sind Medienwirklichkeiten stets kontingent, d. h. immer auch anders denkbar.

Wenn Nachrichten also einerseits Ereignisse normalisieren und andererseits dramaturgisieren, so liegt es nahe, ihnen ein Operieren auf der Basis stark ausgeprägter *common sense*-Strukturen zu unterstellen, wie es beispielsweise auch im Modell des *bardic televison* von John Fiske und John Hartley (1978) anklingt. Fernsehen wird hier eben gerade nicht als Kommunikator distinkter Ereignisse sondern als Mittler zwischen *common sense* und Rezipient verstanden. »The real authority for both bardic and television is the audience in whose language they are encoded« (ebd., 86). In der Instanz des ›Barden‹ kulminiert die narrative Grundlage der Kultur (eben das kommonsensuale Wissen) und wird im Moment der oralen Wiedergabe sowohl abgerufen, variiert als auch wiederum instantiiert. So kann auf die Betonung der Latenz des *common sense* verwiesen werden, also auf die These, dass der *common sense* sich nicht explizit machen muss, dass sich Narrative im Kommonsensualen latent einschreiben und nicht manifest werden.

> The main point is that meaning does not inhere in things, in the world. It is constructed, produced. It ist the result of a signifying practice – a practice that produces meaning, that makes things mean (Hall 1997, 24).

Gehen wir also davon aus, dass eine Karte per se keine symbolische Form der Erzählung darstellt. Dennoch trägt sie implizit Formen kommonsensualen Wissens in sich. Es ist dies aber eben genau nicht das Wissen um die Positionierung eines raumzeitlichen Ereignisses – beispielsweise des Kosovokonfliktes. Wolfgang Müller Funk (2002) umreißt den *common sense* (im Rückgriff auf Clifford Geertz) als eine »Darstellung der Dinge, die beansprucht, die richtige zu sein« (ebd., 156). Kriterien dieser »Darstellung der Dinge« können unter direktem Bezug auf die Geertz'sche Konturierung des *common sense* in fünf Eigenschaften zusammengefasst werden: natürlich, praktisch, dünn, unmethodisch und zugänglich (vgl. Geertz 1997, vor allem 275-286).
Führen wir uns noch einmal eine Nachrichteninsertkarte, wie sie im Zusammenhang mit dem Einmarsch des deutschen Kafor-Kontingents in Prizren am Ende des Kosovo-Konfliktes verwandt wurde, vor Augen (vgl. Abb. 2). Eine solche topographisch strukturierte Karte fällt vor allem unter der Prämisse einer klaren Grenzziehung, einer dezidiert ereignisorientierten Ausschnittwahl und einer Zentrierung auf eine ›Distinktheit‹ der Bildgestaltung auf (im analysierten Beispiel eine deutsche Fahne über dem Punktsymbol der Stadt Prizren). Eine solche Karte konstruiert Natürlichkeit und Zugänglichkeit: Die Karte erscheint uns als natürliches ›Ab-Bild‹ des Raumes, als eine quasi-objektive Repräsentation. Durch eingeübte und naturalisierte Effekte erscheint uns eine solche Karte nicht nur als Abbild des Raumes, sondern auch als Bild des Geschehens. Die Zugänglichkeit einer solchen Darbietung ist der Schlüsselmoment für die kommonsensuale Konturierung einer Medienkartographie. Die Karte erscheint uns – trotz der innewohnenden Generalisierung und Modellierung – durch ihre Referenz auf eine Indizierung des Realen intuitiv lesbar. Daran ankoppelnd kann die unmethodische Argumentation der Karte festgemacht werden. Eine Karte verwechselt methodisch Abbildfunktion und Abbildungsvorschrift, ist eigentlich – wie oben schon angedeutet – arbiträr.[9] Jenseits dieser Kriterien, die zunächst für alle kartographischen Darbietungsformen angenommen werden können, sind es aber vor allem die verbleibenden zwei Kriterien, die am speziellen Beispiel die Konturierung kommonsensualer Formationen verständlich und analysierbar machen. Die von Geertz formulierte Praktischheit lässt sich auch deklinieren als eine emphatische Bezugnahme auf die Lebenspraxis,[10] die im weitesten Sinne durch die Ein-

lösung des ereignisdramaturgischen Impetus der Karte (Stichwort: Deutsche Fahne) hergestellt wird und in diesem Sinne zu einem reduktionistischen Umgang mit komplexen Formationen anregt. Die Simplizität oder Dünnheit der kartographischen Argumentation liegt aber basal in ihrer ›einfachen‹ bzw. polaren Argumentation verborgen. Im Beispiel ist es die Idee der Grenze als Eindeutigkeit: Die Idee der Grenze ist letztlich in ihrer bipolaren Linearität und Distinktion eine generalisierende Argumentationsfigur, die dem zonalen Erleben der Differenz inkompatibel ist und dem eigentlichen Ereignis eine reduktive und generalisierende Perspektive der Reduktion gegenüberstellt.

Sämtliche dieser Perspektiven und Kategorisierungen rekurrieren aber eben nicht genuin auf die Karte selbst, sondern sind interdependent mit Wissensbeständen des kulturellen Wissens: eben, was es ›bedeutet‹ eine Fahne aufzurichten, eine Grenze zu ziehen oder sie zu überschreiten. Wir können daher einen Erzähler benennen (den Nachrichtensprecher als Barden im Fiskeschen Sinne), ebenso wie sich ein Erzähltes benennen lässt, dass sich beispielsweise sehr leicht in die Whitesche Elemente von *plot* und *story* differenzieren lässt. Im Beispiel zeichnet sich eine Dramaturgie ab, hier die Dramaturgie des Konflikts (Sieg des Guten über das Böse) oder der *last-minute-rescue*, ebenso wie Motive der läuternden Queste oder der Expedition ins Unbekannte, der Inbesitznahme des ›Unbekannten‹ oder Missionierung des ›Barbarischen‹. Dies alles ist eingebettet in eine Erzählzeit, die – wiederum jenseits des Faktischen – ein Anfang und ein Ende hat. So verstanden ist eine Karte also Manifestation latenter kommonsensualer Wissensbestände einer Gesellschaft oder Kultur.

> Der *common sense* präsentiert die Dinge – so, als läge das, was sie sind, einfach in der Natur der Dinge. Ein Hauch von ›wie denn sonst‹, eine Nuance von ›versteht sich‹ wird den Dingen beigelegt – aber hier nur ausgewählten, besonders herausgestrichenen Dingen (Geertz 1997, 277).

So perspektiviert lässt sich die Nähe der kommonsensualen kartographischen Narrativität zu ideologischen Strukturen darstellen. Die Erzählung des Kartentextes verwandelt »Geschichte in Natur«, indem er arbiträren Zeichen scheinbar offensichtliche und klare Referentialität verleiht – es findet eine Naturalisierung statt (Eagleton 1993, 230). Diese Naturalisierung setzt am Diskurs selbst an und nicht an der Welt, die den Diskurs hervorbringt.

Erweitern wir die artefaktische Karte um den Kontext ihrer Präsentation, also die bardische Erzählung der Welt durch die Nachrichten, so wird das Narrativ Fernsehkartographie noch deutlicher. Das kartographische Moment im Kontext der Fernsehnachrichten kann im Rückgriff auf kommonsensuale Strukturen und im Kontext eines bardischen-erzählenden Nachrichtenumfeldes in einem bestimmten Sinne auf andere Narrative und allegorisierende Formationen und Praktiken bezogen verstanden werden. Lesen wir aktuelle Medienkartographien (zumindest im besprochenen Beispiel) als eine multiepistemische Aufschreibung von latenten und narrativen Wissensbeständen, die hochgradig in das Wissen ihrer Gesellschaft eingebunden sind und sie je Lektüre sowohl abrufen als auch stabilisieren – was läge näher als sie mit der Traditionslinie der Ebsdorfer Weltkarte zu parallelisieren? Denn im Kern geht es beiden Aufschreibesystemen darum, jenseits der Positionierung Wissensbestände zu artikulieren und zu stabilisieren.

So verstanden wird erkennbar, dass das kartographische Moment im Kontext der Fernsehnachrichten im Rückgriff auf kommonsensuale Strukturen und im Kontext eines bardischen-erzählenden Nachrichtenumfeldes in einem bestimmten Sinne auf die allegorische Karte im Stil der Ebsdorfer Weltkarte zurückweist. Und so etabliert sich auch ein Begriff der Zeugenschaft und der Wahrheit ganz in dem Sinne, wie in John Locke einleitend vorgegeben hat: mit dem großen Unterschied, dass wir nicht mehr auf eine fragwürdige Zeugenschaft in der Konstruktion von Wahrheit angewiesen sind, sondern indem wir uns selbst, unser eigenes Wissen zur Konstitution von Selbstverständlichkeit externalisieren. Die Glaubwürdigkeit des Zeugens ist nun seine natürliche Erzählung der Welt.

ANMERKUNGEN

[1] »Die Sätze ohne die Personalform stellen eine ganz eigenwertige Kommunikationsmöglichkeit dar, deren besondere Leistung darin liegt, in einer kurzen und prägnanten Weise dem Geschehen einen eigenen Modus durch die Unterdrückung der Personalform zu geben« (Rath 1968, 22).

[2] Vertiefend sei zu diesem Bereich verwiesen auf Nohr 2002.

[3] Zur ausführlichen Analyse der Ebsdorfer Karte s. exemplarisch Kugler/Eckhard 1991; Warnke 1998.

[4] So kann beispielsweise auf die Ausführungen Yves Lacostes (1990) verwiesen werden, der für den speziellen Fall des deutschen Geographieunterrichtes nach der Niederlage im Ersten Weltkrieg die Instantiierung revisionistischer geopolitischer Lerninhalte nachweist. »Die Rolle der Geographielehrer hatte für die Anfänge der Geopolitik eine ganz entscheidende Bedeutung, und dies ist auch in Zusammenhang mit der Tatsache zu sehen, dass Deutschland der erste Staat war, der, lange vor Frankreich, die Geographie als Lehrfach an Universitäten und Schulen etablierte« (ders., 20).

[5] Diese Arbitrarität lässt sich zumindest eingeschränkt auf die Kartographie bezogen postulieren. Die (komplexere und bedeutsamere) kartographische Zeichenklasse ist sicherlich die komplex-kodierte (reduzierte) Klasse der etablierten, im eigentlichen Wortsinne arbiträren Zeichen. Farbcodes (Blau = »Wasserfläche«), Beschriftungen (»Marienstraße«) u. a. bedürfen zum einen einer konkreten und je Karte erneue-

rungsbedürftigen Etablierung via Legende und zum anderen der Rekapitulation erlernter und eingeübter kommunikativer Zeichen-Repertoires. Diese Klasse der Kartenzeichen ist sicherlich der textuell-sprachlichen Zeichenklasse näher, so wie die Klasse der selbsterklärenden Zeichen der ikonisch-graphischen Zeichenkategorie näher ist (vgl. bspw. Nöth 1998).

[6] Nach Eagleton (1997, 98) ist es Michail Bachtin, der hier unter dem entliehenen Pseudonym *Vološinov* publiziert.

[7] Diese Auffassung verweist im weitesten Sinne auf die Konzeptionalisierung von Ideologie durch Althusser (1969) beziehungsweise den Hegemonie-Begriff Gramscis (vgl. Hall 1996).

[8] »Naturalisierung wurde innerhalb der Cultural Studies definiert als ein Mechanismus, der arbiträren, kulturell definierten Zeichenkomplexen den Status unbestreitbarer, quasi-natürlicher Gewissheiten verschafft« (Winkler 1999, 57).

[9] Es scheint deutlich, dass das kartographische Zeichen in seinem Objektbezug im weitesten Sinne *arbiträr*, d. h. nicht ein-eindeutig motiviert sondern (weitestgehend) willkürlich und künstlich hergestellt ist. Hier greift die generelle Position de Saussures, die Sprache selbst als grundsätzlich zweigeteiltes System zu begreifen, als ein System zweier differenter Bedeutungskonstellationen. So betrachtet zerfällt Sprache zum einen in ein *Außen* (Syntagmatik), ein intersubjektives und konventionalisiertes Interagieren als codegestütztes Externalisieren von Bedeutung. Zum anderen hat Sprache aber eben auch nachvollziehbarerweise ein *Innen* (Assoziation), nämlich das nichtmaterielle innersubjektive Verhandeln von Bedeutung und Sinn (vgl. de Saussure 1967). »Die Sprache erscheint als eine gesellschaftliche Maschinerie, die die linearen Syntagmen im Außenraum mit der nicht-linearen Struktur der empirischen Gedächtnisse in eine regelhafte Verbindung bringt« (Winkler 1997, 29). Gerade eine solche Konturierung der Arbitrarität konturiert aber m. E. kommonsensuale Unmethodik, Natürlichkeit und Zugänglichkeit als Konstruktion intuitiven Umgehens mit Texten und Sprachformen.

[10] Zur Ausdifferenzierung der Geertzschen Eigenschaften des *common sense* vgl. Müller-Funk (2002, 156).

BIBLIOGRAPHIE

Althusser, Louis, For Marx, Harmondsworth, 1969

Arnheim, Rudolf, Kunst und Sehen. Eine Psychologie des schöpferischen Auges, Berlin / New York 1978 [1954]

Eagleton, Terry, Ideologie – Eine Einführung, Stuttgart / Weimar, 1993

Eagleton, Terry, Einführung in die Literaturtheorie, Stuttgart / Weimar, 1997 [1983]

Fiske, John, Power Plays – Power Works, London / New York, 1993

Fiske, John, Television Culture, London / New York 1987

Fiske John / Hartley, John, Reading Television, London, 1978

Foucault, Michel, Die Ordnung der Dinge. Eine Archäologie der Humanwissenschaften, Frankfurt a. M., 1974

Geertz, Clifford, Dichte Beschreibungen, Frankfurt a. M., 1997

Hall, Stuart, Signification, Representation, Ideology: Althusser and the Post-Structural Debates, in: James Curran / David Morley / Valerie Walkerdine (Hg.), Cultural Studies and Communications«, London / New York / Sydney, 1996, S. 11-34

Hall, Stuart, The Work of Representation, in: Ders., Representation. Cultural Representation and Signifying Practices, London, 1997, S. 15-64

Harley, J. Brian, Silences and Secrecy: the Hidden Agenda of Cartography in Early Modern Europe, in: Imago Mundi, Vol. 40, 1988, S. 57-76

Hartley, John, Discourse, in: Tim O'Sullivan / ders. / Danny Saunders / Martin Montgomery / John Fiske (Hg.), Key Concepts in Communication and Cultural Studies, London / New York, 1994, S. 92-95

Kugler, Hartmut / Michael, Eckhard (Hg.), Ein Weltbild vor Columbus – die Ebsdorfer Weltkarte, interdisziplinäres Kolloquium 1988, Weinheim, 1991

Lacoste, Yves, Geographie und politisches Handeln – Perspektiven einer neuen Geopolitik, Berlin, 1990

Link, Jürgen, Versuch über den Normalismus. Wie Normalität produziert wird, 2. Aufl., Opladen, 1998

Lefebvre, Henri, The Production of Space, Oxford / Cambridge, 1991

Locke, John, Versuch über den menschlichen Verstand. In vier Büchern. Übersetzt und erläutert von J. H. von Kirchmann, Berlin, 1872

Mohr, Howard, TV Weather Programms, in: Journal of Popular Culture, No. 4/1971, S. 628-633

Müller, Eggo / Wulff, Hans J., Aktiv ist gut: Anmerkungen zu einigen empirischen Verkürzungen der British Cultural Studies, in: Andreas Hepp / Rainer Winter (Hg.), Kultur – Medien – Macht: Cultural Studies und Medienanalyse, Opladen 1997, S. 171-176

Müller-Funk, Wolfgang, Die Kultur und ihre Narrative. Eine Einführung, New York / Wien, 2002

Nohr, Rolf F., Karten im Fernsehen. Die Produktion von Positionierung, Münster, 2002

Nöth, Winfried, Kartosemiotik und das kartographische Zeichen, in: Zeitschrift für Semiotik, Band 20, Heft 1-2, 1998, S. 25-40

Rath, Rainer, ›Unvollständige Sätze‹ im heutigen Deutsch – Eine Studie zur Sprache des Wetterberichts, in: Ders. / A. Brandstetter, Zur Syntax des Wetterberichts und des Telegramms, Mannheim, 1968, S. 9-22

Saussure, Ferdinand de, Grundfragen der allgemeinen Sprachwissenschaft, Berlin, 1967 [1916]

Vološinov, Valentin N., Marxismus und Sprachphilosophie. Grundlegende Probleme der soziologischen Methode in der Sprachwissenschaft, hg. u. eingeleitet von Samuel M. Weber, München 1975 [1929]

Warnke, Martin, ›Et mundus, hoc est homo‹. Von einer sehr alten, nun wieder virtuellen Weltkarte, in: Zeitschrift für Semiotik, Band 20, Heft 1-2 1998, S. 119-132

White, Hayden, The Content of the Form. Narrative Discourse and Historical Representation, Baltimore, 1987

Winkler, Hartmut, Docuverse. Zur Medientheorie der Computer, München, 1997

Winkler, Hartmut, Jenseits der Medien. Über den Charme der stummen Praxen und einen verdeckten Wahrheitsdiskurs, in: Hebecker, Eike / Stauff, Markus u. a. (Hrg), Neue Medienumwelten: zwischen Regulierungsprozessen und alltäglicher Aneignung, Frankfurt a. M. / New York, 1999, S. 44-61

Wulff, Hans J., Flow. Kaleidoskopische Formationen des Fern-Sehens, in: montage/av. Zeitschrift für Theorie und Geschichte audiovisueller Kommunikation, 4/2/1995, S. 21-39

Wulff, Hans-J., Kommunikative Formatierung am Beispiel von Wetterkarten, in:

Werner Wehry (Hg.), Wetterinformationen für die Öffentlicheit – aber wie?, Berlin, 1998, S. 33-42

Zahn, Ulf / Kleinschmidt, Verena, Der Schulatlas seit dem 16. Jahrhundert, in: Hans Wolff (Hg.), Vierhundert Jahre Mercator – Vierhundert Jahre Atlas: ›Die ganze Geschichte der Welt zwischen zwei Buchdeckeln‹. Eine Geschichte der Atlanten, München 1995, S. 307-317

Zitat und Rahmen. Leonardo da Vincis *Codex über den Vogelflug* digital

SONJA NEEF

> Folgende Anekdote erzählt man sich über den amerikanischen Maler Robert Motherwell, der zumeist dem abstrakten Expressionismus zugerechnet wird; sie könnte ebensogut über jeden anderen zeitgenössischen Maler erzählt werden. Motherwell, einmal von einem Journalisten gefragt, welche früheren Maler ihn am meisten beeinflusst hätten, gab zur Antwort: »Ich verstehe ihre Frage nicht. *Ich* bin es, der *diese Maler* beeinflusst.« (Fechner-Smarsly/Neef 2002)

Das Konzept von Geschichtlichkeit und historischem »Wandel«, das sich hinter dieser Anekdote verbirgt, gestaltet sich nicht im traditionellen Sinne als eine monolineare Entwicklung von einem historischen »Vorher« zu einem historischen »Nachher«, sondern die Vergangenheit ist gleichermaßen von der Gegenwart durchdrungen wie umgekehrt. Geschichte, wenn sie so verstanden wird, ist »umgekehrt«, vielleicht auch »verkehrt«, auf jeden Fall aber »widersinnig« im Sinne von Mieke Bals Konzeption einer »preposterous history«, »which puts what came chronologically first (»pre-«) as an aftereffect behind (»post«) its later recycling.«[1] (1999: 6-7) »Wandel« hat hier also mit »*recycling*« zu tun, mit dem – um auf das andere zentrale Konzept dieses Buchs zu sprechen zu kommen – *recycling* oder Wieder-in-Verkehr-Bringen von Narrationen, also mit dem Zitat.
Das Konzept der »Narration« entstammt ursprünglich der Literaturwissenschaft, wo es im Allgemeinen als eine Gattungsbezeichnung und zudem als ausschließlich sprachlich verstanden wird. Im Folgenden möchte ich »Narration« weniger als literarischen Gattungsbegriff denn als Diskurstyp und auch nicht als ausschließlich an Sprache gebundene, sondern auch als visuelle Erzählform auffassen. Die Frage nach dem »medialen Wandel« erschöpft sich somit nicht allein in historischen Fragestellungen, sondern interessiert sich auch für den Wechsel oder die Interaktion zwischen den medialen Modi Schrift und Bild.

Abbildung 1:
Basisseite aus: *Der Codex über den Vogelflug*. CD-ROM

Einer Verknüpfung beider Konzepte – medialer Wandel und Narration – möchte ich mich anhand eines kulturellen Objektes annähern, nämlich der CD-ROM *Die Multimedia Manuskripte von Leonardo da Vinci*, die nicht nur als ausgesprochen narrativ verstanden werden kann, sondern die zugleich auch reichhaltiges Material für eine Reflexion über medialen Wandel bietet. Das Hauptanliegen meines Beitrags wäre sodann, zu verstehen, wie das digitale Medium des Computers ein historisches Medium, nämlich ein Renaissance-Manuskript, transkribiert oder zitiert und medial inszeniert, mit anderen Worten, wie »wir« von heute aus auf eine Schreibweise der Vergangenheit blicken, wobei ich den Satz »wir blicken« durchaus als eine Mini-Erzählung im Rahmen einer visuellen Narratologie verstehen möchte.

ZU BESUCH BEI LEONARDO

Die Basisseite dieser CD-ROM zeigt einen virtuellen Raum in 3-D-Graphik, der offensichtlich ein Arbeitszimmer mit einem Bücherregal, einer Bücherkiste und einem Schreibtisch darstellt. Hier und dort befinden sich seltsame Messinstrumente, Pendel, Leinwände, eine Malstaffelei. Mit der Maus kann ich diesen Raum wie mit einer Filmkamera durchschreiten und dabei wechselnde Kamerastandorte einnehmen. Mit einem *Roll-over* berühre ich die Gegenstände im Raum; ein Windrad bringe ich zum Drehen, ein Pendel zum Schwingen. Mit ihm bewegt sich sein Schatten auf dem Fußboden, projiziert vom Licht, das durch das offene Fenster hereinfällt. Gleite ich mit dem Cursor durch das Fenster hinauf in den Himmel, so erscheint dort ein Vogel, dessen Flug naturgetreu wirkt, der sich aber dennoch nicht von der Stelle bewegt. Klicke ich den Himmel an, so schwebe ich durch das Zimmer, ohne Umschweife über den Schreibtisch hinweg, und mache erst am Fenster halt, von wo aus ich den Flug des Vogels näher betrachten kann.

In diesem interaktiven Spiel entfaltet sich eine Erzählung, an der ich als erste Person irgendwie beteiligt bin. Aber wie? Nicht die Rolle der Erzählerin, also derjenigen, die spricht, kommt mir zu, sondern die Rolle derjenigen, die sieht. Diesen Akt des Sehens im Rahmen der Erzählung möchte ich in Anlehnung an Bals *Narratology* als »Fokalisation« bezeichnen, als »the relation between the elements presented and the vision through which they are presented« (1997: 142). Im Falle der Computeranimation beschränkt sich der Akt des Betrachtens, des Fokalisierens, aber nicht auf ein passives Zusehen von einem strikt abgegrenzten Außen her, sondern mithilfe der Maus kann ich den Cursor so über die zweidimensionale Bildfläche gleiten lassen, dass sich diese dreidimensional öffnet und wie mit einer beweglichen Kamera aus verschiedenen Perspektiven durchschreiten lässt. Als körperliches Subjekt bin ich zwar außen, in der historischen Gegenwart; indem ich den Cursor wie eine Kamera mit der Maus von diesem Außen heraus fernsteuere, kann ich aber in das Bild und somit in die simulierte, körperlose, historische Vergangenheit hinein und dort verschiedene Standorte einnehmen, z. B. über den Schreibtisch hinwegschweben, ans Fenster oder ans Bücherregal treten. Und mehr als das: meine Präsenz beschränkt sich nicht auf meine Rolle als *sehendes* Subjekt, sondern ich kann *taktil* in den virtuellen historischen Raum eingreifen, ein Windrad zum Drehen, ein Pendel zum Schwingen bringen. In dieser visuellen Narration bin ich doppelt, außen und innen, körperlich und entkörpert, heute und damals.

Um diese doppelte Position des Blicks genauer bestimmen zu können, möchte ich abermals Bals Konzept der Fokalisation bemühen. Gemäß Bal kann das Subjekt der Fokalisation, »the point from which the elements are viewed« (146), differenziert werden in einen externen Fokalisator außerhalb der Diegese und einen internen Fokalisator innerhalb der Diegese. Für den Fall der Fokalisationssituation in der CD-ROM kann entsprechend der gegenwärtige, »reale«, körperliche Anwender außerhalb des Bildschirms als externer Fokalisator und das multiperspektivische, virtuelle Subjekt innerhalb der dreidimensionalen Graphik des Bildschirms als interner Fokalisator kategorisiert werden. Dabei gestaltet sich das Verhältnis zwischen internem und externem Fokalisator so, dass der externe Fokalisator mit dem internen mitschaut; er schaut sozusagen durch dessen Kameraobjektiv, »mit dessen Augen«. Auf den ersten Blick sieht es danach aus, als fielen interner und externer Fokalisator zusammen, als schlüpfte der Äußere in die Haut des Inneren. Bei genauem Hinsehen werden aber signifikante Unterschiede zwischen internem und externem Fokalisator sichtbar, und zwar sowohl 1. von der Funktion als auch 2. von der Blickperspektive her.

Von der Funktion her tritt der interne Fokalisator als ein körperloser, uneingeschränkt beweglicher, medialer Handlanger auf, dem ein körperlicher, nur bedingt beweglicher Fokalisator mithilfe der Maus seine Kamerafahrten delegiert.[2] Diese Fokalisationspraxis folgt nicht der rhetorischen Struktur der *Metapher*, sie setzt nicht das Innen als Substitut für das Außen, das Entkörperte für das Verkörperte. Stattdessen möchte ich dafür argumentieren, dass Innen und Außen in einem *metonymischen* Verhältnis zueinander stehen, sie sind nach dem Kontiguitätsprinzip *sequentiell* weitergeschaltet, das heißt, dass ein realer, externer Fokalisator in der Gegenwart über die Verlängerung eines körperlosen, internen Fokalisators im virtuellen Raum der Vergangenheit wirkt. Dieses metonymische Verhältnis zwischen externer und interner Fokalisation beschränkt sich zudem nicht auf einen rein visuellen Akt, sondern der Akt des Sehens korreliert mit einem Akt des Berührens, aktiviert doch das Gleiten des fokalisierenden

Blicks – medientechnisch durch das Gleiten des Cursors auf der Bildschirmoberfläche inszeniert – an entsprechend vorprogrammierten Stellen einen *Roll-over*; aus passivem Betrachten wird manipulierendes Eingreifen.
Dieses haptische, manipulative Potenzial des Blicks gewinnt durch das oben angekündigte zweite Unterscheidungskriterium zwischen internem und externem Fokalisator noch eine zusätzliche Bedeutung. Von der Blickperspektive her fällt nämlich auf, dass der externe Fokalisator zwar mit dem internen mitschauen kann, aber nicht umgekehrt. Die Blicke sind nicht-reziprok organisiert. Der externe Fokalisator verweilt, unsichtbar wie ein Voyeur, außerhalb des Bildes, von wo aus er sein Objekt wie durch ein Kameraobjektiv fokalisiert. Diese Unumkehrbarkeit des Blicks bringt eine Art Entkörperung in Gang, gleitet doch der externe Fokalisator für einen Moment ins Körperlose ab, da er – selber unsichtbar – sozusagen »aus dem Rahmen« der Diegese fällt. Zugleich hat dieser Akt des Sehens für den internen Fokalisator geradezu physische Auswirkungen, wenn dieser – wie ein Stock, der dem Blinden als Tastinstrument dient – zur taktilen Verlängerung eines realen Körpers wird. Die Bühler'sche »Ich-jetzt-hier-origo« (1934) verlagert sich vom externen Fokalisator auf den internen, von der realen Gegenwart in die virtuelle Vergangenheit, in der fortan jegliches körperlich-taktiles Wirken angesiedelt ist.

(UN-)LESBARKEIT

Beim Navigieren im System der CD-ROM kann die Benutzerin per Hyperlink eine digitale Graphik von Leonardos *Codex über den Vogelflug* aufrufen. Diese Seite zeigt Leonardos Manuskript, das teilweise mit Skizzen von Vögeln, Zahnrädern, Hebeln, Pendeln oder anderen Maschinenteilen illustriert ist. Von hier aus können über zahlreiche Hyperlinks eine diplomatische Transkription in Maschinenschrift sowie eine englische und eine deutsche Übersetzung aufgerufen werden.
Im System des Computers gelten sowohl Leonardos Handschrift als auch seine Skizzen ohne Rücksicht auf ihre mediale Differenz gleichermaßen als Bild, denn der Computer interpretiert die Handschrift als rein visuellen Modus, als pure »Autographie« im Sinne von Goodman, ohne ihre »allographische« Dimension als buchstabierbare, alphanumerische Schrift zu erfassen.[3] Überhaupt ist Leonardos Handschrift als Schrift geradezu unlesbar, und zwar nicht nur für den Computer, sondern überhaupt für die Leser, denn sie ist rätselhafterweise spiegelverkehrt geschrieben und verläuft zudem entgegen dem Normalverlauf von abendländischer Schrift von rechts nach links anstatt von links nach rechts über den Blattspiegel.
Für diese eigentümliche Schreibweise sind in der Leonardo-Forschung verschiedene Erklärungen vorgetragen worden, von denen ich hier zwei pro-

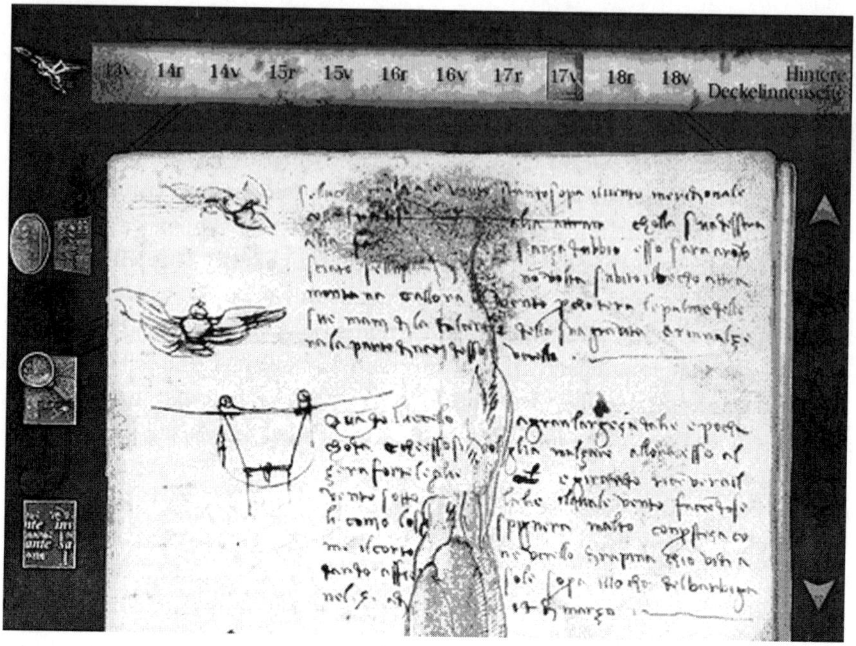

Abbildung 2:
Bildschirmansicht von Folio 17 verso aus *Der Codex über den Vogelflug*.

minente Positionen kurz skizzieren möchte. Vasari argumentiert in seiner zeitgenössischen Leonardo-Biographie (1564-1568), dass Leonardo sich dieser Schreibweise als Geheimschrift bediente, um seine Erfindungen vor Plagiat und sich selber vor dem Vorwurf der Blasphemie zu schützen. Eine zweite Erklärung argumentiert medienhistorisch, dass Leonardos Spiegelschrift als Vorbereitung für den lithographischen Druck gedient habe, dessen Druckplatten eben spiegelverkehrt angefertigt wurden. (Zwijnenberg 1999: 83) Zu beiden Thesen sind eine Reihe von Einwänden eingeworfen worden, auf die ich an dieser Stelle nicht eingehen kann. Worauf es mir ankommt, ist das Moment der Unlesbarkeit von Leonardos Schrift – damals und heute.

Für das digitale Medium des Computers stellt die rückläufige Spiegelschrift kein größeres Problem dar, zählt doch die Umkehrung von links und rechts zu den wohl leichtesten Übungen des Rechners. Im System der CD-ROM wird den Benutzern in der Tat die Möglichkeit geboten, die linke Schrift per Mausklick in rechte Normalschrift umzuwandeln. Zudem können einzelne Stellen des Codex per Zoom vergrößert werden. Trotz all dem ist diese Schrift ohne Hinzuziehung der Transkriptionen auch für die heutigen Leser kaum zu dechiffrieren. Die semiotische Operationsweise dieser Handschrift, so möchte ich argumentieren, beruht nicht primär auf dem Symbolcharakter der Schriftzeichen.[4] Vielmehr ist an dieser Handschrift gerade ihr Autographiecharakter signifikant, ihre physische Materialität als somatische Handschrift. Während die »normale«, lesbare, allographische Schrift zu Kommunikationszwecken stereotypiert, standardisiert und somit als Schrift nahezu unsichtbar gemacht worden ist, schiebt sich bei Leonardo das Bild seines eigenwilligen Schriftzugs unentwegt zwischen Schrift und Bedeutung.[5] Im Gegensatz zur Schreibmaschinenschrift, in der, wie Martin Heidegger schreibt, »alle Menschen gleich aus[sehen]« (zit.n. Derrida 1988:75), fungiert Leonardos persönliche Hieroglyphe als Index im Sinne von Peirce, der nicht auf ein mechanisches, elektrisches oder elektronisches Medium verweist, sondern – wie ein Fingerzeig – auf Leonardos einzigartige und unverwechselbare Schreib- und Zeichenhand.

Die hypertextuelle Inszenierung von Leonardos Handschrift macht sich gerade diese Geste des Fingerzeigs zunutze, indem sie die Schrift in ihrem rein visuellen Modus darstellt, als Bildschirmkopie eines Manuskripts, das noch die Spuren des Aktes des Schreibens in Form von Verwischungen, Flecken und Kratzern und überhaupt den Fingerabdruck seines Schreibers trägt. Das »Bild« der Schrift dient hier nicht bloß der Sichtbarmachung eines Signifikats, sondern es verweist in erster Linie auf das »*Image*« von Leonardo als personifizierter Virtuosität, Kreativität und Brillanz, die sich in der Spur seiner Schrift eingeschrieben haben. Schließlich impliziert die

Inszenierung einer Autographie zwangsläufig auch immer eine Inszenierung des schreibenden Subjekts – auch wenn dieses längst abwesend ist. Leonardo verkörpert bis heute einen Mythos (vgl. Arasse 9-20). »Er«, Leonardo, der »uomo universale« der Renaissance, der brillante Maler, Bildhauer, Architekt, Musiker, Ingenieur und Naturwissenschaftler, er, der geniale Linkshänder, der unkonventionelle Querkopf, Erfinder des Ornithopters und Vordenker des hydrostatischen Gesetzes, das er ganz ohne akademische Ausbildung und lange vor Pascal entwarf. Den Schlüssel zum Rätsel dieses Multitalents von damals halten die heutigen CD-ROM-Benutzer wörtlich *in der Hand*, und zwar in Form der Maus, mit der sie die Schrift von links nach rechts verkehren, transkribieren, entziffern können. Auf dem Bildschirm ist das Unlesbare lesbar gemacht – in digitaler Graphik, eins zu eins und ohne Rest. Leonardo heute: ein »Monitorbild«, flach, sichtbar bishin zum Voyeuristischen, um mit Wetzel zu sprechen »ein Passepartout einer universalisierten Visibilität.« (2002: 86)
Diese expositorische Geste, die Leonardo in Form seiner Handschrift als eine dritte Person »ausstellt«, auf dem Bildschirm zur Schau stellt, möchte ich mit der expositorischen Geste eines Kurators im Museum vergleichen, der, selber erste Person, sein »Objekt« als dritte Person dem Museumsbesucher als zweiter Person vorführt. Eine derartige nicht-reziproke Konstellation von Blicken im Museum kritisiert Bal mit ihrem Konzept der »double exposure«:

> Something is made public in exposition, and that event involves bringing out into the public domain the deepest held views and beliefs of a subject. Exposition is always an argument. Therefore, in publicizing these views the subject objectifies, exposes himself as much as the object; this makes the exposition an exposure of the self. (1996: 2)

In Anlehnung an Bal möchte ich die Inszenierung von Leonardos Handschrift auf dem Bildschirm nicht ohne Reflexion über das Subjekt der Exposition betrachten, *in casu* die Macher des Hypertextes, die Autoren, Programmierer, Herausgeber und Verleger der CD-ROM, die ihre visuelle Erzählung über Leonardo auf den Bildschirm bringen. Die Strategie dieser Erzählung besteht zum einen darin, selber als erzählendes oder exponierendes Subjekt unsichtbar zu sein, keine auffälligen Spuren zu hinterlassen, die die Interessen und Ziele dieses Subjekts verraten könnten. Beispielsweise finden sich keinerlei Anachronismen im virtuellen Museum des Hypertextes; alle exponierten Gegenstände erheben den Anspruch auf historische Authentizität. Stöbert die CD-ROM-Benutzerin in der Rolle der Museumsbesucherin etwa in Leonardos Bücherregal, so trifft sie dort auf Aristoteles' *Meteorologie* und Plinius' *Historia Naturale*, nicht aber auf Vasari, Pascal oder Freud, wodurch eine Reflexion über den tatsächlich stattfindenden Anachronismus dieser Zeitreise – wir, heute, in Leonardos

Arbeitszimmer – in Gang gebracht werden könnte. Dabei ist das erste Ziel der Exposition – das Lesbarmachen von Leonardos Handschrift auf Grundlage unseres heutigen Wissens und Könnens – kaum zu übersehen. Diese Unumkehrbarkeit der Blickkonstellation zwischen erster, zweiter und dritter Person, so möchte ich argumentieren, dient dem Zweck, eine Hierarchie zu begründen zwischen unserer heutigen *visuellen* digitalen Kultur und der historischen *Bild*kultur der Renaissance. Eben diese Spannung zwischen Visualität und Bild arbeitet Wetzel in seiner Gegenüberstellung des Aumont entlehnten Begriffs des »Monitorbildes« und des von Didi-Huberman diskutierten Begriffs des Renaissance-»Tafelbildes« heraus.[6] Dabei hebt Wetzel als Kerncharakteristikum des Tafelbildes »das Bleibende, das Bewahrende, ja das Materielle des Bildes« (76-77) hervor, das sich etwa bei der *Wachstafel* als »Modellierbarkeit« und »Oberflächenglättung« darstellt:

> Entscheidend ist dabei, »dass das Tableau nicht auf eine Oberfläche des sichtbar Dargestellten reduziert wird, sondern ein *Volumen* besitzt, gebildet aus einer [...] Mannigfaltigkeit der Farbschichten als Materialität des Trägers, der sich in Oberfläche und Tiefe differenziert.« (81)

Wenn die digitale Inszenierung von Leonardos Handschrift sich zum Ziel setzt, das Rätsel des Genius lesbar zu machen, so eskamotiert sie dabei genau jenes von Wetzel für das Tafelbild beanspruchte ›Andere‹ des Bildes, und zwar nicht zuletzt, indem sie seine Tiefe, sein Volumen verflacht. Die digitale technische Umkehrung vermag zwar, das Linke ins Rechte zu verkehren, aber nicht, ohne dabei einen gewissen *Rest* hervorzubringen. Dies wird angesichts einer weiteren Eigentümlichkeit von Leonardos Schreib- und Zeichentechnik besonders anschaulich, nämlich einer ungewöhnlichen Praxis der Vorzeichnung bei den Studien zu seinen Gemälden, die Arasse wie folgt beschreibt:

> Indem sie immer wieder über die gleichen Stellen fuhr, ihre Bewegungsmöglichkeiten erprobte, um die ausgewogenste Form zu finden, erzeugte Leonardos Hand schließlich einen unlesbaren Fleck; in diesem Chaos ist nichts mehr zu erkennen. Sein Blick jedoch entdeckte in der Bewegung der Hand die gesuchte, aber verwischte und verborgene, zur Gestalt strebende Form. Leonardo markierte diese Form mit dem Stichel, *wendete dann das Blatt* und machte sie in einem Zug sichtbar. (2002: 285; Hervorhebung SN)

An dieser Zeichenpraxis ist bemerkenswert, dass die im *Volumen* aufbewahrte Form erst durch das *Wenden des Blattes* von der rechten zur linken Ansicht sichtbar wird; erst die Geste des Umdrehens schließt den Akt der Erzeugung der idealen Form als *différent* der anderen, unbrauchbaren Zeichenzüge ab. Eben diese Tiefe, das Relief der Linie, macht das Monitorbild nicht sichtbar. Durch diese Verflachung suggeriert das Monitorbild »uns«, den zweiten Personen in dieser visuellen Narration, das Rätsel dieses

Schriftbildes final entzifferbar zu machen; wir haben wörtlich »das Zeug« dazu. Die Systematik dieses Taktierens beruht auf einem medientechnischen Trick, der das Prinzip der *double exposure* – unser Blick von heute legt sich wie bei einer photographischen Doppelbelichtung palimpsestartig über den Blick von damals – verkennt. Zweck dieser Unsichtbarkeit der medialen Inszenierung ist es, Leonardos Handschrift mitsamt ihrem Anspruch auf Authentizität und Unikatizität buchstabierbar, wiederholbar und somit lesbar zu machen.

Lesbarmachen, dahingehend möchte ich in Anlehnung an Derridas »Signatur Ereignis Kontext« argumentieren, ist aber nicht nur auf bloßes Wiederholen (etwa für spätere Leser) angelegt, sondern jede Wiederholung, jedes »Zitieren« als performative Praxis, birgt die Möglichkeit zum Bruch mit dem Kontext in sich und somit die Möglichkeit, neue Erzählungen und neue Sichtweisen zu generieren. Als eine solche »Bruchstelle« möchte ich den »Rahmen« der digitalen Graphik der CD-ROM interpretieren. Denn die technische Vollendung, mit der Leonardos historische Realität optisch nicht nur simuliert, sondern geradezu perfektioniert wird, macht zwar einerseits den Zitatcharakter der digitalisierten Handschrift nahezu transparent, zugleich aber lässt die spektakuläre visuelle Qualität der Bildschirmgraphik die physische Materialität der Handschrift auch täuschend echt, wenn nicht gar hyperrealistisch erscheinen.

Das Verfahren des medialen Wandels vom Manuskript zur visuellen Bildschirmgraphik ist also einerseits damit beschäftigt, das unlesbare *Bild* von Leonardos Schrift im logozentristischen Sinne des Wortes »lesbar« zu machen, zugleich aber quillt dieses »optische Spektakel« der Computergraphik sozusagen aus allen Poren des Bildschirms hervor – mit einem Vogel am Himmel, der seinen Flügelschlag unendlich wiederholt, ohne jemals von der Stelle zu kommen; mit einer verflachten, künstlichen Dreidimensionalität; mit den Ikons, dem Cursor und der Symbolleiste im »Rahmen« der Bildschirmoberfläche. Wenn ich oben argumentiert habe, das Verhältnis zwischen interner und externer Fokalisation sei nicht-reziprok organisiert, so möchte ich hier ergänzen, dass dieser »Rahmen« den monodirektionalen Blick des Benutzers arretiert und somit die starren Oppositionen zwischen Innen und Außen der Diegese, zwischen einer fokalisierenden unsichtbaren ersten Person von »heute« und einer fokalisierten 3. Person als *unmittelbar* re-präsentiertem historischem Objekt, zu destabilisieren vermag.

DIE LINKE HAND

Als einen solchen »parergonalen« Rahmen, der von einem gewissen Außen doch im Innen des Werkes wirkt, verstehe ich nicht zuletzt das Bild von Leonardos *Hand*-Schrift, seiner »linken Hand«, die dem »rechten Gang« der Schrift – ob als authentisches Manuskript, ob als Monitorbild – ein *Hand*icap ist. Diese aus dem Diskurs über Schrift und ihrer Semiose meist ausgeklammerte linke Hand hat, wenn ihr einmal der Zutritt gewährt worden ist, sogleich ihre eigene Erklärung für Leonardos eigentümliche Schreibweise *bei der Hand*. Dahingehend argumentiert auch der Leonardo-Spezialist Zwijnenberg:

> By writing from right to left a left-handed person prevents his or her hand from wiping through the wet ink. But the form of the letters of our alphabet are adapted to writing that move from left to right. To make writing easier and quicker for most people a right-handed movement was introduced into the structure of these letters. For someone who writes from right to left, however, and tries to do so efficiently, this structure is an obstacle. Leonardo solved this problem for himself by writing the letters in reverse; thus his letters acquired a left-handed structure. (1999: 83)

Dieser körperlichen Dimension von Hand-Schrift möchte ich mich abschließend anhand von Freuds berühmter Leonardo-Biographie »Eine Kindheitserinnerung des Leonardo da Vinci« (1910) nähern. In diesem Essay diskutiert Freud in einer Fußnote eine Leonardo zugesprochene anatomische Zeichnung, die einen Sagittalschnitt eines Koitus zeigt.[7] Unter Bezugnahme auf Reitler deutet Freud diese Zeichnung als Indiz für Leonardos verdrängte Homosexualität, da sie diverse anatomische Mängel enthalte, nicht nur bei der Darstellung der weiblichen Genitalien, sondern es seien auch die unteren Extremitäten der Figuren vertauscht worden:

> Die gröbste Fehlleistung hat [...] Leonardo bei der Zeichnung der beiden unteren Extremitäten begangen. Der Fuß des Mannes sollte nämlich der rechte sein; denn da Leonardo den Zeugungsakt in Form eines anatomischen Sagittaldurchschnittes darstellte, so müsste ja der linke männliche Fuß oberhalb der Bildfläche gedacht werden, und umgekehrt sollte aus demselben Grunde der weibliche Fuß der linken Seite angehören. Tatsächlich aber hat Leonardo weiblich und männlich vertauscht. Die Figur des Mannes besitzt einen linken, die des Weibes einen rechten Fuß. (1910: 99)

Ebenso wie Freud möchte auch ich dafür argumentieren, dass diese anatomische Zeichnung über das Potenzial verfügt, als ein »theoretisches Objekt« zu fungieren, wenngleich ich sie nicht für eine Theorie der Psychoanalyse, sondern für eine Theorie der Schrift operationalisieren möchte. Schließlich bedarf es nur eines winzigen Schritts, um von einer Vertauschung der Füße zu einer Vertauschung der Hände zu kommen. Anders als

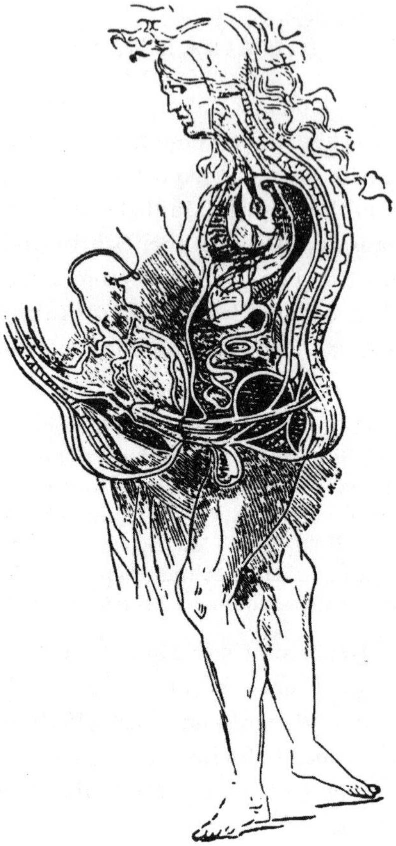

Abbildung 3:
Leonardo da Vinci zugeschriebene Zeichnung *Paarung eines männlichen Halbkörpers mit einem weiblichen Halbkörper*

Freud möchte ich Leonardos Zeichnung aber weniger als »Fehlleistung« im Sinne von »verkehrt herum«, »anders herum« interpretieren, sondern sie zunächst weiter befragen, worin genau ihre visuelle Verwirrung besteht. In diesem Zusammenhang weist Rose darauf hin, »daß der Betrachter nicht weiß, wo er im Verhältnis zum Bild steht. Eine Verwirrung auf der Ebene der Sexualität bringt [somit] eine Verstörung des visuellen Feldes mit sich.« (1996: 229) Übertragen in Bals Terminologie einer visuellen Narratologie könnte man auch sagen, dass die dargestellten Körper aus verschiedenen, einander gegenseitig ausschließenden, internen Fokalisationspositionen gesehen sind. Die Füße der Figuren sind von einem anderen Blickwinkel aus, linksherum, wie durch einen Spiegel betrachtet, während ihre Torsos in der »rechten« Ansicht gesehen sind. Diese plurale Darstellungsweise ist vergleichbar mit der Montagetechnik kubistischer Malerei, die ihre Objekte »im Winkel über Eck« sieht, wie Raphael (1989:74) es ausgedrückt hat.[8] Das Krumme, das »Linkische« dieser Zeichnung resultiert demnach aus dem Bruch zwischen dem Blickwinkel des externen Fokalisators, der unbeweglich vor der Gesamtansicht der Figuren steht, und dem multiperspektivischen Blick des internen Fokalisators, der sein Objekt gleichzeitig von rechts wie von links betrachtet.

SEPARATES DOKUMENT (H.H.)

Eben diesen Bruch möchte ich nicht durch Gleichschaltung der pluralen Fokalisationspositionen normalisieren, sondern ihn für meine Lektüre produktiv machen. Während Freud die Vertauschung von links und rechts als ein bedeutungshaftes somatisches Zeichen versteht, das die binäre Opposition zwischen dem Männlichen und dem Weiblichen destabilisiert, möchte ich zusätzlich dafür plädieren, dass diese Umkehrung eine mit der Geschlechterdifferenz eng verzahnte generelle Kultursemantik aufzubrechen vermag, die die rechte Hand von jeher privilegiert – man sitzt zur rechten Hand Gottes – und die Benutzung der linken Hand – beim Grüßen, beim Schwören, beim Schreiben – mithilfe von strengen Benimmregeln zu exorzieren versucht hat.[9] Wenn Heidegger von der »Hand« des Menschen, immer – wie Derrida in »Heideggers Hand« (1988: 80) bemerkt – im Singular spricht und betont, die Hand sei nicht »leibliches Greiforgan« (65), sondern »[a]lles Werk der Hand beruht im Denken« (69), dann meint er damit bestimmt nicht die linke, sondern die rechte Hand. (zit. n. Derrida 1988)
In meiner Leonardo-Lektüre dagegen stehen links und rechts sich nicht als starre Gegensätze gegenüber, sondern sie nehmen je nach Kontext, je nach Fokalisationsstandort neue Positionen ein und hinterfragen somit die Hierarchie zwischen der rechten Hand einerseits, also der »schreibenden« Hand (auf Englisch könnte man beides zugleich sagen: »the (w)ri(gh)ting

hand«), die für das Lesbarwerden der Schrift zuständig ist, und der linken Hand andererseits, der falschen Hand, die als unfähig eingestuft wird, Denken auf Papier zu fixieren, sondern stattdessen in emphatischer Weise körperlich und »linkshändig« ist und entsprechend eine Schrift hervorbringt, die eher unlesbares Bild als lesbare Schrift ist.

Je unreflektierter die CD-ROM-Benutzer durch den Bildschirm hindurch unbehindert auf das dort exponierte Manuskript blicken, umso verhängnisvoller erfahren sie dort Leonardos linke Hand als Hindernis, da diese ihre körperliche Dimension zwischen Schrift und Bedeutung schiebt und somit den Blick freimacht für den Akt der Inszenierung selber, den medialen Wandel. Dieser »neue Blick« wird sich fortan nicht nur an einem uneingeschränkt sichtbaren historischen »Vorher«, sondern auch an den »supplementären«, materiellen Äußerlichkeiten des aktuellen Mediums der Transkription aufhalten. Der im Monitorbild ausgesparte Rest, die materiellen Bedingungen des Schreibens mit der linken Hand, die Nassheit der Tinte, die Körperlichkeit des Schreibers, die Tiefe des Papiers, wird zu einer Kippfigur im Sinne einer doppelten Exposition, wobei die Verflachung der mit dem Stichel eingeritzten Gravur im visuellen Spektakel des flachen Monitorbildes sozusagen als Aussparung einer Aussparung mitkommuniziert wird. Die CD-ROM von Leonardos *Codex über den Vogelflug* ist beides: final lesbar und unendlich chiffriert.

Jede mediale Wiederholung, jedes Zitat birgt schließlich in der Geste des Transkribierens die Möglichkeit zum Bruch in sich, zur Veränderung im Sinne eines »medialen Wandels«. In dieser Differenz der Medien können die Gegensätze zwischen visuellem Bild und alphanumerischer Schrift, zwischen Unlesbarkeit und Lesbarkeit, links und rechts usw. allerdings nicht aufgehoben oder gar im »Links-rechts«-Gleichschritt final stabilisiert werden. Das Konzept des »medialen Wandels« im Sinne einer »preposterous history« begnügt sich weder mit einer bloßen Beschreibung einer historischen Vorher-nachher-Entwicklung noch mit einer bloßen Umkehr dieser Ordnung. Es bezeichnet auch nicht ausschließlich den Vorgang der Umschrift einer visuellen Erzählung in einer unlesbaren, körperlichen, linken Bilderschrift vorher in eine sprachliche Nacherzählung in einer final lesbaren, rechten Typenschrift nachher. Das Lesbarmachen des Zitats ist nicht das alleinige Interesse dieses Konzepts, sondern es interessiert sich auch und gerade für den »Rahmen«, für das *Hand*icap, wie es in der Bewegung des Schriftzugs zum Ausdruck kommt, und zwar jenseits einer Opposition zwischen links und rechts.

ANMERKUNGEN

[1] Genaugenommen entwickelt Bal dieses Konzept am Beispiel der barocken Kunst Caravaggios und von Zitaten dieser Werke in der Kunst der Gegenwart; »preposterous« verweist somit nicht nur auf eine Konzeption »verdrehter« Geschichtlichkeit, sondern auch auf das dem Barocken oft zugeschriebene Überdrehte oder Verdrehte, Groteske, Geschraubte.

[2] Für die Idee der Beweglichkeit im virtuellen Raum verweise ich auf Manovitch (1995-1996: 129-134).

[3] Als allographisch stuft Goodman geschriebenen *Text* ein, da dieser iterabel, reproduzierbar und buchstabierbar sei. *Bilder* dagegen seien autographisch, da ihre Kerneigenschaften in ihrer Unikatizität und in ihrer Authentizität im Sinne von Fälschbarkeit bestehen. (1998: 101-122)

[4] Gemäß dem Paradigma der strukturalistischen Linguistik beruht dieser Symbolcharakter auf der Vorstellung von Schrift als *Re-präsentation*. In ihrem sekundären visuellen Modus als Signifikant repräsentiert die Schrift primär die Rede, also auditive Sprache, die ihrerseits ein Signifikat designiert. Für eine eingehende Kritik dieser Privilegierung der (unikaten, authentischen) Rede vor der (iterablen) Schrift verweise ich auf Derridas *Grammatologie*. In Hinblick auf Leonardos rückläufige Spiegelschrift könnte sich im Rahmen dieser Kritik zugespitzt sogar die Überlegung aufdrängen, ob der Regress des Textflusses gemäß dem linguistischen Postulat seine auditive Entsprechung in einem rückwärts gesprochenen Sprechakt oder gar in einem rückwärts gedachten Gedanken finden müsste.

[5] Goodmans Modell ist, genauer betrachtet, auf den Fall der Typenschrift zugeschnitten, die sich in der Tat als allographisch im Sinne von iterabel und buchstabierbar erweist. *Hand*schrift operiert zwar – sofern sie lesbar ist – ebenfalls als »Allographie«, fungiert zugleich aber auch als »autographisches Bild«, da sie immer auch Unverwechselbarkeit, Einzigartigkeit und Authentizität für sich beansprucht. Überhaupt steht die Fälschbarkeit der Unterschrift der Fälschbarkeit eines Gemäldes in nichts nach. Und die Reproduktion von Handschrift verlangt immerhin eher nach Reproduktionstechniken für Bilder als für Schrift. (Benjamin 1977)

[6] Wetzel bezieht sich auf Aument *L'image* (1990) und Didi-Huberman *Vor einem Bild* (2000).

[7] Freuds Leonardo-Biographie hat eine Reihe kritischer Reaktionen hervorgerufen, wobei auch die Authentizität dieser Zeichnung in Frage gestellt worden ist; vgl. hierzu etwa Arasse (2002: 488-499); Eissler (1994: 15-29); Schapiro (1956)

[8] Für eine Analyse kubistischer Montagetechnik anhand des Konzepts der Fokalisation verweise ich auf Neef (2000: 226-230).

[9] Für eine wunderbar reiche Kulturkritik des Links-Rechts-Dualismus und deren Korrelation zur kulturell kodierten Geschlechterdifferenz verweise ich auf Sofri (1998).

BIBLIOGRAPHIE

Arasse, Daniel, Leonardo da Vinci, Köln: Dumont 2002

Aumont, Jacques, L'image, Paris: Nathan 1990

Bal, Mieke, Quoting Caravaggio. Contemporary Art, Preposterous History, Chicago/London: University of Chicago Press 1999

Bal, Mieke, Double Exposures. The Subject of Cultural Analysis, New York/London: Routledge 1996

Bal, Mieke, Narratology. Introduction to the Theory of Narrative, Toronto/Buffalo/ London: University of Toronto Press 1997

Benjamin, Walter, Das Kunstwerk im Zeitalter seiner technischen Reproduzierbarkeit, Frankfurt a. M.: Suhrkamp 1977

Bühler, K., Sprachtheorie. Die Darstellungsfunktion der Sprache, Jena: Fischer 1934

Derrida, Jacques, Heideggers Hand, hrsg. von Peter Engelmann, aus dem Französischen von Hans-Dieter Gondek, Wien: Passagen 1988

Derrida, Jacques, Die Wahrheit in der Malerei, Wien 1992

Derrida, Jacques, Grammatologie, aus dem Französischen von Hans-Jörg Rheinbacher und Hanns Zischler, Frankfurt a. M.: Suhrkamp 1998

Derrida, Jacques, Signatur Ereignis Kontext, in: Ders., Limited Inc, hrsg. von Peter Engelmann, aus dem Französischen von Werner Rappl unter Mitarbeit von Dagmar Travner, Wien: Passagen 2001, S. 15-45

Didi-Huberman, George, Vor einem Bild, übersetzt von R. Werner, München: Hanser 2000

Eissler, Kurt R, Leonardo Da Vinci. Psychoanalytische Notizen zu einem Rätsel, München: dtv 1994

Fechner-Smarsly, Thomas und Sonja Neef, Kulturanalyse. Zur interdisziplinären Methodologie Mieke Bals, in Bal, Mieke, Essays zur Kulturanalyse, hrsg. von Thomas Fechner-Smarsly und Sonja Neef, Frankfurt a. M.: Suhrkamp 2002

Freud, Sigmund, Eine Kindheitserinnerung des Leonardo Da Vinci, in: Ders., Studienausgabe, Bd. X, Frankfurt a. M.: Fischer 2000 (1910), S. 87-159

Goodman, Nelson, Sprachen der Kunst. Entwurf einer Symboltheorie, Frankfurt a. M.: Suhrkamp 1998 (1976)

Leonardo da Vinci, Der Codex über den Vogelflug, in: Die Multimedia Manuskripte von Leonardo da Vinci, CD-ROM, Mailand: Giunti Multimedia 1999

Manovitch, Lev, Eine Archäologie des Computerbildschirms, in: Kunstforum 132/1995-1996, S. 124-135

Raphael, Max, Raumgestaltungen. Der Beginn der modernen Kunst im Kubismus und im Werk von Georges Braque, hrsg. von Hans-Jürgen Heinrichs, Frankfurt a. M.: Suhrkamp 1989

Rose, Jacqueline, Sexualität im Feld der Anschauung, aus dem Englischen von Catherina Zakravsky, Wien: Turia und Kant 1996

Neef, Sonja, Kalligramme. Zur Medialität einer Schrift. Anhand von Paul van Ostaijens ›De feesten van angst en pijn‹, Amsterdam: ASCA 2000

Schapiro, Meyer, Leonardo and Freud: an Art-Historical Study, in: Journal of History of Ideas 17/1956

Sofri, Adriano, Der Knoten und der Nagel. Ein Buch zur linken Hand, aus dem Italienischen von Walter Kögler, Frankfurt a. M.: Eichborn 1998

Vasari, Giorgio, Lebensläufe der berühmtesten Maler, Bildhauer und Architekten, Manesse 1993 (1564-1568)

Wetzel, Michael, Die Leonardo-Galaxis: Vom Tafel- zum Monitorbild, in Korrespondenzen. Visuelle Kulturen zwischen Früher Neuzeit und Gegenwart, hrsg. von Matthias Bickenbach und Axel Fliethmann, Köln: Dumont 2002, S. 75-88

Zwijnenberg, Robert, The Writings and Drawings of Leonardo Da Vinci. Order and Chaos in Early Modern Thought, Cambridge: University Press 1999

Computerhystorien.
Szenarien der Digitalisierung und ihre Bühnen in den 80er Jahren

KARIN HARRASSER

> Uns ist vorgeworfen worden, daß wir uns zu oft auf Literaten berufen. Aber beim Schreiben braucht man nur zu wissen, an welche andere Maschine die literarische Maschine angeschlossen werden kann und muß, um zu funktionieren.
>
> *Gilles Deleuze/Félix Guattari* [1]

Dieser Text beschäftigt sich mit dem Verhältnis von Sprache und Technologien, genauer mit dem Verhältnis digitaler Technologien zu ihren Narrativen. Die Leitgedanken für meine Überlegungen stammen aus zwei Büchern: In Deleuze/Guattaris Buch *Mille Plateaus*[2] wird das Verhältnis von sprachlichen und technischen Realitäten als ein reziprok – zirkuläres konzipiert, Sprache und Technologie werden als zwei übereinander liegende Schichten (*Strata*) des Daseins gedacht, das Verhältnis von Menschen zu Maschinen stellt sich als eines der fortschreitenden Vermischung (*Assemblage*) dar. Der zweite wichtige Einfluss ist Bruno Latours *Die Hoffnung der Pandora*[3]. Ein Buch, das auf programmatische Weise die wissenschaftstheoretischen Überlegungen der Actor-Network-Theory zusammenfasst und zu ähnlichen Perspektiven wie Deleuze/Guattari kommt: Latour fasst Wissenschaft und Technik als Instrumentarium zur »Sozialisation nichtmenschlicher Wesen«[4] auf und gesteht damit den Dingen selbst den Status von Agentenschaft zu. Die Art dieser Agentenschaft bleibt bei Latour jedoch etwas im Dunklen, und so bleibt auch das asymmetrische Verhältnis zwischen Dingen und Menschen (aus epistemologischem Kalkül) relativ unreflektiert.[5] Das Konzept vermittelt zwischen zwei konkurrierenden Theorien der (technischen) Medien: Betonen die technikdeterministischen Ansätze[6] in der Tradition McLuhans die diskurs- und gesellschaftsprägenden Eigenschaften von Technik und stellen damit den Subjektstatus menschlicher Akteure in Frage, betonen anthropologische und sozialkonstruktivistische Medientheorie und Technikforschung die Relevanz sozialer und kultureller Signifikationsprozesse bei der Entwicklung neuer (Medien)technologien. Sie beschränken das Privileg des Handelns auf voluntaristische Subjekte (ErfinderInnen, BenutzerInnen von Technologien). Beide Ansätze bleiben jedoch unbefriedigend, weil Erstere die Entstehung von Technologien nicht anders als selbstlaufend und evolutionär erklären können. Letztere Ansätze können hingegen die Auswirkungen von Technologien auf Kultur und Gesellschaft nicht fassen[7] und ihrer Funktion als Diskursdispositive nicht gerecht werden. Praxisorientierte Kulturtheorien wie die Pierre Bourdieus[8], Régis Debrays[9] oder auch Bruno Latours, die Kultur, Gesellschaft und Technologien zirkulär aufeinander beziehen und kulturelle Praktiken als Scharnier zwischen Imaginärem, Symbolischem und Realem ansehen, bilden daher den Denkraum dieses Textes.

ELECTRONIC KINDERGARTEN.[10] DIE 80ER JAHRE

Der Zeitraum seit Mitte der 80er Jahre ist für Überlegungen zum Verhältnis von Science Fiction-Narrativen zu technischen Innovationen deshalb interessant, weil zu dieser Zeit der PC massiv Eingang in den Alltag sehr breiter Bevölkerungsschichten fand und gleichzeitig das World-Wide-Web sein exponentielles Wachstum begann. 1984 gemahnt nicht nur an George Orwells dystopischen Roman, es ist auch das »Geburtsjahr« einer Art Literatur, die unter dem Begriff »Cyberpunk« subsummiert wird: William Gibsons Roman *Neuromancer*[11], der zu einer Bibel der Programmierer/Hackerkultur wurde und dessen Autor nicht nur den Begriff des Cyberspace erfand, sondern diesen auch mit Metaphysik füllte, erschien in diesem Jahr. Wise[12] weist außerdem darauf hin, dass der Populärkultur der 80er Jahre Momente innewohnen, die ein Überdenken der modernen Episteme und des Verhältnisses von Menschen und Maschinen im Sinne Deleuze/Guattaris für ein Massenpublikum andeuteten. Eine der Hauptthesen dieser Arbeit ist deshalb, dass parallel zur technischen und sozio-kulturellen »Schließung«[13] der digitialen Technologien in den 90er Jahren auch die innovativen Narrative der Digitalisierung, die das Verhältnis von Menschen zu Maschinen neu erzählen wollten, einen diskursiven Ab- und Ausschluss erfahren haben. Was in das kulturelle Archiv einer Gesellschaft aufgenommen wird und was diskursprägend wird, ist abhängig davon, wie sehr es in (von Machtverhältnissen informierten) Praktiken einen Echoraum findet.

SZENARIEN, BÜHNEN UND NARRATIVE

> This is a particular moment in the history of digital networks, one when powerful corporate actors and high-performance networks are strengthening the role of private electronic space and altering the structure of public electronic space. Electronic space has emerged not simply as a means for communicating, but as a major new theatre for capital accumulation and the operations of global actors.
>
> *Saskia Sassen*[14]

Den Terminus Szenario verwende ich deshalb zur Beschreibung diskursiver Formationen, weil das Zukunftsszenario eine der häufigsten Erzählstrategien sowohl von Kulturschaffenden (SF-AutorInnen, FilmemacherInnen etc.) als auch von Wissenschafts- und Technologieschaffenden (MedientheoretikerInnen, ComputerwissenschafterInnen, ProgrammiererInnen) im Feld der Informationstechnologien ist. Diese Szenarien können unterschiedliche Teleologien haben (Utopie, Apokalypse, Dystopie, Erlösung), sind aber grundsätzlich alle einer szientistischen Weltsicht verhaftet. Malmgren[15] hat auf die gemeinsamen erzählerischen Grundlagen von Science Fiction und Historiographie bzw. Evolutionstheorie hingewiesen: Die Annahme eines kausalen Zusammenhangs zwischen Vergangenheit, Gegenwart und Zukunft ausgedrückt in der Definition von SF als Literatur des »Was wäre wenn« und die Methode der Extrapolation wurzeln im Fortschrittsnarrativ der Moderne. Klassische SF ähnelt deshalb den traditionellen Narrativen der Wissenschafts- und Technikgeschichte, die technische und wissenschaftliche Innovation als heroisch-triumphales Überwinden eines naturgebundenen Daseins begreifen. Zukunftsszenarien spielen eine entscheidende Rolle bei der Durchsetzung von Forschungsvorhaben und Geschäftsinteressen – kaum ein AI-Forscher kommt ohne das Zukunftsszenario aus, wenn er die Relevanz seiner Arbeit unterstreichen möchte. Die Darstellung einer noch zu entwickelnden Technologie als unvermeidbare Notwendigkeit und/oder Segnung der Menschheit ist eine vielversprechende Strategie im Konkurrenzkampf um Forschungsgelder und Kunden. Der Gestus des Vorgriffs auf die Zukunft eignet den politischen und ästhetischen Avantgarden mit ihrem Willen zu Gestaltung der Gesellschaft. Die Technoavantgarden, wie ich manche digitalen Kulturen der 80er und 90er Jahre nennen möchte, sind an der Schnittstelle von künstlerischem und wissenschaftlich-technischem Feld anzusiedeln und partizipieren deshalb an beiden Innovationsdiskursen: dem der ästhetischen Avantgarden und dem des technischen Fortschritts.

Den Begriff der Bühnen habe ich deshalb gewählt, weil in dem untersuchten Diskurs Motive und Erzählungen in verschiedenen sozialen und intellektuellen Umfeldern unterschiedlich inszeniert werden: Bestimmte Narrative der SF wurden in der US-amerikanischen SF geprägt und tauchten verändert in der europäischen Medienphilosophie und -theorie (Baudrillard, Virilio) wieder auf, um dann wieder rückimportiert zu werden. Sie erscheinen in anderen Kostümen und sind unterschiedlich akzentuiert, enthalten aber ähnliche Charaktere und Plots. Das SF-Inventar wurde zu einem Kulturgut, das via subkultureller Zuschreibungen Aus- und Einschlüsse der globalisierten Digitalen Kulturen organisiert.

Beide Begriffe (Bühnen und Szenario) verweisen darauf, dass technische Entwicklungen und Erkenntnisse sowohl innerhalb der begrenzten wissenschaftlich-technischen Öffentlichkeit, aber auch, um ihre breite Nutzung möglich zu machen, in verschiedensten Formen inszeniert werden müssen. Damit meine ich nicht, dass es einen authentischen, wahren aber bitteren Kern von Tatsachen und Technologien gibt, der »den Massen« mit bunten Bildern und Erzählungen schmackhaft gemacht werden muss, ich denke vielmehr, dass die Inszenierungen bis zum vermeintlichen Kern der Tatsachen reichen. Wie Bruno Latour[16] in einem anderen Zusammenhang – dem Labor – anhand der Entdeckung der Milchsäurebakterien durch Pasteur zeigen konnte, ist erfinderische und entdeckerische Tätigkeit stets mit kreativer Inszenierung verbunden. Pasteur musste mit Hilfe von Versuchsanordnungen nach und nach eine Bühne errichten, um seine Bakterien erstmals als Lebewesen *erscheinen* zu lassen und sie anschließend der wissenschaftlichen Welt präsentieren zu können. Das Bauen solcher Bühnen erfordert große Geschicklichkeit und eine gute Kenntnis des potentiellen Publikums: Welche Geschichten kennt es bereits und wie verhält sich die eigene dazu? Es erfordert aber auch einen hohen Grad an Aufmerksamkeit für das zu Inszenierende: Die Arbeit des Wissenschafters/Technikers ähnelt damit ein wenig der Arbeit eines Regisseurs, einer Regisseurin[17], der/die das Beste aus »seinen/ihren« SchauspielerInnen machen möchte. Der/die SchauspielerIn ist für das Publikum dann am »authentischsten«, wenn er/sie gleichzeitig ganz bei sich ist und ganz in der Rolle aufgeht. Forschungsergebnisse erscheinen dann am verlässlichsten und interessantesten, wenn der/die ForscherIn die Eigenschaften des Beforschten so inszeniert, dass sich der Zusammenhang selbst erklärt und beweist. Eine Technologie ist dann erfolgreich, wenn die Möglichkeiten der Technologie (Material, Zusammensetzung der Teile etc.) bestmöglich genutzt *und* mit den Wünschen und Bedürfnissen der BenutzerInnen abgestimmt sind. Dieser Prozess der Abstimmung ist gar nicht anders denkbar als ein in kulturelle

Muster eingebetteter, von sozioökonomischen Bedingungen abhängiger etc. Latour hat aber auch deutlich gemacht, dass dies nicht die »Realität« von Gegenständen untergräbt (Sozialkonstruktivismus), sondern ihre Realität erst beweist.

Noch eine Konnotation ist mit dem Begriff der »Bühne« verbunden: Die Tendenz digitaler Technologien, Realitäten (Landschaften und Räume, menschliche Kommunikation) durch mediatisierte Formen zu ersetzen. Doch hier soll nicht die Geschichte des Verlusts »authentischen« Lebens und Kommunizierens, die kulturpessimistische Geschichte der Entfremdung erzählt werden, die so viele Medientheorien apokalyptisch grundiert, noch die Geschichte von der zunehmenden Vergeistigung des Menschen, die notwendigerweise zur totalen Informatisierung der Wahrnehmung führen muss. Die Bühnenmetapher soll als Denkfigur dienen, um die Prozesse der Kommunikation von ForscherInnen und ProgrammiererInnen mit ihren Gegenständen, mit ihren AuftraggeberInnen, den zukünftigen BenutzerInnen, aber auch mit ihrer eigenen spezifischen Geschichte und Kultur zu beschreiben. Es soll deutlich werden, dass dies ein kreativer und produktiver Prozess ist, der verschiedenste Akteure involviert und verbindet, ein Prozess, der als Dialog und nicht als Determination verstanden werden muss und der rationale wie affektive Prozesse inkludiert, »Große Erzählungen« und kleine Episoden.

SF-Welten bieten einzigartige Möglichkeiten für die Inszenierung technischer Artefakte. Ich möchte zeigen, wie vielfältig, widersprüchlich und wirkungsmächtig die Narrative der Digitalisierung in einem Moment (Mitte der 80er Jahre) waren, in dem noch nicht so klar wie heute war, welche Rolle digitale Technologien spielen würden (ökonomisch, politisch, auf der Ebene der alltäglichen Nutzung).

NARRATIVE UND TECHNISCHE ARTEFAKTE

Während frühere Studien Technologie entweder als einen besonders verhärteten Teil einer sozialen Realität im Basis-Überbau-Modell dachten, dem sich die Ästhetik »anpassen« müsse um nicht auf der Strecke zu bleiben[18], oder die relative Autonomie von technischer Realisierung und dem Technoimaginären[19] betonten, mehren sich in den Cultural Studies, den Science and Technology Studies und in den Äußerungen der Digitalen Kulturen selbst die Befunde, dass das Technoimaginäre, das Symbolische, das Soziale und die technischen Realisierungen sehr viel enger miteinander verzahnt sind.

Die Gründe für diese Neukonfiguration sind vielfältig:

Erstens ist dafür der erweiterte Kulturbegriff der Cultural Studies verantwortlich, welche Kultur als »Structure of Feeling« (Raymond Williams) begreifen und die Ebenen der Alltagskultur und der kulturellen Praktiken miteinschließen. Zweitens problematisieren die Cultural Studies, Gender Studies und die STS die scharfe Trennung von Natur und Kultur und damit auch eine eindeutige Trennung von Natur- und Kulturwissenschaften. Drittens kam es in den letzten Jahren zu Verschiebungen im Technikbegriff hin zu einem *systemischen* Technikbegriff. Man spricht in der Technikforschung inzwischen gerne von Technologien wie dem Internet als soziotechnischen System. Viertens hat die Actor-Network-Theory nahe gelegt, in der Praxis des wissenschaftlichen Arbeitens nicht einen Widerspruch von Diskurs und Material zu sehen, sondern eine *Fabrikaktion* von Wissen und Technologien. Der bis dahin passiv gedachten Dingwelt wird eine Art Agentenschaft zugeschrieben, Ideen ergeben sich nicht einfach als objektives Wissen aus dem Faktischen, können den Dingen aber auch nicht einfach »appliziert« werden, wie es sozialkonstruktivistische Überlegungen nahe legten. Die Trennung der Welt in eine kulturalisierte und eine natürliche wird dadurch endgültig problematisch, denn der Kultur geht damit ihr definitorischer Widerpart verloren. Fünftens haben die digitale Technologien selbst diesen Paradigmenwechsel ermöglicht: Computer bestehen aus Hardware und aus Software: Erstere wird ganz traditionell von Ingenieuren konstruiert (dass auch in diesem Prozess soziokulturelle Faktoren wesentlich sind, konnten z. B. Arbeiten zur Metrologie bestätigen). Ausschlaggebender für die »kulturalistische Wende« in der Erforschung von Technikentwicklung ist die Tatsache, dass Computer, um arbeiten zu können, »Software« brauchen. Software ist ein Zeichengewebe, sie besteht aus Symbolen, sie übersetzt über mehrere Zwischenschritte menschliches Denken und Wollen in binäre Zahlenreihen, die der Computer »versteht«. Um diese Zahlenreihen herstellen zu können, sind komplexe kulturelle Praktiken vonnöten: Logik und Mathematik, die Entwicklung von Programmiersprachen, die etwa auf halbem Weg zwischen Computersprachen und Menschensprachen angesiedelt sind etc. Seit der/die EinzelverbraucherIn und NichttechnikerIn als potentielle/r ComputernutzerIn entdeckt wurde, ist außerdem eine ganze Industrie damit beschäftigt, User-Interfaces herzustellen. Also Möglichkeiten zu schaffen, dass Menschen ohne wesentliche Kenntnisse des Rechnerinnenlebens mit ihm kommunizieren können. So eine Kommunikation ist nur über Metaphern möglich, die sich wiederum aus vorhandenen kulturellen Mustern speisen[20].

Es sei hier nur so viel festgehalten, dass der Computer als symbolverarbeitendes System notwendigerweise ein sehr viel engeres Verhältnis zu anderen symbolverarbeitenden Systemen (wie der Literatur, der Mathematik etc.) haben muss, als zum Beispiel ein Automobil. Soziales, Imaginäres und Technisches sind auch hier zirkulär aufeinander bezogen, sie stabilisieren sich gegenseitig[21]. Symbolisch vermittelte Machtverhältnisse bleiben

in diesem Prozess in Kraft. Die Entwicklungslogik von Geräten selbst hat folglich Geschichte und braucht Geschichten.
Mein Ansatz wendet sich gegen die Idee einer »evolutionären« Entwicklungslogik von Geräten, einer Geschichte, in der sozialer Kontext als Störgeräusch, das wahre Erkenntnis und gute Technik verhindert, aufgefasst wird und gegen eine triumphale Technikgeschichte, in der Ingenieure in heroischen Anstrengungen, separiert von ihren sozialen Kontexten Neues »erfinden«; er richtet sich aber auch gegen radikal- konstruktivistische Ansätze, die die Existenz einer anderen als der sprachlichen Realität bezweifeln oder für irrelevant befinden.
Das Verhältnis von Narrativen und technischen Artefakten soll in der Folge als eines der wechselseitigen Prägung angesehen werden.

COMPUTERHYSTORIEN

Wenn vom *Computernarrativen* die Rede ist, können nach Bell drei verschiedene Arten derselben unterschieden werden: materielle Geschichten (diese werden üblicherweise von der Technikgeschichte erzählt), symbolische Geschichten (die ihre Organisationsformen zum Teil aus der SF beziehen) und Geschichten des alltäglichen Umgangs mit Technologien (Studien in diese Richtung gibt es in der empirischen Forschung über Computernutzung, untersucht werden z. B. Technobiographien).[22]
N. Katherine Hayles[23] diskutiert analog dazu ihre »virtuellen Kreaturen« mit Hilfe dreier »Modi der Befragung«: Sie befragt sie, was sie sind, was sie bedeuten und was sie tun. Ein Ansatz, der Technologien durch ihre Geschichten erforscht, macht deren Definition zwar schwieriger, hat aber den Vorteil, möglichst viele Aspekte von technischen Entwicklungen abzudecken: die Arbeit an den Technologien selbst, die wissenschaftlichen Ideen, die kommerziellen Erwartungen, den alltägliche Umgang mit ihnen und nicht zuletzt die Träume und Alpträume, die mit ihnen verbunden sind[24].
Eine Analyse des Technoimaginären kann sich folglich nicht nur auf eine formale Analyse von Narrativen verlassen, sie muss auch fragen, wer die Personen sind, die die Geschichten produzieren und rezipieren, in welchen Kontexten (sozialen, technologischen) dies erfolgt, wer welche Geschichten dann wie aufgreift und weiterschreibt, aber auch was in den Geschichten *nicht* erzählt wird, welche Geschichten *nicht* aufgegriffen werden. Kurz: Es geht um rhetorische und pragmatische Dimensionen von Narrativen.
Computerhystorien nenne ich jene Narrative, die durch massenmediale Verbreitung eine besondere Wirksamkeit entfalten können. Der Begriff »Hystorie« ist von Elaine Showalter[25] entliehen, die damit Geschichten meint,

die auf reale Erfahrungen von Menschen bezogen werden können, diese aber nicht einfach reflektieren oder repräsentieren, sondern nach Genremustern überformen.
Der nächste Teil meines Beitrags wird sich mit einigen Narrativen der Science Fiction beschäftigen, die ein besonderes Nahverhältnis zur Computerentwicklung haben. Ich werde dabei Zusammenhänge zwischen einigen Aspekten des Technoimaginären der 80er Jahre und der Entwicklung des Desktopcomputing durch die konkurrierenden Betriebssysteme Windows, Macintosh und Linux skizzieren.

CYBERPUNK ALS »SELF-FULFILLING PROPHECY«

> Cyberpunk fiction has become a self-fulfilling prophecy in which we understand cyberspace through its fantasies but then we find that cyberspace is in fact like cyberpunk.
>
> *Tim Jordan*[26]

Gibsons *Neuromancer* hat in vielerlei Hinsicht den Charakter eines Gründungsdokuments für die Digitalen Kulturen der 80er und 90er Jahre: Nicht nur »erfand« er im Roman den Ausdruck Cyberspace und stattete diesen mit einer psychedelisch angehauchten Metaphysik aus. Er entwarf in dem Roman auch gleich ein Leitbild und Rollenmodell für die jugendlichen, männlichen Programmierer: den »Konsolencowboy« *Case*, der in Robin-Hood-Manier im Netz gegen mächtige Konzerne kämpft.
Es gehört zu den Legenden der Hackerkultur, dass Gibson 1) keine Ahnung vom Stand der Technik hatte, als er das Buch schrieb, 2) den Roman auf einer alten Schreibmaschine tippte, 3) computerspielende Kids die wichtigste Inspiration für ihn waren. – Die neue Technologie »erscheint« in dieser Erzählung als geradezu losgelöst von ihren sozioökonomischen Voraussetzungen: Keine Rede ist davon, dass gerade der erste Boom am Computermarkt stattfindet. Als Gründungsmythos begünstigt diese Herkunftserzählung eine Art professionelles Vergessen der Kontexte, die die Computertechnologie damals prägten (Militär, Kapitalinteressen, gesetzliche Normierung etc.) und führt zu einer Auratisierung der Informationstechnologien als widerständig, individualistisch, der Selbstentfaltung und Lustbefriedigung dienend. Punk eben. Im Zentrum der Selbsthistorisierung der Digitalen Kultur, die in den letzten Jahren zu beobachten ist, stehen dann auch nostalgische kulturelle Artefakte (Filme, Spiele und alten Maschinen selbst), während sozioökonomische Aspekte weiterhin ausgeblendet bleiben.
Der Rekurs auf die Geburt des Cyberspace aus Computerspielen ist trotzdem nicht ganz verkehrt: Nicht nur für Gibson waren Computerspiele ein

wichtiges Eingangsportal in die Computerwelt, auch für die »Nerds« und »Geeks«, die inzwischen in den Softwareschmieden über neue Programme brüten und in Nachtschichten Computernetze administrieren, ist das der Fall. McCafferey beschreibt den kulturellen Hintergrund der Cyberpunks folgendermaßen:

The cyberpunks were the first generation of artists for whom the technologies of satellite dishes, video and audio players and recorders, computers and video games (...), digital watches and MTV were not exoticisms, but part of a daily ›reality matrix‹. They were also the first generation of writers (...) who had grown up immersed in technology but also in pop culture, in the values and aesthetics of the counterculture associated with drug culture, punk rock, video games, (...) comic books, and (...) gore-and splatter SF/horror films.[27]

Weitere Stichworte zu dieser 80er Jahre Subkultur, die im wesentlichen von weißen, männlichen Jugendlichen hervorgebracht wurde, können in etwa so lauten: benützen und ausreizen der ersten Homecomputer (Commodore C64, Amiga), Kommunikation über das gerade entstehende Internet; Kino: *Krieg der Sterne* (1977-83), *Tron* (1982), *War Games* (1983); Bücher: Wilsons *Die Illuminatentrilogie*, Tolkiens *Der Herr der Ringe*, Cyberpunk, Computerspiele.

Wesentlich ist wohl der Rückzug dieser männlichen Jugendlichen ins Kinder- und Jugendzimmer und das Entstehen einer weltweit vernetzten und exklusiven Geek/Nerd Subkultur, die eine Art »Geheimwissen«, das als »Herrschaft über die Maschinen« buchstabiert werden kann, erzeugt und verbreitet. Der Rückzug ins Kinderzimmer und die indirekte Kommunikation der Community im Netz lässt sich aus gegenwärtiger Perspektive als Triumphzug lesen. Aus dem *Evil Nerd* (dem jungen komplexbeladenen Brillenträger) ist der coole Nerd *Neo* aus dem Blockbuster *The Matrix* (1999) geworden. »Als Erfolgsstory lässt sich die ›Rache der Nerds‹ (...) in die Popkultur integrieren. Dabei ist bemerkenswert, dass nicht der Nerd sein Heiligtum verlässt, sondern sein Wissen in gesellschaftliche Anerkennung übersetzt wird.«[28]

Die Kids von damals sind inzwischen erwachsen geworden, sie haben häufig hohe Positionen in der Computerbranche inne, gehören aber jedenfalls jener New Economy an, die an der Oberfläche auf Teamgeist und Enthierarchisierung setzt, die aber soziale Asymmetrien perpetuiert oder neu schafft[29]. Teil der egalitären Spaßgesellschaft sind nach altem Subkulturmuster eben nur die *Members*, diejenigen die – im wörtlichen Sinn – den Code kennen.

Auf der Ebene der Technologien findet sich die gleiche eigentümliche Spaltung von Wissen wieder: Auf der einen Seite werden die Benutzer Innen von den Gestaltern der digitalen Technologien als von bunten Bildern getäuschte Opfer imaginiert, während an der Innenseite der Technik die mit Geheimwissen ausgestatteten Programmierer operieren. Der Entstehung dieses »elektronischen Klassensystems«, das in die Geschichte von GUIs (Graphic User Interfaces) eingeschrieben ist, soll nun ein wenig genauer nachgegangen werden.

REALITÄT, SIMULATION UND CODE. NARRATIVE DES DESKTOPCOMPUTING

Mit dem Cyberpunk kommt es zu einer eigenartigen Dreiteilung der Welt in Realität, Simulation und Code. Ich werde diese Dreiteilung anhand des Films *The Matrix* erläutern, da hier das Konzept überdeutlich verwendet wird. Es liegt eine dreischichtige Realität vor: eine, die so aussieht wie unsere Alltagsrealität, aber reine Computersimulation ist, von den Maschinen programmiert, um die Menschen ruhig zu halten, dann die wirkliche Wirklichkeit: die Wüste des Realen, wie sie einer der Protagonisten – *Morpheus* – nennt. Die von Menschen belebbare Welt ist vollkommen zerstört worden und die Menschen werden als Batterien für die Maschinen verwendet. Die Realitätsebene, auf der die meiste Action stattfindet – die Matrix –, ist eine Zwischenwelt, am ehesten vielleicht identifizierbar als »Programmspeicher«. Hier lernt der Protagonist *Neo* nach seiner Initiation die Funktionsweise der sichtbaren Welt als programmierte Scheinwelt begreifen und diese manipulieren. Er begreift es als seine Aufgabe, die Menschheit als ihr Erlöser von ihrem falschen Bewusstsein zu befreien.

In eine Psychosoziologie der Geeks übersetzt entspricht das einer gnostischen Weltauffassung: Die reale Realität wird als feindlich, leidvoll und unveränderbar angesehen und im Film mit einer verschlingenden Sexualmetaphorik, die an die von Klaus Theweleit herausgearbeitete Struktur der *Männerphantasien*[30] gemahnt, dargestellt. Wirklichkeit 2 ist eine medial vermittelte Oberfläche, die in etwa der Vorstellung der Kritischen Theorie von der Popularkultur entspricht oder auch Jean Baudrillards Simulationstheorie[31], während die Ebene des Programmcodes jene Welt ist, die vom gewitzten Programmierer unendlich manipuliert und gestaltet werden kann. Hier und nur hier ist Veränderung und ein Eingreifen in das Weltgeschehen möglich.

Die Tätigkeit des Programmierens/Codierens wird auf SF-Narrative abgebildet und damit symbolisch aufgeladen. Sie wird narrativ mit der Tätigkeit des »social engineering« assoziiert: Manipulation des Codes = Gestaltung der Wirklichkeit, ein Narrativ, das den Cyberpunk von Grund auf strukturiert. In *The Matrix* findet es seine heroische Zuspitzung und seine heilsgeschichtliche Akzentuierung. Einziger Ausweg aus der Ausbeutung durch die Maschinen ist eine Erlöserfigur: Der Name der Hauptfigur *Neo* spielt nicht nur mit den Konnotationen von Innovation, er ist eine Permutation von the One, der Eine, der Einzige und seine Geliebte heißt wenig überraschend *Trinity. Neos* Fähigkeit die Matrix zu verändern wird mit mythischen Kräften gleichgesetzt. Der Kampf gegen Unterdrückung und Ausbeutung kann nur auf der Ebene des Programmcodes, des Diskurses, der Symbole stattfinden: Der vollkommene Rückzug aus der Realität und wird durch das Phantasma von Allmacht durch Manipulation des Programmcodes erkauft.

Die Herkunft dieses Phantasmas der gleichzeitigen Entgrenzung und Kontrolle kann verschieden tief in der Vergangenheit gesucht werden: Hillis[32] ortet eine Verlängerung alter Eroberungsphantasien und des Frontier-Mythos, der sich nun, da geographisch die letzte Grenze eingeholt wurde, auf den Virtuellen Raum erstreckt. Stephenson[33] assoziiert die zweischneidige Ethik der Cybercowboys mit »Bayarea Babyboomdom«, also mit jenem kalifornischen »Way of Life«, der an der Oberfläche bunt und antibourgeois daherkommt, sich aber als politisch ambivalent, weitgehend wirkungslos oder sogar konservativ entpuppt hat. Apple benützt diese Ästhetik des Widerstandes (oder auch den Widerstand mit den Mitteln der Ästhetik) immer noch gern in seinen Werbesujets.

Aber auch die eigentümliche Stellung der Programmierer in der New Economy mag mit der (politischen) Ambivalenz dieser Kultur zu tun haben: Programmierer sind auf geradezu paradoxe Weise mit »dem System« verbunden: Einerseits sind sie eine Elite (oder waren es jedenfalls in den 80er Jahren), eine versprengte Community gut ausgebildeter Männer, die kreative Arbeit verrichtet und sich deshalb gern als eine neue Generation von Bohemiens sah. Eine Generation, die aufgrund ihrer technischen Kompetenz gute Chancen hatte, die Macht der Väter frühzeitig zu übernehmen. Aber ihr Tätigkeitsfeld bindet sie außerordentlich eng an die Zentren der Macht (Militär, Wirtschaft), auf die sie angewiesen sind und vice versa – eine klassische Doublebind-Situation.

Diese Konstellation musste zu einer einigermaßen gespaltenen Selbstwahrnehmung führen, nämlich der hier skizzierten, eigenartigen Mischung von Technomythen und Revolutionsphantasien und zu den Topoi des Robin-Hood-Hackers oder des Hackers als »Enemy within«. Auch die überaus weitverbreiteten konspirativen und verschwörungstheoretischen Erzählungen (in Romanen, Serien wie den *X-Files*, der öffentlichen Berichterstattung über Hacker-Attacken) partizipieren an dieser soziokulturellen Struktur. Der Film *23* (1998), der die Biographie des deutschen Hackers Karl Koch als Spielfilm umarbeitete, enthält prototypisch das Narrativ eines zunehmenden Kontrollverlusts des Protagonisten in der realen Welt, der zu einer Flucht in eine elektronische und drogengesättigte Parallelwelt führt, in der Karl vorübergehend das Gefühl der Allmacht hat. Wie in vielen anderen popkulturell einflussreichen Artefakten der Hackerkultur steht auch hier ein ödipales Narrativ im Mittelpunkt. Die Auseinandersetzung des Hackers mit der Vatergeneration wird als Grund für Karls Absturz angeführt, aber auch die oben beschriebene typische Doublebind-Situation des Hackers ist handlungsbestimmend, eine Konstellation die als »Verführung durch die Macht« in *Star Wars* und im *Herrn der Ringe* symbolisch codiert wurde.

Der Aspekt der Täuschung durch die Oberfläche (pejorativ auf die BenützerInnen von Interfaces projiziert) wurde ein strukturierendes Prinzip der Auseinandersetzung um die Entwicklung von GUIs, der wiederum den Betriebssystemkampf von Linux vs. Microsoft informiert.

Cyberpunk-Autor und Programmierer Neil Stephenson hat in seinem Essay *In the Beginning was the Command-Line*[34] diese Narrative der Programmiererkultur in einem nichtfiktionalen Modus niedergeschrieben: Auch er schreibt darin von Graphic User Interfaces als einer systematischen Verblendung der Benutzer: Diese sollen mittels bunter Bilder und schlechter Metaphern davon abgehalten werden, ihre Geräte zu verstehen, und begeben sich damit in die Hände der Programmierer und Softwarekonzerne (die er in Anlehnung an H. G. Wells *Morloks* nennt). Der Desktop wird mit der normierenden und manipulierenden Scheinwelt Hollywoods und Disneylands verglichen. In der Manier des Bildungsromans erzählt Stephenson seine eigene Konversion von einem betrogenen Mac-Nutzer zu einem »aufgeklärten«, selbstbestimmten Linux-Programmierer. Windows wird als eine Art »Imagined Community« stilisiert, die sich selbst betrügt, indem sich die Benutzer gegenseitig glauben machen, dass Windows funktioniert.

Stephensons rückblickende Erzählung von der Entwicklung der Betriebssysteme und den GUIs ist überaus aufschlussreich, da er aus der Innenperspektive die Technologie und ihre Kultur beschreibt und damit Aufschluss über die Übersetzungsprozesse gibt, die im Spiel sind, wenn Sprache und Kultur mit Technologie zusammenkommen.

Leider hat Stephenson wie der größte Teil der Mitglieder der Digitalen Kulturen keinen Begriff für kulturökonomische Asymmetrien, die die Verwendung von Symbolen und Maschinen ebenfalls strukturieren und deshalb müssen die UserInnen in dieser Erzählung auch stets als Betrogene enden: Er übersieht gefliessentlich, dass BenutzerInnen und ProgrammierInnen verschiedene ökonomische Interessen an Computern haben. Für die Einen bedeutet die Zeit, die sie in das Erlernen von Befehlen, Syntax und Programmen stecken, nicht nur ein besseres Verständnis der Geräte, sondern führt auch zur Akkumulation von symbolischem und sozialem Kapital auf ihren professionellen Konten. Die Verknappung dieses Wissens ermöglicht ihnen erst eine Selbstwahrnehmung als Spezialisten mit Geheimwissen, während das Wissen um die Installation dieses oder jenes Webservers für den/die übliche UserIn so gut wie kein symbolisches Kapital einbringt, es sich für ihn/sie also nicht »auszahlen« würde, dieses Wissen zu erwerben.

Diese Geschichten von Hackern, Geeks und Crackern sind Beispiele von *Computerhystorien*, wie ich sie weiter oben definiert habe: Es handelt sich dabei um einander amplifizierende massenmediale Erzählungen, die auf soziale Befindlichkeiten verweisen, diese jedoch nach spezifischen Schemata (die den Regeln des Genres Science Fiction gehorchen) überformen. Nur Narrative, die in *Praktiken* eine Anwendung finden, werden weitererzählt. Sie entfalten ihre Wirksamkeit bei der Ausbildung von geschlechtlichen und beruflichen Identitäten und helfen bei der Fabrikation und Inszenierung spezifischer technisch-sozialer Systeme in diesem Fall des Desktopcomputing. In diesem, und nur in diesem Sinn, ist sowohl Gibsons Konsolencowboy als auch sein Cyberspace Realität geworden.

ALTERNATIVE ERZÄHLUNGEN: CYBORGS, TERMINATOREN, REPLIKANTEN

Die Narrationen der Geeks bleiben, wie diese wenigen Beispiele zeigen, weitgehend einer Dialektik von Beherrschen und Beherrscht-Werden, Kontrolle und Kontrollverlust, der traditionellen Geschlechterdichotomie, einer ödipalen Identitätskonstruktion, dem gnostischen Ideal von reinem Wissen versus schmutziger Realität, den großen Narrativen von Heilsgeschichte, Apokalypse und Revolution verpflichtet.

Die 80er Jahre brachten aber auch gegenläufige Geschichten hervor: Geschichten von Vermischungen von Menschen und Maschinen, vom Zweifel an den modernen Epistemen und ihren Ordnungssystemen. Stehen für die erste Gruppe Filme wie *Star Wars* und bestimmte Cyberpunkromane, dann stehen für den zweiten, sehr vielfältigeren, Erzählstrang beispielsweise Donna Haraways *Cyborg-Manifest*[35] und die Filme *Blade Runner* (1983) sowie *Terminator 2* (1989). Man könnte hier von einem Fenster im Technoimaginären sprechen, das für kurze Zeit (Mitte der 80er Jahre bis Mitte der 90er Jahre) ein ganz anderes Nachdenken über Technologien möglich machte, ein Nachdenken, welches das Verhältnis von Menschen und Maschinen nicht in den Begriffen von Sklaverei und linearem Fortschrittsparadigma denken mochte. Hierher gehört auch der Cyberfeminismus, der versuchte, digitale Technologien feministisch umzudeuten. Dazu gehören aber auch einige Teilaspekte des Cyberpunk: Die weiblichen Hackerfiguren, die Stephenson in seinen ersten beiden Romanen entwirft[36], die Einführung von Ada Lovelace als zentraler Figur in Gibsons und Sterlings *Differenzmaschine*[37]. Dieser Variantenreichtum in der Darstellung von Mensch-Maschine-verhältnissen und den dazugehörigen Erkenntnismodellen hat damit zu tun, dass zur Entstehungszeit der Artefakte ein Prozess der »Schließung« digitaler Technologien erst im Gange war, ein Prozess, der von multiplen Interessen geprägt war (ökonomischen, militärischen, politischen) und der technische und rechtliche Standards festlegte (Übertragungsprotokolle, Codierungssysteme, »inoffizielle Standards« wie das Betriebssystem Windows, Copyrightgesetze, Zensur etc.) Dieser Prozess ist zwar auch jetzt noch nicht abgeschlossen, hat aber in den 80er Jahren seine wesentlichen Prägungen erhalten, die Konflikte und die Rollen der involvierten AkteurInnen relativ festgelegt und bewegt sich derzeit schnell auf eine zunehmende Regulierung sämtlicher Bereiche zu. Als 1999 *The Matrix* in die Kinos kam, waren die digitalen Technologien längst reterritorialisiert. Das Hollywoodkino hat in *The Matrix* die Ästhetik des Cyberpunk mit dem Uralt-Plot von Apokalypse und Erlösung versöhnt und hat damit die widerstreitenden Narrative über Form und Nutzung von Technologien, Körpern und Identitäten zu einem einfachen Universalmodell der Welt mit religiös-aufklärerischen Untertönen gemacht. Standardisierung und Schließung findet als dialektischer Prozess gleichzeitig auf den Ebenen der Technologien *und* des Imaginären statt.

Dass die Cyborgisierung der Welt die Form von Lara Croft und Co[38] angenommen hat, dass es 2001 weniger Informatikstudentinnen gibt als in den 80er Jahren, dass Frauen auch im Informationszeitalter und auch in der Softwareindustrie schlechtere Berufschancen als ihre männlichen Kollegen haben und dass trotz der Parole von »Information für alle« bei weitem nicht alle Teil der schönen neuen Datenwelt sind, gibt Anlass für einige abschließende Überlegungen, die meine narratologischen Analysen informieren. Was mir wichtig erscheint ist,

- dass formal und inhaltlich innovative Narrative (trotz ihres sozialrevolutionären Gestus) nicht automatisch sozio-politisch innovative Effekte haben.
- dass die soziale Stellung der ProduzentInnen und KonsumentInnen des Technoimaginären ausschlaggebend für ihre Rezeption und dass diese gebrochen in verschiedenen sozialen Kontexten erfolgt.
- dass Interventionen, die die Digitalen Technologien nicht zum Spielzeug einiger weniger verkommen lassen wollen, auf allen drei Ebenen der kulturellen Produktion (dem Imaginären, dem Symbolischen und dem Materiellen) ansetzen müssen.
- dass es kein deterministisches Verhältnis zwischen dem Technologischen, dem Imaginären und dem Sozialen/Ökonomischen gibt, sondern wechselseitige Abgleichungsprozesse, eine »kontinuierliche, wechselseitige Stabilisierung«.
- dass das Technoimaginäre voll von Ungleichzeitigkeiten, Widersprüchen und Ungereimtheiten ist, genauso wie das Soziale und das Tech-

nologische selbst, nur dass wir das angesichts der Faktizität der Gegenstände gerne vergessen.

ANMERKUNGEN

[1] Gilles Deleuze, Félix Guattari, Tausend Plateaus. Kapitalismus und Schizophrenie, Berlin 1997, 13.
[2] ebd.
[3] Bruno Latour, Die Hoffnung der Pandora, Frankfurt a. M. 2000.
[4] An anderer Stelle spricht er von Wissenschaft als der »fortschreitenden Vermischung von menschlichen und nichtmenschlichen Wesen«.
[5] Régis Debray hingegen schlägt vor, die Geschichte der Menschen und die der Dinge zwar zu parallelisieren und aufeinander zu beziehen, besteht aber darauf, dass beide einer unterschiedlichen Ordnung unterliegen: Die Geschichte der Dinge unterliege der Ordnung der *episteme*, sie verlaufe akkumulativ und die Geschichte der Menschen der Ordnung der *doxa*, diese sei stets zirkulär. Intelligibel wird die Welt der Dinge erst, wenn sie organisierte Materie oder materialisierte Organisation wird. Régis Debray, Transmitting Culture, New York 2000, 10-15.
[6] Zur Unterscheidung zwischen technikdeterministischen und sozialkonstruktivistischen Ansätzen vgl. Hartmut Winkler, Die prekäre Rolle der Technik. Technikzentrierte versus ›anthropologische‹ Mediengeschichtsschreibung 1997, www.uni-paderborn.de/~winkler/henne.html, Zugriff vom 3.2.2002. Winkler schlägt hier ebenfalls einen zirkulären Ansatz vor, orientiert diesen allerdings am Modell der Sprache und wird deshalb an dieser Stellen nicht weiter verfolgt.
[7] Oft kommt es deshalb zu einer Dämonisierung von Medienwirkungen.
[8] Pierre Bourdieu, Outline of a Theory of Practice, Cambridge 1977.
[9] Debray, Transmitting.
[10] »Electronic Kindergarten« hieß eine Veranstaltung (Ausstellung und Symposion) des Wiener Vereins [d]vision 2001, die diese Phase der Digitalen Kulturen dokumentierte.
[11] William Gibson, Neuromancer, München 1987.
[12] John Macgregor Wise, Exploring Technology and Social Space, Thousand Oaks, London, New Delhi 1997.
[13] Zum Begriff der Schließung von Technologien vgl. z. B. Werner Rammert, Technik aus soziologischer Perspektive 2. Kultur – Innovation – Virtualität, Wiesbaden 2000, 59-70.
[14] Saskia Sassen, Digital networks and power. in: Spaces of Culture. City, nation, world, M. Featherstone and S. Lash (Hrsg.), London 1999, 49.
[15] Carl D. Malmgren, Worlds Apart. Narratology of Science Fiction, Bloomington, Indianapolis 1991, 15-30.
[16] Latour, Pandora, 137-174.
[17] Die Metapher des Regisseurs/der Regisseurin geht nicht ganz konform mit Latours Konzepten, sie erscheint mir dennoch adäquat, weil sie das asymmetrische Verhältnis zwischen Dingen und Menschen auszudrücken im Stande ist.
[18] Vgl. dazu Arbeiten zu den frühen Avantgarden z. B. Carl Wege, Buchstabe und Maschine. Beschreibung einer Allianz, Frankfurt a. M. 2000.
[19] Z. B. Birgit Wagner, Technik und Literatur im Zeitalter der Avantgarden. Ein Beitrag zur Geschichte des Imaginären, München 1996.

[20] Zu einer Diskursanalyse des Interface vergleiche zum Beispiel Lev Manovich, The Language of New Media, Cambridge (M), London 2002.
[21] Die Dynamik techno-kultureller Entwicklungen kann mit deleuzoguattarischer Terminologie als ein Zyklus mit deterritorialisierenden und reterritorialisierenden Phasen begriffen werden.
[22] David Bell, An Introduction to Cybercultures, London, New York 2001.
[23] N. Katherine Hayles, Simulating Narratives: what virtual creatures can teach us, Critical Inquiry 1999(26), 1-26, hier 2.
[24] Bell, Introduction, 7
[25] Elaine Showalter, Hystorien. Hysterische Epidemien im Zeitalter der Medien 1997.
[26] Tim Jordan, Cyberpower: the culture and politics of cyberspace and the internet, London, New York 1999, 33.
[27] Larry McCaffery (Hrsg.), Storming the Reality Studio: a casebook of cyberpunk and postmodern science fiction. Durham 1991, hier: Introduction, 12.
[28] Bernhard Rieder, Mirko Tobias Schäfer, Der 80-er-Jahre Kern der Sache. (Das ist halt Geschichtsschreibung), sinn-haft 2001(10), 43-44, hier 44.
[29] Vgl. z. B. Saskia Sassens Konzept von »information poor und information rich«. Sassen, Digital Networks.
[30] Klaus Theweleit, Männerphantasien. Bd. 1: Frauen, Fluten, Körper, Geschichte, München 1977. Ders., Männerphantasien. Männerkörper. Zur Psychoanalyse des weißen Terrors, München 1978.
[31] Der Film enthält eine explizite Referenz an Baudrillard: *Neo* versteckt seine gehackten Disketten in einer hohlen (!) Ausgabe von *Simulations and Simulacra.*
[32] Ken Hillis, Digital Sensation: space, identity, and embodiment in Virtual Reality, Minneapolis, London 1999.
[33] Neil Stephenson, In the Beginning ... Was the Command Line, New York 1999.
[34] ebd.
[35] Donna Haraway, Ein Manifest für Cyborgs. Feminismus im Streit mit den Technowissenschaften, in: dies., Die Neuerfindung der Natur. Primaten, Cyborgs und Frauen. Herausgegeben und eingeleitet von Carmen Hammer und Immanuel Stieß, Frankfurt, NY 1995, 33-72.
[36] Neil Stephenson, Diamond Age. Die Grenzwelt, München 1998. Ders., Snowcrash, München 1994.
[37] William Gibson, Bruce Sterling, Die Differenzmaschine, München 1992.
[38] Vgl. dazu die Studie von Gabriele Winker: Geschlechterverhältnisse und vernetzte Systeme, Zeitschrift für Frauenforschung 1999, 17(1 + 2), 9-25.

BIBLIOGRAPHIE

David Bell, An Introduction to Cybercultures, London, New York 2001.
Pierre Bourdieu, Outline of a Theory of Practice, Cambridge 1977.
Régis Debray, Transmitting Culture, New York 2000.
Gilles Deleuze and Félix Guattari, Tausend Plateaus. Kapitalismus und Schizophrenie, Berlin 1997.
William Gibson, Neuromancer, München 1987.
William Gibson, Bruce Sterling, Die Differenzmaschine. Mit einem Nachwort von

Michael Nagula und Abbildungen der Maschine nach Charles Babbage, München 1992.
Donna Haraway, Ein Manifest für Cyborgs. Feminismus im Streit mit den Technowissenschaften, in: dies., Die Neuerfindung der Natur. Primaten, Cyborgs und Frauen. Herausgegeben und eingeleitet von Carmen Hammer und Immanuel Stieß, Frankfurt, NY 1995, 33-72.
N. Katherine Hayles, Simulating Narratives: What virtual creatures can teach us, Critical Inquiry 1999(26), 1-26.
Ken Hillis, Digital Sensation: space, identity, and embodiment in Virtual Reality, Minneapolis, London 1999.
Tim Jordan, Cyberpower: the culture and politics of cyberspace and the internet, London, New York 1999.
Bruno Latour, Die Hoffnung der Pandora, Frankfurt a. M. 2000.
Carl D. Malmgren, Worlds Apart. Narratology of Science Fiction, Bloomington, Indianapolis 1991.
Lev Manovich, The Language of New Media, Cambridge (M), London 2002.
Larry McCaffery (Hrsg.), Storming the Reality Studio: a casebook of cyberpunk and postmodern science fiction. Durham 1991.
Werner Rammert, Technik aus soziologischer Perspektive 2. Kultur – Innovation – Virtualität, Wiesbaden 2000.
Bernhard Rieder, Mirko Tobias Schäfer, Der 80-er-Jahre Kern der Sache. (Das ist halt Geschichtsschreibung), sinn-haft 2001(10), 43-44.
Saskia Sassen, Digital Networks and Power, in: Spaces of Culture. City, nation, world, M. Featherstone and S. Lash (Hrsg.), London 1999.
Elaine Showalter, Hystorien. Hysterische Epidemien im Zeitalter der Medien 1997.
Neil Stephenson, Snowcrash, München 1994.
Ders., Diamond Age. Die Grenzwelt, München 1998.
Ders., In the Beginning ... Was the Command Line, New York 1999.
Klaus Theweleit, Männerphantasien. Bd. 1: Frauen, Fluten, Körper, Geschichte, München 1977, 1978.
Ders., Männerphantasien. Männerkörper. Bd. 2: Zur Psychoanalyse des weißen Terrors, München 1977, 1978.
Birgit Wagner, Technik und Literatur im Zeitalter der Avantgarden. Ein Beitrag zur Geschichte des Imaginären, München 1996.
Carl Wege, Buchstabe und Maschine. Beschreibung einer Allianz, Frankfurt a. M. 2000.
Gabriele Winker, Geschlechterverhältnisse und vernetzte Systeme, Zeitschrift für Frauenforschung 1999, 17(1 + 2), 9-25.
Hartmut Winkler, Die prekäre Rolle der Technik. Technikzentrierte versus ›anthropologische‹ Mediengeschichtsschreibung 1997, www.uni-paderborn.de/~winkler/henne.html, Zugriff vom 3.2. 2002
John Macgregor Wise, Exploring Technology and Social Space, Thousand Oaks, London, New Delhi 1997.

Politik der Form. Korrelationen und Brüche im lesbaren Text der Avantgarde

ANNA SCHOBER

In einer autobiografischen Schilderung hat der französische Cineast Serge Daney folgendes Resumee seiner Kinoerfahrungen gezogen: »Deswegen habe ich auch denjenigen nie geglaubt – selbst wenn ich sie gefürchtet habe –, die nach der Filmclubvorführung am Gymnasium verachtungsvoll von den armen Irren sprachen, die sich des ›Formalismus‹ schuldig machten, weil ihnen der Genuß der ›Form‹ mehr bedeutete als der ›Inhalt‹ des Films. Nur derjenige, der früh genug auf die Gewalt des Formalen gestoßen ist, wird schließlich wissen – aber dazu braucht es ein Leben, das eigene Leben –, inwiefern diese Gewalt auch einen ›Inhalt‹ hat.«[1] Serge Daney beschreibt hier einen säkular verwandelten Akt des Glaubens an das Erleben des Formalen. Diese von ihm angesprochene Gewalt des Formalen ist im 20. Jahrhundert wiederholt als eine politische Gewalt verstanden worden.
So haben der russische konstruktivistische Künstler Alexander Rodchenko und seine rund um die Zeitschrift *Novyi Lef* tätigen Kolleginnen und Kollegen die visuelle Verfremdung alltäglicher Objekte als revolutionären Akt gesehen: »When I present a tree taken from below like an industrial object such as a chimney, this is a revolution in the eyes of the philistine and the old connoisseur of landscapes.«[2] In dieser Hinwendung zum alltäglichen Leben traf sich das Lef-Kollektiv mit den in Berlin und Zürich zeitgleich aktiven Dadaisten, die allerdings die ästhetischen Kunstgriffe der Groteske und der Montage[3] von herkömmlicherweise nicht zusammen auftretenden Dingen bevorzugten und als Mittel verstanden, um den sogenannten »Sinn des Durcheinanderjagens« aller Dinge zu erkennen und die Verwirklichung neuer Ideale zu ermöglichen.[4] Und die französischen Surrealisten praktizierten einen »Automatismus« des Schreibens oder Sprechens, die Collage bzw. die Montage als Verfahren, um die Imagination aus der »Versklavung« zu befreien.[5]

Aber nicht nur in den blühenden Avantgarde-Kulturen zu Beginn des 20. Jahrhunderts, sondern auch in den sich selbst als »gegenkulturell« verstehenden Bewegungen in der zweiten Jahrhunderthälfte finden sich Ab-wandlungen eines solchen Konzeptes: bei den *Situationisten*, im französischen *Cinéma Lettriste*, im österreichischen *Expanded Cinema*, bei den italienischen *Indiani Metropolitani*, den US-amerikanischen *Vietnam Veterans Against the War Campaigns* oder den *Punks*. So wendet sich das Wiener *Expanded Cinema* mit einer »nicht-affirmativen Kunst« gegen bestimmte Ideologien und Kulturpraktiken der Gegenwart: »Mit Abstinenz oder Verkauf von Seele und Traum, mit Diffamierung oder Besudelung von Schönheit und Würde, mit einer umfassenden Zersetzung der ›höheren Werte‹ etc. kann nicht-affirmative Kunst das Individuum loseisen aus dem allgemeinen Prozeß der Verschleierung, der Entfremdung und Verdinglichung.«[6] Und eine der letzten aufsehenerregenden Manifestationen dieses Konzeptes findet sich einige Jahrzehnte später in einem wieder anderen Kontext: Neo-Avantagarde-Gruppen in den Gebieten des ehemaligen Yugoslawiens wie *ŠKART*, *Otpor!*, *Led Art* und *Magnet* versuchten ebenfalls, die herkömmlichen Bedeutungen der Dinge zu unterbrechen und neu zu organisieren, indem sie ähnliche ästhetische Kunstgriffe verwendeten. Die Gruppe *ŠKART* war beispielsweise seit 1992 Teil der lebhaften, sich nun entwickelnden breiten Protestbewegung in Serbien und parodierte herkömmliche Kommunikationssituationen im öffentlichen Raum – etwa mit der öffentlichen Verteilung von Hilfs-Gutscheinen zum Überleben, auf denen »más/mehr«, »strah/frikë/fear« oder »masturbacija/ masturbation« geschrieben stand, und stellte ironische Straßenschilder auf, die vor nun so alltäglichen »Ereignissen« wie dem Fallen von Bomben warnten.[7]

KONNOTATIONSLINIEN

Wenn man unter »Narration«, nach Jerome Bruner, »a conventional form« versteht, »transmitted culturally and constrained by each individual's level of mastery and by his conglomerate of prosthetic devices, colleagues, and mentors« bzw. sie versteht als »a version of reality whose acceptability is governed by convention and ›narrative necessity‹ rather than by empirical verification and logical requireness«,[8] dann können wir diese von den unterschiedlichen Avantgarde-Gruppen in Umlauf gebrachten und in Umlauf gehaltenen Geschichten als solche Narrationen begreifen.

All diese Texte argumentieren auf durchaus vergleichbare Weise, dass mit Hilfe ästhetischer Kunstgriffe, wie der forcierten Montage, der Verfremdung oder der Ironie, eine von Gewohnheit abgestumpfte Wahrnehmung aufgefrischt, »falsche« Vorstellungen und Ideologien durchbrochen und eine »wahrere«, »gerechtere« oder »emanzipiertere« Schau der Dinge erreicht werden kann. Bestimmte ästhetische Verfahren werden mit einer entlegitimierenden Wirkung auf politischer[9] oder sozialer Ebene in kausale Beziehung gesetzt. In dieser immer ähnlichen Wiederholung dessen, dass

bestimmte ästhetische Kunstgriffe gebraucht werden können, um politische Emanzipation zu erreichen, gibt es eine erste Korrelation zwischen all diesen unterschiedlichen Texten, eine Korrelation, die so eng ist, dass gleichsam eine »These« aus all diesen Manifesten und Bekenntnissen extrahiert werden kann. Eine solche »These« ist uns allerdings nur in der je milieuspezifischen Ausformulierung greifbar, die sie in den einzelnen Gruppenzusammenhängen erfahren hat. Diese Spannung zwischen augenfälliger Wiederholung des immer Ähnlichen und der je partikularen Ausformulierung ist – wie Vladímir Propp aufgezeigt hat – für Narrationen überhaupt kennzeichnend: Die einzelnen Teile einer Erzählung dienen als »Funktionen« der narrativen Struktur als Ganzes; und zugleich kann das Ganze nur unter Bezugnahme auf diese Partikularitäten konstruiert werden.[10] Diese Spannung zwischen dem Allgemeinen dessen, was man »avantgardistisches Narrativ« nennen könnte und seiner je milieuspezifischen partikularen Ausformulierung, wird in der Analyse also nicht in eine Richtung hin aufgelöst werden können, sondern produktiv in Schwebe gehalten werden müssen.
Im folgenden werde ich eine ganze Reihe weiterer Konnotationslinien zwischen diesen Texten unterschiedlicher Avantgarde-Bewegungen aufzeigen und dafür Text-Beispiele aus dem Umfeld der russischen Revolutionskunst, des Dadaismus, des Surrealismus, des *Expanded Cinema* und neo-avantgardistischer Bewegungen im Serbien der 90er Jahre heranziehen. Dabei geht es mir nicht darum, aus all diesen Texten eine einzige Erzählung bzw. – damit zusammenhängend – einen einzigen Sinn herauszufiltern, sondern indem Konnotationslinien[11] gezogen und Brüche aufgezeigt werden, wird Zugang zu einem »Dazwischen« geschaffen und die Spur eines gewissen Pluralen abgesteckt, das sich in diesen Texten äußert.

ZURÜCKWEISUNGEN UND NEU-AUFRICHTUNGEN

Im August 1922 verfassten die Mitglieder der russischen *Kinoki*-Gruppe eine Streitschrift mit dem Titel *Wir. Variante eines Manifestes*. In diesem Text wenden sich die Vertov-Brüder und Elizaveta Svilova gegen das, was sie als überkommene Kulturauffassung verstanden wissen wollten: »Wir säubern die Filmsache von allem, was sich einschleicht, von der Musik, der Literatur und dem Theater; wir suchen ihren nirgendwo gestohlenen Rhythmus und finden ihn in den Bewegungen der Dinge. Wir fordern auf: – Weg – von den süßdurchfeuchteten Romanzen, vom Gift des psychologischen Romans, aus den Fängen des Liebhabertheaters, mit dem Rücken zur Musik! – Weg – ins reine Feld, in den Raum der vier Dimensionen (drei + Zeit)! Auf zur Suche nach ihrem Material, ihrem Jambus, ihrem Rhythmus! Das ›Psychologische‹ stört den Menschen, so genau wie eine Stoppuhr zu sein, es hindert ihn in seinem Bestreben, sich mit der Maschine zu verschwägern.«[12] Film wird hier programmatisch von seinen Bezügen zu den eher traditionellen Künsten Musik, Literatur und Theater befreit. Letzere werden mit Verführung, Vergiftung und Betrug gleichgesetzt. Die Verbindung dieser traditionellen Kunstformen zum »Psychologischen« wird hervorgestrichen, dieses allerdings allein als Hindernis in Szene gesetzt. Zugleich weisen die russischen Revolutionskünstler aber auch konkurrierende Kunstformen der Gegenwart als »bürgerlich« oder »ästhetizistisch« zurück. So schreibt Alexander Rodchenko 1915: »Yet I held the bourgeoisie in contempt and despised their favorite art as well as the aesthetes of the Association of Russian Artists and *Mir Iskusstva*.«[13]

Was durch die ständige Wiederholung zunächst ins Blickfeld gebracht wird, ist die diesen Texten eigene Geste der Zurückweisung überkommener und zeitgenössisch konkurrierender Kunstformen – weniger die immer unterschiedlichen Qualitäten, die hier zurückgewiesen werden, auf die ich erst später zu sprechen kommen werde. Denn eine ähnliche Geste der Zurückweisung findet sich auch in den Texten der Surrealisten und Dadaisten. Diese bestreiten mit ihrer Praxis einer »Kunst als Verfahren« ebenfalls lineare Formen der Narration oder sogenannte »naturalistische« Formen der bildlichen Darstellung, die sie als »gestrig«, »ästhetizistisch«, »konformistisch« bzw. »bürgerlich-ideologisch« oder »kapitalistisch« bezeichnen: »Wir leben dem Unsicheren« heißt es beispielsweise in einem *Pamphlet gegen die Weimarische Lebensauffassung* aus dem Jahr 1919, »wir wollen nicht Wert und Sinn, die dem Bourgeois schmeicheln – wir wollen Unwert und Unsinn! Wir empören uns gegen die Verbindlichkeiten des Potsdam-Weimar, sie sind nicht für uns geschaffen. Wir wollen Alles selbst schaffen – unsere neue Welt!«[14] Zugleich wenden sich die Dadaisten mit ihren ästhetischen Verfahren ebenfalls gegen zeitgenössische andere, sich als »oppositionell« verstehende Formen der Narration – etwa die des Realismus, die von den zeitgenössischen kommunistischen und sozialistischen Bewegungen forciert werden.[15] Hier verläuft eine Konnotationslinie zu den Programmschriften des Wiener *Expanded Cinema*, wo ebenfalls gegen eine »affirmative Kunst«[16] argumentiert wird. Die Aktionen richten sich dabei insbesondere gegen die Verschränkung von Kunst mit einer »bürgerlich-idealistischen Philosophie …, deren Seelen- & Gedankenfreiheit die gesellschaftliche Unfreiheit verdeckt, deren formaler & inhaltlicher Humanismus einen konkreten & äußeren aufhebt und negiert.«[17] Und noch die Neoavantgarde-Bewegungen in den Gebieten des ehemaligen Yugoslawiens bekämpfen eine gesellschaftliche und ästhetische Dominanz. So hat die Gruppe *Otpor!* seit 1989 an Demonstrationen in Belgrad mit Flugblättern teilgenommen, auf denen »Bite the system« zu lesen stand und öffentliche Performances organisiert wie »I am Alexander the Great, and who are you«, »National-Hero-Decoration« or »The Commodity Reserves of Serbia«. Auf diese Weise forderten sie beispielsweise in der Programmschrift *Decisions of Otpor! Congress*, alle politischen Faktoren Serbiens – jene an der Macht und jene in der Opposition – auf: »Get real!«[18]

In all diesen Texten wird Zurückweisung mit Begriffen wie »wir säubern«, »wir fordern auf: – Weg –«, »I ... despised«, »wir wollen nicht«, »wir empören uns gegen ...«, »Leben wir auf eigene Kosten«, »muß destruiert werden«, »zertümmern«, »soll ... attackiert werden«, »Bite the system«, »calls for« etc. ausgeübt. Mit diesen Vokabeln der Zurückweisung sind all diese Gruppen jedoch an die jeweils angesprochenen, attackierten herrschenden Konformismen und anderen Optionen für die Gegenwart auch gebunden. Diese Gruppen benötigen dominante und alternative Ästhetiken, um sich in ihrer Bestreitung selbst aufrichten und ein je anders bestimmtes »Neues« befreien zu können. Zugleich sind sie angewiesen auf das Publikum dieser Kunstformen bzw. auf Vertreter und Vertreterinnen dieser Ideologien und auf Bewohner und Bewohnerinnen dieser Gesellschaftssysteme, um diese irritieren, aufklären oder anderweitig didaktisch »bearbeiten« zu können. In diesem Sinn ist die Avantgarde »eine Familienangelegenheit« und transportiert, wie alle Familienangelegenheiten, »eine eingeschränkte Aggressivität«.[19]

Jerome Bruner hat in seiner Untersuchung erzählerischer Realitätskonstruktionen herausgearbeitet, dass eine solche Verletzung des Kanons ganz generell ein zentrales Merkmal der Narration ist.[20] Denn nicht jede Sequenz von Ereignissen konstituiert gleichsam automatisch eine Narration – ganz im Gegenteil: Um wert zu sein, erzählt zu werden, muss eine Geschichte sich darum ranken, wie ein Kanon zerstört oder zumindest verändert wird. Nur durch solche Verletzungen – seien sie nun linguistischer Art oder geschehen sie durch ein plötzlich hereinbrechendes Ereignis im Plot – entstehen ästhetische Innovationen, die dann unsere narrativen Versionen alltäglicher Realität verändern. All die oben genannten Erzählungen zehren von solchen Zurückweisungen und Zerstörungen, wobei das, was zurückgewiesen wird, immer neu und anders bestimmt ist: die russischen Revolutionskünstler wenden sich gegen einen psychologischen Naturalismus der traditionellen Künste, die Dadaisten gegen Kapitalismus und Kommunismus, das *Expanded Cinema* gegen das Bürgertum und seine Wahrnehmungsapparate und die Neo-Avantgarde-Gruppen in Serbien gegen »das System«. Die erfinderischen Erzählungen der Avantgarde konstituieren sich demnach – wie Narrative überhaupt – vor allem, indem sie die Narrationen der Tradition und von konkurrierenden Gruppen der Gegenwart problematisieren, deren Legitimität in Frage stellen und das Publikum mit neuen Ansprüchen konfrontieren.

Die bisher verwendeten Textbruchstücke haben demonstriert, dass – auch wenn diese Avantgarde-Bewegungen traditionelle narrativ konstruierte Weltsichten bekämpfen – sie ihre Erlebnisse, Erinnerungen und Zukunftsvorstellungen dennoch wiederum in Form von neuen Narrativen organisieren – Geschichten, Entschuldigungen, Mythen, Utopien, Begründungen, warum so und nicht anders gehandelt wird, oder warum das bzw. jenes abgelehnt wird. Ihre Manifeste, Fotos von ihren Aktionen, Geschichten, Relikte und in Museen ausgestellte Kunstwerke haben an der narrativen Konstruktion einer je »neuen Realität« teil.[21] Diese »neue Realität« soll jedoch nicht – und das verbindet all diese Gruppen so eng miteinander – als ein »Ganzes« formuliert vorgelegt, sondern durch eine auf das abgelehnte Überkommene bzw. Gegenwärtige gerichtete »Störungsarbeit« hindurch erahnbar werden.

Wie jedoch dasjenige, was die einzelnen Gruppen zurückweisen, stets anders bestimmt ist, so wird auch die zu erreichende »neue Welt« immer neu definiert und erscheint von höchst unterschiedlichen Qualitäten gekennzeichnet. Bei den russischen Revolutionskünstlern ist es »das Offene«, »der vierdimensionale Raum«, »das eigene Material, Maß und der eigene Rhythmus«, ein »Präzise-Sein wie eine Stoppuhr« und ein »Begehren der Ähnlichkeit mit der Maschine«; die Dadaisten erstreben eine mit »geistigen Machtmitteln« vollkommen »selbst geschaffene Neue Welt«; das *Expanded Cinema* intendiert eine »Perzeption neuer Relationen« und eine »befreite Sinnlichkeit«; und die neo-avantgardistischen Gruppen in Ex-Yugoslawien peilen ein mittels »kritischer Kommunikation«[22] erreichtes friedliches, nicht-nationalistisches Zusammenleben an.

DER MODUS OPERANDI DES ERZÄHLENS WIRD ZUR DISPOSITION GESTELLT

Auch wenn die Verletzung eines Kanons ganz generell Merkmal von Narrationen ist, so haben die in diesem Beitrag untersuchten Narrationen der Avantgarde darüber hinaus gemeinsam, dass in ihnen der Modus Operandi des Erzählens zur Disposition gestellt wird. In all den in diesem Text angesprochenen Narrativen wird nicht mehr nur eine Verletzung der Fabula, also im Plot der Erzählung, in Szene gesetzt, sondern die Art und Weise, wie wir dazu kommen, Realität zu konstruieren und zu verstehen, wird problematisiert.[23] Als zentrales Mittel der Zurückweisung überkommener und konkurrierender Kunstformen werden von all diesen Gruppen Kunstgriffe genannt, welche die Form des Erzählens verändern würden. Alexander Rodchenko etwa macht den Kunstgriff der Verfremdung für eine »Revolution in den Augen«[24] verantwortlich, die Dadaisten setzen auf die Montage als »radikale neufilmtechnische An- und Raumordnung«[25] und die

Surrealisten auf einen »psychischen Automatismus, durch den man mündlich oder schriftlich oder auf jede andere Weise den wirklichen Ablauf des Denkens auszudrücken sucht«[26] sowie auf Collagen und Assemblagen[27]. Das *Expanded Cinema* forciert dagegen vor allem Verfahren der Destruktion, der Parodie und der »Zertrümmerung«: »Der tradierte Apperzeptionsapparat muß destruiert werden, damit die Perzeption neuer Relationen möglich werde. Die Begriffe zertrümmern, um die Sinnlichkeit zu befreien.«[28] Und die Studentin Milja Janovich beschreibt die parodistische ästhetische Taktik von *Otpor!* in einem 1999 geführten Interview folgendermaßen: »Wir können machen, was keine Organisation und keine Partei tun kann, die subversive Karte ausspielen, sprayen gehen und Farbeier auf JUL-Plakate-Wände schmeißen. ... An Milosevics Geburtstag am 20. August werden wir ein kleines Happening veranstalten, ihm symbolisch ein Geschenk überreichen und parallel zur Kampagne der Sozialistischen Partei ›1 Dinar für die Ernte‹ ›1 Dinar für den Rücktritt‹ sammeln. ... Gleichzeitig organisieren wir schon seit längerem eine Happeningreihe. Der Arbeitstitel lautet ›Vampire vertreiben‹. Wir geben den Termin immer einen Tag vorher bekannt, und es kommen die unterschiedlichsten Leute. Sie sprechen sehr offen und sagen zum Teil überraschende Sachen. Manchmal bleibt mir der Mund offen stehen.«[29]
Verfremdung, psychischer Automatismus des Schreibens, Assemblagen, Collagen, Zertrümmerung, Parodie werden hier als Verfahren genannt, mit deren Hilfe gewohnte Formen des öffentlichen Sich-Austauschens – der Wahrnehmung, der Selbstdarstellung, des Erzählens, des Abbildens und künstlerischen Formens überhaupt – problematisiert werden können. Von einer solchen Problematisierung erwartet man sich dann eine soziale und politische »Revolution« (Rodchenko), eine »Befreiung der Imagination« (die Surrealisten), eine »Perzeption neuer Relationen« und eine »Befreiung der Sinnlichkeit« (das *Expanded Cinema*) sowie ein »offenes Sprechen« und »überraschende Aussagen« (*Otpor!*).

IM NETZ EINER WAHRNEHMUNGSGESCHICHTE DES 20. JAHRHUNDERTS

Diese Problematisierung des Modus Operandi des Erzählens kann selbst als Indiz historischer Umbrüche gelesen werden, was zeigt, dass Narrationen Realität nicht nur repräsentieren, sondern auch konstituieren. So stellen beispielsweise nicht nur die Dadaisten und Surrealisten in ihren Manifesten eine sogenannte Krise des Erzählens und der Wahrnehmung fest, sondern auch der Kulturkritiker Walter Benjamin spricht von einer »Krisis des Romans«,[30] die er mit dem Sich-Formieren des klassischen Hollywoodkinos und den nun neu aufkommenden Medien Fotografie und Film ebenso in Zusammenhang bringt wie mit den neuen Formen der Arbeitsorganisation und den neuen Transportmitteln. Und von einer Aufwertung des Sehens und einer Hinwendung zur Sichtbarkeit und den Dingen in der Welt zeugen nicht nur die Texte der russischen Revolutionskünstler und der Dadaisten,[31] sondern auch die Texte Rilkes und die Analysen des Soziologen Georg Simmel[32] stellen Ähnliches fest. So beschreibt ersterer beispielsweise das Wahrnehmungregime moderner Großstädte folgendermaßen: »Ich lerne sehen. Ich weiss nicht, woran es liegt, es geht alles tiefer in mich ein und bleibt nicht an der Stelle stehen, wo es sonst immer zu Ende war ... Habe ich es schon gesagt? Ich lerne sehen. Ja, ich fange an. Es geht noch schlecht. Aber ich will meine Zeit ausnutzen.«[33] Konnotationslinen können also nicht nur zwischen den Narrationen der verschiedenen Avantgarde-Bewegungen des 20. Jahrhunderts gezogen werden – sie verlaufen auch zu anderen, nicht weniger »klassischen« Texten der Moderne. All diese Korrelationen in den Problematisierungen der Form der Erzählung, von Wahrnehmung und von Sehen zeugen davon, dass die hier untersuchten Avantgarde-Bewegungen zugleich Ausdruck wie auch Agenten eines sich veränderten Perzeptionsapparates sind.

Dies verweist darauf, dass die avantgardistischen Narrative zum einen deshalb »erfolgreich« waren und Faszinationsgeschichten nach sich gezogen haben, weil sie die Zwangslagen und Zustände des Individuums in der Moderne offenbar in einer Weise dargestellt haben, die Menschen angeregt hat, ihr Leben in ähnlicher Weise zu erfahren. Die provokanten und innovativen Formen der avantgardistischen Narrationen haben ihre Rezipienten offenbar disponiert, ihre Sensibilitäten und ihren Wahrnehmungsapparat in einer bestimmten Weise zu gebrauchen.[34]

Die auffällige Permanenz der Umschreibung der »Politik-der-Form-These« in Moderne und Postmoderne kann demnach aus einer Geschichte der Wahrnehmung seit dem 19. Jahrhundert heraus erklärt werden. Mit dieser historischen Einbettung knüpfe ich an kulturwissenschaftliche Untersuchungen wie diejenigen von Jonathan Crary an, der eine Fülle von Korrelationen unterschiedlicher Diskurse der Moderne – der Medizin, der Optik, der Physik und jener der literarischen und künstlerischen Kommunikationsformen – hinsichtlich Sehen und Wahrnehmen rekonstruiert hat. Mit dieser Archäologie der Wahrnehmung konnte Crary[35] zeigen, dass das Wahrnehmungsregime der Moderne von einem radikalen Bruch gegenüber früheren Techniken des Betrachters gekennzeichnet sind, wie sie beispielsweise für die Camera Obscura typisch waren. Der Bruch hin zur Moderne betrifft demnach das Erscheinungsbild von Kunstwerken genauso wie das Wissen und die Erkenntnis bezüglich des Sehens und der sozialen Praktiken. All dies strukturiert die produktiven und kognitiven Fähigkeiten des Menschen und seine Bedürfnisstruktur auf vielfältige Weise neu.

Es entsteht eine ganz bestimmte Formung der Wahrnehmung und der Ausrichtung von Aufmerksamkeit, die für die Moderne charakteristisch geworden ist:[36] Der Blick ist gegenüber allem Sichtbaren aufmerksam, gleichzeitig zerstreut und auf Details fixiert. Dieses nun aufgewertete Sehen ist zugleich von einer neuartigen Ereignishaftigkeit gekennzeichnet, d. h. mit einem »intensiven« und uns oft selbst »überraschenden« Sehen wird nun dem Vergänglichen des Wirklichen und einer zunehmenden Ferne des Realen entgegengetreten. Und umgekehrt wird durch dieses »intensive Sehen« die Bedeutsamkeit von Anschaulichkeit und Gegenständlichkeit wiederum bestätigt. Diese Aktivität des Auges in der Moderne ist dabei auch in einer veränderten Weise mit »Glauben« verbunden: Dieser bezieht sich nun allerdings nicht mehr auf einen Gott außerhalb der Welt, sondern auf die greifbaren Dinge in der Welt. Etwas hat jetzt sichtbar, zeigbar und im Licht des Tages angesiedelt zu sein, um uns gläubig zu stimmen und in Bewegung zu versetzen.

Avantgardistische Bewegungen reagieren auf diese Verschiebungen im Bereich von Wahrnehmung, Glauben und Selbstdarstellung und treiben einen solchen Bruch selbst mit voran, indem sie mit den so aufgewerteten »sichtbaren« Formen und/oder Ereignissen der Wahrnehmung auf ihre je eigene Weise Politik machen. Gruppen wie die Dadaisten, aber auch das *Expanded Cinema*[37] nutzen die veränderten Wahrnehmungskonstellationen der Moderne demnach mit einer utopistischen Sensibilität und mit Engagement für das Erreichen einer »neuen«, d. h. »besseren« und »befreiteren« Gesellschaft. Zugleich gibt es im Kontext der modernen Metropolen vielfältige andere Institutionen und soziale Kräfte, die versuchen, diese Wahrnehmungskonstellationen zu nutzen, sie zu kalkulieren und zu beherrschen und in Unternehmens- und Erziehungsstrategien einzubinden.

Die Narrationen der avantgardistischen Gruppen sind notwendiges und zentrales Instrument für solche Verhandlungen, da – wie Jerome Bruner herausstreicht – Narrationen eine spezifische Kontext-Sensitivität aufweisen, die es ihnen ermöglicht, effektiv die Kohärenz und Abhängigkeit einer »Kultur« mit zu konstituieren. Denn Narrationen enthalten Bezüge zu den Hintergrund-Wissens-Feldern der Rezipienten genauso, wie sie Ignoranz, Zweifel, Nächstenliebe und Annahmen von Relevanz in Rechnung stellen oder wie sie versuchen müssen, den Kriterien von Konsistenz und Verifikation zu genügen, und all diese Merkmale machen sie so besonders geeignet für kulturelle Verhandlungen. Die Avantgarde-Gruppen treten über solche Erzählungen mit den unterschiedlichsten Institutionen und Kräften – der Werbung, der Hollywoodfilmindustrie, den Erziehungsdiskursen der Schulen und Universitäten, verschiedenen Kunstrichtungen etc. – in Auseinandersetzung um gesellschaftliche Dominanz, wobei es in diesem Streit immer auch um eine ästhetische Dominanz bzw. Marginalisierung geht.

Auch neo-avantgardistische Gruppen wie *Otpor!* oder *SKART* können innerhalb einer solchen Wahrnehmungsgeschichte[38] verortet werden. Ihre ästhetischen Praktiken legen wie das Internet, das nun dasjenige Medium ist, auf das sich diese Gruppen zentral beziehen, Zeugnis ab von weiteren Wahrnehmungsverschiebungen und sind zugleich ebenso wieder deren Agenten: *SKART* und *Otpor!* veröffentlichen ihre Aufrufe im Internet, gestalten parodistische Web-Pages, stellen dort ein Archiv mit Kommentaren zu und Berichterstattungen von ihren Aktionen zur Verfügung und verteilen über e-mail Informationen an Interessierte in der ganzen Welt. Die Internet-Projekte von Gruppen wie *SKART* oder *Otpor!*[39] sind jedoch nicht isoliert zu sehen, sondern stehen in einem Verbund mit der Nutzung einer Vielzahl von Medien gleichzeitig – etwa Telefon, Radio und Fernsehen, Computer, Werbung und Live-Auftritten. All diese über die verschiedenen Medien vermittelten Eingriffe definieren nun ebenfalls wieder – wie Film, Fotografie und veränderte Arbeitsbedingungen zur Jahrhundertwende – die Beziehung von Menschen und Information auf neue Weise: »Electronic remote monitoring and summoning technologies widen the range of options, change the payoffs and dangers, and require us to rethink our architectural and legal mechanisms for getting the balance right.«[40] Sichtbarkeit und Präsenz im öffentlichen Raum ist nun zum Beispiel nicht mehr nur ausschließlich auf die physische Präsenz einer Menschenmenge angewiesen, sondern kann jetzt zudem über e-mail und Internet erzeugt werden. Zugleich werden die traditionellen Foren der Äußerung von Staatsbürgerschaftsrechten und von Öffentlichkeit durch die neuen Medien auch in ihrer Bedeutsamkeit reduziert. Innerhalb dieses sich transformierenden Wahrnehmungskontextes treten *SKART* und *Otpor!* mit Parodien und ironischen Kommentaren wieder in eine Verhandlung mit anderen Kräften und ästhetischen Sprachen ein, die im Kontext Belgrads der 90er Jahre die Wahrnehmung der Menschen nun ebenfalls auf neue Weise beanspruchen. Sie streiten damit etwa gegen die im Fernsehen nun omnipräsenten »Turbofolk-Queens« und ihre nationalistischen Songs, gegen die JUL-Plakate und gegen Ethno-Nationalismus in Form von Nachrichten, CDs, T-Shirts oder Konzerten.

DAS UNERNSTE UND DIE GEWÖHNLICHE SPRACHE

Die genannten Avantgarde-Bewegungen wenden sich in ihren narrativen Konstruktionen an ein Gegenüber: an ein »du« bzw. an ein »ihr« und zwar mit dem Anspruch, auf diese Adressaten einwirken zu können – entweder durch Verführung und Einladung oder durch Hinterfragung und Erschütterung, durch die Gewalt des Zertrümmerns, durch Aufrufe und Forderungen. Ganz deutlich kommt ein solcher didaktischer Anspruch in folgendem

Text von Lázló Moholy-Nagy zum Ausdruck: »We, who today have become one with the necessity and condition of class-struggle in all respects, do not think it important that a person should find enjoyment in a picture, in music, or in poetry. The primary requirement is that those who have not yet reached the contemporary standard of mankind should be enabled to do so as soon as possible through our work.«[41] Und selbst die Surrealisten bekennen sich in ihrem zweiten Manifest in einer Art Resümee der Ziele der Bewegung zu einem solchen didaktischen Anspruch: »Wird man letztlich doch zugestehen müssen, dass er (der Surrealismus, A.S.) nichts so sehr erstrebte, als in intellektueller und moralischer Hinsicht eine Bewußtseinskrise allgemeinster und schwerwiegendster Art auszulösen.«[42] Auf ähnliche Weise haben dann auch die Aktivisten und Aktivistinnen des *Expanded Cinema* ihre Verfahren ausführlich in Texten, Manifesten und Interviews didaktisch begründet. Gottfried Schlemmer hat Anfang der 70er Jahre als Programm formuliert: »Einem produktionsorientierten System mit seinen Kaufs- und Verkaufszwängen soll in einer ›Gegengesellschaft‹ – mit in freier Organisation entstehenden neuen Produktions- und Distributionsformen – subversiv begegnet werden.«[43] Valie Export hat die Aktion *Tapp & Tastkino* selbst in den Jahren ihrer Durchführung folgendermaßen beschrieben: »tapp und tastfilm ist ein beispiel für die aktivierung des publikums qua neue interpretation, taktile statt visuelle kommunikation. ... die sinne werden befreit und dieser prozess läßt sich in keiner weise in die staatlichen regeln integrieren. denn er führt zur direkten befreiung der sexualität.«[44] Und *ŠKART* inszeniert die Bezugnahme auf die klassische Avantgarde nicht nur durch in Schaufenstern plazierte kleine Drucker-Pressen-Plakate auf recyceltem Papier im 20er-Jahre-Stil, mit »alt« aussehenden Survival-Coupons auf denen statt »Mehl« oder »Zucker« allerdings »fear« und »masturbacija« geschrieben stand, sondern auch in didaktisch ausgerichteten Slogans wie »kritische Kommunikation.«

In all diesen Zitaten wird eine Kausalität angenommen zwischen einer ästhetischen Intervention – in Form der Verfremdung, der Parodie, des Brüchig-Machens – einerseits und einem erzielten Ergebnis auf einer politisch-ideologischen Ebene andererseits. Diese mehr oder weniger ausführliche Begründung eines solchen didaktischen Anspruchs stellt eine weitere augenfällige Korrelation zwischen all diesen unterschiedlichen Narrationen avantgardistischer Gruppen dar. Dabei steht einer solchen in den Texten behaupteten Kausalität ganz offensichtlich die Schwierigkeit entgegen, die Effekte der eigenen avantgardistischen Verfahren wirklich kontrollieren zu können. Denn die in den Manifesten, Begleit-Texten und Interviews mehr oder weniger vehement artikulierte Intention kann die den Aktionen innewohnenden Handlungen und Äußerungen nicht so vollständig beherrschen, wie die darüber verbreiteten Erzählungen uns glauben machen

möchten. Die ästhetischen Interventionen dieser Gruppen sind demnach »performative Akte«, wie Jacques Derrida sie versteht, d. h. Kommunikationsakte, was die Mitteilung einer ursprünglichen Bewegung, eine Operation und das Hervorrufen einer Wirkung impliziert und nicht die Beförderung oder Übermittlung eines Bedeutungsinhaltes.[45] Diese ästhetischen Interventionen haben ihren Referenten außerhalb ihrer selbst, vor sich, sich gegenüber. All diese ästhetische Taktiken können demnach als »zwiespältig« bezeichnet werden, d. h. auch wenn sie von bestimmten narrativ erzeugten Utopien und Mythen geleitet und darauf ausgerichtet sind, anderen, ebenfalls narrativ erzeugten Mythen und Ideologien zu widersprechen, so entziehen sie sich der Kontrolle der Subjekte und gehen für alle unerwartete Verknüpfungen auf ideologischer Ebene, »Artikulationen« genannt, ein. Es gibt keine a priori Garantie dafür, dass diese Artikulationen eine bestimmte Gestalt annehmen werden: die einer »Bewußtseinskrise«, »einer sozialisierung von sexualität« oder eines »kritischen Bewußtseins«.
Wenn, wie Derrida nahelegt, jede Intervention zu solchen kontingenten Artikulationen führt, was macht dann aber noch einen Unterschied aus zwischen den Interventionen der Avantgarde und anderen, alltäglicheren Interventionen? Worauf bezieht sich das in den Narrationen so vehement geäußerte Beharren auf einer Möglichkeit der didaktischen Einwirkung bzw. der Parodie und des Brüchig-Machens? Zur Klärung dieser Fragen schlage ich vor, einen Begriff von »Parodie« und »Ironie« zu verwenden, den Paul de Man geprägt hat. Dieser versteht unter »Ironie« eben nicht ein Konzept, sondern genau dasjenige, was jeder Definition, jedem Versuch, es sprachlich zu fassen, entgleitet: Gerade das Erklären der Ironie zu einem Konzept war einer derjenigen Kunstgriffe mit der sie entschärft worden ist.[46] Ironie kann demnach zwar als eine »Unterbrechung« der narrativen Illusion beschrieben werden – ähnlich dem »buffo« der Comedia del'Arte, wo das Anwesend-Sein des Publikums die narrative Illusion bricht – ist zugleich aber immer schon eine permanent mögliche Unterbrechung der Kohärenz und Systematik von Erzählung. Das Unernste ist also immer schon eine Möglichkeit der gewöhnlichen Sprache, es lässt sich nicht an einem gesellschaftlichen Ort festbinden, sondern taucht unter Umständen und überraschend auf, verweist auf ein Jenseits von Bedeutung und setzt Zweifel an den Möglichkeiten des Verstehens in Gang.
Diese Möglichkeit des ästhetischen Eingreifens in das Wahrnehmungsgefüge verwandeln die Avantgarde-Gruppen in ihren Narrationen in eine Gewissheit. Eine der Verführungsstrategien avantgardistischer Narrative scheint darin zu bestehen, die Unkontrollierbarkeit der eigenen Verfahren und Handlungen zu überspielen und sich in den um solche Interventionen herum erfundenen Erzählungen und Geschichten als schon dort angelangt zu zeigen – in der Befreiung, in der Aufklärung, im Bruch, in der Dekon-

struktion, im Unsinn – wohin man mit den eigenen Verfahren doch offenbar erst gelangen möchte.

UM-ORDNUNGEN VON MASKULINITÄT UND VON WEIBLICHKEIT

Die ästhetischen Verfahren der Avantgarde produzieren und verwandeln eine Situation – kurz: Sie wirken. Deshalb ist die Positionierung des Rezipienten bzw. der Rezipientin eines solchen ästhetischen Eingriffs immer schon eine plurale: diese/r kann zugleich Flaneur/Flaneuse, Konsument/Konsumentin, Angestellter/Angestellte, Kunstliebhaber/Kunstliebhaberin, begehrender Mann/begehrende Frau sein – welche dieser Positionen mit der Aktion korreliert, kann nicht vorab festgelegt werden und meistens sind es zugleich mehrere Positionen, die in die Rezeption involviert sind. Das Ensemble dieser Positionen kann demnach nicht vereinheitlicht werden, sondern die Beziehungen zwischen diesen Positionen werden zu einer offenen Artikulation. Dies zeigt sich beispielsweise, wenn man die ästhetischen Aktionen der Avantgarde-Bewegungen in Hinblick auf ihre Geschlechter-Inszenierungen befragt. Die Aktivisten und Aktivistinnen der Avantgarde bringen Aufrufe wie »Geben sie die Geschlechtsromantik auf«[47] und Analysen wie die folgende in Umlauf: »indem ein busen nicht mehr das eigentum des mannes ist, sondern die frau selbständig über ihn verfügt, wird die moralität der staatlichen vorschriften (staat, familie, eigentum) durchbrochen.«[48] Damit sind diese Gruppen insbesondere seit den 60er Jahren des 20. Jahrhunderts angetreten, eine Neu-Ordnung in die bezüglich der Geschlechter-Hierarchien immer schon in Unordnung geratene Welt der Moderne (bzw. der Postmoderne) zu bringen. Die Surrealisten haben dem Publikum nackte Frauenpuppen zu sehen gegeben, den Frauenakt in Collagen integriert bzw. ihm psychologische Betrachtungen gewidmet. Und im *Expanded Cinema* wurde der nackte weibliche Frauenkörper nicht nur auf provokante Weise öffentlich sichtbar, sondern – etwa in der Aktion TAPP UND TASTKINO – auch öffentlich berührbar gemacht. Diese Interventionen haben mit dem Zur-Schau-Stellen und Anfassbar-Machen des nackten Frauenkörpers einen Tabubruch in Szene gesetzt. Zugleich bleiben diese Interventionen zwiespältig und haben als solche eine dichotome Struktur affirmiert, in der »Weiblichkeit« mit Sinnlichkeit, Nacktheit, Buntheit und Sexualität verbunden und einer »Männlichkeit« gegenübergestellt ist, die in diskrete, graue Schutzmasken – Anzüge, die ein komplexes, reiches und unternehmerisches »Inneres« bewachen – gehüllten erscheint. Und die mit Androgynität spielenden Produktionen der Dadaisten haben eine neuartige Auftrittsweise der Geschlechter mitinitiiert, die von Philippe Ariès beispielsweise als »eingeschlechtliche Geseschaft«, die sich an »Männlichkeit« orientiert, bezeichnet worden ist.[49] Die Inszenierung der Geschlechter, die von avantgardistischen Bewegungen vorgenommen wird, ist demnach nicht ausschließlich »anders«, wie (von ihnen selbst und anderen) oft behauptet wird, sondern vor allem hier gibt es vielfältige Artikulationen und unter Umständen auch Zustimmungen zu den Geschlechter-Bildern jener Kulturen, gegen die sich die avantgardistischen Praktiken so vehement wenden. Aus diesem Grund zieht beispielsweise Susan Rubin Suleiman[50] in ihrer Untersuchung des Verhältnisses von Gender, Politik und Avant-garde den Schluss, dass die Subjektposition des Surrealismus in hohem Grad eine »männliche« sei. Dieser Schluss ist jedoch insofern zu hinterfragen, als damit in ihrer Untersuchung die mögliche Pluralität von Lese-Ereignissen und kontingenten Artikulationen ebenfalls auf eine einzige Lesart – »die Subjektposition des Surrealismus ist eine männliche« – festgeschrieben wird. Gegen ein solches Vergessen-Machen der Zwiespältigkeit dieser Aktionen kann darauf verwiesen werden, dass diese ästhetischen Eingriffe ein endloses Potential für Manipulationen, Artikulationen, Phantasien und Projektionen von Seiten des männlichen und weiblichen Publikums bergen. Für die diesbezüglich vonstatten gehenden Artikulationen steht eine genauere Untersuchung jedoch noch aus.

ANMERKUNGEN

Dieser Artikel stellt eine erste Formulierung von Überlegungen und Teilergebnissen eines größeren Forschungsprojektes dar, das derzeit vom ›FWF. Der Wissenschaftsfonds‹ gefördert wird. Ich möchte mich hiermit beim FWF für die Finanzierung bedanken, bei meinem Kollegen Vrääth Öhner sowie bei den Mitwirkenden an der Graduiertenkonferenz ›Narrationen im medialen Wandel‹ 2002 für die anregenden Diskussionen zum Thema.

1 Serge Daney, Das Travelling des Kapo, in: Ders., Im Verborgenen. Kino – Reisen – Kritik, Wien 2000, S. 37

2 Alexander Rodchenko, Downright Ignorance or a Mean Trick, in: Novyi Lef Nr. 6 (1928). Zitiert nach: Victor Margolin, Struggle for Utopia: Rodchenko. Lissitzky. Moholy-Nagy. 1917-1946, Chicago und London 1997, S. 133

3 Bezeichnet als »radikale neufilmtechnische An- und Raumordnung«. Zitiert nach: John Heartfield, Ein wiederentdeckter Brief über expressionistische Filmpläne, in: kintop 8. Film und Projektionskunst (Hrsg. Kessler/Lenk/Loiperdinger), Frankfurt a. M. 1999, S. 174

4 Richard Huelsenbeck, Das dadaistische Manifest, zitiert nach: Raoul Hausmann, Am Anfang war Dada (Hrsg. Riha/Kämpf), Steinbach bei Gießen 1972, S. 24

5 Erstes Manifest des Surrealismus (1924), in: André Breton, Die Manifeste des Surrealismus, Reinbek bei Hamburg 1996 (1962), S. 38

6 Peter Weibel, Kritik der Kunst. Kunst der Kritik, Wien und München 1973, S. 37f.

[7] Jasmina Cubrillo, *ŠKART*-Group, unveröffentlichtes Manuskript 2001

[8] Jerome Bruner, The Narrative Construction of Reality, in: Critical Inquiry Nr. 18, Herbst 1991, S. 4

[9] Unter dem »Politischen« verstehe ich jenen Moment der Offenheit und Unentscheidbarkeit, der dann vorhanden ist, wenn Strukturprinzipien der Gesellschaft in Frage gestellt werden; »Politik« dagegen ist ein separater sozialer Komplex, der diese prekäre Logik des Politischen verhandeln muss. Dazu: Ernesto Laclau, New Reflections on the Revolution of Our Time, London und New York 1990, S. 68ff.

[10] Vladímir Propp, Morphologie des Märchens (Hrsg. Karl Eimermacher), Frankfurt a. M. 1975 (1969), insbes. S. 12ff.

[11] Die Konnotation ist, so Roland Barthes, Grundlage dessen, was er als »lesbaren Text« bezeichnet: Sie ist das Konventionelle, gut Bekannte am Text, das in Einklang mit dem Kanon steht. Roland Barthes, S/Z, Frankfurt a. M. 1987 (1970), insbes. S. 12

[12] Wir. Variante eines Manifestes (1922), in: Texte zur Theorie des Films (Hrsg. Franz-Josef Albesmaier), Stuttgart 1973, S. 20

[13] Alexander Rodchenko, zitiert nach: German Karginov, Rodchenko, London 1986, S. 13

[14] Zitiert nach: op. cit., Anm. 4 , S. 77

[15] »Der Kommunismus ist die Bergpredigt, praktisch organisiert, er ist eine Religion der ökonomischen Gerechtigkeit, ein schöner Wahnsinn. Der Demokrat aber ist gar nicht wahnsinnig, er möchte leben auf Heller und Pfenning. Immerhin ist Wahnsinn schöner als blasse Vernunft, doch seien wir alle wir selbst! Leben wir auf eigene Kosten!« Pamphlet gegen die Weimarische Lebensauffassung (1919) zitiert nach: op. cit., Anm. 4, S. 76

[16] Gottfried Schlemmer, Anmerkung zum Undergroundfilm, in: Avantgardistischer Film 1951-1971: Theorie (Hrsg. Ders.), München 1973, S. 18

[17] op. cit., Anm. 6, S. 37f.

[18] Decisions of Otpor! Congress, Belgrad, unveröffentlichtes Manuskript 1999

[19] Siehe: Roland Barthes, Das französische Avantgardetheater, in: Ders., »Ich habe das Theater immer sehr geliebt, und dennoch gehe ich fast nie mehr hin«, Berlin 2001, S. 253

[20] op. cit., Anm. 8, S. 11f.

[21] Vgl. Birgit Wagner, Auslöschen, vernichten, gründen, schaffen: zu den performativen Funktionen der Manifeste, in: »Die ganze Welt ist eine Manifestation«. Die europäische Avantgarde und ihre Manifeste (Hrsg. Asholt/ Fähnders), Darmstadt 1997, S. 39ff.

[22] »critical communication« lautet ein Slogan von *ŠKART*

[23] Die russischen Formalisten wie Tzvetan Todorov unterscheiden zwischen einem Plot der Erzählung, ihrer »Fabula«, und der Art und Weise, wie diese erzählt wird – was sie als »sjužet« bezeichnet haben. Siehe: Jerome Bruner, Actual Minds. Possible Worlds, Cambridge 1986

[24] op. cit., Anm. 2, S. 133

[25] op. cit., Anm. 3, S. 174

[26] op. cit., Anm. 5, S. 26

[27] op. cit., Anm. 5, S. 38

[28] op. cit., Anm. 6, S. 42

[29] Katja Diefenbacher, Belgrade Interviews. Gespräche und Texte, Berlin 2000, S. 153

[30] Walter Benjamin, Krisis des Romans. Zu Döblins ›Berlin Alexanderplatz‹, in: Ders., Angelus Novus. Ausgewählte Schriften Bd. 2, Frankfurt a. M. 1988, S. 437ff.
[31] »The objects receive a meaning, they become friends and comrades of humans and humans beginn to learn how to laugh, to rejoice and to converse with objects.« Alexander Rodchenko, zitiert nach: op. cit., Anm. 2, S. 10. »DADA ist das Schild der Abstraktion; Werbung und Geschäfte sind auch poetische Elemente.« Dada Manifest 1918, in: Tristan Tzara, Sieben Dada Manifeste, Hamburg 1979, S. 44
[32] »Die wechselseitige Beziehung der Menschen in den Großstädten ... zeichnet sich durch ein ausgesprochenes Übergewicht der Aktivität des Auges über die des Gehörs aus. Die Hauptursache davon sind die öffentlichen Verkehrsmittel. Vor der Entwicklung der Omnibusse, der Eisenbahnen, der Tramways im neunzehnten Jahrhundert waren die Leute nicht in die Lage gekommen, lange Minuten oder gar Stunden sich gegenseitig ansehen zu müssen, ohne aneinander das Wort zu richten.« Georg Simmel, zitiert nach: Walter Benjamin, Charles Baudelaire. Tableaux parisiens, in: Ders., Gesammelte Schriften, Bd. 10, Frankfurt a. M. 1980, S. 35f.
[33] Rainer Maria Rilke, Die Aufzeichnungen des Malte Laurids Brigge. Kommentierte Ausgabe, Stuttgart 1997 (1910), S. 8
[34] Nach Jerome Bruner sind narrative Genres nicht nur auf eine Konventionalisierung menschlicher Zustände spezialisiert, sondern stellen auch eine Art »Führer« bereit dafür, wie wir unser Gehirn benutzen sollen. Op. cit., Anm. 8, S. 14
[35] Jonathan Crary, Techniken des Betrachters. Sehen und Moderne im 19. Jahrhundert, Dresden und Basel 1996, insbes. S. 14f.
[36] Dazu siehe: Anna Schober, Blue Jeans. Vom Leben in Stoffen und Bildern, Frankfurt a. M. und New York 2001, S. 54f.
[37] Das *Expanded Cinema* wendet sich ganz programmatisch den »Foren der Sichtbarkeit«, den Kinos und der filmischen Repräsentation, zu.
[38] Zu den Wahrnehmungsverschiebungen in Zusammenhang mit den neuen Computermedien: William J. Mitchell, @-topia. »Urban Life, Jim-But Not As We Know It«, Cambridge/MA und London/GB 1999, S. 12ff. und S. 96ff.
[39] http://www.otpor.net/documents/090100.html (25.6.2002) Und: http.//www.skart.avalon.hr/skart.html (25.6.2002)
[40] op. cit., Anm. 38, S. 117
[41] László Moholy-Nagy, On the Problem of New Content and New Form, in: Krisztina Passuth, Moholy-Nagy, London 1985, S. 286ff.
[42] Zweites Manifest des Surrealismus 1930, in: André Breton, Die Manifeste des Surrealismus, Reinbek bei Hamburg 1986, S. 55
[43] op. cit., Anm. 16, S. 18
[44] Valie Export, TAPP UND TASTFILM, unveröffentl. Manuskript, o.O. o.J.
[45] Jacques Derrida, Signatur, Ereignis, Kontext, in: Ders., Randgänge der Philosophie, Wien 1999 (1972), S. 305
[46] Wie Ironie auch entschärft worden ist, indem man sie zu einem Kunstmittel erklärt hat, das den ästhetischen Apeal eines Werkes erhöht; indem man sie als eine Spiegelstruktur begriffen hat, in der das Selbst auf sich selbst von einer gewissen Distanz aus schaut oder indem man sie in einer Dialektik der Geschichte integriert hat. Siehe: Paul de Man, The Concept of Irony, in: Aesthetic Ideology. Paul de Man (Hrsg. Warminski), Minneapolis 1996, S. 163f.
[47] Raoul Hausmann, Der deutsche Spießer ärgert sich, in: DADA total. Manifeste, Aktionen, Texte, Bilder (Hrsg. Merte/Riha/Schäfer), Stuttgart 1994, S. 110
[48] op. cit. Anm. 44

[49] Philippe Ariès, Überlegungen zur Geschichte der Homosexualität, in: Die Masken des Begehrens und die Metamorphosen der Sinnlichkeit (Hrsg. Ariès/Béjin/Foucault), Frankfurt a. M. 1986, S. 82

[50] Susan Rubin Suleiman, Subversive Intent. Gender, Politics, and the Avant-Garde, Cambridge (Mass.)/London 1990, S. 20f.

BIBLIOGRAPHIE

Philippe Ariès, Überlegungen zur Geschichte der Homosexualität, in: Die Masken des Begehrens und die Metamorphosen der Sinnlichkeit (Hrsg. Ariès/Béjin/Foucault), Frankfurt a. M. 1986, 80-96

Roland Barthes, Das französische Avantgardetheater, in: Ders., »Ich habe das Theater immer sehr geliebt, und dennoch gehe ich fast nie mehr hin«, Berlin 2001, 253–264

Roland Barthes, S/Z, Frankfurt a. M. 1987 (1970), insbes. S. 12

Walter Benjamin, Charles Baudelaire. Tableaux parisiens, in: Ders., Gesammelte Schriften, Frankfurt a. M. 1980, Bd. 10, 7-64

Walter Benjamin, Krisis des Romans. Zu Döblins ›Berlin Alexanderplatz‹, in: Ders., Angelus Novus. Ausgewählte Schriften Bd. 2, Frankfurt a. M. 1988, 437-443

André Breton, Die Manifeste des Surrealismus, Reinbek bei Hamburg 1996 (1962)

Jerome Bruner, Actual Minds. Possible Worlds, Cambridge 1986

Jerome Bruner, The Narrative Construction of Reality, in: Critical Inquiry Nr. 18, Herbst 1991, 1-21

Jonathan Crary, Techniken des Betrachters. Sehen und Moderne im 19. Jahrhundert, Dresden und Basel 1996

Jasmina Cubrillo, *ŠKART*-Group, unveröffentlichtes Manuskript 2001

Dada Manifest 1918, in: Tristan Tzara, Sieben Dada Manifeste, Hamburg 1979, 35-60

Serge Daney, Im Verborgenen. Kino – Reisen – Kritik, Wien 2000

Decisions of Otpor! Congress, Belgrad, unveröffentlichtes Manuskript 1999

Jacques Derrida, Signatur, Ereignis, Kontext, in: Ders., Randgänge der Philosophie, Wien 1999 (1972), 291-314

Katja Diefenbacher, Belgrade Interviews. Gespräche und Texte, Berlin 2000

David Gillespie, Early Soviet Cinema. Innovation, Ideology and Propaganda, London 2000

Raoul Hausmann, Am Anfang war Dada (Hrsg. Riha/Kämpf), Steinbach bei Gießen 1972

Raoul Hausmann, Der deutsche Spießer ärgert sich, in: DADA total. Manifeste, Aktionen, Texte, Bilder (Hrsg. Merte/Riha/Schäfer), Stuttgart 1994, 109-112

John Heartfield, Ein wiederentdeckter Brief über expressionistische Filmpläne, in: kintop 8. Film und Projektionskunst (Hrsg. Kessler/ Lenk/ Loiperdinger), Frankfurt a. M. 1999, 169-180

German Karginov, Rodchenko, London 1986

Ernesto Laclau, New Reflections on the Revolution of Our Time, London und New York 1990

Paul de Man, The Concept of Irony, in: Aesthetic Ideology. Paul de Man (Hrsg. Warminski), Minneapolis 1996, 163-184

Victor Margolin, Struggle for Utopia: Rodchenko. Lissitzky. Moholy-Nagy. 1917-1946, Chicago und London 1997

William J. Mitchell, @-topia. »Urban Life, Jim-But Not As We Know It«, Cambridge/ MA und London/GB 1999

Krisztina Passuth, Moholy-Nagy, London 1985

Vladímir Propp, Morphologie des Märchens (Hrsg. Karl Eimermacher), Frankfurt a. M. 1975 (1969)

Rainer Maria Rilke, Die Aufzeichnungen des Malte Laurids Brigge. Kommentierte Ausgabe, Stuttgart 1997 (1910)

Gottfried Schlemmer, Anmerkung zum Undergroundfilm, in: Avantgardistischer Film 1951-1971: Theorie (Hrsg. Ders.), München 1973, 18-23

Anna Schober, Blue Jeans. Vom Leben in Stoffen und Bildern, Frankfurt a. M. und New York 2001

Susan Rubin Suleiman, Subversive Intent. Gender, Politics, and the Avant-Garde, Cambridge/Massachusetts und London/England 1990

Birgit Wagner, Auslöschen, vernichten, gründen, schaffen: zu den performativen Funktionen der Manifeste, in: »Die ganze Welt ist eine Manifestation«. Die europäische Avantgarde und ihre Manifeste (Hrsg. Asholt/Fähnders), Darmstadt 1997, 39-57

Peter Weibel, Kritik der Kunst. Kunst der Kritik, Wien und München 1973

Wir. Variante eines Manifestes (1922), in: Texte zur Theorie des Films (Hrsg. Franz-Josef Albesmaier), Stuttgart 1973, 19-23

Historische Fallstudien

Erzählte Geschichte im Bild

Die narrative Darstellungsweise der Trajanssäule als Vermittlung historischer Ereignisse*

BARBARA ZIMMERMANN

Die Bilder der schrecklichen Ereignisse vom 11. September 2001 in Amerika, die im Herbst in unseren Medien allpräsent waren, uns live berichteten von dem, was ab nun ›Geschichte‹ ist, stehen uns noch klar vor Augen. Ihre Rolle in der Berichterstattung belegt sehr anschaulich, wie unsere Unmittelbarkeit zum Geschehen in aller Welt erzeugt wird. Das ist einerseits symptomatisch für unsere Mediengesellschaft, andererseits dokumentiert es, wie stark unser Bedürfnis ist, Geschichte über Bilder zu definieren. Diese erscheinen wie selbstverständlich auf unseren Bildschirmen: der amerikanische Präsident richtet seine Ansprachen an die Welt, gefolgt von Berichten mit immer gleichbleibenden Bildsequenzen: die Flugzeuge, die in das WTC fliegen, als Zeichen für das Unfassbare, Rettungsmannschaften beim Einsatz in den Trümmern; Bilder, die beim Betrachter die ganze Geschichte einer entsetzlichen Tragödie abrufen. Auch mit Bildern aus der arabischen Welt sind wir konfrontiert. Sie zeigen beispielsweise Demonstranten, die Steckbriefbilder des Präsidenten verbrennen und haben eine eindeutige Intention, ein – vermeintlich objektives – Bild des ›Feindes‹ zu vermitteln.

Diese Bilderflut unseres Medienzeitalters ist einer der Hauptträger der Konstruktion von Wirklichkeit im Sinne einer kollektiven symbolischen Sinn- bzw. Lebenswelt, die neben wirtschaftlichen, sozialen und politischen Umständen Handeln und Denken einer Gesellschaft prägt[1]. Im Sinne einer konstruktivistischen Methode können die Bilder auf ihren prospektiven Wert hin befragt werden, d. h. in welchem Maße und wie sie an der Konstituierung von kollektiven Wahrnehmungen bzw. Vorstellungen und in Folge an kulturellen Entwicklungsprozessen beteiligt sind. Sie sind aber auch unter dem retrospektiven Aspekt Zeugnisse einer Wirklichkeit, in der sie entstehen[2]. Das Drama des 11. September hatte für die westliche Welt identitätsstiftenden Charakter wie wohl kaum ein Ereignis in den letzten

Jahren. Die seitdem neu und intensiv geführten Diskurse über religiöse und politische Identität haben zusammen mit den Bildern eine Wirklichkeit konstruiert, die historische Entwicklungsprozesse eingeleitet hat.
Die Berichterstattung des 21. Jh., die chronologisch vor- und zurückspringt, Szenen direkt aneinander reiht, die an verschiedenen Schauplätzen zu unterschiedlichen Zeitpunkten spielen, setzt sich aus realen Bilder zusammen und ruft so beim Betrachter die Illusion einer objektiven Berichterstattung hervor. Nur der informierte, kritische Betrachter erkennt die Manipulation und das politische Konzept und hat dank der grenzenlosen Medialität die Möglichkeit, diesem Prozess auf die Schliche zu kommen. Einzelne Bilder bzw. Bildsequenzen reichen oft aus, um beim Betrachter die ganze dramatische Geschichte wachzurufen. Der Betrachter wird so zum Erzähler von Geschichten, die an verschiedenen Enden der Welt anders erzählt werden; Geschichten, die gesellschaftliche Verhaltensmuster und kollektive Wahrnehmung bestimmen, ein Wertesystem untermauern, das der Gesellschaft als Identifikationsmodell dient. Das ist die Macht der Bilder, die uns mittlerweile so selbstverständlich geworden ist, das sie oftmals nicht mehr hinterfragt wird.
Der Mensch in der Antike lebte ebenfalls mit Bildern. Durch ihre Allpräsenz in unterschiedlichen Medien und basierend auf einer statischen und daher leicht verständlichen Bildsprache[3], trugen sie bei, kollektive Vorstellungen von Wirklichkeit zu vermitteln bzw. zu verfestigen. Für die Frage, in welchem Maße und wie sie Teil des Prozesses der Wissensvermittlung waren, bieten sich die sog. historischen Darstellungen in besonderem Maße an. Denn sie geben schon per se Ereignisse mit gesellschaftsprägendem Charakter wieder, in denen auch Fremde und Feinde im Sinne einer politischen Ideologie zur Darstellung kommen[4].
Dieser Beitrag befasst sich mit der Frage, wieweit an den unterschiedlichen Darstellungsweisen historischer Ereignisse in der römischen Kunst Aussageintentionen zu differenzieren sind; ob diese mit einem Medienwandel zu tun haben und ob dieser sich erst vollzog, um den intendierten Aussagen gerecht zu werden. Mit anderen Worten, kann man durch eine Analyse der Darstellungsweisen erschließen, welche Rolle historische Darstellungen im Prozess der Wissensvermittlung als Teil der Wirklichkeitskonstruktion spielen. Die Annäherung erfolgt über eine Untersuchung der Erzählstruktur[5].
Die Anfänge der römischen Repräsentationskunst, d. h. einer Kunst mit ausschließlich politischen Zielen, liegen am Ende des 4. und Anfang des 3. Jhs. v. Chr.[6] Hierzu zählen auch Monumente mit historischer oder besser kommemorativer Intention. Die Darstellung historischer Ereignisse fand Eingang in die unterschiedlichsten Medien. Sehr früh findet man sie in der Sepulkralmalerei, wo sie sich auf spezifische Kriegsereignisse beziehen

können[7] oder in mehreren Szenen die Gründungsmythen Roms erzählen[8]. Ein wichtigstes Medium zur Verbreitung politischer Botschaften bzw. zu Propagandazwecken sind Münzen. Auf Münzbildern erscheinen Personifikationen, Gegenstände, Kombinationen beider, aber v. a. auch szenische Darstellungen wie etwa der opfernde Kaiser meist im Beisein einer Personifikation, sein adventus (feierlicher Einzug), adlocutio (Ansprache), profectio (Aufbruch) usw. Diese Münzbilder stehen in enger Verbindung mit den Legenden. Die Legende bzw. das Bild können durch die jeweilige Verbindung unterschiedliche Deutungen erfahren. Mit dem opfernden Kaiser beispielsweise ist meist seine Frömmigkeit (pietas) gemeint, doch kann das Opferbild auch von Legenden begleitet sein, die auf die Eintracht der Kaiser (concordia augustorum), seinen Sieg (victoria augusti) oder den Kaiser als Friedensgründer (fundator pacis) verweisen[9]. Umgekehrt kann die Legende virtus (Tugendhaftigkeit, Tüchtigkeit) durch die Darstellung eines Kampfes, einer Jagd oder einer profectio (Aufbruch) begleitet sein[10]. Im Falle eines Bezuges des Münzbildes zu einem konkreten historischen Ereignis geht dieser nicht aus dem chiffrenhaften Bild selber hervor, sondern aus der Beischrift. Eine wichtige Gattung historischer Darstellungen ist die Triumphalmalerei, die allerdings materiell gänzlich verloren und nur aus literarischen Quellen zu erschließen ist[11]. Allenfalls sind ihre Reflexe in oben genannten Sepulkralmalereien zu erschließen und in den sog. historischen Reliefs. Schon in der Republik war die Mitführung solcher Malereien integraler Bestandteil des Triumphzuges. Auf großen Paneelen vermittelte man der Bevölkerung einen visuellen Bericht über das, was sich während des Feldzuges ereignet hatte. Vor allem erfolgreiche Schlachten, aber auch Bilder des eroberten Feindeslandes wohl in kartographischer Manier waren Hauptthemen, zudem kamen Ereignisse zur Darstellung, die zu diesen wichtigen Schlachten und Eroberungen führten, sowie deren Konsequenzen. Diese großen Paneele wurden in Folge an öffentlichen Plätzen und in Tempeln ausgestellt. Intention dieser Malereien war die Information der Bevölkerung über den Hergang der großen Triumphe der Feldherrn und Kaiser. Zur Darstellung kam selbstredend nur das, was deren Ruhm und Ansehen zuträglich war. So waren diese Bilder in besonderem Maße daran beteiligt, eine kollektive gesellschaftliche Wirklichkeit zu konstruieren, basierend auf den identitätsstiftenden Ereignissen der unmittelbaren Zeitgeschichte. Im Allgemeinen werden diese Malereien als typisch für die dokumentarisch-narrative Tradition in der römischen Kunst bezeichnet. Im Vordergrund stand jedoch auch hier die ›Dokumentation‹ der Tapferkeit, Schlagkräftigkeit, Stärke, des Mutes und der Frömmigkeit des Heeres und des Feldherren bzw. Kaisers. Daher vermitteln solche rein politischen Kunstwerke mit propagandistischen Zielen schon per se ein gesell-

Abb. 1:
Hassel, Franz Josef, Der Trajansbogen in Benevent, Mainz 1966, Taf. 6, 2

Abb. 2:
Hassel 1966, Taf. 13

schaftskonstituierendes Wertesystem. Die wichtigste Gattung aufgrund des Überlieferungs- bzw. Erhaltungszustandes stellt die der historischen Reliefs dar mit ihren Wurzeln in der frühen Republik[12]. Vor allem anhand dieser Gattung entstand die Diskussion um den in den Bildwerken römischer Kunst auszumachenden Geschichtsbegriff. Man unterteilte die Reliefs in zwei Gruppen[13]: einerseits solche mit zeremoniellen repräsentativen Charakter, die in immer gleichbleibenden Bildtypen bzw. festgeprägten Szenen politische Leitvorstellungen wiedergeben und den Großteil der Reliefs ausmachen. Auf der anderen Seite wird eine Gruppe postuliert, die historische Ereignisse festhält in narrativ-dokumentarischer Weise, die auf die oben genannte Triumphalmalerei zurückgehen und deren Hauptvertreter die Triumphsäulen darstellen sollen. Man sah einen Zusammenhang mit literarischen Kriegskommentaren, die – teilweise von den jeweiligen kriegsführenden Kaisern verfasst – überliefert sind, wie etwa der jedem Gymnasiasten bekannte Bericht Caesars über seinen Gallischen Krieg. Der von Trajan selbst verfasste Kommentar über die Dakerkriege ist leider verloren. Bekannt ist, dass Feldherrn bzw. Kaiser Historiker mit dem Verfassen eines Kommentars beauftragten[14]. So wird bei diesen ›dokumentarischen‹ Darstellungen, die schon in der Antike geführte Diskussion über das Verhältnis zwischen Bild und Text immer wieder aktuell[15].

Beide Traditionsstränge gingen bis in die frühe Republik zurück. Um den Rahmen nicht zu sprengen, führe ich ein Beispiel aus trajanischer Zeit an, womit wir uns chronologisch dem Hauptthema des vorliegenden Beitrages nähern.

Der 114 n. Chr. fertig gestellte Trajansbogen in Benevent zeigt in seinen figürlichen Reliefs diverse Szenen, in welchen der Kaiser Trajan mit Personifikationen bzw. Göttern und Göttinnen als Protagonist auftritt[16]: In den Reliefs der Landseite des Bogens schließt er im Beisein Jupiters Verträge mit Nachbarvölkern; er gibt seinen Soldaten Weisungen; er mustert vor den Augen von schwer bestimmbaren Personifikationen seine Soldaten; eine Idealfigur mit Mauerkrone, nur allgemein als Göttin des Wohlergehens bestimmbar, pflügt im Beisein des Kaisers, von Mars und Provinzpersonifikationen die Erde (Abb. 1, unten); in einem weiteren Relief kniet eine Provinzpersonifikation flankiert von zwei Flussgöttern vor dem Kaiser (Abb. 2); schließlich steht Trajan den Schutzgöttinnen der Provinzen gegenüber. Auf der Stadtseite des Bogens ist sein feierlicher Einzug (adventus) zu sehen, wobei er vom Genius des Senates und des römischen Volkes empfangen wird; es sind Entlassung von Veteranen dargestellt und der Kaiser, der sich um den Handel kümmert, auch hier immer im Beisein von verschiedensten Personifikationen, Göttern bzw. Genien, und schließlich ein weiterer adventus des Kaisers, der nun von der kapitolinischen Trias empfangen wird, wobei ihm Jupiter den Blitz überreicht. Für unsere Fragestellung interessant ist v. a. die Frage nach der Intention der Reliefs: Alle Versuche, in ihnen konkrete historische Ereignisse zu sehen, können nicht überzeugen, denn geht man von den Darstellungen selber aus, finden sich keine Hinweise auf topographische, chronologische bzw. kausale Umstände[17]. Schon die Unbestimmheit der durchgängig anwesenden Personifikationen und Göttergestalten, die den Reliefs einen allegorisch ›überzeitlichen‹ Charakter verleihen, ist signifikant für die ›historische Unbestimmtbarkeit‹ der Ereignisse. Die Komposition der Szenen mit ihrer räumlichen Tiefe ist auf die Protagonisten zentriert, bleibt innerhalb der Bildgrenzen bzw. schließt zwei Reliefs zu einer Gruppe zusammen. Die Darstellungen gehen nicht über die Bildgrenzen hinaus, finden ihren inhaltlichen Mittelpunkt, ihre zentrale Aussage innerhalb der jeweiligen Darstellung. Die Reliefs bilden so ein komplexes Programm, das die Grundlagen der kaiserlichen Herrschaft im Sinne von Werten, Tugenden, Handlungen des Kaisers vorführt. Dem Betrachter werden die Grundideen durch allegorische Szenen vor Augen geführt, die da sind: die Friedensidee, die Reichsidee und die Romidee, all dies gipfelt schließlich in der zentralen Idee vom Gottgnadentum[18]. Insofern führen diese sog. historischen Reliefs nicht ›Ereignisgeschichte‹ vor, sondern ein politisches Konzept und sind daher besser als ›politische‹ Reliefs zu bezeichnen. Sie stehen hier nur exemplarisch für eine ganze Gruppe solcher Darstellungen.

Nun kann man diese Art der Darstellungen mit Münzbildern vergleichen, die – zwar chiffrenhaft reduziert – dieselben festgeprägten Szenen wiedergeben. Die dort agierenden Personifikationen erhalten erst durch die Legenden eine Konkretisierung, ikonographisch sind sie ebenso offen wie die Idealfiguren auf den Beneventer Reliefs. Diese Offenheit war sicher intendiert und bestimmte das Wesen der römischen Repräsentationskunst mit[19]. So sind diese Bilder in extremen Maße daran beteiligt, die kollektive Wahrnehmung der römischen Gesellschaft in Bezug auf die Legitimierung der kaiserlichen Herrschaft zu konstruieren. Diese basiert auf den Tugenden und Handlungen des Guten Kaisers. Dies führte zu dem Schluss, dass es in der triumphalen Staatskunst der römischen Kaiserzeit, die sich über Jahrhunderte hinweg einer statischen Bildsprache im Sinne eines semantisches Systems bediente[20], nur in geringem Maß um die Aufzeichnung historischer Realitäten geht, sondern vor allem um den Ausdruck gedanklicher Idealvorstellungen. An feststehenden Bildtypen werden v. a. zeremonielle, repräsentative Vorgänge ins Bild gesetzt, die die Tugenden des ideologischen Wertesystems ausdrücken[21].

Diese Beobachtungen werden aus den angesprochenen Monumenten bzw. Gattungen bestätigt. Problematisch ist jedoch, diesen Geschichtsbegriff generell auf alle historischen Darstellungen umzulegen. Denn neben solchen repräsentativen Darstellungen tauchen in geringerer Zahl in der römischen

Triumphalkunst auch narrative Darstellungen auf, deren Charakter und formale Struktur es zu definieren gilt. Paradebeispiel hierfür ist die jedem Rombesucher bekannte Triumphsäule des Trajan am Trajansforum in Rom[22]. Sie befindet sich zwischen den beiden Bibliotheksgebäuden des zwischen 107 und 113 n. Chr. anläßlich des Sieges über die Daker errichteten Trajansforums. Auf einem Sockel, der die Grabkammer für den Kaiser Trajan aufnimmt, erhebt sich der ca. 40 m hohe Säulenschaft, der in der Tradition der Ehrensäulen die heute verlorene Bronzestatue des Kaisers trug. Auf dem Säulenschaft steigt der Relieffries spiralenförmig in 23 Windungen an. Die Ereignisse der beiden Dakerkriege werden in kontinuierend aneinander gereihten Szenenfolgen erzählt. Für unsere Fragestellung ist v. a. von Bedeutung, dass es sich hierbei um eine völlige Neuschöpfung handelt. Die Ehrensäule mit einem Reliefband, das auf ca. 200 m die Erzählung der Dakerkriege aufnimmt, stellt ein gänzlich neues Medium ohne Vorläufer dar, wodurch schwer zu beantworten ist, woher die Idee zu solch einem Kunstwerk stammt, auf welche Modelle sie zurückgeht, für wen die Säule errichtet wurde und v.a mit welcher Intention. Die ›Unlesbarkeit‹ der Bildgeschichte stellt eines der Hauptprobleme dar. Um der Bilderzählung zu folgen, musste man 23 Mal die Säule umrunden, durfte dabei ›die Zeile nicht verlieren‹, was v. a. im oberen Schaftbereich äußerst schwierig war. Die Fülle an beschreibenden Details, die Figurendichte, die große Anzahl an topographischen Angaben waren vom Standpunkt des Betrachters am Fuße der Säule v. a. im oberen Bereich nicht mehr rezipierbar. Eine Neuerung stellt auch die Art der Darstellungsweise der Bilderzählung dar. Sie wird generell als episch-dokumentarisch bzw. narrativ bezeichnet, und ihre Wurzeln werden in republikanischer Zeit angenommen. Als Vorläufer ist v. a. thematisch die Gattung der Triumphalmalereien in Anspruch zu nehmen. Doch eine kontinuierende Darstellung in dieser Ausprägung hat keine Vorläufer[23]. Die fast filmische Abspulung der Szenen legte den unhistorischen Vergleich mit dem Medium Film nahe, der es erleichtert, die Erzählstruktur zu begreifen[24]. Wie im Film folgt eine Szene der anderen in kontinuierendem Ablauf, verschiedene Etappen der Handlungen schließen sich zu größeren Sequenzen zusammen, die eine einheitliche Zeitspanne im selben Raum einnehmen können. Der Raum wird zum Träger der Zeitkomponente, so zeigt jede Änderung des Ortes mit demselben Protagonisten einen chronologischen Fortschritt an. Die Zeitkomponente kann beschleunigt werden durch die schnellere Abfolge der Aktionen, ohne die Klarheit und Kontinuität der Erzählung einzubüßen. Auch Anfang und Ende der einzelnen Szenen können wie im Film durch unterschiedliche Mittel angezeigt werden: Es gibt klare Szenentrennungen, etwa durch Landschaftselemente oder durch die Gegenüberstellung zweier Szenen als Ende bzw. Anfang einer gänzlich neuen Episode. Szenen können sich überlappen, wenn eine neue Szene noch in der vorangehenden ihren Ausgang nimmt. Interessant sind auch die Fälle, in welchen man von Montagen sprechen kann: Beispielsweise können Szenen zusammengestellt werden, die gleichzeitig an verschiedenen Orten spielen, etwa derselbe Moment bei den Römern und bei den Barbaren. Sowohl im Film als auch auf der Säule sind diese nacheinander angeordnet.

Nicht nur der Vergleich mit modernen Medien, auch der Monumentenvergleich innerhalb der Antike führt die Charakteristika des kontinuierenden Reliefbandes deutlich vor Augen: Es sind hier zwar dieselben Motive, Bildformulare, Bildtypen und standardisierten Szenen verwendet wie auf der oben kurz vorgestellten Gruppe der sog. historischen Reliefs mit zeremoniell-repräsentativen Darstellungen bzw. auf Münzen, doch werden diese auf der Trajanssäule mit visuellen narrativen Mitteln erweitert[25]. Als Beispiel dient der Abschnitt der Reise Trajans zum Kriegsschauplatz am Beginn des 2. Dakerkrieges: Die Sequenz beginnt in Ancona mit der Einschiffung des Kaisers, der selber am Steuerruder steht (Abb. 3); an der Mole der Hafenstadt erwartet ihn bereits die Bevölkerung, im Hintergrund verweist der noch brennende Altar und der tote Stier auf das vollzogene Opfer für seine glückliche Ankunft (Abb. 4). Die angedeutete Hafenarchitektur erweitert sich nach rechts zur Porticus des städtischen Tempelbezirkes der folgenden Szene, die die Begegnung der zivilen Bevölkerung mit dem Kaiser zeigt (Abb. 5). Die Bewegung eines Teiles der Menge zeigt die Leserichtung an. Die folgende Reiseetappe des Kaisers ist nur durch einen Teil der Flotte zeichenhaft ins Bild gesetzt (Abb. 6). Die Festprozession in der Ankunftsstadt bewegt sich zusammen mit dem schnell voranschreitenden Kaiser durch eine Bogenarchitektur zum Opferplatz (Abb. 7). Die Opferdiener sind bereit für den Opfervollzug (Abb. 8). Die vom Wasser umspülten Ruder eines Schiffes zeigen in abgekürzter Form die nächste Reiseetappe an. Die eben ankommenden Soldaten folgen dem Kaiser schnellen Schrittes über die Hafenmole (Abb. 9). Trajan vollzieht bereits vor urbaner Architektur ein weiteres Opfer in Anwesenheit seiner Soldaten und der Zivilbevölkerung (Abb. 10). In der nächsten Szene hat die Flotte an felsigem Ufer angelegt, und die eben ausgeschifften Soldaten folgen in Eile dem Kaiser (Abb. 11), dem ein Begleiter den Weg weist. Diese Geste führt gleichzeitig den Betrachter zur nächsten Reiseetappe (Abb. 12), die nun reitend zu Lande fortgesetzt wird. Das Gefolge des Kaisers ist noch in Vorwärtsbewegung begriffen (Abb. 13), Trajan selbst wird bereits von der Zivilbevölkerung unterwürfig empfangen (Abb. 14).

Die standardisierten Szenen sind hier weit von dem chiffrenhaften Charakter der Münzbilder entfernt, denn sie sind durch topographische Angaben in einen konkret definierten Raum gestellt, die Kontinuität der Erzählung, der chronologische Fortschritt der Ereignisse wird durch die Änderung des

Abb. 3:
Settis, Salvatore, Adriano La Regina, Giovanni Agosti, Vincenzo Farinella, La Colonna Traiana, Torino 1988, Taf. 140

Abb. 4:
Settis 1988, Taf. 143

Abb. 5:
Settis 1988, Taf. 144

Abb. 6:
Settis 1988, Taf. 146

Abb. 7:
Settis 1988, Taf. 148

Abb. 8:
Settis 1988, Taf. 149

Abb. 9:
Settis 1988, Taf. 152

Abb. 10:
Settis 1988, Taf. 153

Abb. 11:
Settis 1988, Taf. 155

Abb. 12:
Settis 1988, Taf. 156

Abb. 13:
Settis 1988, Taf. 158

Abb. 14:
Settis 1988, Taf. 159

Raumes erreicht, in welchem der immer wiederkehrende Protagonist Trajan agiert. Im Gegensatz zu den repräsentativen ›politischen‹ Darstellungen gehen die einzelnen Szenen über die Szenengrenzen hinaus, beziehen sich durch Gesten, Blicke und die Bewegungsrichtung der agierenden Personen auf vorangehende oder folgende Szenen. Die unglaubliche Fülle an beschreibenden Details sowohl topographischer als auch architektonischer Natur betont noch einmal mehr den dokumentarischen, ›realen‹ Charakter der Erzählung und legt es nahe, an die bildliche Umsetzung eines schriftlichen Berichtes zu denken[26].

Der Bild-Text-Bezug ist eines der häufig diskutierten Probleme in der Auseinandersetzung mit den Reliefs und steht in unmittelbarem Zusammenhang mit der Frage nach der Herkunft bzw. der Vorlage der Bilderzählung. Schon 1907 wurde die Trajanssäule mit einer ausgerollten Buchrolle in Verbindung gebracht, als Th. Birt sie als Bilderbuch über Trajans Kriege bezeichnete: »Der Reliefstreifen ... erzählt continuo in zeitlicher Folge die ganze Kriegsgeschichte, wie sie ganz analog in dem Prosawerk des Kaisers gestanden haben muss ... Das Buch ist bis zum Ende aufgerollt, und keine Falte der Rolle bleibt leer.«[27] Zum Aufstellungsort schreibt er: » ... [Trajan] machte sie zum Zentrum seiner Bibliothek. Ist das Zufall? Gewiss nicht! .... [Zwischen den Bibliotheken] die Säule mit dem erhöhten Buch, das den Ruhm des Kaisers erzählt und alle Bücher überragt, die in den Büchersälen rechts und links stecken: die großartigste Publikation, die ich kenne.«[28] Birts Theorie stieß teils auf Zustimmung, teils auf Ablehnung. Die Existenz solcher kontinuierender Rotuli erschien vor dem Hintergrund der von Weitzmann rekonstruierten Geschichte der Buchillustration unmöglich[29]. Aber auch die Achsbezüge, die eine vertikale Lesung der Säule ermöglichen, sollten gegen eine solche Vorlage sprechen[30]. Über die reine Vorlagenfrage hinaus wurde die Diskussion auf die Frage des Geschichtsbegriffes ausgedehnt. G. Koeppel sieht den Unterschied zwischen den Reliefs der Trajanssäule und der Gruppe der repräsentativen zeremoniellen Darstellungen v. a. in der Intention[31]. Im Vergleich zu diesen wollte die Trajanssäule dokumentieren, erzählen, was, wie, wann in den Dakerkriegen vorgefallen ist. In der aktuellen Forschungsmeinung neigt man dazu, die Trajanssäule als Verbildlichung eines ideologischen Wertesystems anzusehen[32]. Ausgehend von T. Hölschers semantischem System werden die Bildtypen als topoi für die kaiserlichen Tugenden angesehen, so verbildlichen etwa die unzähligen Opferszenen die pietas Augusti[33]. Ausgangspunkt für diese Interpretation sind Münzbilder mit den zugehörigen Legenden. Konkret wird etwa die eben vorgestellte Reise des Trajan als Verbildlichung der Frömmigkeit des Kaisers angesehen. Die Opferszenen im Verband mit römischen Soldaten und Zivilbevölkerung sollen die Loyalität der Provinzen dem Kaiser gegenüber bekunden bzw. das gegenseitige Treueverhältnis.

Beleg für diese Deutung sind hadrianische (also spätere) Münzbilder, die den Kaiser zusammen mit einer Provinzpersonifikation am Altar stehend zeigen, wobei in diesem Fall die Personifikation das Opfer innerhalb einer gänzlich abgeschlossenen Komposition vollzieht[34]. T. Hölscher lehnt es ab, die Reliefs als Umsetzung eines schriftlichen Kriegsberichtes zu sehen, da das Reliefband mit seinen stereotypen Szenenfolgen und der Hervorhebung der zeremoniellen Szenen überhaupt nicht als literarischer Bericht vorstellbar sei und dessen Lektüre schwer erträglich gewesen wäre. Historische Treue stünde nicht im Vordergrund, sondern der Ausdruck des Wertesystems[35]. Eine etwas abweichende Meinung vertritt S. Settis: Er sieht das Spiralband als bildliche Umsetzung eines Wertekataloges für den Guten Kaiser, der auch bei antiken Autoren überliefert ist. Es handle sich dabei aber nicht um die Illustration eines solchen Textes, sondern um eine textunabhängige Bilderzählung, die eben besagte Tugenden und Werte programmatisch ins Bild setzt[36].

Nun ist eine Bildgeschichte in derartigem Umfang mit einer vom Betrachter nicht rezipierbaren Dichte an beschreibenden Details kaum ohne zugrunde liegenden Text vorstellbar. Kehren wir noch einmal zum Vergleich mit dem Medium Film zurück. A. Malissard parallelisierte auch den Entstehungsprozess der Bilderzählung der Trajanssäule mit dem eines Filmes[37]: So musste ein Bericht über die Dakerkriege zur Verfügung stehen, den man auf die wichtigsten Ereignisse reduzierte, um dann mit entsprechenden Bildern dieses Drama zu illustrieren, wobei die gewünschte Länge des Reliefs ausschlaggebend für die Konzeption war. Wie beim Film musste demnach ein Basistext zur Verfügung stehen, eine Redaktion des ›Drehbuches‹ stattfinden, mit der Beschränkung auf die geplante Dauer des ›Filmes‹, sprich auf die vorgegebene Länge des Reliefbandes. Schließlich musste die Umsetzung des ›Drehbuches‹ in Bilder erfolgen.

Der Vergleich mit dem modernen Medium Film ist insofern ertragreich, als die Idee eines Drehbuches, d. h. eines Basistextes, der in Hinblick auf eine Umsetzung in Bilder bearbeitet wurde, zu einem anderen antiken Medium führt, zur Buchmalerei. K. Weitzmann rekonstruierte die Existenz von Rotuli narrativen Inhaltes mit in die Textkolumnen eingefügten Illustrationen analog den Illustrationen wissenschaftlicher Texte[38]. Diese Meinung dominierte jahrzehntelang die Forschung, und die von Birt am Beginn des 20. Jhs. postulierten Rotuli mit kontinuierenden Illustrationen durften nicht mehr in Erwägung gezogen werden. De facto kennen wir illustrierte Bücher narrativen Inhaltes aber erst aus der Spätantike, wobei 13 – in Codexform – erhalten sind[39]. Sie weisen jeweils gänzlich unterschiedliche Illustrationssysteme auf, sowohl in Bezug auf die formale Disposition als auch bezüglich des Bild-Text-Verhältnisses[40]. Auffällig ist, dass eine kontinuierende Darstellung nur einmal vorkommt, obwohl sie oftmals als typisch für Buchillustrationen in Anspruch genommen wird. Die sog. Wiener Genesis, eine Purpurhandschrift aus dem 6. Jh, vereint auf den einzelnen Codexseiten den respektiven Text mit darunter stehenden Miniaturen[41]. Diese zeigen in engem Zusammenhang mit dem dazugehörigem Text mehrere Szenen in kontinuierender Folge, die den oben genannten narrativen Charakteristika der Trajanssäule entsprechen und ebenfalls dem ›Filmvergleich‹ standhalten. Auch hier bewegen sich die Personen von einer Szene zur nächsten, deren Verbindung durch Gesten, Blicke, Bewegungsrichtung erfolgt. Die Gegenüberstellung von Szenen zeigt Anfang und Ende an, wenn etwa derselbe Protagonist einer Szene dem eigenen Ich der folgenden Szene den Rücken kehrt. Ebenso sind auch Szenentrennungen durch Architekturen oder Landschaftselemente zu finden. Perspektivenänderungen oder Invertierung der Bewegungsrichtung sind vergleichbare Kunstgriffe. Der Fortschritt der Zeitkomponente wird durch das Auftreten desselben Protagonisten in verändertem Raum in der darauf folgenden Szene wiedergegeben.

Auch zur Wiener Genesis gibt es ein Pendant aus derselben Kunstgattung und demselben geographischen und chronologischen Kontext, den sog. Codex Rossanensis, eine neutestamentliche Handschrift mit Illustrationen, die allem Anschein nach aus demselben Atelier wie die Wiener Genesis stammt[42]. Auch hier macht die Gegenüberstellung der Handschriften wie bei den Beneventer Reliefs und der Trajanssäule die Charakteristika der kontinuierenden Miniaturen noch einmal deutlicher. Die ganzseitigen Miniaturen des Codex Rossanensis sind dem Evangelientext vorangestellt, nehmen oben neutestamentliche Szenen, unten alttestamentliche Prophetenfiguren mit Spruchbändern auf, deren Texte sich auf die dargestellten Ereignisse beziehen. Jede Seite bildet eine abgeschlossene theologische Sinneinheit. Dieser entspricht die Komposition der narrativen Szenen. Im Gegensatz zu den Miniaturen der Wiener Genesis, in welchen die Zielpunkte der Figuren in den darauf folgenen Szenen oder außerhalb der Bildgrenzen zu suchen sind, bewegen sich die Protagonisten der Rossanensis Bilder innerhalb der Bildgrenzen, finden dort einen Ziel- oder Mittelpunkt. Wie bei den Reliefs des Beneventer Bogens und denen der Trajanssäule wurde in diesem ›Handschriftenpaar‹ dasselbe Bildformular verwendet, die narrative Fortsetzung des Erzählflusses aber mit kompositorischen Mitteln erreicht. Besonders interessant ist aber in Bezug auf den Vergleich mit dem Medium Film eine weitere Besonderheit der Wiener Genesis, nämlich die Textredaktion: der Septuaginta-Text wurde stark gekürzt im Sinne des Erzählflusses der Ereignisse der Genesis[43]. Er beschränkt sich auf die wichtigsten Handlungselemente der Erzählung. Diese entsprechen exakt den im Bild dargestellten Ereignissen. Mit dieser Entsprechung sind auch durchgängig alle Ungereimtheiten in den Darstellungen zu verstehen[44]. Eine derartige Harmonisierung von Bild und Text konnte nur im Rahmen eines Entwurfes für das Codexformat erreicht werden, der gleichzeitig eine Bild- und Textredaktion umfasste. Hier wurde also ein Basistext – der Septuagintatext – im Sinne eines Drehbuches für die narrative Szenenfolge redigiert. Diese ›Drehbuchredaktion‹ war einerseits durch den Willen zur Erzählung bestimmt, wodurch nur konkrete Ereignisse bzw. Handlungen stehen blieben, andererseits natürlich durch Format und geplanten Umfang des Codex.

Ein vergleichbares Monument ist der sog. Josua-Rotulus aus dem 10. Jh.[45] In kontinuierender Bildfolge reihen sich hier die Ereignisse aus dem 6. Buch der Bibel aneinander, eng verbunden mit dem darunter stehenden Text, der im Sinne des Erzählflusses paraphrasiert ist. Zwischen den Szenen und dem gekürzten Bibeltext ist eine Harmonie erreicht, die die Entstehung des Zyklus in vorliegender Friesform auch nur zugleich mit der Textredaktion zulässt. Erst den neuesten Arbeiten von J. Lowden und O. Kresten sind diese Ergebnisse zu verdanken[46], denn Jahrzehnte lang dominierte die Meinung, der Rotulus sei eine Neuschöpfung der makedonischen Renaissance, geschaffen in Anlehnung an die römischen Triumphalsäulen aus Vorlagen im Codexformat. Doch auch hier sind Ungereimtheiten und Fehler nur mit dem respektiven Text zu erklären[47].

Auffällig ist nun, dass die einzigen beiden illustrierten Bücher mit kontinuierenden Darstellungen mit oben beschriebenen, dem Medium Film vergleichbaren narrativen Charakteristika paraphrasierte Texte aufweisen. Alle anderen erhaltenen illustrierten Codices narrativen Inhaltes nehmen den Volltext der jeweiligen Werke auf. Ausführliche erzählende Texte mit literarischem Charakter verbinden sich also nicht mit kontinuierenden Bilderzählungen!

Was kann dies nun aber für die Reliefs der Trajanssäule bedeuten? Die Gegenargumente Hölschers, in den Reliefs eine bildliche Umsetzung eines Kriegsberichtes zu sehen sind zwei: Erstens führt er die durchgehende Verwendung typisierter Einzelszenen an, die ebenso etwa auf Münzbildern in Verbindung mit Legenden bzw. Triumphbögen vorkommen und seiner Meinung nach daher durchwegs ideologische Bedeutung haben. Das zweite Argument ist, dass das Reliefband gar nicht als literarischer Bericht vorstellbar sei: »Die starke Hervorhebung zeremonieller und repräsentativer Szenen und die stereotype Abfolge der kriegsentscheidenden Vorstöße stehen der Dynamik und der dramatischen Verknüpfung der Literatur fern.[48]«

Die Verwendung von bestimmten Bildmotiven bzw. feststehenden Szenentypen charakterisiert generell die römische Kunst bis in die Kaiserzeit. Die Gleichsetzung der Bedeutung etwa der Opferszenen auf der Trajanssäule mit solchen auf repräsentativen zeremoniellen Denkmälern und besonders auf Münzbildern kann nur mit Vorbehalt geschehen, denn der kontinuierenden Darstellungsweise wird man hierbei nicht gerecht. Durch die Beifügung von Personifikationen oder anderen Idealfiguren erhalten sie dort ihren ›überzeitlichen‹ zeremoniellen Charakter. Anders auf der Trajanssäule, wo gerade durch die Erweiterung der Motive durch reale Personen deren Gesten, Bewegungen und Blicke den Erzählfluss tragen, die Wiedergabe einer ›realen‹ Situation intendiert ist. Diese wird weiters erreicht durch die Situierung der Szenen in Raum und Zeit. Die beschreibenden Details v. a. topographischen Charakters verstärken noch einmal mehr den Eindruck des realen Geschehens. Dass die Bilder nun historisch reale Treue im eigentlichen Sinne (sowohl in der Wiedergabe von Lokalitäten, in der genauen Abfolge von Riten, in Realien wie Bewaffnung oder Ausrüstung) entbehren, ist mit der Umsetzung in die Bildsprache zu verstehen. Diese muss mit sowohl dem Künstler als auch dem Betrachter bekannten Motiven arbeiten, um überhaupt ›lesbar‹ zu sein. Gerade die augenfälligen Unterschiede in der Darstellungsweise lassen aber sehr wohl den Schluss zu, dass es in den Reliefs der Trajanssäule um die Dokumentation von unmittelbarer Ereignisgeschichte ging. Dass die Vermittlung dieser auf öffentlichen Denkmälern im Sinne politischer Propaganda stand und einen ideologischen ›Wertekatalog‹ implizierte, darf als selbstverständlich gelten. Sowohl durch antike als auch durch moderne Umstände lässt sich dies untermauern: Dass auch die literarische Geschichtsschreibung unter propagandistischen Gesichtspunkten verfasst wurde, belegt u. a. die Korrespondenz des Lucius Verrus mit Frontin, in welchem der Kaiser bei dem Schriftsteller einen Bericht über seine Partherkriege bestellt[49]. Für diese Auftragsarbeit werden dem Literaten diverse Dokumente, Briefe, Bilder etc. zur Verfügung gestellt. Abschließend schreibt der Kaiser, dass seine Taten nur so groß erscheinen werden, wie sie der Verfasser erscheinen lässt. Die herausragende Rolle des Kaisers und die Betonung seiner Tugenden und Leistungen in dem Bildfries widerspricht in keiner Hinsicht literarischen Kriegskommentaren. Wie eingangs angesprochen, liefert auch die moderne ›objektive‹ Berichterstattung durch ›reale‹ Bilder nur den Eindruck eines authentischen Berichtes. Der Eindruck der durch Bilder vermittelten ›Realität‹ lässt Manipulation und Propaganda in den Hintergrund treten[50].

Das zweite Argument, dass die Bilderzählung als literarischer Bericht nicht erträglich gewesen sei bzw. der Dynamik der Literatur entgegenstünde, wird entkräftet durch die einzigen erhaltenen Vergleichsbeispiele zu der kontinuierenden Darstellungsweise auf der Trajanssäule, durch die Wiener Genesis und den sog. Josua-Rotulus. Der Basistext wurde – ähnlich einem Drehbuch – auf die wichtigsten Ereignisse reduziert und büßte damit seinen literarischen Wert ein. Ein Blick auf die erhaltenen illustrierten Bücher narrativen Inhaltes zeigte darüber hinaus, dass sich literarischer Volltext eben nicht mit kontinuierenden Bilderzählungen verbindet.

Kann man also den Entwurf für die Trajanssäule als Drehbuch bezeichnen? Wenn ja, wie könnte dieses ausgesehen haben? Die prominente Position der Säule zwischen den beiden Bibliotheken, die auch eine Art Staatsarchiv beinhalteten[51], der spiralförmige Fries, der sich um den Säulenschaft windet, all das hat schon sehr früh die Assoziation mit einer ausgerollten Buchrolle nahegelegt. Nun durfte man an illustrierte Rotuli mit kontinuierenden Illustrationen vor der von Weitzmann rekonstruierten Geschichte der Buchmalerei nicht mehr denken. Diese ist heute großteils widerlegt[52], und es zeigt sich, dass Texte narrativen Inhaltes erst sehr spät illustriert waren, dass alle illustrierten Bücher einen ausgesprochenen Luxuscharakter hatten und es keineswegs eine typische Illustrationsweise gab. Jeder illustrierte Codex war wohl eine Auftragsarbeit, die bestimmten Ansprüchen gerecht werden musste. Vor diesem Hintergrund wird man für ein Monument wie die Trajanssäule von höchstem politischen Rang und kaiserlichem Auftrag sehr wohl daran denken können, dass man ein neues Medium schuf: Eine kontinuierend illustrierte Buchrolle, als Entwurf, sozusagen als Drehbuch für das neue Medium Triumphsäule. Diese Neuschöpfung basierte auf der Tradition der Triumphalmalerei zur Dokumentation historischer Ereignisse und der Wertschätzung von Luxusausgaben von Büchern. Hiermit war ein Medium vorhanden, das zur Wiedergabe historischer Ereignisse bzw. von dem was als Ereignisgeschichte der Gesellschaft vermittelt werden sollte, geeignet war. Paraphrasierte literarische Texte als ›Drehbuch‹ für Bilderfolgen sind aus der Spätantike überliefert, die zugehörigen Bildzyklen folgen denselben ›filmischen‹ Regeln wie die kontinuierende Bilderzählung der Trajanssäule. Die Vorstellung, dass man nun dieses ›Drehbuch‹, eine illustrierte Buchrolle, in den öffentlichen Bibliotheken aufbewahrte, ist zwar spekulativ, aber reizvoll: Die Unlesbarkeit der Reliefs könnte der interessierte ›Leser‹ durch Hinzuziehung der Buchrolle überwinden. Der hohen Wertschätzung für illustrierte Prachtausgaben entsprechend hätte sie in den kaiserlichen Bibliotheken eine würdige, archivarische Aufbewahrung gefunden, wodurch der Eindruck eines authentischen Berichtes, der in den Reliefs formalen Niederschlag fand, auch durch den Kontext unterstrichen worden wäre[53].

Die Dokumentation der Ereignisse auf dem Relieffries unter ideologischen Gesichtspunkten zielt durch die räumliche und zeitliche Fixierung der Szenen darauf, den Eindruck eines authentischen Berichtes zu vermitteln, »... so soll doch vor allem gezeigt werden, daß die Ideologie des Sieges und der Herrschaft unter Traian Wirklichkeit geworden ist.«[54] Diese Ergebnisse T. Hölschers sprechen nicht dagegen, in den Reliefs einen illustrierten paraphrasierten Kriegskommentar zu sehen, denn die Vergleichsbeispiele, die in der Darstellungsweise denselben narrativen Regeln folgen, sind Bildzyklen mit paraphrasierten Begleittexten. Die Umsetzung letzterer erfolgte naturgemäß unter rein visuellen Gesichtspunkten. So muss die ideologische Botschaft der Bilderzählung nicht der von P. Zanker formulierten Idee widersprechen: »Es ist faszinierend zu denken, der Fries sei eine Bildparaphrase dieser (Trajans) Commentarii. ... Durch die Reliefs werden Trajans Taten für alle Zeiten dokumentarisch festgehalten, und der Beweis, die Urkunde dafür, daß alles wirklich so gewesen ist, wie es die Bilder berichten, ist in der Bibliothek hinterlegt«[55].

Mit anderen Medien aber durch ›reale‹ Bilder wurde damals wie heute die Illusion einer objektiven Berichterstattung vermittelt. In den modernen Medien wird diese durch fotografische bzw. filmische Abbildung der Realität erreicht; in der Antike ist die kontinuierende Darstellungsweise mit der Situierung der Ereignisse in Raum und Zeit ihr Träger. Die in diesen ›objektiven Berichten‹ implizierten ideologischen Botschaften waren und sind Teil der gesellschaftlichen Wirklichkeitskonstruktion.

ANMERKUNGEN

[*] Die hier nur in aller Kürze präsentierten Überlegungen fassen erste Teilergebnisse eines Forschungsprojektes mit dem Titel *Erzählte Geschichte im Bild* zusammen, das im Rahmen einer Hertha Firnberg-Nachwuchsstelle am Institut für Klassische Archäologie in Wien durchgeführt wird. Mein Dank gilt dem BMBWK und dem FWF. Den VeranstalterInnen der Graduiertenkonferenz danke ich für die Möglichkeit, Teilergebnisse meines Projektes in diesem Rahmen präsentieren zu können.
Abkürzt zitierte Zeitschriften:
AA = Archäologischer Anzeiger
AnnEconSocCiv = Annales. Economies, sociétés, civilisations
AnzWien = Anzeiger. Österreichische Akademie der Wissenschaften
ArtB = The Art Bulletin
BJb = Bonner Jahrbücher des Rheinischen Landesmuseums in Bonn und des Vereines von Altertumsfreunden im Rheinlande
JbKuHistSamml = Jahrbuch der Kunsthistorischen Sammlungen in Wien
JdI = Jahrbuch des Deutschen Archäologischen Instituts
RM = Mitteilungen des Deutschen Archäologischen Instituts, Römische Abteilung

[1] Von den Hoff, Ralf, Stefan Schmidt (Hg.), Konstruktionen von Wirklichkeit. Bilder im Griechenland des 5. und 4. Jahrhunderts v. Chr., Stuttgart 2001, S. 11-19
[2] Von den Hoff, Schmidt 2001, S. 18
[3] Hölscher, Tonio, Römische Bildsprache als semantisches System, Abhandlungen der Heidelberger Akademie der Wissenschaften. Philosophisch-Historische Klasse 2, Heidelberg 1987; Alföldi, Maria R., Bild und Bildersprache der römischen Kaiser, Beispiele und Analysen, Mainz 1999

[4] Stellvertretend für zahlreiche Arbeiten zu Fremdvölker- bzw. Feindesdarstellungen in der römischen Kunst: Krierer, Karl R., Sieg und Niederlage. Untersuchungen physiognomischer und mimischer Phänomene in Kampfdarstellungen der römischen Plastik, Wien 1995

[5] Eine ausführliche Analyse der Erzählstruktur an Einzelbeispielen soll an anderer Stelle erscheinen, da dies den vorgesehen Rahmen des Konferenzbeitrages sprengen würde, vgl. auch Anm. *

[6] Hölscher, Tonio, Die Anfänge römischer Repräsentationskunst, in: RM 85 (1978) S. 315-357; Ders., Die Geschichtsauffassung in der römischen Repräsentationskunst, in: JdI 95 (1980) S. 265-321, bes. S. 269-273

[7] Die Wandmalereien in dem um 300 v. Chr. zu datierenden Fabiergrab vom Esquilin geben Ereignisse aus den Samnitenkriegen wieder; Brilliant, Richard, Visual Narratives. Storytelling in Etruscan and Roman Art, Ithaca and London 1984, S. 26f. mit Lit.

[8] Borda, Mario, Il fregio pittorico delle origini di Roma, in: Capitolium 34 (1959) S. 3-10; Brilliant 1984, S. 30

[9] Hölscher 1980, S. 265-321, bes. 299f.

[10] Hölscher 1980, S. 303f.

[11] u. a. Holliday, Peter J., Roman Triumphal Painting: Its Function, Development, and Reception, in: ArtB 79 (1997) S. 130-147 mit Lit.; Settis 1988, S. 93-100

[12] Koeppel, Gerhard, Official State Reliefs of the city of Rome in the Imperial Age. A Bibliography, in: Aufstieg und Niedergang der römischen Welt II Prinzipat, 12.1 (1982) S. 477-506; Torelli, Mario, Typology and Structure of Roman Historical Reliefs, Ann Arbor 1982

[13] Torelli 1982, S. 119-136

[14] Vgl. Anm. 49

[15] Zusammengefasst bei Brilliant 1984, S. 16-20; und zuletzt: Stansbury-O'Donnell, Mark D., Pictorial Narrative in Ancient Greek Art, Cambridge 1999

[16] Hassel, Franz Josef, Der Trajansbogen in Benevent, Mainz 1966

[17] Hassel 1966, unternimmt den Versuch, in den Darstellungen konkrete historische Ereignisse festzumachen; dagegen Fittschen, Klaus, Das Bildprogramm des Trajansbogens in Benevent, in: AA (1972) S. 742-788

[18] Fittschen 1972, S. 785-788

[19] Hölscher 1980, S. 265-321

[20] Hölscher 1987

[21] Hölscher 1980

[22] Ausgewählte Lit. mit ausführlicher Bibliographie: Lehmann-Hartleben, Karl, Die Trajanssäule. Ein römisches Kunstwerk am Beginn der Spätantike, Berlin – Leipzig 1926; Settis, Salvatore, Adriano La Regina, Giovanni Agosti, Vincenzo Farinella, La Colonna Traiana, Torino 1988; Koeppel, Gerhard, Die historischen Reliefs der römischen Kaiserzeit 8, in: BJb 191 (1991) S. 135-198; ders., dass. 9, in: BJb 192 (1992) S. 61-122; Coarelli, Filippo, La colonna Traiana, Roma 1999; zuletzt: Hölscher, Tonio, Bilder der Macht und Herrschaft, in: Nünnerich-Asmus, Annette (Hg.), Traian. Ein Kaiser der Superlative am Beginn einer Umbruchzeit, Antike Welt Sonderbd. Mainz 2002, S. 127-144

[23] Der Begriff der kontinuierenden Darstellungsweise wurde von F. Wickhoff in Zusammenhang mit den Miniaturen der Wiener Genesis geprägt und folgendermaßen definiert: »Hier wird nicht ein entscheidender Moment gewählt … Nicht einzelne, epochemachende Augenblicke treten zu einem Zyklus zusammen, sondern, wie der

Text strömt, begleiten ihn die jeweiligen Helden der Erzählung in continuierlich sich reihenden Zuständen unbekümmert um das Gesetz der Erfahrung, daß nur dasjenige zugleich gesehen werden könne, was zur gleichen Zeit vor sich geht ... «. Wickhoff, Franz, Wilhelm Ritter von Hartel, Die Wiener Genesis, JbKuHistSamml, Beilage 15-16 (1895) S. 7f. Zusammenfassende Diskussion zum Problem der narrativen Darstellungsweisen und besonders der kontinuierenden: Zimmermann, Barbara, Überlegungen zur Textabhängigkeit kontinuierender Darstellungen in der römischen und spätantiken Kunst, in: Akten des 9. Österreichischen Archäologentages, Salzburg 6.-8.12.2001 (im Druck).

[24] Malissard, Alain, Une nouvelle approche de la Colonne Trajane, in: Aufstieg und Niedergang der römischen Welt II Prinzipat, 12.1 (1982) S. 579-606

[25] Hierzu detailliert Settis 1988, S. 132-182

[26] Brilliant 1984, S. 90-109

[27] Birt, Theodor, Die Buchrolle in der Kunst. Archäologisch-antiquarische Untersuchungen zum antiken Buchwesen, Leipzig 1907, S. 270

[28] Birt 1907, S. 271

[29] Weitzmann, Kurt, Illustrations in Roll and Codex, Princeton [1]1947, Princeton [2]1970; Ders., Ancient Book Illumination, Princeton 1959

[30] Farinella, Vincenzo, La Colonna Traiana. Un esempio di lettura verticale, in: Prospettiva 26 (1981) S. 2-9

[31] Koeppel, Gerhard, The Grand Pictorial Tradition of Roman Historical Representation during the Early Empire, in: Aufstieg und Niedergang der römischen Welt II Prinzipat, 12.1 (1982) S. 507-535, bes. S. 517

[32] Hölscher 1980, S. 265-321, bes. S. 290-297; Baumer, Lorenz E., Tonio Hölscher, Lorenz Winkler, Narrative Systematik und politisches Konzept in den Reliefs der Trajansäule. Drei Fallstudien, in: JdI 106 (1991) S. 261-295

[33] Baumer, Hölscher, Lorenz 1991, S. 271-277

[34] Baumer, Hölscher, Lorenz 1991, S. 274

[35] Hölscher 1980, S. 292f.

[36] Settis, Salvatore, Le colonne Trajane. Invention, composition, disposition, in: AnnEconSocCiv 40 (1985) S. 1151-1194; Settis 1988, S. 188-202

[37] Malissard 1982, bes. S. 581

[38] Vgl. Anm. 29

[39] Sörries, Reiner, Repertorium der christlich – antiken Buchmalerei, Wiesbaden 1992

[40] Zimmermann, Barbara, Die Codexillustration als neuer Kunstzweig – Spiegel einer geänderten Funktion des Buches in der Spätantike, in: Rutgers, Leonard V., Pieter W. Van der Horst, H. Havelaar, Lieve Teugels (Hg.), The Use of Sacred Books in the Ancient World, Leuven 1998, S. 263-285

[41] Gerstinger, Hans, Die Wiener Genesis. Textband zur Faksimile, Wien 1931; Mazal, Otto, Kommentar zur Wiener Genesis, Wien 1983; Zimmermann, Barbara, Die Wiener Genesis im Rahmen der antiken Buchmalerei. Ikonographie, Darstellungsweise, Illustrationsverfahren und Aussageintention, Diss. Wien 1996 (i. Dr.).

[42] Codex purpureus Rossanensis, Faksimile Graz 1985; Commentarium a cura di Cavallo, Guglielmo, Jean Gribomont, William C. Loerke (1987); Sevrugian, Petra, Der Rossano – Codex und die Sinope-Fragmente, Worms 1990

[43] Ausführlich zur Textredaktion Mazal 1983, S. 86-92

[44] Diese ›Fehler‹ bzw. Ungereimtheiten wurden Jahrzehnte lang mit einem Archetyp der Handschrift aus hellenistisch-jüdischen Kreisen erklärt, der die von Weitzmann

postulierte Form eines Rotulus mit in den Textkolumnen eingefügten Illustrationen aufwies; vgl. u. a. Mazal 1983

[45] Cod. Vat. Pal. gr. 431. Weitzmann, Kurt, The Joshua Roll. A Work of Macedonian Renaissance, Princeton 1948; Mazal, Otto, Kommentar (zur) Josua-Rolle. Vollständige Faksimile-Ausgabe im Originalformat des Codex Vaticanus Palatinus graecus 431 der Biblioteca Apostolica Vaticana, Wien 1984

[46] Lowden, John, The Octateuchs. A Study in Byzantine Manuscript Illustration, Pennsylvania 1992; Kresten, Otto, Die Hinrichtung des Königs von Gai (Jos. 8,29). Der realienkundliche Beitrag des Skylitzes Matritensis zur Klärung eines ikonographischen Problems im Josua-Rotulus der Bibliotheca Apostolica Vaticana (Cod. Vat. Pal. Gr. 431), in: AnzWien 126 (1989) S. 111-130; ders., Parerga zur Ikonographie des Josua-Rotulus und der illuminierten byzantinischen Oktateuche. I. Die ›Grabstele‹ von Jericho, in: Sode, Claudia, Sarolta Takács (Hg.), Novum Millenium. Studies on Byzantine History and Culture, dedicated to P. Speck, Ashgate 2001, S. 185-212

[47] Auf den engen Bild-Text-Zusammenhang verwies bereits Lietzmann, Hans, Zur Datierung der Josuarolle, in: Mittelalterliche Handschriften, Festschrift H. Degering, Leipzig 1926, S. 181-185

[48] Baumer, Hölscher, Lorenz 1991, S. 293

[49] Hierzu ausführlich Settis 1988, S. 105f.

[50] Hierzu auch Hölscher 2002, S.132-134

[51] Zanker 1970, S. 527

[52] Geyer, Angelika, Die Genese narrativer Buchillustration. Der Miniaturenzyklus zur Aeneis im Vergilius Vaticanus, Frankfurt am M. 1989; Zimmermann 1996

[53] Die Ähnlichkeiten mit den Reliefs der Markussäule könnten ebenfalls mit diesem ›Entwurf‹ erklärt werden, der in diesem Falle auch noch nach Jahrzehnten zur Hand gewesen wäre.

[54] Hölscher 2002, S. 120

[55] Zanker, Paul, Das Trajansforum in Rom, in: AA (1970) S. 499-544, bes. 527f.

BIBLIOGRAPHIE

Baumer, Lorenz, Hölscher 1991 = Baumer, Lorenz E., Tonio Hölscher, Lorenz Winkler, Narrative Systematik und politisches Konzept in den Reliefs der Trajansäule. Drei Fallstudien, in: JdI 106 (1991) S. 261-295

Birt 1907 = Birt, Theodor, Die Buchrolle in der Kunst. Archäologisch-antiquarische Untersuchungen zum antiken Buchwesen, Leipzig 1907

Brilliant 1984 = Brilliant, Richard, Visual Narratives. Storytelling in Etruscan and Roman Art, Ithaca and London 1984

Fittschen 1972 = Fittschen, Klaus, Das Bildprogramm des Trajansbogens in Benevent, in: AA (1972) S. 742-788

Hassel 1966 = Hassel, Franz Josef, Der Trajansbogen in Benevent, Mainz 1966

Hölscher 1978 = Hölscher, Tonio, Die Anfänge römischer Repräsentationskunst, in: RM 85 (1978) S. 315-357

Hölscher 1980 = Hölscher, Tonio, Die Geschichtsauffassung in der römischen Repräsentationskunst, in: JdI 95 (1980) S. 265-321

Hölscher 1987 = Hölscher, Tonio, Römische Bildsprache als semantisches System,

Abhandlungen der Heidelberger Akademie der Wissenschaften. Philosophisch-Historische Klasse 2, Heidelberg 1987

Hölscher 2002 = Hölscher, Tonio, Bilder der Macht und Herrschaft, in: Nünnerich-Asmus, Annette (Hg.), Traian. Ein Kaiser der Superlative am Beginn einer Umbruchzeit, Antike Welt Sonderbd. Mainz 2002, S. 127-144

Malissard 1982 = Malissard, Alain, Une nouvelle approche de la Colonne Trajane, in: Aufstieg und Niedergang der römischen Welt II Prinzipat, 12.1 (1982) 579-606

Mazal 1983 = Mazal, Otto, Kommentar zur Wiener Genesis, Wien 1983

Settis 1988 = Settis, Salvatore, Adriano La Regina, Giovanni Agosti, Vincenzo Farinella, La Colonna Traiana, Torino 1988

Torelli 1982 = Torelli, Mario, Typology and Structure of Roman Historical Reliefs, Ann Arbor 1982

Von den Hoff, Schmidt 2001 = Von den Hoff, Ralf, Stefan Schmidt (Hg.), Konstruktionen von Wirklichkeit. Bilder im Griechenland des 5. und 4. Jahrhunderts v. Chr., Stuttgart 2001

Weitzmann 1970 = Weitzmann, Kurt, Illustrations in Roll and Codex, Princeton ^{2}1970

Zanker 1970 = Zanker, Paul, Das Trajansforum in Rom, in: AA (1970) S. 499-544

Zimmermann 1996 = Zimmermann, Barbara, Die Wiener Genesis im Rahmen der antiken Buchmalerei. Ikonographie, Darstellungsweise, Illustrationsverfahren und Aussageintention, Diss. Wien 1996 (i. Dr.)

InFormA(k)tionen. *Metamorphosen* als intertextuelles Prinzip

URSULA REBER

> The real problem lies [...] in the notion of »classical simplicity« that we have fathered onto the ancients in the last two centuries, which makes us want to see them as more simple than they really were. Ovid [...] was a *doctus poeta*, not a Hans Andersen in verse.[1]

Hans-George Ruprecht greift für seinen Aufsatz *The Reconstruction of Intertextuality*[2] auf den ›Gottvater‹ der Intertextualität, Ovid, mit der Erzählung der in ihrer poetologischen Kunstfertigkeit konkurrierenden Webmeisterinnen Minerva und Arachne zurück. Die Praxis des *intertextum*, der Verflechtungsfigur oder des verflechtenden Ornaments, verweist nicht nur »to the borderline phenomena of closure«[3], sondern auch auf ihre Funktion, in (Ausdrucks)Form und Inhalt den Prozess der Bedeutungsproduktion und die (poetische) Semiose in Gang zu halten.

Wie sich die Ovidischen *Metamorphosen* in den Rahmen römischer intertextueller Praxis fügen, gilt es zu umreißen. Erzähltheoretisch betrachtet, folgt die Metamorphose einem komplexen intertextuellen Verfahren. Aus den Ovidischen *Metamorphosen* kann eine Erzählweise gewonnen werden, die auf andere Texte übertragbar ist und ein Muster für ›metamorphosisches Erzählen‹ abgibt. In Ergänzung dazu verlangt das Plötzlich-Fantastische und Unverständlich-Erschreckende des Verwandlungs-Sujets, auf die Verflechtungspotenziale der ›Metamorphose‹ zwischen Bild- und Textdiskurs zu rekurrieren. Indem ich das Verwandlungsmoment als Bild begreife, wird ein Moment der Dynamik erkennbar, das von der spannungsgeladenen Gleichzeitigkeit zweier disparater und widersprüchlicher Körper in einem Übergangsmoment geprägt ist, wobei die Dynamik wiederum durch die Erzählung in einen verständlichen und motivierten Vorgang aufgelöst wird.

ANTIKE INTERTEXTUALITÄT IM SPANNUNGSFELD VON *AEMULATIO* UND *IMITATIO*

Mit der Bloomschen[4] Kategorie *clinamen*, der Abweichung oder der Richtungsänderung an einem gewissen Punkt einer Narration, kann die antike ›Arbeit am Mythos‹[5] umrissen werden. Der Mythos als je spezifisch aktiviertes Narrativ und explizite Narrationsvariante eines ›Vorgängers‹ unterliegt der ständigen Neuinterpretation, deren Geheimnis im jeweiligen *clinamen* liegt. Im Kontextwechsel oder der Kontextverschiebung wird der Gehalt eines mythischen Narrativs jedesmal neu akzentuiert. Legt z. B. Euripides bei seiner *Medea* das Gewicht auf das übersteigerte Unrechtsbewusstsein der Heldin, das sie zum Kindsmord aus Rache treibt, akzentuiert Seneca das Barbarische an der Fremden, die aus mangelnder Kultur Lust an der Grausamkeit verspürt. Die jeweils mittransportierte ideologische Erzählung könnte trotz des gemeinsamen Plots unterschiedlicher nicht sein. Die eine Medea hat ungeachtet ihrer ethnischen Zugehörigkeit gegenüber dem treulosen Gatten »Recht« innerhalb einer Weltauffassung, die von der Universalität athenischen Rechts und platonisch geprägten Gleichheitsvorstellungen ausgeht. Nur in der Ausblendung von Medeas »Nationalität«, Sozialisation und kultureller Prägung ist es möglich, der Fremden nicht nur ein mit athenischem Gesetz und Humanismus konformes Gerechtigkeitsempfinden, sondern sogar die bessere Einsicht in Recht und Ehre als dem griechischen Gatten zuzusprechen. Für den Römer Seneca existiert diese Form eines universalen Gesetzes allgemeiner ›Menschlichkeit‹ (als Gleichheit) nicht mehr: Seine Kaukasierin wird gerade durch die von Euripides übergangenen Eigenschaften der ethnischen und kulturellen Fremdheit bestimmt. In die Wildheit dieses Fremdseins hat der vom Römer interpretierte Grieche keinen Einblick mehr, die andere Welt ist ihm so unzugänglich, dass die ausländische Königstochter zum oppositionell Anderen des Eigenen wird, zur unkultivierten Hexe, die in der fremden Kultur nicht gelernt hat, ihre Affekte zu zügeln, und durch verbotenes magisches Wissen äußerst gefährlich wird. Senecas *Medea* ist das bis ins Absurde übersteigerte Fehlverhalten nach den Werten und Lehren seiner eigenen philosophischen Schule, der Stoa. Das ›Andere‹, das sie verkörpert, ist zunächst das Andere im Eigenen, nicht das vollkommen Unbekannte, doch das Surplus der fremden Herkunft aus dem weiten und unbekannten Nordosten potenzieren dies zum genuin Fremdartigen.

Exakter, wenn auch nicht ähnlich weitreichend, lässt sich das *clinamen* im Falle der Orpheus-Darstellung bei Ovid und Vergil ausmachen, weil im Gegensatz zum strittigen Hypotext Senecas die intertextuelle Beziehung zwischen den *Georgica* Vergils (iv 453-527) und dem Buch x der *Metamor-*

phosen fest steht. Vergil lässt Aristaeus dadurch, dass er sie begehrlich verfolgt, Eurydices Tod verschulden. Der zweite Verlust Eurydices wird durch einen Anfall von Wahn (*dementia*) begründet, auf den Eurydice aktiv reagiert und Orpheus wegen seines *furors* Vorwürfe macht. Der ovidische Erzähler hingegen tilgt Aristaeus aus der Erzählung; Eurydice tritt zufällig auf die Schlange, an deren Biss sie stirbt, so dass die Faten als regellose und blinde Mächte in den Vordergrund treten. In weiterer Abweichung dreht Orpheus sich nicht in momentaner Verwirrung, sondern aus Liebe und Sorge (*amor* und *metuens, ne deficeret*) nach der Gattin um, die sofort klaglos entschwindet. Die Abweichungsabsicht gegenüber Vergil wird unmissverständlich expliziert, da der Erzähler versichert, Eurydice habe, weil Liebe keine Anklage verdiene, Orpheus *nicht* beschuldigt. Durch das *clinamen* wird Eurydices Reaktion aus dem Lebens- in den Liebes-Kontext verlagert.

Im Zuge seiner chronotopischen und dialogischen Theorie des Romans[6] schreibt Bachtin dessen Entstehung gesellschaftlichen Formen zu, die eine gewisse, in der antiken Gesellschaft nicht gegebene Privatheit verlangen. Auch Bachtin geht also mit einem lang verteidigten Gemeinplatz der Klassischen Philologie von einer extroversiven und nicht-subjektiven Verfasstheit des antiken Menschen aus, dem seine Identität über seine Öffentlichkeit, über das Bei-allem-gesehen-Werden und seine gesellschaftlichen Funktionen und Ämter zusätzlich zur Vermögenskonstitution sicher ›gegeben‹ sei, auf Grund der Konstanz und geringen Wandelbarkeit des öffentlichen Standes, die ein komplexes Gebilde einer mehrschichtigen Persönlichkeit verhindere. Zwar bezieht sich dies nur auf die literarische Form der (Auto)Biografie, doch spricht die Theorie, die für die Antike literarische Monologizität konstatiert, implizit auch für Monologizität der »realen« Biografie, wenn sich Umwelt und Literatur in transtextuellem Zusammenhang befinden.

Erste komplexere literarische Formen bindet Bachtin an das Thema der Metamorphose mit ihrem folkloristischen Bezug unbestimmbaren Alters und ihrer Nähe zum Mythos[7]. Obwohl die Metamorphose vordergründig einen Aspekt der Ungleichzeitigkeit[8] (Sprunghaftigkeit und Stockung der Entwicklung mit entsprechenden Zeitreihen) und Disparatheit in die »wie aus Marmor gegossene« Einheitlichkeit der antiken Lebensgeschichte bringt, kommt Bachtin dennoch – wie auch einer der heutigen »klassischen« Ovidphilologen, Ernst August Schmidt[9] – zu dem paradoxen Ergebnis, dass dennoch die sich selbst gleich bleibende Identität nicht aufgehoben, sondern bestätigt wird, was sich erzählerisch in der Stimmeneinheit und in der Vereinheitlichung durch einen in Ton und Wissensperspektive gleich bleibenden Erzähler niederschlägt, der das metamorphosische Ge-

schehen einem fantastischen Raum des Ontologisch-Allegorisch-Gleichnishaften oder Märchenhaft-Folkloristischen einschreibt.
In der »mechanisch« gereihten Enzyklopädie von Erstaunlichem der Ovidischen *Metamorphosen* kommt weder ein exoterischer (Öffentlichkeits-) noch ein autobiografischer, allenfalls ein exotischer Diskurs zustande. Da die mythische, durch ihre Ur-Vergangenheit zeitlose Narration aufgehoben ist, innerhalb derer die Metamorphose eine organische Aufgabe erfüllt, und an ihre Stelle keine lebensgeschichtlich begründete Narration tritt, entsprechen die Ovidischen *Metamorphosen* eher dem vom Zufall und von der Ortlosigkeit geprägten Chronotopos des griechischen Abenteuerromans als dem gegenwartsbezogenen des Romans. Die metamorphosische Erzählweise befindet sich demnach mehr im Dialog mit anderen literarischen Texten und Narratologien als mit ihrer konkreten Umwelt.

NARRATOLOGIE DER *METAMORPHOSEN*/METAMORPHOSE

Die ›*Metamorphosen*-Erzählung‹ ist eine Art, sichtbare Naturwirklichkeit abzubilden (›mimetische Funktion‹) bzw. in mythischen Entstehungszusammenhängen herzustellen (›konstruktive Funktion‹). Dabei dienen heterogene Kategorien wie ›das Wünschbare‹ – dass z. B. pietätvolles Handeln wie im Falle von Philemon & Baucis belohnt wird (viii 611-724) – ›das Erlebte‹ in einer allgegenwärtigen römischen Alltagskultur,[10] ›das Erkannte‹ in Sentenzen und Maximen und ›das Halluzinierte‹, worunter das Fantastische des metamorphotischen Vorgangs ebenso fällt wie das Fantasma unerbittlicher, machtbesessener Gottheiten und blutrünstiger Menschen. Literatur als »professionelles Erzählen« enträt weiterhin nicht der Selbstreferenzialität, die aus produktionsästhetischer Sicht mehr oder weniger zufällig ist (im Zuge der Textauswahl des *doctus poeta* Ovid unterstelle ich ein Weniger).
Die Transtextualität[11] der *Metamorphosen* betrifft alles, was als zeitspezifisch gefasst werden kann, d. h. die literarische Reflexion auf die jeweilige historische, soziologische, kulturelle Situation (oder ihr Fehlen) der jeweiligen Entstehungsumgebung.[12] Andererseits stehen die rhetorischen und narratologischen Verfahren zur Debatte, die die *Metamorphosen* zur Herstellung von Realität aufbieten. Durch die serielle Natur aneinander gereihter Einzelerzählungen gewinnt die Art, wie der Text sich selbst strukturiert, Bedeutung. Der extremste Fall besteht in der ›Ipseität‹, die in ihren unterschiedlichen »Treueformen« vom strengen Selbstzitat bis zur variierten Formelbildung reicht.[13] Metamorphosen werden vermittels Ipseität »sichtbar« gemacht. Ihre Überzeugungskraft und ihren Effekt von »Wirklichkeit« erhalten sie erst in der Wiederholung, nicht als »einzelne[] isolierte[] Erscheinungen«, die »den Charakter einer äußeren wundersamen Verwand-

lung im besonderen Einzelfall [annehmen]«[14]. Parallelität, Wiederholung und Selbstzitat überzeugen gleichsam den Rezipienten von der Wahrscheinlichkeit des Geschilderten, auch wenn dies in totalem Gegensatz zur erfahrbaren Lebensrealität steht.

In jedem neuen Narrativ einer (thematischen) Serie wird ein frischer Aspekt aufgerissen; die Serie lebt nicht nur von der Wiederkehr des Gleichen, sondern in diesem Gleichen von der Variation. Die Monotonie der Ipseität macht durch teilweise minimale Kontrastierung das Andere im Gleichen erst sichtbar.[15] In die erzählte Möglichkeitswelt wird das fantastische, der kommonsensualen Alltags- und »Erfahrungs«welt widersprechende Element der Verwandlung und der mit ihr verbundenen »Lügengestalten« in steter Perspektivenverschiebung mit einem hohen Aufwand an erzählter Sinnlichkeit (Metaphern, Vergleiche u. a. Textbilder) und strenger Blickführung eingebracht. Zugleich wird durch die ständig mitlaufende, ironisierende Kommentartätigkeit des Erzählers die Skepsis über den Wahrheits-, Wahrscheinlichkeits- oder Lügengehalt des Erzählten aufrechterhalten. Beide Momente sind notwendig, um die Monotonie von Seriellem und Ipseität in die Lust am Lesen/Hören zu überführen.

In der metamorphosischen Narration erfolgt die Herstellung eines ›künstlich Natürlichen‹[16] für die transportierte Erzähllehre (Narratologie) der *Metamorphosen* mit den Merkmalen der Vernatürlichung des fantastischen Elements in der seriellen Häufung des Unglaublichen und der Reduktion komplizierter Plots auf einen narrativen Kern, wie z. B. »die verfolgte Nymphe«. Die Kunst oder Künstlichkeit liegt einerseits in der Transtextualität, dem Einbruch bspw. moderner Technik, wie dem geborstenen Wasserrohr als *tertium comparationis* zur Blutfontäne aus Pyramus' Brust, in die Möglichkeitswelt,[17] und andererseits der alexandrinischen Intertextualität, die keine noch so entlegene mythische Figur auslässt.

ARCHITEXTUALITÄT

Das metamorphosische Erzählen ist mit satirischen Techniken verbunden, die vom Spielerischen bis zum Grotesken reichen. Es will durch architextuelle[18] Transformationsakte in gewissem Sinne »Subversions«effekte erzielen. Die Grenzen einer Gattung werden ausgelotet, für welche die Reduktion der Tragödie[19] durch Ovid beispielhaft ist: Eine Figur tritt im dramatischen Monolog auf und lässt den Rezipienten am Kampf der Affekte mit der anschließenden Verfehlung teilhaben (erste Reduktion: Verkürzung auf den zentralen dramatischen Monolog), wobei die Katharsis ausgespart und die Verfehlung umgedeutet wird (zweite Reduktion).

Sorgfältig weist der Handlungsaufbau der *Dryope*-Erzählung (ix 324-393) darauf hin, dass diese nichts von der Heiligkeit des Lotusbaumes wissen kann. Dryopes Wunsch, ihrem Sohn mit Lotusblüten eine Freude zu machen, beinhaltet alles andere eher als eine Erkenntnisverfehlung, es sei denn, man würfe ihr vor, nicht in jeder mythologischen Variante oder dem Text, dem sie selbst entstammt, gelehrtengleich beheimatet zu sein, weil sie nicht weiß, dass »Lotis« nicht nur der Name dieses Baumes, sondern auch derjenige einer von Priap verfolgten Nymphe ist, die sich in den Baum verwandelt hat. Auch die Erzählerin der Geschichte weiß davon nichts und wird nur durch das Schauspiel vor ihren Augen vor dem gleichen Fehler bewahrt. Dryopes Schwester ist also keine Kontrastfigur zum Metamorphosen-Opfer, die mehr erkennte oder richtiger handelte. Die Verwandlung erfolgt aus der Figurenperspektive unmotiviert, wenn Dryopes harmlose und alltägliche Handlung des Blumenbrechens, als versteckter Frevel enttarnt und sie ihrerseits in einen Baum verwandelt wird. Die Motivation für die Strafe liegt nicht in einer falschen oder verweigerten Erkenntnis wie beim sophokleischen *Ödipus*, auch nicht in einem fehlerhaften Charakter, der ein marginales Gut zum Absoluten erhebt, – Dryope tritt sogar als besonders fromme Frau in Erscheinung, die vor dem Unglück den Nymphen Blumenopfer dargebracht hat –, sondern sie liegt einzig in einem ›fatalen‹ Namen versteckt, der sich nur aus dem Text selbst erklärt. Ein Geschöpf des Textes hat aber keine Chance, den Kosmos, in den es eingewoben ist, zu durchschauen.

Mit der Ankündigung, von der Weltentstehung an bis zur Gegenwart Weltgeschichte zu erzählen,[20] schreiben die *Metamorphosen* sich selbst allerdings kein Tragödien-, sondern ein episches und ein historisches Projekt zu. Aber auch in den entsprechenden Partien gehen mythische und ›historische‹ oder eher bereits historiografisch verwertete Stoffe ineinander über: Historisches Geschehen und historische Personen werden in den mythischen und fantastischen Kontext so sehr mithineingezogen, dass sie jeden Bezug zu ihrer eigentlichen (Lebens)zeit verlieren. Die Figuren Caesar und Augustus werden ihrer Taten, dessen, was eine *historia rerum gestarum* ausmachte, beraubt und als »passive Akteure« gestaltet, die fremden und höheren Mächten – wenn auch in positivem Sinne (Apotheose) – ausgeliefert sind. Zwar fügt sich das Verfahren, weithin und allgemein Bekanntes, wozu die historischen Leistungen Caesars und Augustus' unzweifelhaft gehören, zu verschweigen oder in wenigen, äußerst reduzierten Sätzen zu übergehen, zu den narrativen Techniken, wie sie im Falle besonders populärer Mythen angewendet werden – einem historiografischen Projekt aber ist es gegenläufig.

Die *Metamorphosen* präsentieren auf einer anderen Ebene narratologische Muster der Geschichtsschreibung: *historia* wird *per se* nicht als einheitlicher Zusammenhang organisch auseinander hervorgehender Ereignisse, sondern als Kette unverbundener Einzelereignisse begriffen, die durch erzählerische Interpretation erst zu einem einheitlichen Konzept gelangen kann. Die *Metamorphosen* behalten eine literal verstandene *historia rerum gestarum* bei. In ständigem Wechsel wird im Reihungsprinzip Historisches und Mythisches bis zur scheinbaren Identität miteinander verwoben, wobei jede einzelne *Metamorphosen*-Erzählung eine *res gestae* abbildet. Die Leseerwartung, die sich an der Ankündigung einer Geschichtsdarstellung ausgerichtet hat, wird in ihren Grundzügen durch die leichthin verbundene Reihung einzelner, sehr grob in einer chronologisch fortschreitenden Reihe angeordneter, in sich abgeschlossener und erwähnungswürdiger Geschehnisse bestätigt. Die Wahl des Sujets ›Metamorphose‹ impliziert eine verfließend-dynamische Weltsicht mit einer Vielzahl gestaltwandlerischer, »passiver Akteure«. Im Fortlauf der Erzählungen verlassen die menschlichen Figuren allerdings immer mehr ihren »Opferstatus« und beginnen zu handeln. Der Bereich dieses Handelns liegt allerdings gerade nicht im politisch-öffentlichen, für die Geschichtsschreibung interessanten, sondern im privat-erotischen Bereich. Insofern bleiben die *Metamorphosen* in Aufbau und geschilderter Zeitspanne dem Weltgeschichte-Anspruch treu, nicht jedoch in dem, was erzählt wird. Entgegen einem historiografischen Programm, das öffentliche Personen und besondere (kriegerische) Ereignisse in den Vordergrund rückt, die durch die mitgelieferten Interpretamente (Tugenden & Überlegenheit) der *gloria* des Imperiums dienen, erzählt, trotz allem kriegerischen Beiwerk und trotz historischer Persönlichkeiten, der *Metamorphosen*-Erzähler von Privatpersonen, Menschen wie Gottheiten, die ihr erotisches Schicksal zu meistern haben. In einem narrativen Gewand, das parodistisch an die Historiografie angelehnt ist, schreiben die *Metamorphosen* Privatgeschichte, durch die eine spezielle ›Weltgeschichte‹ hindurchschimmert: Die Erzählung, wie Eros Mars und Pluto domestiziert. Nebenbei werden in dieser Weltgeschichte die ursprünglichen Herrschafts- und Machtverhältnisse verkehrt: Die Gottheiten, die sich durch extremes Machtbewusstsein und Lust an der Herrschaft auszeichnen und ihre Lebensart ungebeten leidvoll auf den menschlichen Bereich ausdehnen, erweisen sich als weniger änderungsfähig oder -bedürftig als die Menschen, die durch die Kultur des Eros an Entscheidungskraft gewinnen. Dies geht m. E. über eine bloße »Aufklärungsgeschichte«, wie bspw. Lukrez sie betreibt, hinaus,[21] da die erotische Kultur fähig zu sein scheint, die nach wie vor ungebrochene Plötzlichkeit des Fatums in ihrer metamorphotischen Sichtbarkeit und Wirksamkeit zu für die Betroffenen positiven Effekten zu wenden, wie z. B. den verschiedenen Apotheosen, aber auch dem erfolgreichen Geschlechtswandel von der Frau zum Mann im Fall von Iphis (ix 666-797), die/der daraufhin die Geliebte Ianthe ehelichen darf.

Die historisch-epischen Personen leiht Ovid sich aus anderen Texten aus, die einerseits Epen sind, andererseits einem Fundus der von Schriftstellern und Politikern hergestellten und unterstützten Identitäten entstammen. Auch hinsichtlich der Archigattung ›Epos‹ arbeiten die *Metamorphosen* grenzüberschreitend. Eine Zuteilung zum Untergenre ›historisches‹ oder ›mythisches‹ Epos versagt, was nicht nur am beschriebenen Ineinander von mythischen und historischen Figuren liegt, zwischen denen solcherart hinsichtlich eines »Wahrheits-« oder »Tatsächlichkeitsgehaltes« keine Wertung sichtbar wird, sondern auch an der reflexiven Bezugnahme auf die epische Gattung. Diese Art von spielerisch-theoretischem Reflex auf das Epos als Königin unter den antiken Literaturgattungen ist kein unübliches Verfahren; innerhalb der epischen Dichtung selbst tritt er jedoch i. d. R. nicht auf, sondern ist in der kallimacheischen Kleindichtung beheimatet, die sich entstehungsgeschichtlich bewusst gegen die Königsgattung ›Epos‹ wandte. Dass der Erzähler in sein episches Projekt epenkritische Momente einfügt, korrespondiert damit, dass er das Heroische als genuine Sphäre des Epos narrativisch unterläuft und der *mock-epic* annähert, wenn er Kampfeshandlungen aus dem Zufall hervorgehen lässt, Sieg oder Niederlage dem ins Positiven gewendeten Ungeschick eines »Helden« zuschreibt und den Blick außerdem in der Konzentration auf die Diskrepanz zwischen Intention und Situation auf das Grotesk-Grausame und Komische heldischer Kampfeshandlungen etc. lenkt, und so in einem Akt der Travestie eine ernste Transformation erzeugt, die die Semantik des zu Grunde liegenden Architextes ins glatte Gegenteil verkehrt.[22] Erweiterungen um einen literaturkritischen Metatext, bzw. die Verlagerung und Einbettung eines literaturtheoretischen Intertextes aus einer anderen Gattung in die kritisierte selbst, führt beide in transformatorischer Absicht zu einer Art Exempelum zusammen.

KONTEXT ›MYTHOS‹

Die Verflechtungsgattung zwischen den architextuellen Gattungen Tragödie, Historiografie und Epos, bilden offensichtlich die Mythen, die in einem gemeinsamen narrativen und kosmologischen Kontext stehen. Die agonale Interpretation ihrer Handlungen erfolgte während der »mythischen Zeit« selbst (die v. a. Griechenland betrifft) durch Neu-Erzählen und Sichtbarmachung auf der Bühne und war in mehr oder weniger unveränderliche kultische Praktiken eingebunden.[23] Für Rom gestaltet sich die Eingrenzung von ›Mythos‹ einesteils komplizierter, andernteils aber auch einfacher, als es für Griechenland der Fall ist. Die Spezialität der von Griechenland »erborgten« und auf die etruskische Welt von *fairies* applizierten Mythen räumt ihnen von Beginn an einen Sonderstatus ein. Einerseits kamen sie bereits als philosophisch Gedeutete und politisch-kultisch Instrumentierbare auf die Römer, andererseits gaben sie sich immer schon als li-

terarische Tätigkeit zu erkennen. Sollten die zu Mythologien verschriftlichten Mythen im Rahmen homerischer und hesiodischer Überlieferung jemals mehr als literarische Geltungskraft und Verbindlichkeit besessen haben, ist es spätestens in der augustäischen Zeit damit vorbei, nicht nur durch die bei Ovid und den Neoterikern merkbare Fragmentarisierung und Verkünstlichung einzelner Mythen und Mytheme, die als narratives Erbe im preziös-erschöpfenden Wiedererzählen künstlich-archaische Räume eröffnen, sondern paradoxerweise v. a. durch das Nationalepos Vergils, das die Lücke zwischen *Ilias* und *Odyssee* geschlossen, die romanisierten Gottheiten Homers um spezifisch römische ergänzt und Rom in der mythopoetischen Geschichte den Status des Siegers verliehen hat. In diesem Nationalepos – gipfelnd in der *gens Iulia* – tritt Rom in ein mythisches und heroisch-geschichtliches Zeitalter zugleich ein, was jedoch keine nachhaltigen Auswirkungen auf den Kultus hatte. Die *Aeneis* hatte letztlich die Superiorität der römischen Kultur über die griechische bewiesen und den Fundus an wiedererzählbaren Geschichten um diejenigen von Aeneas, Turnus, Dido und die Sibylle erweitert, nicht mehr, aber auch nicht weniger.
Die *Metamorphosen* als Konkurrenzprojekt zur *Aeneis* füllen auf ihre Art mythologische Lücken, indem entlegene Figuren zu Akteuren ihrer jeweiligen Erzählung erhoben werden, indem im Vergleich zu den Epen Homers und Vergils Wichtigkeiten verschoben und die direkte *aemulatio* mit ihnen vermieden wird: Nicht Odysseus erzählt von seinen Abenteuern, sondern ein ehemaliger Begleiter (xiv); Aeneas und Dido werden ihrer Singularität beraubt, indem ihre kurze Verbindung ohne *happy end* in einem Satz abgehandelt wird, als ginge es um x-beliebige Personen (xiv 78-81); Aeneas' Gang in die Unterwelt mitsamt der Teichoskopie werden zu Gunsten der Erzählung der Sibylle von ihrer missglückten Liebesgeschichte mit Apoll extrem verkürzt (xiv 116-119) etc. Ovid bedient sich der alten und der neuen vergilischen Mythen gleichermaßen, geht allerdings von der kallimacheisch-neoterischen Partikularisierung ab und arbeitet an einer neuen ›Mythologie‹, für die bezeichnend ist, dass die abgeschlossenen *Metamorphosen*-Erzählungen nach dem Prinzip des Lehrgedichts durch einen quasi-philosophischen Überbau und durch die spezifische metamorphosische Narratologie zusammengehalten werden. Die Selbstreflexivität der Mythen entsteht v. a. durch die kommentierende Erzählerstimme, die in rezeptionsästhetischer Hinsicht Distanz zum Geschilderten hervorruft und solchermaßen ununterbrochen auf die Fiktionalität der Erzählungen verweist. Diese Erzählhaltung im Rahmen eines *carmen* ist nicht notwendig, da der römische Hörer/Leser von der Fiktionalität des Erzählten ausging und also nicht extra auf sie hingewiesen werden musste. Die Durchsetzung einer fiktiven Erzählung mit Erzählerkommentaren steht wiederum im Zeichen einer »innertextuellen Agonalität«[24] oder der Bloomschen ›*tessera*‹.

Mythen sind in sich agonal aufgebaut, indem zwei Einzelpersonen, zwei Gruppen oder eine Person und eine Gruppe gegeneinander agieren, woraus sich die Dynamik der mythischen Erzählung ergibt. Die *Metamorphosen* als Stoffsammlung verarbeiten Mythen, so dass sich diese agonale Struktur auch hier findet.[25] Die beharrlich kommentierende Stimme des Erzählers leistet in diesem Zusammenhang teilweise die Aufgabe des gelehrten Philosophen, der in einem Traktat Distanz schafft und die korrigierte Meinung anderer wiedergibt, zum anderen übernimmt sie eine didaktische Funktion[26], und zum dritten setzt sie sich an die Stelle des Chores. Der Erzähler schließt folglich einen ›Pakt mit dem Leser‹ und tritt mit diesem zusammen gegen den Text an. Mit einer auf diese Art paktierenden Erzählhaltung, wiederum aus der ständigen Verschmelzung verschiedener Gattungen herrührend, wird eine narratologische Lücke in den Erzählhaltungen der Vorgänger gefüllt. Diese hybride metamorphosische Narratologie verhindert eine sog. »lebensweltliche« Revitalisierung der Mythen oder gar des »Mythos«, sondern eröffnet das literarische, unendlich kombinatorische Spielfeld der Mythenerzählungen.

›VERWANDLUNG‹ ODER ›WANDELBARKEIT‹?

Metamorphose, Verwandlung, kann sowohl den Wechsel des Gewands, der Gestalt, des Mediums als Ausdrucksform als auch die genuine Essenzlosigkeit, die reine Alterität bezeichnen. Im Falle von ›Verwandlung‹ ist etwas Gleich-Bleibendes, mit sich selbst Identisches notwendig, an dem sich die Verwandlung vollzieht. Verzichtet man auf den »festen Kern«, bestünde keine Möglichkeit, sie zu erkennen, weder für den Betrachter noch für den/die sich Verwandelnde/n. Der Zusammenhang zwischen dem ersten und dem zweiten Status wäre nicht gegeben und somit beide füreinander kontingent. ›Wandelbarkeit‹ hingegen kann auf solche Konstanz und Identität verzichten. Was mit diesem Begriff evoziert wird, verhindert in seiner umfassenden Wirkkraft jede Form von Identität (oder lässt sie doch nur auf einer so abstrakten Ebene zu, dass sie verzichtbar wird). ›Wandelbarkeit‹ bezeichnet ein Gesetz, das nur die ständige Verschiedenheit von allem anderen, von sich selbst und jedem zeitlich fassbaren Zustand zulässt, das genauso gut auf der totalen Kontingenz wie auf der totalen kumulierenden Einheit und Quasi-Identität beruhen kann.

Die »erzählte Verwandlung«[27] braucht ein Moment der Identität. Die Erzählung ruft einerseits durch die grammatische Struktur mit Gleich-, Neben- und Unterordnungen der Sprache, andererseits durch semantische Isotopien im Sinne der Lesbarkeit und Verständlichkeit identitäre Zustände hervor. In diesem Sinne liegt es nahe, wie Schmidt[28], Pianezzola[29], Harzer[30] u. a. von der Metamorphose als Metapher auszugehen, die in gewissem Sinne die der Sprache inhärente identitäre »Prädikatenlogik« beispielhaft repräsentiert: Lycaon ist ein Wolf, Arachne ist eine Spinne. Aus diesen Attribuierungen des wölfischen Lycaon oder der Spinnerin Arachne entwickelt die *Metamorphosen*-Erzählung ein ›Aition‹ als »entzerrte« Metapher im erzählenden Gewand. Die der Metapher inhärente Dynamik relationiert sich im Medium der Erzählung zeitlich-diskursiv, wobei Ausgangs- und Endgestalt der Metamorphose erzählerisch miteinander identifiziert werden. Auf der narrativen Ebene – das Problem begegnete in Form erzählter Geschichten – sind bspw. Frauen und Bäume syntaktisch verbunden[31], so dass sich eine (scheinbare) Kernidentität ergibt.

Zahlreiche *Metamorphosen*-Erzählungen, auch die von Dryope, konstruieren allerdings unmögliche Identitäten: Dryope ist Lotus ist Lotis. Eine solche Dreifachidentität nähert sich bereits wieder der ›Wandelbarkeit‹ des steten Übergangs und Wechsels. Die Metamorphose als Verwandlungsmoment kann insofern auch als Überschneidung verschiedener Formen gefasst werden, die präsentiert wird. Vieles spricht für den präsentativen Aspekt der einzelnen *Metamorphosen*: der aitiologische Anspruch, das Körper-Sujet und die zentrale Stellung der Verwandlung. Der Ausschnitt eines Übergangsstadiums zwischen zwei Identitäten als reine Alterität ähnelt dem Effekt, der entsteht, wenn zwei Bilder übereinander projiziert werden: Auf dem einen ist Dryope als menschliche Gestalt, auf dem anderen ein Baum abgebildet; im changierenden Überlappen wird aus zweien eines gemacht. Die optischen Qualitäten, welche in den *Metamorphosen*-Erzählungen evoziert werden, sprechen gemeinsam mit dem präsentativen Aspekt für eine Bildqualität der Verwandlung. Als Bild ist ihr eine nicht-narrative Dynamik eigen, die anders als über die Metapher erschlossen werden kann. Sie liegt in der Kategorie der ›Alterität‹, insofern das Bild es leichter hat als die Narration, von einem Neben- oder Ineinander der Gegebenheiten auszugehen. Das »stumme« Bild fordert weniger die psychologisierende Figurenperspektive heraus als die erzählte Verwandlung, so dass im Diskurs über das Bild die Wandelbarkeit als Alterität, wenn überhaupt, nur eine schwache Konstruktion von Identität benötigt. Das Bindeglied »Lotus« zwischen Dryope und Lotis lässt die beiden Frauen sowohl nebeneinander existieren als auch im Baum ineinander fallen, ohne dass eine Kernidentität, an der sich der Gestaltwandel vollzieht, suggeriert werden muss. Das Bild scheint geeignet, eine Gesamtheit an komplexer und widersprüchlicher InFormA(k)tion wiederzugeben, wohingegen der Text in der Lektüre auf ein vorausgreifendes und retrospektiv-korrigierendes Verfahren des Nacheinander angewiesen ist.

KIPPBILD ›VERWANDLUNG‹

Die *in nova corpora mutat[ae] form[ae]* (i 1f.) transportieren zweierlei Bestimmungen: Einerseits glaubt man, einen Reigen an Figuren und Gestalten vor sich zu haben, die allmählich ineinander übergehen, wobei die eine Gestalt immer schon in die andere eingefaltet zu sein scheint. Augenfälligstes Beispiel hierfür sind die sog. »proteischen« Gestalten in den *Metamorphosen*, die das Verwandlungsvermögen von Geburt an in sich tragen, – aber auch Doppelwesen wie Ocyroe (ii 633-675), die sozusagen die unvollständige, nicht vollzogene Demarkation bis zur Verwandlung mit sich trägt. Ihre Metamorphose in ein Pferd trägt Merkmale einer Entscheidung, Vereinheitlichung und Harmonisierung. Im Sinne des ›Eingefaltet-Seins‹ der einen Gestalt in die andere, des windbebenden Lorbeers in die prüde und scheue Daphne (i 452-567) oder der nachtaktiven Fledermäuse in die lichtscheuen Minyastöchter (iv 389-415), tragen die meisten Verwandlungen »harmonische« Elemente in sich; die Evokation eines organischen Verwandlungsvorgangs in Formeln der Ipseität tut das Ihrige dazu:[32] Immer werden Arme zu Ästen, Finger zu Zweigen, Haut zu Rinde, Zehennägel zu Wurzeln etc. Auch die Bewegung derer, die sich in Vögel verwandeln, sind harmonisch, und es bedarf nur eines Augenschlags, um statt der fallenden Frau (Scylla viii 6-154) oder des rennenden Mannes (ibid.) den in der Luft segelnden bzw. sich aufschwingenden Vogel zu erblicken.[33] Der Übergang scheint nahtlos, vorbestimmt und organisch; wie eine Verkleidung wird der menschliche Körper abgelegt, damit sich der »wahre« pflanzliche oder tierische in befreiter Bewegung (die auch Stillstand, Verharren heißen kann) entfaltet. Insofern trägt der in Bildern gefasste Verwandlungsvorgang das von Deleuze für die Antike veranschlagte »Posenhafte« sehr wohl in sich.[34] Die Stadien der Metamorphose sind zunächst im Sinne der Pose herausgehobene Momente, in ihrer seriellen Reihung gleichen sie einem Fries ineinander verflochtener Figuren in unendlich wiederholter und nur leicht variierter *varitatio mutatae formae*.

Aber Organizität und Pose täuschen. Der Körper ist nicht nur Subjekt der Metamorphose, sondern auch Ausdrucksform und Medium der Verwandlungsursache, sei diese »vorher« schon gegeben oder entstehe sie erst mit ihr.[35] Der in der Verwandlung eingefangene Übergangsmoment präsentiert ein Monster, ein unmögliches Wesen. Was in den menschlichen Körper eingefaltet ist und in aufeinander folgenden Bildern de-monstriert wird, entspricht keiner antiken Idealität, sondern einem Abgrund. In der Metamorphose »kippt« ein Zustand in den anderen in einer nichtzeitlichen Dynamik. Das bebilderte Kippmoment ist mit Leerstellen und Hybridem markiert, mit einem Noch-Nicht, aber Auch-Nicht-Mehr an verflüssigten Demarkationslinien, die noch nicht wieder erstarrt sind. Insofern liegt im Metamorphosevorgang ein Ensemble von Bildern und Einstellungen, die nicht genuin zeitlich strukturiert sind, aber auf diese verweisen und sie mit sich transportieren. Die Perspektivierung springt von der Figur zum erzählenden Beobachter hin und her, und in diesem Oszillieren eröffnet sich die Geschichte des Monstrenkörpers als psychosomatische Motivation. In der Vorstellung des Zeitstrahls hat die Verwandlung gefasst, wird sie fassen den einen Punkt »Gegenwart«, der immer schon vorbei ist und immer gerade kommt. Aus dem Zugleich disparater Formen bezieht die Metamorphose ihre Dynamik, wie sie den sich verwandelnden Körper zur Ausdrucksform macht und dabei auf die Figur verweist, deren gestörte Gestalt von einer gestörten, in der Überschreitung befindlichen Person spricht. Der Blick, den die Figuren auf sich selbst werfen, zeigt, dass die Verwandlung die Betroffenen sich selber fremd macht und sich selbst gegenüberstellt, so dass sie sich für die kurze Zeit der Verwandlung mit fremden Augen als mit sich selbst nicht mehr ganz Identische (*pertimuit seque exsternata refugit* [i 641] [Sie, sc. Io, erschrak und floh entsetzt vor sich selbst; Übers. UR]) sehen.

Ut vero vultus et cornua vidit in unda, / ›me miserum!‹ dicturus erat: vox nulla secuta est; ingemuit: vox illa fuit, lacrimaeque *per ora / non sua* fluxerunt; *mens tantum pristina mansit*. [...] heu famulos fugit ipse suos! Clamare libebat: ›Actaeon ego sum, dominum cognoscite vestrum!‹ / verba animo desunt: resonat latratibus aether. (iii 200-231) [Sowie er aber das Gesicht und die Hörner im Wasser erblickte, wollte er ausrufen ›Weh mir Ärmstem!‹: aber keine Worte kamen aus seinem Mund – er röhrte: Das war seine Stimme. Tränen flossen über die Wangen, die nicht die Seinen waren; Verstand und Psyche nur blieben die früheren. [...] Oh weh, er floh vor seinen eigenen Zöglingen! Er versuchte, dem Wunsch, ›Actaeon bin ich! Erkennt euren Herrn!‹ auszurufen, nachzugeben, aber dem Willen fehlten die Worte: Vom Hundegebell nur ertönte die Luft.] [Übers. u. Hervorh. UR]

Der Zweifel an der Identität betrifft allerdings nicht die Personenidentität, sie betrifft Rolle (z. B. Arachne, Ocyroe), Aufgabe (z. B. Iphis, Minyastöchter) und v. a. den Körper (z. B. Arethusa), der das einzig verfügbare Instrument der Identität als Gewissheit abgibt. Dieser Körper aber kippt in einen anderen in ungeheurer Plötzlichkeit und Gewaltsamkeit. Der Zwischenzustand, der Moment des Kippens bringt sich in bildlicher ›Präsentationsform‹ zum Ausdruck. Der Körper-Akzent als sicht- und fühlbare Gewissheit, der sich in beliebigen Momenten der Verwandlung in die Ungewissheit entgrenzt, trägt eine nichtprozessuale Verwandlungsdynamik, die an Filmbilder erinnert. Die Metamorphose schafft eine optische Situation, in der sich eine monströse Figur selbst beobachtet, für die alle Marsyas mit seiner Frage *quid me mihi detrahis?* (vi 385) [Was ziehst du mich mir selber ab?] spricht. In diese optische Situation ist die Zeitlichkeit als kontingenter Prozess, als heimlicher Gegenspieler eingeflochten: Die Verwandlung geschieht plötzlich, sie ist unmotiviert und kann nicht aufgehalten oder rückgängig gemacht werden. Am ehesten lässt sich das Phänomen mit Deleuzes ›Chrono-Zeichen‹ in Verbindung bringen, die »nicht von den Lekto-Zeichen zu trennen [sind], die uns auffordern, im Bild eine Vielzahl von Symptomen zu lesen und somit das optische [...] Bild auch als etwas Lesbares aufzufassen. Aber nicht nur das Visuelle [...], sondern auch Gegenwart und Vergangenheit, das Hier und Dort konstituieren Elemente und innere Beziehungen, die dechiffriert werden müssen [...]«.[36] Deleuze führt das Chrono-Zeichen anhand des realistischen Films Antonionis ein, der in seinen Bildern die Präsenzfunktion und -definition des Bildes durchbricht, bzw. den Nicht-Ort des Präsens mit den Worten, die auch eine Zusammenfassung der *Metamorphosen* sein könnten, wiedergibt:

> Wenn wir am Eros kranken, dann [...] deswegen, weil der Eros selber krank ist; und krank ist er nicht einfach, weil er alt und im Innern verbraucht ist, sondern weil ihn die reine Form einer Zeit gefangenhält, die zwischen einer schon beendeten Vergangenheit und einer ausweglosen Zukunft zerrissen ist. [...] Chronos ist die Krankheit selbst.[37]

Im Moment der Verwandlung, deren Krankheit gleichfalls den Namen »Eros« trägt, offenbart sich in der Tat keine Präsenz, sondern nur Übergang, die Erinnerung der vergangenen menschlichen und die Ahnung der zukünftigen tierischen, pflanzlichen, mineralisch-kristallinen Gestalt. Insofern kann Deleuzes Satz abgeändert werden in: »Chronos ist die Verwandlung selbst«.

Das ›Motiv‹ der Metamorphose als *movens* liegt in der Ungewissheit der Relationen des Körpers zu sich selbst, seinen Demarkationen in sich selbst und gegenüber einem möglichen Außen. Der Außenraum, in dem sich der Körper bewegt, wird im Kippbild ausgeschlossen bzw. tritt als leerer Raum auf. Im Bild ist nur – um bei Rilke eine Anleihe zu machen – ein »Körperinnenraum«, der sich in der Auflösung befindet. Parallel zu den ungefestigten Relationen des Innenraums tritt der Außenraum ebenfalls nur als Potenzialität, als Absenz oder ornamentaler Hintergrund auf. Die Kippfigur wird in einen narrativen Raum überführt, der die freien Relationen gewissermaßen in einer Narration verortet. Der prozessual-diskursive ›Raum‹ in der Funktion des »Körperinnenraums« wird psychosomatisch und habituell besetzt mit einer Entstehungsgeschichte der erwähnten Rollen-, Geschlechts- und Körperkonflikte. Die Erzählung aber, die die Metamorphose mit ihrem Nichts und Schrecken erfordert, kann wegen der Unbestimmtheit der Relationen nur eine ›mythische‹ im leeren Raum sein. Der Außenraum zu diesen konfliktuösen Körpern tritt als sozial kodierter Raum auf; als Ort, »an dem die Geschichte spielt«, bleibt er ornamental in einer einfachen Überkodierung durch exakte Namensnennung (Theben, Athen, Palast des Minos etc.) oder Unterkodierung ([irgend]ein Wald, [irgend]ein Hain, irgendwo). Im narrativen Rahmen und Ornament wird die Verwandlung in einen diskursiven Vorgang rückgebettet und dem gleichfalls diskursiven Verstehen zugänglich macht. Die Momentaufnahme Verwandlung als ›Opto-Zeichen‹ enthüllt ihre Motivation und verbirgt sie zugleich. Als reines Bild der Präsentation mit der Funktion, »etwas Untragbares und Unerträgliches faßbar [zu machen]«, wobei »es um etwas [geht], was zu gewaltig, zu ungerecht, aber manchmal auch einfach zu schön ist und von nun an unsere sensomotorischen Vermögen übersteigt«[38], birgt es eine verschwiegene Geschichte, deren Unverständlichkeit und Schrecken die Umwandlung in eine motivierte Narration erfordern. Die Präsentation des Unerklärlichen bedarf einer Kontextualisierung, die beiden Körper müssen in einen Verweisungszusammenhang gebracht werden. Das Kippbild ›Verwandlung‹ ist kein Bild der Fülle, sondern ein Bild des Mangels und Schreckens. Es zeigt nicht etwas, sondern nichts, den exakten Moment des Übergangs vom einen ins andere, vom Eigenen ins Fremde. »Das Nicht ist nicht da, aber indem es derart das Nicht eines Da ist, ist es nicht einfach Nicht, sondern zugleich das Nicht-Da. Als solches hält es das Nicht bei sich nicht aus, ist vielmehr aufs Da eines Etwas treibend bezogen. Das Nicht ist Mangel an Etwas und ebenso Flucht aus diesem Mangel; so ist es Treiben nach dem, was ihm fehlt.«[39]

ANMERKUNGEN

1 Ahl 1985, S.51.
2 Ruprecht 1991.
3 Ibid.
4 Bloom 1973.
5 Cf. Blumenberg 1996.
6 Ich beziehe mich im Folgenden sowohl auf *Formen der Zeit im Roman* als auch auf *Die Ästhetik des Wortes*.
7 Bachtin 1989, S.39f.
8 Ibid., S.41.
9 Schmidt 1991.
10 Cf. zur Theatermetaphorik und zu römischen Schmink- und Kleidungsgewohnheiten mythischer Figuren v. Albrecht 2000.
11 Ich wähle diesen Begriff in Absetzung zum gebräuchlicheren der ›Kontextualität‹, um Vorsicht gegenüber der Konstruktion eines *texte génerale* anzudeuten, bzw. um merklich zu machen, dass zwischen einer kulturellen und einer literarisch-schriftlichen Textualität nicht nur Grad-, sondern auch kategoriale Unterschiede bestehen.
12 Die ›Transtextualität‹ ist im Falle der ovidischen *Metamorphosen* auf Reflexe, auf die Alltagskultur und die politische u. evtl. kultische Öffentlichkeit beschränkt. Für

eine originelle Lektüre der *Metamorphosen* als anti-augustäisch u. röm. Kultus verpflichtet möchte ich exemplarisch auf die eingangs zit. Untersuchung von Ahl 1985 verweisen.

[13] tendebam bracchia caelo: bracchia coeperunt levibus nigrescere pennis (Corvus ii 580f.) [ich streckte die Arme gen Himel: Die Arme begannen von leichten Federn zu erdunklen] [Übers. UR].

.tendebat bracchia supplex: bracchia coeperunt nigris horrescere villis (Callisto ii 476f.) [Sie senkte die Arme zu Boden: Die Arme begannen von schwarzen Zotteln zu starren] [Übers. UR].

[14] Bachtin 1989, S.41.

[15] Cf. Spencer 1997 u. Wheeler 2000.

[16] Cf. Plett 1991 u. Plett 1985, bes. S.97.

[17] cruor emicat alte, / non aliter, quam cum vitiato fistula plumbo / scinditur et tenui stridente foramine longas / eiaculatur aquas atque ictibus aera rumpit. (iv 121-124) [Das Blut schoss in die Höhe, nicht anders, als wenn in einem beschädigten Bleirohr ein Riss aufbricht und in zischendem Strahl durch die Öffnung das Wasser weit emporschießt und in Stößen die Luft durchbricht. Übers. UR] – Die Drastik des transtextuellen Vergleichs und der hyperbolischen Schilderung untermalen die bloße Zufälligkeit des Geschehens und die Sinnlosigkeit der Tode, die von keinem Fluch hervorgerufen, von keinem Gott unterstützt und gewollt wurden. Pyramus u. Thisbe rennen in ein zufällig-grausames und a-personales Schicksal, das sie auf keine Weise hätten vermeiden können.

[18] Genette 1993.

[19] Cf. Genette 1990, S.24ff.

[20] adspirate meis primaque ab origine mundi / ad mea perpetuum deducite tempora carmen. (i 2f.)

[21] Bei einer Beurteilung der kultischen Praxis in der Antike begibt sich jede kategoriale Aussage auf Glatteis; Augustus war jedenfalls um die Wiederbelebung zahlreicher marginalisierter öffentlicher Kulte bemüht, was sich in der mythischen Vielfalt der *Metamorphosen* und *Fasti* widerspiegelt. Cf. dazu Galinsky 1996.

[22] Die Gruppe von Erzählungen rund um Meleager mit dem Kernstück der Eberjagd (viii 260-444) haben Eitelkeit zum Anlass, so dass ein mörderischer Streit um eine Jagdtrophäe ausbricht und in eine groteske Schlacht unter Freunden mündet. Grausamkeit und Brutalität beherrschen in *trash*-Form die Erzählung.

[23] Cf. zu diesem gesamten Komplex Larmour 1999, der zwischen Veranstaltungen die nur sportlich, die sportlich und musikalisch, die sportlich, musikalisch und dramatisch und solchen, die sportlich und dramatisch strukturiert sind, unterscheidet.

[24] Nach Larmour 1999, S.56ff. u. S.86ff.

[25] Agon zw. zwei Personen: z. B. Meleager und Atalanta, zw. zwei Gruppen z. B. Lapithen und Kentauren, zw. Person und Gruppe z. B. Perseus mit dem Haupt der Medusa gegen die Verräter um Phineus.

[26] Warnung an jugendliche Leserinnen bei Myrrha: procul hinc natae, procul este parentes, / aut, mea si vestras mulcebunt carmina mentes, / desit in hac mihi parte fides, nec credite factum; vel, si credetis, facti quoque credite poenam. (x 300-303) [Haltet euch fern von hier, Mädchen, bleibt auch fern, ihr Eltern, oder – wenn schon meine Verse eure Sinne bezaubern – so schenkt mir wenigstens beim jetzt folgenden Teil keinen Glauben und haltet das Geschehene nicht für wahr; oder, wenn ihr es doch tut, glaubt genauso an die Strafe für die Tat.] [Übers. UR].

[27] So der Titel einer jüngeren Publikation zur Metamorphose in narratologischer Hinsicht: cf. Harzer 2000.
[28] Schmidt 1991.
[29] Pianezzola 1999.
[30] Harzer 2000.
[31] Dass die Syntax bei Ovid nicht immer linear die zwei Wesen vor und nach der Verwandlung verbindet, sondern a-grammatische Wege beschreitet, zeigt Haege 1976 mit Hilfe des »*ipse-suus*-Systems«.
[32] per ungues porrigitur radix, longi firmamina trunci, ossaque robur agunt, mediaque manente medulla sanguis it in sucos, in magnos bracchia ramos, in parvos digiti; duratur cortice pellis (Myrrha x 489ff.);
haeserunt radice pedes; convellere pugnat nec quicquam nisi summa movet. Subcrescit ab imo, totaque paulatim lentus premit inguina cortex. Ut vidit, conata manu laniare capillos fronde manum inplevit: frondes caput omne tenebant. (Dryope ix 351ff.)
[33] Die Verwandlung als Augen-Blick nimmt bspw. E.T.A. Hoffmann mit dem Archivar/Geier Lindhorst in *Der goldene Topf* auf, hier: S.32.
[34] Deleuze ^{2}1998, S.13 u. S.18.
[35] Im ersten Fall handelt es sich um die einfacher zu erschließenden metaphorisch oder symbolisch ›motivierten‹ Metamorphosen, zu denen bspw. Daphne, Niobe, Midas und Clytie zählen, im zweiten Fall um die ›unmotivierten‹ und über keine Ähnlichkeitsbezüge zu begründenden oder die sog. »missglückten« (unechten) Metamorphosen wie im Falle des Actaeon (die Verwandlung erfolgt nach dem Prinzip der Inversion; der Jäger wird zum Gejagten), des Marsyas (unechte Metamorphose), des Narziss (kontingente Begründung über den erst zu installierenden Blumennamen), der Philomela, der Callisto (Gestalt ist unmotiviert) etc.
[36] Deleuze 1991, S.39.
[37] Ibid.
[38] Ibid., S.32.
[39] Bloch 1985, S.356.

BIBLIOGRAPHIE

Ahl, Frederick, Metaformations: Soundplay and Wordplay in Ovid and Other Classical Poets, Cornell UP 1985

Albrecht, Michael v., Das Buch der Verwandlungen. Ovid-Interpretationen, Düsseldorf, Zürich 2000

Bachtin, Michail M., Formen der Zeit im Roman. Untersuchungen zur historischen Poetik, hg. v. Edward Kowalski u. Michael Wegner, aus d. Russ. v. Michael Dewey, Frankfurt a. M 1989

Bachtin, Michail M., Die Ästhetik des Wortes, hg. u. eingel. v. Rainer Grübel, aus d. Russ. v. Rainer Grübel u. Sabine Reese, Frankfurt a. M. 1979

Bloch, Ernst, Das Prinzip Hoffnung, Frankfurt a. M 1985

Bloom, Harold, The Anxiety of Influence. A Theory of Poetry, Oxford UP 1973

Blumenberg, Hans, Arbeit am Mythos, Frankfurt a. M 1996

Deleuze, Gilles, Das Bewegungs-Bild. Kino 1, übers. v. Ulrich Christians u. Ulrike Bokelmann, Frankfurt a. M ^{2}1998

Deleuze, Gilles, Das Zeit-Bild. Kino 2, übers. v. Klaus Englert, Frankfurt a. M 1991

Galinsky, Karl, Augustan Culture. An Interpretive Introduction, Princeton UP 1996
Genette, Gerard, Palimpseste. Die Literatur auf zweiter Stufe, aus d. Frz. v. Wolfram Bayer u. Dieter Hornig, Frankfurt a. M 1993
Genette, Gerard, Einführung in den Architext, aus d. Franz. v. J.-P. Dubost, G. Febel, H.-Ch. Hobohm, U. Pfau, Stuttgart 1990
Haege, Hansjörg, Terminologie und Typologie des Verwandlungsvorgangs in den Metamorphosen Ovids, Göppingen 1976 (Göppinger Akademische Beiträge 99)
Harzer, Friedmann, Erzählte Verwandlung. Eine Poetik epischer Metamorphosen (Ovid – Kafka – Ransmayr), Tübingen 2000 (Stud. z. dt. Lit. 157)
Hoffmann, E.T.A., Der goldene Topf (1813/14), in: Ders., Märchen, Berlin 1991. S.7-90
Larmour, David H. J., Stage and stadium: drama and athletics in ancient Greece, Hildesheim 1999 (Nekephoros: Beihefte 4)
Ovidius, Metamorphoses, ed. by William S. Anderson, Stuttgart, Leipzig ^{6}1996
Pianezzola, Emilio, Ovidio. Modelli retorici e forma narrativa, Bologna 1999 (Testi e manuali per l'insegnamento univer. del latino. Coll. dir. da A. Traina 60)
Plett, Heinrich, Intertextualities, in: Ders., Intertextuality, Berlin, New York 1991 (Research in text theory 15). S.3-29
Plett, Heinrich, Sprachliche Konstituenten einer intertextuellen Poetik, in: Ulrich Broich / Manfred Pfister (Hg), Intertextualität. Formen, Funktionen, anglistische Fallstudien, Tübingen 1985 (Konzepte d. Sprach- u. Literaturwiss. 35). S.78-98
Ruprecht, Hans George, The Reconstruction of Intertextuality, in: Plett, Heinrich F. (Hg), Intertextuality, Berlin, New York 1991 (Research in text theory 15). S.60-134.
Said, Edward W., Orientalism. Western Conceptions of the Orient, Harmondsworth ^{2}1995
Schmidt, Ernst August, Ovids poetische Menschenwelt: die Metamorphosen als Metapher und Symphonie, Heidelberg 1991 (Sitzungsber. d. Heidelberger Akad. d. Wiss. Phil.-Hist. Klasse 2)
Spencer, Richard A., Constrast as Narrative Technique in Ovid's Metamorphoses, Lampeter 1997 (Studies in Classics 6)
Wheeler, Stephen M., Narrative Dynamics in Ovids Metamorphoes. Tübingen 2000 (Classica Monacensia 20)

»Geistiges Gebären« als Narrativ der Frauenmystik: Die Transposition des Genießen Gottes durch Mechthild von Magdeburg

STEFANIE RINKE

> Vision: »Mutterschaft aus dem Geiste und dem Wasser«
> »Deshalb siehst du nun ein Weib von so hoher Gestalt, dass es anzuschauen ist wie eine große Stadt. [...] Netzartig öffnet sich der Schoß des Weibes in vielen Spalten, durch die eine große Menschenmenge einzieht. Das ist die Mutterliebe, die sich zum Fang der gläubigen Seelen öffnet. [...] Du siehst nur, dass helles Licht sie ganz durchstrahlt und schimmender Glanz sie rings umfließt. [...] Und nun breitet die Gestalt ihren Glanz aus wie ein Gewand und sagt, sie müsse [...] Kinder empfangen und gebären im Bade der Wiedergeburt aus dem Geiste und dem Wasser. [...] Daher tut die Gestalt einen tiefen Atemzug – ihr Atem ist der Heilige Geist – und zieht sie [die Menschen] empor zu ihrem Haupte, wo sie aus ihrem Munde [wieder] hervorgehen. Sie selber bleibt dabei ganz unversehrt.«[1]
>
> *(Hildegard von Bingen)*

1. EINLEITUNG

In der mittelalterlichen Frauenmystik des 13. Jahrhunderts lässt sich beobachten, dass sich Mystikerinnen in ihren Schriften zu jungfräulichen »Medien Gottes« stilisierten. Die Begine Mechthild von Magdeburg (1208-1282/97) zum Beispiel erzählte in ihrem Werk »Das fließende Licht der Gottheit« von der innigen Liebe ihrer minnenden Seele zu Gott, wobei sie ihre Visionen und Erfahrungen als das »Genießen Gottes« beschrieb. Gleichzeitig thematisierte sie ihre eigene Funktion in der Rolle derjenigen, die diese Erzählung niedergeschrieben hatte. So ergeben sich heute narrative Auffälligkeiten, die vor allem um die Thematik des Schreibens kreisen. Laut Mechthild habe sie ihr Beichtvater dazu gezwungen, das Buch zu schreiben, so sei es gekommen, dass sie Gottes Ehre durch ihr Werk preise. Aber eigentlich sei Gott selbst der Autor des Buches.[2] Darüber hinaus weist sie darauf hin: »Dieses Buch ist dreifaltig und bezeichnet alleine mich« (II,

26). Aus heutiger Sicht, die durch die historische Distanz zu den Schriften der Frauenmystik bestimmt ist, sind diese Selbstbezüge und Stilisierungen irritierend, weil Mechthild einerseits Gott als den Autor benennt, aber andererseits ihr Buch als ihr Produkt markiert. Was verbirgt sich hinter diesen Widersprüchlichkeiten? War Mechthild von Magdeburg nur Überbringerin oder hat sie dem Wort Gottes eine eigene Körperlichkeit verliehen, was sie legitimierte, indirekt einen Anspruch auf die Autorschaft zu erheben?

Um dieser geschlechter- und kulturwissenschaftlichen Fragestellung im Folgenden nachzugehen, wird die Erzählung der Mechthild von Magdeburg anhand ihrer Einbettung in das übergeordnete frauenmystische Narrativ analysiert. Narrative konstruieren nämlich die Zusammengehörigkeit und die Identität einer Gemeinschaft dadurch, dass sie als Ensemble erzählter Geschichten und kultureller Praktiken schon selbstverständlicher Teil des *common sense* einer Gruppe geworden sind.[2] Zum Beispiel mussten Askese- und Ekstasepraktiken innerhalb des Narrativs der Frauenmystik nicht mehr ständig kognitiv vergegenwärtigt und religiöse Grundvorstellungen wie das Mysterium Mariens nicht mehr ständig wiederholt werden, sondern das Ensemble war schon quasi in ›Fleisch und Blut‹ der teilnehmenden Mystikerinnen übergegangen. Auch die einzelnen Erzählungen und Schriften der Mystikerinnen gehörten in dieses Ensemble, so dass sie das übergeordnete, frauenmystische Narrativ selbst erzählend reproduzierten. Das Erzählen kann hier also als performativer Akt verstanden werden[3], durch den die Möglichkeit der Veränderung gegeben ist.

Aus heutiger Sicht kann durch die Analyse der überlieferten frauenmystischen Erzählungen ein Zugriff auf das damalige Narrativ der Frauenmystik erfolgen, wenn neben der Handlung der Erzählung auch ihre Narration mit eingebunden wird. Die Narration gehört zur Struktur des Erzählens und bezeichnet den Verweis der Erzählung auf die eigene »spezifische Kommunikationssituation.«[4] Im Text von Mechthild von Magdeburg besteht die Narration in dem Hinweis auf ihr »uneigentliches Schreiben« und den materiellen Anfertigungsvorgang ihrer Schriften. Auf der Handlungsebene geht es hingegen um die Visionen von Gott, die in eine Bildersprache übersetzt wurden. Wie in der Analyse gezeigt werden soll, überschneiden sich beide Ebenen im Ausdruck »Genießen Gottes«, welcher zum einen eine Metapher für Gottes Gegenwärtigkeit ist, und zum anderen die fließende, körperliche Erfahrung Mechthilds während ihrer ekstatischen Vermittlung des göttlichen Wortes benennt.

Anhand der Analyse des »Genießen Gottes« soll in diesem Artikel gezeigt werden, dass sich Mechthild von Magdeburg durch ihre Stilisierung als »geistige Gebärerin« des göttlichen Wortes verstand, was die Gleichzeitigkeit des »technischen Anfertigungsprozesses« der Schriften und der Ver-

mittlung der göttlichen Visionen impliziert. Sie »gebar« das Wort Gottes in Form des mystischen Buches. Durch die Thematisierung und den Anspruch des geistigen Gebärens wurde eine Umstrukturierung innerhalb des frauenmystischen Narrativs eingeleitet. Dadurch wurde das Wissen der Frauenmystik anderen historischen Formationen zugeführt, wie am Beispiel des Kommunikationssystems des Buchdrucks ersichtlicht werden soll.
Um den Übersetzungsvorgang des geistigen Gebärens zu zeigen, wird es darum gehen, zunächst zwei Aspekte des religiös-historischen Kontexts des 13. Jahrhunderts zu beleuchten, denn in diesen war das frauenmystische Narrativ eingebettet. Die Mystikerinnen adaptierten religiöse Grundvorstellungen der Zeit, entwickelten sie weiter und integrierten sie in ihr religiöses Selbstverständnis. Zum Beispiel galt Maria den Mystikerinnen als Vorbild für ihr mystisches Erleben, denn sie repräsentierte das Auratische des Empfangens und Tragens des göttlichen Wortes. Ferner ließen sich die Mystikerinnen auf den multisensorischen, medialen Kirchenraum ein, um während der Eucharistie das sinnliche »Genießen Gottes« in der Gemeinschaft als Sich-durchfließen-Lassen zu praktizieren. Inwiefern die Vorbildfunktion Mariens und die Praktik des »Genießen Gottes« das frauenmystische Narrativ unterfütterten, wird im dritten Kapitel anhand der Analyse des Textes von Mechthild von Magdeburg gezeigt. Es soll deutlich werden, dass sich Mechthild durch ihre Verschriftlichung als geistige Gebärerin des göttlichen Wortes verstanden hat. Damit erhob sie den Anspruch als die auserwählte Jungfrau das vorzügliche Medium Gottes zu sein. Dies veränderte den Rahmen des frauenmystischen Narrativs, wodurch das frauenmystische Wissen, wie ausblickend hypothetisch gezeigt wird, auf die neue mediale Reproduktionstechnik des Buchdrucks und die daran anknüpfende Vorstellung einer auf dem gedruckten Buch basierenden Gemeinschaft wirkte.

2. RELIGIÖS-HISTORISCHE GRUNDLAGEN DES »GEISTIGEN GEBÄRENS«

2.1. Mystisches Vorbild: Maria und das Buch

In ihrer umfangreichen Untersuchung der Verkündigung an Maria stellt die Historikerin Maria Elisabeth Gössmann fest, dass abgesehen von der Kreuzigung Christi die Verkündigung an Maria die am meisten dargestellte und beschriebene Glaubensthematik des Mittelalters war.[5] Das Verkündigungsgeschehen geht auf das Lukasevangelium zurück, wo der Engel Gabriel Maria das Wort Gottes überbringt und sie durch ihren Glauben Jesus Christus empfängt. Dieses Verkündigungsgeschehen galt den Mystikerinnen schlechthin als Vorbild für das mystische Erleben.[6] Denn die Thematik der *unio mystica* beinhaltete die Vorstellung der Ehe zwischen der *ecclesia* als *sponsa* und Christus als *sponsus*. Diese Vereinigung zwischen Braut und Bräutigam geht auf Ephesus 5, 22 und vor allem auf das alttestamentliche Hohelied Salomos zurück. Die *Cantica Canticorum* wird als der christliche Urtext der Liebe schlechthin angesehen. Die frühchristliche Exegese bezog einerseits diese Liebe auf die Beziehung zwischen Kirche und Christus, andererseits deutete Origines (um 185-253) die Braut als die Seele des Menschen und den Bräutigam als den überhistorischen *logos*; Seele und Schrift waren für ihn mystisch miteinander vermählt. Beide Auslegungsrichtungen wirkten stark bis ins Mittelalter hinein.[7] Für das 12. Jahrhundert lässt sich die Tendenz, die Braut der Brautmystik durch eine konkrete weibliche Gestalt zu personifizieren, anhand der Spezifizierung der *ecclesia* als Maria beobachten. »Braut Christi« wurde äquivalent mit dem Wort »Maria« verwendet.[8]

Neben der »Braut Christi« war Maria in der Heimsuchung Trägerin der Inkarnation Jesus Christi. Die Heimsuchungsskulptur am Dom von Bamberg aus dem 13. Jahrhundert zeigt Maria nicht etwa wie in der Verkündigungsdarstellung im schlichten Gewand, sondern das Gewand der Heimsuchung umschließt ihren Körper in vielen üppigen Falten. Die Größe und Würde Mariens beim Tragen Christi wurde plastisch als üppiger Faltenwurf veranschaulicht.[9]

Ein ähnliches Bild findet sich im »Marienlob« aus dem 12. Jahrhundert. Der Leib Christi wird dabei aus Mariens Fleisch als ihrem Kleid zusammengelegt und -gefaltet: »Godes sun, allerreinste wif, inde kleit sich bit dem kleide dines vleischs vol reinicheide«.[10] Das reine Kleid Mariens ist der von ihr gesponnene und gewebte Purpur, den sie laut frühchristlicher Quellen für den Tempelvorhang angefertigt hatte.[11] In der Heimsuchung wird also durch das Einströmen der göttlichen, dreifaltigen Kraft, Jesus Christus aus dem Gewebe, dem stofflichen, reinen Fleisch Mariens zusammengesetzt, so dass ihr Körper in diesem Moment einer Verwandlung unterliegt.

Das reine Fleisch Marias wurde nicht nur als Stoff verstanden, sondern auch als weißes, reines Pergament, aus dem die Heilige Schrift gefertigt wurde. Seit der sogenannten »Karolingischen Renaissance« war Maria auf zahlreichen Verkündigungsdarstellungen lesend oder mit einem Buch als Symbol für die unverbrüchliche Einheit der *ecclesia* mit Gott abgebildet.[12] Diese Zusammenhänge werden in einem Passionstraktat des 15. Jahrhunderts mit dem Titel »Das Buch des Lebens« beschrieben:

»Ez wirt auch gehaissen dez lebens, wan es von dem iunckfrawenlichen permant durch wurken dez heiligen gaistes hubslich aussgeczogen ist. Daz selbig puch vnsser her Ihesus Christus verspot ist [worden] vnd hertiglich geslagen mit spiczigen dornern, sein haut durch stochen mit gaisseln vnd ruten durch hawen vnd mit den haubpt pustaben der heiligen funfbunden durch graben vnd mit lewchtenden pustaben mancherley rot vnd swarcz durch schriben vnd mid eisenen stilen, alz der lieb Job begeret, vnd auf dem pulpet dez heiligen crewcz [awf gestellet], daz ietczunt nit verslossen noch bezaichent oder verporgen ist, sunder auf getan vnde enplost ist mit allen sigellen vns czu lesen, daz in im beslossen hat vil vnd mancherlay heilikait vnd haimlickait daz weder menslich noch engeli[s]ch vernunft begraiffen kan. In dem puch wer do stetiglich vnd vil lesen ader studiren ist ains in der wochen andechtiklich an czwaifel, wen der alt der tagen czu richten kumen wirt vnd der thron den richtern geseczet wirt vnd die pucher der gewissen auf werden getan, so wirt auch geoffent daz puch dez lebens, in dem sein nam geschriben ist.«[13]

Aus dem jungfräulichen Pergament und dem Wirken des heiligen Geistes wird also das Buch Jesus Christus. Hier ließe es sich vorstellen, dass jede Seite eine stoffliche Falte bildet. Die Allegorie des Christus-Buches lässt deutlich werden, dass Maria und Christus ineinander übergehen. Mariens Haut wird als Pergament genauso bearbeitet, das heißt, »durchstochen«, »illuminiert« und »gebunden«, wie Jesus in seiner Passion gelitten hat.[14] Maria selbst wurde ebenfalls als »Buch des Lebens« angesehen, da sie es war, die das Geheimnis der Verwandlung vollzog.[15]

Die Aura des Mysteriums Mariens hatte also viele Komponenten: Als Braut Christi kam Maria mit Gott zusammen, um das Wort Gottes zu empfangen, in der Heimsuchung wurde aus ihrem reinen Gewebe Jesus Christus gebildet, und als reines Pergament wurde sie durch das Wirken des heiligen Geistes zum Buch Jesus Christus. Es wird deutlich, dass ihre jungfräuliche Materialität eine Textur bildete, die unabhängig von der göttlichen Einschreibung verschiedene Formen annehmen konnte. Die Äquivalenz von stofflicher Textur, dem Textil, und der Textur von Pergament und Geist, dem Text, ist offensichtlich. Beide wurden durch den jungfräulichen Leib Mariens geboren. Es liegt nahe, dass solche Formen des Mysteriums bei den Mystikerinnen den Wunsch nach mystischem Erleben inspirierten, welcher zudem durch die kulturelle Praktik des Genießen Gottes unterstützt wurde.

2.2. Das Fließen Gottes in den multisensorischen Kirchenräumen

Da im Mittelalter die meisten Menschen weder Schreiben noch Lesen konnten, war es nötig, das Wort Gottes und damit den Glauben mündlich und sinnlich zu vermitteln. Diese Vermittlung der Erfahrung der göttlichen Spiritualität vollzog sich in den Kirchenräumen, in denen ein auf dem Hören basierender multisensorisch-medialer Raum[16] geschaffen wurde, der alle fünf Sinne ansprechen sollte. Die Kirche wurde zum Schauraum: die prachtvollen Kirchenfenster und die Bilder sollten den Glanz Gottes widerspiegeln. Die Kirche wurde zum akustischen Raum: durch die besondere Architektur wurde ein Schall erzeugt, der zu einem bestimmten

Tempo während des Redens und des Singens zwang. Ein spezieller Rhythmus ermöglichte Trancezustände und das Gefühl des Aus-der-Welt-Seins. Weiterhin war die Kirche ein Duftraum, der durch Weihrauch und Gewürze erzeugt wurde. Der Geschmacksraum kam dadurch zustande, dass während der Eucharistie Brot und Wein den Geschmack der Heiligkeit annahmen, welches auch als Empfangen einer göttlichen Süßigkeit empfunden wurde. Die Kirche als erfühlender Raum: hier ging es um das Ertasten, Küssen und Berühren von Reliquiaren.[17] Die Erfahrbarkeit des Heiligen für alle Sinne gab dem Numinosen gleichsam einen Körper, der physisch-sensorisch erfahren werden konnte und durch den Gott geschaut werden sollte. Ihren Höhepunkt hatte diese Verkörperung während der Zeremonie des heiligen Abendmahls. Diejenigen, die während der Eucharistie an Leib und Blut Christi partizipierten, waren unmittelbar miteinander verbunden, und es entstand ein die Körper umschließender medialer Raum, in dem sich ein Aus-der-Welt-Sein als ein Schwindelzustand ereignete.[18] Fand hier nun ein fließendes Gefühl der gemeinsamen Teilhabe statt, dann kann, wie im folgenden erläutert wird, von einem »Genießen Gottes« gesprochen werden.

Der Begriff »Genießen« meint: »etwas nutzen, in Gebrauch nehmen, Erstrebtes ergreifen oder fangen und gleichzeitig Freude daran haben«.[19] Er ist im Zusammenhang mit religiösen Opferkulten gebräuchlich und wurde in der christlichen Religion von Apostel Paulus als das gemeinsame Genießen von Leib und Blut Christi während des heiligen Abendmahls bekannt (vgl. 1. Kor. 10, 16). Zwei Funktionen konstituieren das Genießen: einerseits geht es um die einheitliche, körperliche Gemeinschaft während der Kommunion. Die Gemeinde wird zu *einem* Leib und empfängt das Wort Gottes. Andererseits geht es um die Übertragung dieses Wortes, welches symbolisch als Blut und Leib Christi während des heiligen Abendmahls zirkuliert, so dass das Wort auch sinnlich durch die einzelnen Körper der Teilnehmenden fließt. Der Gemeinschaftsaspekt kommt heute noch in dem Begriff »Genosse«[20] zum Ausdruck.

Die Kirchengemeinde wurde durch Frauen, den »typischen Laien«[21] repräsentiert, da sie vom Priesteramt ausgeschlossen waren und deshalb eine rezeptive Frömmigkeit entwickelt hatten, die die Rolle der Empfangenden im hohen Maße ausgebildet hatte. Man erwartete von Frauen förmlich, dass sie ihren Glauben über ihre somatischen Fähigkeiten der Askese und Ekstase zum Ausdruck brachten, so die Historikerin Caroline Walker Bynum.[22] Hier kann von einem latenten *common sense* gesprochen werden, der sich auf ein mittelalterliches Alltagswissen beziehen lässt.[23] Da letztlich die gesamte Kirchengemeinde aus Laien bestand, repräsentierte die empfangsfähige Weiblichkeit im Mittelalter die Gemeinschaft aller Gläubigen.

Die Kirchengemeinde selbst wird in Texten und Bildern des Mittelalters als Braut Gottes betrachtet.
Vor diesem Hintergrund ist es nicht verwunderlich, dass im 13. Jahrhundert die Hauptthemen der Mystikerinnen Visionen und Wundererlebnisse während der heiligen Messe waren. Einige Bilder der Mystikerinnen für die *unio mystica* sind hierfür sehr bezeichnend: Gott wie süßen Honig auf der Zunge schmecken, ihn als einen süßen Duft empfangen, mit Gott in einem Hochzeitslager des Herzens vereint sein oder ihn in der Gestalt eines Kindes auf dem Arm halten.[24] Allgemein kann man sagen, die Frauen »aßen« oder »tranken« Gott.

3. DAS »FLIESSENDE LICHT DER GOTTHEIT« VON MECHTHILD VON MAGDEBURG

3.1. Das »Genießen Gottes« als Raum des Imaginären

Vor diesem Hintergrund entstand im 12. und 13. Jahrhundert eine religiöse Frömmigkeits- und Frauenbewegung vor allem in Nordeuropa, die ein volkssprachliches mystisches Schriftgut hervorbrachte. In der Volkssprache und nicht mehr in Latein beschrieben die Mystikerinnen nun ihre Visionen von Gott und drückten ihre Körperzustände, die sie in der *unio mystica* erlebten, als das »Genießen Gottes« aus. Die niederländische Begine Hadewijch beschrieb in ihren »Visioenen« als erste das »Genießen Gottes« nicht als lateinisch »fruitio dei«, sondern als mnl. »gebruken«.[25] In ihrer Nachfolge verwendete auch Mechthild von Magdeburg den Begriff »gebruchunge«,[26] das mit dem Verb »gebrauchen« zusammenhängt und als das »Genießen« oder »Verkosten« Gottes übersetzt werden kann. Mechthild von Magdeburg lebte im 13. Jahrhundert und stammte aus adeliger Familie, so dass sie höchstwahrscheinlich über eine breite Bildung verfügte. Sie lebte als Begine in Magdeburg und wurde vom Dominikanerbeichtvater Heinrich von Halle betreut. Auf sein Drängen hin, begann sie 1250 mit der Niederschrift ihres Buches »Das Fließende Licht der Gottheit«, an dem sie dreißig Jahre lang schrieb. Die heutige Überlieferung beruht auf der Übersetzung der verlorenen niederdeutschen Originalfassung ins Alemannische durch Heinrich von Nördlingen.[27]
Der Text weist keinen einheitlichen Charakter auf, sondern es sind viele Textformen integriert wie Dialoge zwischen Gott und der minnenden Seele, Verse in Reimform und kleine analytisch-religiöse Abhandlungen, die die Liebe zu Gott zum Gegenstand haben. Ihr Text zeichnet sich zudem durch eine äußerst sinnlich-erotische Sprache aus. Mit zwölf Jahren erreichte Mechthild zum ersten Mal der Gruß Gottes, also die göttliche Zuwendung, welche sie als das Genießen Gottes beschreibt:

Diese gnadenvolle Anrede [durch Gott] hat viele Adern
und strömt aus dem fließenden Gott
in die arme, dürre Seele hinein
zu allen Zeiten
mit neuer Erkenntnis
und mit neuer Schau
und mit einzigartigem Genuß
der neuen Gegenwärtigkeit. (I, 2.)

Das Fließen Gottes in der Seele wird an anderer Stelle als spielende Minneflut bezeichnet. Diese Fluiditätsmetapher analysiert Margot Schmidt als ein Bild Mechthilds für das Fließen der Dreifaltigkeit Gottes: »Die dreifaltige Dynamik beschreibt Mechthild als »spilende« oder »vliessende« »minnevlut«, die die Liebe Gottes als etwas Beseligendes und Erquickendes ausdrückt.« [...] »Das Wesen göttlicher Liebe erklärt Mechthild als eine in sich fruchtbringende Kraft des Sichmitteilens, des Aussichheraustretenmüssens.«[28] Dieses dynamische und kommunikative Prinzip muss auf der Grundlage der christlichen Metaphysik gesehen werden. Gott ist gleichzeitig als der Eine in der Dreifaltigkeit, in Vater, Sohn und heiligem Geist, enthalten wie auch umgekehrt die Dreifaltigkeit als der eine Gott betrachtet werden kann.

Das göttliche Fließen führt zu einem kaum in Worte zu fassenden Überwältigtsein. Mechthild weist darauf hin, dass dies eine Erfahrung ist, die man körperlich erlebt haben muss:

Wer hiervon sprechen will, der lege sich in das Feuer
Und sehe und koste, wie die Gottheit fließt
Und wie die Menschheit gießt,
Wie der Heilige Geist ringt
Und manches Herz bezwingt,
Damit es Gott übertrunken minnt. (VI, 29.)

Der heilige Geist, der für die Dreifaltigkeit steht, ist nun in den Leib eingeflossen und wird dort als Rausch erlebt. Die Seele ist betrunken, weil sie das Fließen Gottes aufgenommen und sich die Einheit mit Gott ereignet hat.

Der Rausch kann hier mit der enormen Sinnlichkeit des Genießen Gottes im multisensorischen Kirchenraum in Verbindung gebracht werden, wo die Seele während der Zirkulation von Wein und Brot zur Braut Gottes wird. Es handelt sich um ein Spiel zwischen Distanz und Nähe, wobei es immer wieder um das Erreichen der Nähe und Gegenwärtigkeit Gottes im Fließen geht. Dabei spricht die minnende Seele dann zu Gott und Gott antwortet der Seele.

16. Gott vergleicht die Seele mit vier Dingen
Du schmeckst wie eine Weintraube,

du duftest wie ein Balsam,
du leuchtest wie die Sonne,
du bist ein Wachstum meiner höchsten Minne.

17. Die Seele lobt Gott an fünf Dingen
O du gießender Gott in deiner Gabe!
O du fließender Gott in deiner Minne!
O du brennender Gott in deiner Sehnsucht!
O du schmelzender Gott in der Einung mit deinem Lieb!
O du ruhender Gott an meinen Brüsten!
Ohne dich kann ich nicht mehr sein. (I, 19.)

In diesem Dialog wird der Bezug zur erotischen Sprache des Hohelieds der Liebe des Alten Testaments deutlich. Gott und die Seele kreisen im gegenseitigen Preisen umeinander, und durch die Beschreibung formt Mechthild einen Raum der inneren Imagination aus, der immer weiter bildhaft ausgearbeitet wird. Gott wird als körperliches Fließen wahrgenommen und muss in eine eigene Bildlichkeit und damit Materialität gekleidet werden, um vorstellbar und anschaulich zu werden. Was hier vorliegt, ist eine Spaltung des »Ichs« in ein »Je-moi«[29], wie es Luce Irigaray für die Frauenmystik gezeigt hat. Gott wird zum Partner und zum Spiegel des anderen. Die Mystikerinnen öffneten somit durch ihr Schreiben die Gemeinschaft mit Gott als einen imaginären Raum, der, in die Schrift übersetzt, einem Publikum zugänglich gemacht wurde. Die Leser und Hörer der frauenmystischen Texte konnten eigene Bezüge zu ihrem Inneren bilden, was ihnen eine vormals nicht gekannte Gemeinschaft mit Gott vorstellbar machte.

3.2. »Geistiges Gebären« als Transposition

Die Mystikerinnen waren in der Situation, zwar wie Maria den heiligen Geist empfangen, aber natürlich die leibliche Verwandlung zu Jesus Christus nicht durchführen zu können. Als Ersatzmöglichkeit, die durch die Äquivalenz der Texturen von fleischlichem Gewebe und textuellem Gewebe gegeben war, schrieben sie einen Textkörper, der sich aus ihren Körperzuständen und Visionen von Gott zusammensetzte. Anhand des Verhältnisses von Leiblichkeit und Text kann Mechthilds Aussage, »Dieses Buch ist dreifaltig und bezeichnet alleine mich« (II, 26), nachvollzogen werden. Mechthild ging es darum, ihre Vertrautheit mit Gott und seiner Dreifaltigkeit, Mechthild spricht von ihrer »heimlichkeit«,[30] deutlich zu machen. Diese Vertrautheit sollte durch ihren »Textkörper« als Zeichen des Bundes mit Gott bezeugt werden. Mechthild beanspruchte also einen qualitativen Stellenwert für ihr Buch, welches als äquivalentes Zeichen zur Menschwerdung Jesus Christi angesehen werden sollte. Wegen dieses Anspruchs stand sie wahrscheinlich auch immer zwischen Verehrung und Häresieanklage.

Dadurch, dass sie Gott selbst zum eigentlichen Autor ihres Buches narrativ stilisierte – »Diese Schrift ist aus Gott geflossen« (VI, 43)[31] –, gab sie sich indirekt selbst die göttliche Autorisation, das ausgesuchte Medium Gottes zu sein. Als Medium war sie die auserwählte Jungfrau, die die Stellung Marias und damit der geistigen Empfängerin und Gebärerin des Wortes Gottes beanspruchen konnte.

Die Geburt des frauenmystischen Buches kann hierbei als Übersetzung bzw. Transposition ekstatischer, individueller Erfahrungen und Visionen Gottes in die Schrift gelesen werden. Das Fließen Gottes im Körper und die auftretenden Visionen und Körperzustände bilden die »originale« Erfahrung Gottes, welche wie das Mysterium Mariens von einer Aura umgeben ist. Um diese Erfahrungen zu übersetzen, reicht es nicht, sie nur zu beschreiben, sondern der Übersetzung muss es darum gehen, eine Form zu finden, die das »Nicht-Mitteilbare«[32] des auratischen Moments in der Übersetzung zu verbergen und gleichzeitig erfahrbar zu machen versucht, wie es Walter Benjamin fordert. »So umgibt die Sprache der Übersetzung ihren Gehalt wie einen Königsmantel in weiten Falten. Denn sie bedeutet eine höhere Sprache als sie ist und bleibt dadurch ihrem eigenen Gehalt gegenüber unangemessen, gewaltig und fremd.«[33] Es geht um die materielle Form der Übersetzung, die innerhalb des frauenmystischen Narrativs in dem durch Gott autorisierten, jungfräulichen Gewand bestand, welches technisch wie ein Buch gefertigt wurde. Die Aura wird durch das Technische also nicht zerstört, sondern beide bedingen sich gegenseitig, wie ich Benjamins Ausführungen zur Photographie hier lesen möchte. Die »Aura« des Photos besteht in dem technisch-exakten Moment des »Fünkchens Zufall, Hier und Jetzt«[34] der Aufnahme. Erst durch die mechanische Hervorbringung erhält die Aura ihren »magischen Wert.«[35] Dieser wird durch den Augenblick der technischen Präzision getragen. »Magie« und »Technik«[36] gehen hier also Hand in Hand, wobei ihre Differenz nie aufgelöst wird, sondern sie sich in der gegenseitigen Abhängigkeit erhalten.

Die Produktion des auratischen Moments lässt sich auch im Körper Mechthilds finden. Wie in der Photographie wird das Bild Gottes aus dem göttlichen Fließen herausgeschnitten. Ihren Rausch hält Mechthild an, die Zeit wird auf den Punkt gebracht, um mit Hilfe des Auslösers einen Moment herauszuschießen, der wie das Photo einen imaginären Raum eröffnet. Das visionäre Bild wird dann in die Schrift gesetzt, in Pergament gekleidet und später zum Buch gebunden. Dabei ist es ihr eigener Leib, der durch sie selbst quasi »durchstochen«, »illuminiert« und zu einem Faltengewand gefertigt wird. Wie ein Photoapparat ist Mechthild eine textuelle Übersetzungsmaschine, die präzise und technisch die Momente göttlicher Gegenwärtigkeit aufzeichnet. Hierbei genießt sie sich selbst, so dass mit Irigaray von einer »(Auto-)Erotik«[37] gesprochen werden kann, die aber nicht in der spezifisch frauenmystischen Sprache – sofern es diese überhaupt gibt –, sondern in der Gleichzeitigkeit von mechanischer Anfertigung der imaginären Räume und ihrer rauschhaften Konsumtion besteht. Durch ihre Selbststilisierung zum Medium Gottes und ihr Genießen der Übersetzungstätigkeit verließ Mechthild den Rahmen, der den Laien und Mystikerinnen zugewiesen worden war,[38] denn sie begnügte sich nicht mit dem Empfangen und der einfachen Vermittlung des göttlichen Wortes, sondern thematisierte die Praktik der Anfertigung ihrer Schriften. Durch diese Materialität beförderte Mechthilds Erzählen nun die Zementierung und den Höhepunkt des frauenmystischen Narrativs in eines des geistigen Gebärens. Dieses birgt in sich den Primat des Medium-Seins. Denn das Medium verschwand nicht hinter den visionären Inhalten, sondern das Wort Gottes wurde »technisch reproduzierbar«, ohne den Moment des Auratischen einzubüßen. Ausblickend soll nun hypothetisch gezeigt werden, inwiefern das Narrativ des geistigen Gebärens auf drucktechnische Verfahren der frühen Neuzeit gewirkt haben könnte.

4. FRAUENMYSTIK UND DIE MEDIALE HERAUSFORDERUNG DES BUCHDRUCKS

Durch die frauenmystische Selbststilisierung zu »Übersetzungsmaschinen« des göttlichen Fließens und Genießens gaben die religiösen Frauen die Vorstellung der Gemeinschaft mit Gott und die technische Reproduzierbarkeit des göttlichen Wortes an ein religiöses, meist volkssprachliches Publikum weiter. Betreut wurde solch ein Publikum durch männliche Seelsorger, die auch für das Kopieren der Schriften in den klösterlichen Skriptorien sorgten.[39] Mystiker waren in diesem »Aufschreibesystem« also nicht als weibliche »Medien Gottes«, sondern männlich als Distributoren codiert – hier ließe sich die Frage nach der kulturellen Konstruktion von Geschlecht in der Frauenmystik stellen. Die Mystiker predigten und verbreiteten auf ihren Reisen mystische Bücher, die als technisch angefertigte, unmittelbare Zeichen des Bundes mit Gott eine auratische Anziehungskraft ausstrahlten.

Es ließe sich die hypothetische Frage formulieren, ob sich die Technik des Buchdrucks ab 1455 hier deshalb so gut einfügen und als Beschleuniger der Verbreitung von religiösen Schriften fungieren konnte, weil sich in der Frauenmystik schon mentale Veränderungen im Hinblick auf mediale Techniken entwickelt hatten. Auch die Vermittlung des Fließen Gottes wurde durch das auf dem gedruckten Buch beruhende Kommunikationssystem adaptiert.

Gutenbergs zentrale Neuerung innerhalb des Buchdrucks bestand darin, dass er das Drucken mit beweglichen Lettern erfunden hatte. Diese Technik markierte den Beginn aller weiteren Mechanisierungen in der Neuzeit und der Moderne.[40] Die Erfindung dieser Drucktechnik »beruhte auf der neuen Wahrnehmung, dass die semantisch-morphologische Einheit des Wortes eine Sache ist, der Prozess seiner Verschriftlichung aber eine andere. [...] Vor der technischen Synthese lag also der mentale Schritt der Segmentierbarkeit von Wörtern und Texten«[41], so analysiert es treffend Wolfgang Neuber. Ein solcher mentaler Schritt war durch den frauenmystischen Übersetzungsvorgang gegeben. Das Buch wurde nicht als Einheit, sondern als Schriftansammlung der verschiedenen Momente der von Gott in der Ekstase eingeprägten und nacheinander niedergeschriebenen Visionen angesehen.

Zudem bestand das Wesentliche am neuen Handgießinstrument Gutenbergs in der Erfindung der einheitlichen Gussform bzw. Matrize. Das Vorbild der Matrize lieferte der Körper der Mystikerin. Hildegard von Bingen hat sich zum Beispiel als Wachstafel verstanden, in die das Fließen Gottes als Vision Gottes eingeprägt und anschließend verschriftlicht wurde.[42] Äquivalent wurde flüssiges Metall in die Matrize gegossen, um Buchstabenrohtypen anzufertigen. Die Matrize gab diesen Buchstabenrohtypen eine präzise und einheitliche Form, welche später für ein »reines« Druckbild unerlässlich war.[43] Dem einmaligen mit der Hand geschriebenen Buchstaben wurde damit das Individuelle entzogen und einer reproduzierbaren Reinheit in Form des gedruckten Buchstabens zugeführt. Hier käme also die Vorstellung der reinen Körperlichkeit der Jungfrau Maria zum Tragen.

Die Körperlichkeit Mariens spielte auch für das mediale Kommunikationssystem des Buchdrucks eine wichtige Rolle. Maria wurde im 12. Jahrhundert durch den Mystiker Bernhard von Clairvaux (1090-1153) mit einem technischen Wasserleitungssystem, einem Aquädukt, verglichen, durch das das göttliche Wort als das Fließende zu den Menschen gebracht werden sollte: »›Eine starke Frau, wer findet sie?‹ (Spr 31,10) Dem Menschengeschlecht fehlten nämlich die Ströme der Gnade deswegen so lange, weil dieser so erwünschte Aquädukt, von dem wir sprechen, sie noch nicht weiterleitete.«[44] Bernhard weist auf die Notwendigkeit der weiblichen Vermittlung des göttlichen Fließens durch den jungfräulichen Körper Mariens hin. Diese Vermittlung wurde dann durch das frauenmystische, das Fließen vermittelnde Buch umgesetzt. Später wurden religiöse Schriften wie ein Wasserstrom über die Kanäle der Druckkunst zu möglichen Empfängern geleitet, so dass ein zirkulierendes Gemeinschaftsgefühl entstand. Die metaphorische Verknüpfung von Bewässerung und Kommunikation geht auf die christliche Taufe zurück, durch die die Menschen in das Kommunikationssystem der christlichen Gemeinde aufgenommen wurden. Wie Giesecke nachweist, wurde der Kommunikationsraum in der frühen Neuzeit mehr und mehr durch das gedruckte Buch übernommen und getragen.[45] Dies könnte auch auf den frauenmystischen Hintergrund der Vermittlung des Fließen Gottes durch den jungfräulichen Körper als Buch zurückzuführen sein. Bücher stellten imaginäre Räume bereit, die wie das Fließen Gottes durch die Buchdrucktechnik mechanisch vermittelt wurden, und ermöglichten die Kommunikation zum Beispiel innerhalb religiös-reformatorischer Gruppen. So ließe sich vorstellen, dass durch die Partizipation an dem gedruckten Buch ein neues imaginäres Gemeinschaftsgefühl aufkam.[46]

ANMERKUNGEN

[1] Hildegard von Bingen, Wisse die Wege. Scivias, nach dem Originaltext des illuminierten Rupertsberger Kodex der Wiesbadener Landesbibliothek ins Deutsche übertr. und bearb. von Maura Böckeler, 5. Aufl., Berlin 1963, S. 161-171.

[2] Vgl. Mechthild von Magdeburg, Das fließende Licht der Gottheit, übersetzt von Margot Schmidt, 2., neubearbeitete Auflage, Stuttgart-Bad Cannstatt 1995, (I) S. 9. Im folgenden werden die Textstellen direkt im Text angegeben.

[3] Vgl. Müller-Funk, Wolfgang, Die Kultur und ihre Narrative. Eine Einführung, Wien/New York 2002, S. 13-14.

[4] Vgl. Müller-Funk, Die Kultur und ihre Narrative, S. 54-56.

[5] Vgl. Müller-Funk, Die Kultur und ihre Narrative, S. 54.

[6] Vgl. Gössmann, Maria Elisabeth, Die Verkündigung an Maria. Im dogmatischen Verständnis des Mittelalters, München 1957, S. 119.

[7] Vgl. Gössmann, Verkündigung, S. 189.

[8] Vgl. Stein, Heidrun, Die romanischen Wandmalereien in der Klosterkirche Prüfening, Regensburg 1987, S. 49; in ihrer Untersuchung der *ecclesia*-Darstellung in Prüfening erläutert die Autorin sehr aufschlussreich Geschichte und Bedeutung der *ecclesia*, vgl. S. 39-106.

[9] Vgl. Stein, Romanische Wandmalerei, S. 52.

[10] Vgl. Gössmann, Verkündigung, S. 202.

[11] Gössmann, Verkündigung, S. 182.

[12] Vgl. Gössmann, Verkündigung, S. 27-29.

[13] Vgl. Schreiner, Klaus, »... wie Maria geleicht einem puch«. Beiträge zur Buchmetaphorik des hohen und späten Mittelalters, in: Archiv für Geschichte des Buchwesens 11 (1971), Sp. 1438.

[14] Das puch des lebens, Berlin, Stiftung Preußischer Kulturbesitz, ms. Germ. 8° 467, fol. 208-249; zitiert nach Wenzel, Horst, Die Schrift und das Heilige, in: Die Verschriftlichung der Welt. Bild, Text und Zahl in der Kultur des Mittelalters und der Frühen Neuzeit, hrsg. von Ders., Wilfried Seipel, und Gotthart Wunberg, Wien 2000, S. 36.

[15] Vgl. Bynum, Caroline Walker, Jesus as Mother: Studies in the Spirituality of the High Middle Ages, Berkeley 1982.

[16] Schreiner, Klaus, Maria. Jungfrau, Mutter, Herrscherin, Wien 1994, S. 151.

[17] Vgl. Wenzel, Horst, Hören und Sehen. Schrift und Bild. Kultur und Gedächtnis im Mittelalter. München 1995, S. 95-127.

[18] Vgl. Wenzel, Hören und Sehen, S. 95-115.
[19] Vgl. Braun, Christina von, Versuch über den Schwindel. Religion, Schrift, Bild, Geschlecht, Zürich/München 2001, S. 23.
[20] Vgl. Kluge, Friedrich, Etymologisches Wörterbuch der deutschen Sprache, bearbeitet von Walther Mitzka, Berlin 1967.
[21] Binder, Wolfgang, »Genuss« in Dichtung und Philosophie des 17. und 18. Jahrhunderts, in: Archiv für Begriffsgeschichte 17 (1973), S. 68: Genossen sind die, »die das Vieh gemeinsam nutzen«.
[22] Bynum, Caroline Walker, Fragmentierung und Erlösung. Geschlecht und Körper im Glauben des Mittelalters, Frankfurt a. M. 1996, S. 124.
[23] Vgl. Bynum, Fragmentierung und Erlösung, S. 124-125.
[24] Vgl. Müller-Funk, Die Kultur und ihre Narrative, S. 156.
[25] Vgl. Bynum, Fragmentierung und Erlösung, S. 118.
[26] Hadewijch, Das Buch der Visionen, hrsg. von Gerald Hofmann, Stuttgart-Bad Cannstatt 1998.
[27] Vgl. Mechthild von Magdeburg, »Das fließende Licht der Gottheit«, nach der Einsiedler Handschrift in kritischem Vergleich mit der gesamten Überlieferung, hrsg. von Hans Neumann, besorgt von Gisela Vollmann-Profe, München 1990, I, 44.
[28] Vgl. Ruh, Kurt, Geschichte der abendländischen Mystik. Bd. 2: Frauenmystik und Franziskanische Mystik der Frühzeit, München 1993, S. 248-252.
[29] Schmidt, Margot, »die spilende minnevlut«. Der Eros als Sein und Wirkkraft in der Trinität bei Mechthild von Magdeburg, in: »Eine Höhe, über die nichts geht«. Spezielle Glaubenserfahrung in der Frauenmystik?, hrsg. von Margot Schmidt und Dieter R. Bauer, Stuttgart-Bad Cannstatt 1986, S. 75.
[30] Irigaray, Luce, Speculum. Spiegel des anderen Geschlechts, Frankfurt a. M. 1980; hier der Originaltitel des Kapitels »Das Mystische – Hysterische«, S. 239.
[31] Mechthild von Magdeburg, Das fließende Licht der Gottheit, Einleitung, S. XXX.
[32] Vgl. zum Thema Autorschaft: Grubmüller, Klaus, Sprechen und Schreiben. Das Beispiel Mechthild von Magdeburg, in: Festschrift für Walter Haug und Burghart Wachinger, Bd. 1, Tübingen 1992.
[33] Benjamin, Walter, Die Aufgabe des Übersetzers, in: Ders., Gesammelte Schriften, hrsg. von Tillman Rexroth, Bd. IV, 1, Frankfurt a. M. 1972, S. 19.
[34] Benjamin, Aufgabe des Übersetzers, S. 15.
[35] Benjamin, Walter, Kleine Geschichte der Photographie, in: Ders., Das Kunstwerk im Zeitalter seiner technischen Reproduzierbarkeit, Frankfurt a. M. 1977, S. 57.
[36] Benjamin, Geschichte der Photographie, S. 50.
[37] Benjamin, Geschichte der Photographie, S. 50.
[38] Irigaray, Speculum, S, 252.
[39] Vgl. Bynum, Fragmentierung und Erlösung, S. 160-161.
[40] Vgl. Weitlauff, Manfred, »dein got redender munt machet mich redenlosz ... «. Margareta Ebner und Heinrich von Nördlingen, in: Religiöse Frauenbewegung und mystische Frömmigkeit im Mittelalter, hrsg. von Peter Dinzelbacher und Dieter R. Bauer, Köln/Wien 1988, S. 303-352.
[41] Vgl. McLuhan, Marshall, Die magischen Kanäle. Understanding Media, 2., erweit. Aufl., Dresden/Basel 1995, S. 186.
[42] Neuber, Wolfgang, Ökonomien des Verstehens. Markt, Buch und Erkenntnis im technischen Medienwandel der Frühen Neuzeit, in: Die Verschriftlichung der Welt. Bild, Text und Zahl in der Kultur des Mittelalters und der Frühen Neuzeit, hrsg. von Horst Wenzel, Wilfried Seipel, und Gotthart Wunberg, Wien 2000, S. 183.

[43] Vgl. Wenzel, Hören und Sehen, S. 385.
[44] Vgl. Giesecke, Michael, Der Buchdruck in der frühen Neuzeit. Eine historische Fallstudie über die Durchsetzung neuer Informations- und Kommunikationstechnologien, Frankfurt a. M. 1991, S. 78-80.
[45] Bernhard von Clairvaux, Sämtliche Werke lateinisch/deutsch, hrsg. von Gerhard B. Winkler, Bd. VIII, Innsbruck 1997, S. 625 und 647.
[46] Vgl. Giesecke, Buchdruck, S. 157-159.
[47] Vgl. Anderson, Benedict, Die Erfindung der Nation. Zur Karriere eines folgenreichen Konzepts, 4., erw. Aufl., Berlin 1998; im Originaltitel »Imagined Community«.

BIBLIOGRAPHIE

Anderson, Benedict, Die Erfindung der Nation. Zur Karriere eines folgenreichen Konzepts, 4., erw. Aufl., Berlin 1998

Bernhard von Clairvaux, Sämtliche Werke lateinisch/deutsch, hrsg. von Gerhard B. Winkler, Bd. VIII, Innsbruck 1997

Benjamin, Walter, Die Aufgabe des Übersetzers, in: Ders., Gesammelte Schriften, hrsg. von Tillman Rexroth, Bd. IV, 1, Frankfurt a. M. 1972, S. 9-21

Benjamin, Walter, Kleine Geschichte der Photographie, in: Ders., Das Kunstwerk im Zeitalter seiner technischen Reproduzierbarkeit, Frankfurt a. M. 1977, S. 47-67

Braun, Christina von, Versuch über den Schwindel. Religion, Schrift, Bild, Geschlecht, Zürich/München 2001

Binder, Wolfgang, »Genuss« in Dichtung und Philosophie des 17. und 18. Jahrhunderts, in: Archiv für Begriffsgeschichte 17 (1973), S. 66-92

Bynum, Caroline Walker, Fragmentierung und Erlösung. Geschlecht und Körper im Glauben des Mittelalters, Frankfurt a. M. 1996

Bynum, Caroline Walker, Jesus as Mother: Studies in the Spirituality of the High Middle Ages, Berkeley 1982

Giesecke, Michael, Der Buchdruck in der frühen Neuzeit. Eine historische Fallstudie über die Durchsetzung neuer Informations- und Kommunikationstechnologien, Frankfurt a. M. 1991

Gössmann, Maria Elisabeth, Die Verkündigung an Maria. Im dogmatischen Verständnis des Mittelalters, München 1957

Grubmüller, Klaus, Sprechen und Schreiben. Das Beispiel Mechthild von Magdeburg, in: Festschrift für Walter Haug und Burghart Wachinger, Bd. 1, Tübingen 1992

Hadewijch, Das Buch der Visionen, hrsg. von Gerald Hofmann, Stuttgart-Bad Cannstatt 1998

Hildegard von Bingen, Wisse die Wege. Scivias, nach dem Originaltext des illuminierten Rupertsberger Kodex der Wiesbadener Landesbibliothek ins Deutsche übertr. und bearb. von Maura Böckeler, 5. Aufl., Berlin 1963

Irigaray, Luce, Speculum. Spiegel des anderen Geschlechts, Frankfurt a. M. 1980

Kluge, Friedrich, Etymologisches Wörterbuch der deutschen Sprache, bearbeitet von Walther Mitzka, Berlin 1967

McLuhan, Marshall, Die magischen Kanäle. Understanding Media, 2., erweit. Aufl., Dresden/Basel 1995

Mechthild von Magdeburg, Das fließende Licht der Gottheit, übersetzt von Margot Schmidt, 2., neubearbeitete Auflage, Stuttgart-Bad Cannstatt 1995

Mechthild von Magdeburg, »Das fließende Licht der Gottheit«, nach der Einsiedler Handschrift in kritischemVergleich mit der gesamten Überlieferung, hrsg. von Hans Neumann, besorgt von Gisela Vollmann-Profe, München 1990

Müller-Funk, Wolfgang, Die Kultur und ihre Narrative. Eine Einführung, Wien/New York 2002

Neuber, Wolfgang, Ökonomien des Verstehens. Markt, Buch und Erkenntnis im technischen Medienwandel der Frühen Neuzeit, in: Die Verschriftlichung der Welt. Bild, Text und Zahl in der Kultur des Mittelalters und der Frühen Neuzeit, hrsg. von Horst Wenzel, Wilfried Seipel, und Gotthart Wunberg, Wien 2000, S. 180-211

Ruh, Kurt, Geschichte der abendländischen Mystik. Bd. 2: Frauenmystik und Franziskanische Mystik der Frühzeit, München 1993

Schmidt, Margot, »die spilende minnevlut«. Der Eros als Sein und Wirkkraft in der Trinität bei Mechthild von Magdeburg, in: »Eine Höhe, über die nichts geht«. Spezielle Glaubenserfahrung in der Frauenmystik?, hrsg. von Margot Schmidt und Dieter R. Bauer, Stuttgart-Bad Cannstatt 1986, S. 71-93

Schreiner, Klaus, Maria. Jungfrau, Mutter, Herrscherin, Wien 1994

Schreiner, Klaus, » ... wie Maria geleicht einem puch«. Beiträge zur Buchmetaphorik des hohen und späten Mittelalters, in: Archiv für Geschichte des Buchwesens 11 (1971), Sp. 1437-1464

Stein, Heidrun, Die romanischen Wandmalereien in der Klosterkirche Prüfening, Regensburg 1987

Weitlauff, Manfred, »dein got redender munt machet mich redenlosz ... «. Margareta Ebner und Heinrich von Nördlingen, in: Religiöse Frauenbewegung und mystische Frömmigkeit im Mittelalter, hrsg. von Peter Dinzelbacher und Dieter R. Bauer, Köln/Wien 1988, S. 303-352

Wenzel, Horst, Die Schrift und das Heilige, in: Die Verschriftlichung der Welt. Bild, Text und Zahl in der Kultur des Mittelalters und der Frühen Neuzeit, hrsg. von Ders., Wilfried Seipel, und Gotthart Wunberg, Wien 2000, S. 14-57

Wenzel, Horst, Hören und Sehen. Schrift und Bild. Kultur und Gedächtnis im Mittelalter, München 1995

Printing Press as Agent of Change Redux: A Thought Experiment about the Origins of Objectivity in Reformation Historical Narratives[1]

SUSAN BOETTCHER

A text probably unknown to most modern readers of history remains an essential prerequisite for anyone seeking entry to Reformation historical narratives: the biblical dream narrated in Daniel 7 of the four gruesome violent animals defeated in turn by their successors and then finally by an old man with white hair, a prophecy identified repeatedly by Reformation intellectuals with the past and future trajectory of world history.[2] The tendency of historical writers before the advent of historicism to rely on characteristic narrative tropes like the »four ages« emplotment is typically criticized by scholars of historicism as fundamentally ahistorical.[3] Insofar as such historical narratives are governed by construction of historical narratives widely considered ahistorical, history writing before historicism is assumed to be compromised, teleological, unoriginal, and occasionally »tendentious« or »fundamentalist.«[4] It would be false, however, to regard the continued persistence of such tropes as evidence of the backward quality of Reformation histories, for by the middle of the sixteenth century, German histories show the emergence of recognizable narrative structures in alternative to such tropes, as well as decided struggles with the problems created by adherence to the tropes at their disposal. This essay explores the character of the divergence that German Reformation narratives made to then common tropes and historical methodology and suggests possibilities for the origins of those challenges related to the medial transformation created by the printing press. Textual traces from Reformation histories and chronicles reveal potential ways in which the printing press influenced the presentation and content of these texts through the creation of new markets and hypothetical new audiences. An examination of the foreword to the monumental history of the Reformation constructed by Johannes Sleidan allows us to illuminate this connection.

Sleidan appears to have wrestled with the nature of the act of writing history in a way that makes his work both sympathetic and intriguing to us. He writes:

> From time to time, writers of histories have presented us with many and several occurrences of the human race and astounding changes in the Empire. Long before such things occurred, however, God gave us to know and demonstrated finely, primarily through the Holy Prophet Daniel and as if with his own voice, the four mightiest empires of the world along with their transformations and the way in which one follows the other. [...] Similarly St. Paul also clearly prophesied the changes and conflicts in doctrine and religion before and after his time.[5]

This statement, with which he begins the *Vorrede* to his history, rhetorically paints him into a corner from which he spends a good deal of time trying to extract himself; that is, this clear reference to »Four Ages« trope draws heavily into question the possibility of writing a Reformation history. If all of history has been prophesied or at least hinted at in its details in the Bible, the task of the historian and the scope of his powers is extremely limited: he does not construct or reconstruct history by fashioning a narrative that accounts for diverse events, but rather explains those events in light of programmatic goals with pre-ordained patterns and content. The historian is formally reduced to the construction of an evidential *Schlüsselroman*, even if authors influential upon the genre of history writing in the Reformation like Philip Melanchthon understood this action more specifically as the human demonstration of the influence of divine Providence.[6] Sleidan, a historical expert who in 1556 had written *De quatuor summis imperiis libri iii*, a textbook explanation of the »Four Ages« emplotment, nonetheless recognizes the rhetorical problem that his adherence to it causes, for he spends a great deal of the remainder of his *Vorrede* arguing the case for writing history despite the determinate patterns of biblical prophecy. For instance, he makes a move toward giving paramount priority in his research to sources:

> Nothing befits a history or historical account better than truth and sincerity, on account of which I have exerted myself to the furthest extent of my abilities so that no lack may be perceived in me in this matter. For I have taken nothing from empty talk or gossip, but rather I have industriously brought together the documents, which gave me cause and instruction to write, and which in truth are to be believed. (Sleidan, Vorrede)

This statement is odd, not because it appears unusual from the perspective of the modern historian, but rather and paradoxically because it appears so familiar, that is, because it sounds much more like the nineteenth century than we might have expected. In a manner similar to his insistence on the primacy of his documents, Sleidan also emphasizes that he can write history »prout quaeque res acta fuit,« curiously similar to the Rankean program of writing history »als es eigentlich gewesen.«[7] Sleidan continues, »Here many foreign things are remembered, namely things that happened in France and England. In these matters I have dealt in the same way and have added nothing that did not sufficiently prove its worth and that in reality was not so.«[8] Important here is the willingness not only to collect sources (shared with works like Hartmann Schedel's so-called Nuremberg Chronicle, which left the evaluation of the sources presented to the discretion of the reader)[9] but the eagerness to weigh and sort the conclusions drawn from documents that could not be taken separately but had to be compared with each other and evaluated respectively, even if this action did not always happen in the service of a historically-oriented motivation. If scholars like Heinrich Bünting, the author of the Braunschweigische und Lüneburgische Chronica, collected details from different histories to support their narratives, this was not for the mere sake of antiquarian interest, but at least in Bünting's case, in order to compare them so as to thank God for the religious changes that allowed the Gospel to reappear in his territory. The goal of publishing such a history, Bünting continues, is to share the possibility of such reflections with a wider audience.[10] The use of sources and *Urkunden* was a clear selling point for his work; its title page included the statement that the book was not only decorated with beautiful figures and coats of arms and drawn from believable histories, but also »drawn from valuable *Urkunden* and documents laboriously brought together.«

Even if his execution is imperfect, as many commentators note, still Sleidan shared important assumptions with those of historicist methodology, including the need for source examination and critique, an explicit rhetorical move toward objectivity grounded in a statement about comparison of sources and questioning the legitimacy of differing interpretations, and finally the pursuit of the project of being able to describe history in its real actuality. That is, traces of the fundamental characteristics of historicism as a methodology are clearly already present in the sixteenth century. Although Sleidan's Reformation history is remarkable in the 1550s for the extent of its adherence to this standard, it does not hold an anomalous status within the contemporary genre at anywhere near the level of (*mutatis mutandis*) Augustine's Confessions in the fifth century. To a greater or lesser extent, German history writers in the sixteenth century use such techniques frequently, even those who are not writing narrative histories: the Mansfeld Chronicle of Cyriakus Spangenberg, which claims to use »books, letters and old monuments« in order to create a history for the people of Mansfeld equivalent to those created by other authors for other peoples, is a good example.[11]

The vast literature on the origins of historicism does not deal well with this tendency in the sixteenth century, giving an annihilating judgment on the soteriological underpinnings of even the most apparently »modern« authors as detrimental to their historical qualities.[12] Still, it is emphatically not the case that these writers, for instance, are still hopelessly mired in the generic conventions of the medieval chronicle, that they are uninterested in causes or origins, or that they lack a sense of historical transformation. Spangenberg even thinks that »it has been planted in each person's nature, that he yearns and desires to know of the origin of his ancestors and what has happened from the beginning with the people into which he was born,« which is the reason that God calls historians.[13] Sleidan was not the only author to struggle with the inadequacy of medieval conventions, and even Spangenberg, who never adopted a recognizable narrative style, still developed particular unique narrative trajectories related to his own understanding of soteriology, within texts that were dominated by conventions related to humanist exempla collections and late medieval hagiographies.[14] To charge that Spangenberg is unconcerned by historical transformation, causes or source critique in his activities as is typically done by commentators flies in the face of clear traces of these matters in the text. In fact, as the Magdeburg Centuries of Matthias Flacius Illyricus demonstrate, concern over such matters could coexist with the soteriological emplotment.[15]

The question of why both recognizable historical narratives and a methodology with similarities to historicism emerge so powerfully in this period remains, and among a multitude of reasons for this situation that might be postulated, I wish to turn in particular to abbreviated brainstorming about two possible explanations that relate explicitly to the presentation of these texts in the relatively new medium of the printing press.[16] It would be foolish to attempt to present a putatively universal and blatantly mechanistic or technologically determinant explanation; instead, this thought experiment in its truest sense is intended as a response to recent debates about the meaning of the printing press for the early modern European intellectual world and as a suggestion for an area of future research.

The first explanation for the emergence of interest in causality and origins and the documents and sources that explained them clearly relates to the legal problems created by the emergence of a new confession. Most Protestant Reformation historians are fundamentally concerned with explaining the emergence of a historical phenomenon that appears to be new (even if some of them argue that it is really related to something much older).[17] Thus it is significant that Old Church controversialist critiques of the Reformation often sought to explain it as the re-eruption of a long-condemned ancient heresy, and hence not something that needed or could claim a respectable history. We can see an example of this interest in causes and origins in a series of histories of the Reformation written in East Frisia at the end of the sixteenth century that mark the emergence of narrative history writing there.[18]

Multi-confessional East Frisia accepted both the Lutheran and Reformed confessions in different local communities after 1555, as well as a good number of non-confessional groups and religious refugees officially prohibited from practicing their religion but unofficially tolerated. Brothers, Johann (a Calvinist) and Edzard (a Lutheran), co-governed the territory after 1561, but Edzard pursued a Lutheran program after Johann's death in 1593.[19] After 1593, in the context of a controversy about the Eucharist, East Frisian pastors began to take part in the historical debate. Lutheran pastors published a »Truthful Counterreport,«[20] taking a position on one of the histories published by the Bremen church superintendent Christoph Pezel, and the Emden Reformed pastors published in response their own history, »Basic Truthful Report of the Evangelical Reformation, the Christian Churches in Emden and in East Frisia.«[21] Each tract argued that its own respective confession had been the first present in the East Frisian territorial state, and each argued based on historical sources such as church ordinances and other official documents, which were cited and sometimes even reproduced completely in the histories. The Lutheran history argued that the East Frisian Reformation had begun shortly after the Saxon one, and that the churches in Norden and several neighboring communities had embraced Lutheranism after 1520; a 1528 Calvinist confession accepted in some East Frisian congregations was introduced by pastors who lacked a proper calling. Pezzel's arguments about the course of the Reformation in East Frisia are countered with particular sources and arguments stemming from their interpretation. The Calvinist history argued, in contrast, on the basis of *Patronatsrecht*, a branch of secular law concerning the rights of cities granted to them by the local lord, that congregations were empowered to determine their own religious practice and that an attempt to impose the Lutheran confession upon cities with a Calvinist tradition would counter legal and historical precedent.[22] After 1520, the authors argue, local churches progressively accepted the Calvinist confession, perpetuating it by city ordinance.

No one today would argue that these histories were »objective«; although each work claimed to offer the truth drawn from a legal and documentary basis; the authors were openly partisan in a way different from Sleidan's rhetorical claims of objectivity. Two points, however, are interesting about these histories: first, despite the fact that authors of all of the tracts were pastors or churchmen, neither confession argued for its position based on the intrinsic truth of the confession, but instead each claimed that it was the legitimate confession of the territory because it had been there first, a claim substantiated by documents. Secondly, this method of argument explicitly ties the present together with the past in a way that would have been impossible for a medieval historian to consider: the theologians cum historians who wrote these histories saw their legitimacy as deriving from a particular interpretation of the past which they produced based on historical sources and critical, often adversarial, interpretations of them.[23] The growth of a narrative history from the legal needs of the writer is not limited to East Frisia; the *Vorrede* to Timotheus Kirchner's history of the Augsburg Confession functions similarly, not according to the need to defend the rightness of the doctrine (which the author admittedly does in the polemical tract preceding the history), but rather according to the perceived need to get the story straight for purposes of legal negotiation.[24] Specifically, Kirchner warns Calvinists that they should not expect to have their heresy confirmed in the true history of the confession, even though they »try to creep away under the cover of the Augsburg Confession like an ostensible fig leaf«; publishing the true story will »explode« this possibility[25] and support the position of Lutheran sovereigns.[26] Here we see an important intellectual change responding to medial transformation, for the actual decision about a territory's confession was until 1648 always legally subject to the local lord's *jus reformandi*, a matter upon which printed historical arguments could not be expected to have much influence unless the authors assumed the presence of a wider audience for their arguments than merely the territorial decision-maker, an audience made possible by the intervention of the printing press and its production of legal arguments not merely for the purposes of jurists but as a mass product for the consumption of a broader group of readers.

The understanding of printed books and the logic behind their production postulated by Michael Giesecke as the first example of the mass production of wares[27] presents another meaningful possibility for explaining historians' struggles with issues of narrative and objectivity in the sixteenth century. To my knowledge, despite extensive debate about the nature of the changes caused by the introduction of printing for European intellectual life, no one has considered what it could mean for historical narratives. The vituperative debate between Elisabeth Eisenstein and Adrian Johns shows that historians are far from agreed on what exactly was changed by printing. Critiques of Eisenstein's work have focused (too?) heavily on her controversial contention that printing led to previously unavailable standardization and reliability based on the fixity of the text that came to the greatest benefit of the natural and physical sciences, ultimately changing not only the content and practice of the sciences but also the markets for scientific readings. These critics charge that printing was unreliable and that it exploited established modes for the dissemination of ideas.[28] Johns' response to Eisenstein's argument is heavily conditioned upon his contention that any kind of knowledge is the same and will be affected in the same way by the introduction of the printing press (assuming it is affected at all).[29] In correlation to the following points, we might argue instead that the sort of standardization and objectivity apparently in demand from hypothetical audiences for historical works (as reflected in the remarks of authors about this objectivity) differs strongly from the kind that Johns and Eisenstein essentially agree was desired by the audiences for works of natural science (whether that objectivity, as represented in reliable standardization and fixity, was ultimately achieved or not). The objectivity being marketed in the works of the authors of Reformation narratives resulted from the author's faithfulness in transmitting materials to which the reader would not otherwise have access and the judiciousness of his narrative presentation; the novelty in this action consists not in the act of transmission itself, which was possible before the press, but in the possibility of reaching wider audiences with the information and in the creation of markets for the information that the author himself was responsible for providing, in the sense in which sold books created information that itself had a social character different and wider than that disseminated in manuscripts.[30]

Thus, the form of Reformation narrative and the move away from typically medieval emplotments could potentially be enhanced by the printing press. Several features of the chronicle and the traditional emplotment are called into question by printing. An obvious example is the function of the chronicle as a historical textbook or workbook of sorts. That is, when chronicles were printed initially (a good example is the tremendously popular *Chronica carionis*, lauded by Philip Melanchthon as exemplary), they could include blank pages for the reader to enter his or her own observations about passing time up till the approaching apocalypse.[31] This form is at least theoretically hostile to the further sale of printed materials because it suggests that once the pattern of history is explained to the reader, the reader is just as qualified as the author to interpret events according to the established pattern. While this practice squares well with some of the more idealistic features of the Protestant scriptural hermeneutical principle, it puts the role of the author as privileged interpreter at risk by suggesting that the reader's insights are just as valuable. The buyer of a chronicle is thus not purchasing historical insights, but ostensibly only information about the content of the past events to aid him as tools in his historical thinking. The consumer of a narrative, in comparison, is purchasing precisely the insight of the author as creator of the narrative, scholar of the documents, privileged presenter of information to which the reader would not have access without his analytical and creative activities. It is exactly this possibility that Sleidan addresses when he writes, after considering the possibility that other writers might conceivably have done a better job of writing this work than he could, »I wanted to construct this history because I really had a desire to, on account of which my nature would excite me to disseminate something fruitful in it.«[32] Narrative increases the natural authority of the author in general and specific (successful) authors in particular over their audience(s).

Moreover, it could be postulated that the need for printers to reach wider markets and subsidize their efforts is ultimately hostile to chronicle style in history writing. Chronicle writing did focus on matters of universal interest, but primarily within the context of local matters.[33] Moreover, it seemed unable to distinguish events of general significance from those of purely local meaning. Insofar as these events are only of a local value, a printer with broad ambitions might not want to print them because they have no value to a larger audience. Instead, larger historical narratives like Sleidan's were quickly translated into multiple languages and forms and printed repeatedly because of their applicability to wider audiences and their challenge to the local quality of memory embodied in the chronicle – once again, the implication to the reader that the privileged author possesses a perspective on events that he or she cannot hope to create or reproduce, and hence Sleidan's stress on the centrality of his own experiences and access to the documents. The rhetorical move toward objectivity and reconstruction of events is thus not at first intimately related to the objective qualities of scientific discourses or to the desired fixity of scientific data (and their popularization), but rather to the opportunity for the commodification and possible sale of the narrator's objectivity as a desirable product for the »smarter« consumer. History is a product for consumption, in which the consumer (just as if he were buying wheat or livestock) must be protected from dishonest dealings. Sleidan writes:

> I thought, I have to continue, and not allow that such events be treated falsely and with lies, either in our time or in the future. For what is more scandalous and less to be suffered, than that the material about which the reader should be reportedly and reminded correctly be counterfeited with lies and deception? And it would be seemly for the authorities to have a glimpse into such affairs, so that this does not happen so frivolously. (Sleidan, Vorrede, A iij verso)

This is not to say that the anecdotal aspects of chronicle writing disappear (monstrous births, ominous portents, oddly shaped vegetables, bad weather, and so on), but rather that they move into other genres (»Newe Zeittung«, »Prophecyung«) with different audiences.[34] Unlike histories, they are not marketed on the basis of the privileged perspective of the historical narrator but rather by perpetuating (in the case of prophecies) the action of the reader as interpreter OR the primacy of the strange and remarkable over the broad and generalizable. Significant here, I think, is that printers poach each other's histories to widespread protest (which underlines that the author's perspective is being consumed), while the materials of the other genres are spread on a »word of mouth« basis in the absence of such protests. Piracy of histories in this context takes on a different meaning than in Johns' description of the theft and unreliable reproduction of scientific data.[35]

Finally, it is arguable that authors see in the rhetorical move toward objectivity a sort of protection from criticism guaranteed precisely by the action of the audience as consumer and thus financer of the historian's activities. Sleidan, for example, spends a good deal of time emphasizing his honesty and sincerity as a historical writer; he suggests that he should have the trust of the reader because his activities in writing were not subsidized by any of the parties to the religious dispute and thus he was not writing to please a patron.[36] Sleidan thus makes the explicit move towards characterizing his audience as the consumer and guarantor of his objectivity: he responds to the demands of his imagined audience.

The attempt to replace the particularist aspect of chronicles, which reproduce local memories, with the generalizable content of history writing (dominated by a small class of history writers) has been much commented on by historians of memory like Pierre Nora. This contrast, like the supposedly unique qualities of historicism, has been overdrawn, but the suggestion that early modern historical narratives undertake some of the same activities as historicist ones erodes this distinction, furthermore giving (as has been postulated above) the potential reader reason to consume the product. Historical authors thus have to enhance their authority and it is in the financial interest of printers to encourage them to do so. In so far as the printing press transformed and broadened markets for knowledge, then, it may also be thought to have affected the content and presentation of that knowledge itself in the form of a push toward »objectivity« and recognizable narrative structures.

NOTES

[1] This essay utilized collections at the Forschungsbibliothek Gotha, the Herzog August Bibliothek Wolfenbüttel, and the Niedersächsische Staats- und Universitätsbibliothek Göttingen. Special thanks to William Sederholm of the University of Texas at Austin, without whose timely logistical help it could not have been submitted, as well as to the suggestions of the paper respondent and audience at the conference. All translations from the German are my own.

[2] For example, Jacob Andreae, Dreyzehen Predigen vom Türcken, Tübingen 1568, 33-66; the theme is discussed more extensively by Robin Barnes, Prophecy and Gnosis, Stanford 1988, 103-115, and Volker Leppin, Antichrist und Jüngster Tag, Gütersloh 1999, 59-63.
[3] Hayden White, Tropics of Discourse, Baltimore 1978, 102; Paul Avis, Foundations of Modern Historical Thought, London 1986, 7-8. A discussion of the meaning of the term »historicism« must be omitted here for reasons of space; the reader is referred to the basic discussions in Georg Iggers, »Historicism: The History and Meaning of the Term,« Journal of the History of Ideas 56 (1995): 129-152 and Hayden White, Metahistory: The Historical Imagination in Nineteenth-Century Europe, Baltimore 1973, and the debates associated with each author's position.
[4] Bruce Gordon, ed., The Changing Face of Protestant History and Identity in the Sixteenth Century, in: Protestant History and Identity in Sixteenth Century Europe: The Later Reformation, Aldershot 1996, 4; Donald Kelley, »Johann Sleidan and the Origins of History as a Profession,« Journal of Modern History 52 (1980): 573-598, here 573.
[5] Johann Sleidan, Warhafftige Beschreibung aller Geistlichen unnd Weltlichen sachen / so sich unter dem jetzigen Grosmechtigsten Keyser Carolo V. verlauffen haben. [...], Basel 1557, A ij recto.
[6] E. Menke-Glückert, Die Geschichtsschreibung der Reformation und Gegenreformation, Leipzig 1912; A.G. Dickens et al., The Reformation in Historical Thought, Cambridge 1986, 7-9.
[7] Dickens, Reformation in Historical Thought, 13.
[8] Sleidan, Vorrede to Warhafftige Beschreibung.
[9] Christoph Reske, Die Production der Schedelschen Weltchronik in Nürnberg, Wiesbaden 2000, 165; Klaus A. Vogel, »Hartmann Schedel als Kompilator. Notizen zu einem derzeit kaum bestellten Forschungsfeld,« in: Stephan Füssel, ed., 500 Jahre Schedelsche Weltchronik, Nürnberg 1994, S. 73-98.
[10] Heinrich Bünting, Braunschweigische und Lüneburgische Chronica. Darinnen man eigentlich nacheinander Beschreiben findet was lange für und nach Christi geburt in diesen Landen für herrliche thaten geschehen [...] alles mit schönen Figuren Brustbildern / und Wapen gezieret / und aus vielen glaubwirdigen Historien / auch gewerten urkunden und Documenten / auffs fleissigste zusammen gezogen, Magdeburg 1584,)(iij verso.
[11] Cyriakus Spangenberg, Mansfeldische Chronica. Der Erste Theil, Eisleben 1572, iij. Spangenberg also includes an extensive list even before the text begins of the numerous sources he consulted in preparing the chronicle.
[12] Ulrich Muhlack, Geschichtswissenschaft im Humanismus und in der Aufklärung, Munich 1991; Stefan Fisch, »Auf dem Weg zur Aufklärungshistorie: Prozesse des Wandels in der protestantischen Historiographie nach 1600,« in Geschichte und Gegenwart 23 (1997): 115-133.
[13] Spangenberg, Mansfeldische Chronica, iij.
[14] Susan R. Boettcher, »Martin Luthers Leben in Predigten: Johannes Mathesius & Cyriakus Spangenberg,« in: Rosemarie Knape (Hg.), »von daher bin ich«—Martin Luther und der Bergbau im Mansfelder Land« Eisleben 2000, 163-183; on the assumptions of these conventions, Eckhard Kessler, Theoretiker humanistischer Geschichtsschreibung, Munich 1971; Rüdiger Landfester, Historia magistra vitae: Untersuchungen zur humanistischen Geschichtsschreibung des 14. bis 16. Jahrhunderts, Geneva 1977.

[15] Matthias Pohlig, Lutheraner vor Luther? Modelle protestantischer Geschichtsdeutung am Beispiel von Vitensammlungen der zweiten Hälfte des 16. Jahrhunderts, M.A. thesis, Humboldt University 1999, 51-60.
[16] The poles of this debate are represented by the works of Elisabeth Eisenstein, The Printing Press as an Agent of Change: Communications and Cultural Transformations in Early-Modern Europe, 2 vols, Cambrige 1979 and idem, The Printing Revolution in Early Modern Europe, Cambridge 1983, and the challenge presented by the works of Adrian Johns, most particularly in The Nature of the Book: Print and Knowledge in the Making, Chicago 1998, as well as the recent debates in the American Historical Review. Various critiques of both positions are presented below, with an orientation toward an introduction of the research of Michael Giesecke, Der Buchdruck in der frühen Neuzeit, Frankfurt 1998[2], which both of these authors ignore.
[17] Gordon, ibid.
[18] On the course and meaning of this historical debate, see Heinrich Garrelts, Die Reformation in Ostfriesland nach der Darstellung der Lutheraner in 1593, Aurich 1925; Heinz Schilling, »Calvinismus und Freiheitsrechte: die politisch-theologische Pamphletistik der ostfriesisch-groningischen »Patriotenpartie« und die politische Kultur in Deutschland und in den Niederlanden,« in Bijdragen en Mededelingen betreffrende de Geschiedenis der Nederlanden 102 (1987): 403-434; Nicole Grochowina, Durch historische Erinnerung zur konfessionellen Identität, in: Steffen Bruendel et al. (Hg.), Kulturelle Identität, Berlin 2000, 88-106.
[19] On the ecclesiastical history of the territory, see Menno Smid, Ostfriesische Kirchengeschichte, Pewsum 1974, as well as Heinrich Schmidt, Politische Geschichte Ostfrieslands, Leer 1975.
[20] [Johannes Ligarius], Warhafftiger Gegenbericht der rechtgläubigen Predicanten in Ostfrießland auff des D. Petzels Vorrede, Emden 1593.
[21] [Menso Alting, et al.], Gründtlicker Wahrhafftiger Bericht Van der Evangelischen Reformation, der Christlicken Kercken tho Emden un in Ostfrießland van 1520 beth up den hüdigen dag, Bremen, 1594. Alting and Gerhard Geldenhauer were assisted by the East Frisian chronicler Ubbo Emmius (author of the Rerum Frisicarum historia).
[22] Alting, 84.
[23] Think, for example, of Gregory of Tours' arguments for the rightness of Roman Christianity over against Arianism in his *Historia Francorum*; Gregory argues that the orthodox faith is correct because kings who have espoused it are still alive while Arian leaders have been defeated or died miserable deaths.
[24] [Timotheus Kirchner], Gründtliche Warhafftige HISTORIA: Von der Augspurgischen Confession / wie die Anno 1530. geschrieben / Keyser Carolo ubergeben / und von dero verwandten Stenden und zugethanen / ... / je und allwege verstanden / und inn offentlichen Religionshandlungen / erkleret und verteidiget worden [...] Leipzig 1584.
[25] Ibid.,)(iij verso.
[26] Ibid.,)(iiij verso-recto. Like Sleidan, Kirchner also emphasizes his relationship to the documents, as it appears, for legal or legalistic reasons,)(iij recto-)(iiij verso.
[27] Giesecke, Buchdruck, 640-643, 954.
[28] Rosamund McKitterick, »Books and sciences before print,« in Marina Frasca-Spada and Nick Jardine, eds., Books and the Sciences in History, Cambridge 2000,

13-34 and the literature cited there, as well as many of the essays in the same volume.

[29] Johns, Nature of the Book, 6.

[30] Giesecke, Buchdruck, 641.

[31] On Melanchthon's understanding of history instruction and the textbook uses of the Chronica carionis, see the oeuvre of Emil Scherer, especially »Die letzten Vorlesungen Melanchthons über Universalgeschichte,« Historisches Jahrbuch 47 (1927): 359-366.

[32] Sleidan, Vorrede to Warhafftige Beschreibung, A iij verso.

[33] Pace Johns' comments about the local qualities of developing print culture, it cannot be denied that the ultimate goal of (whether successfully achieved or not) of the author was to reach over local audiences. Obviously, a general history like Sleidan's is more relevant to such efforts than a local one like Spangenberg's.

[34] Spangenberg, for example, was also the occasional author of items in the Newe Zeittung genre: for example, Newe Zeittung. [...] vom dem Beylager eines Mönches mit einem Marienbilde / Von der Barfüsser Holtzschuch / Wovon die gemacht, Eisleben n.d.; the standard for such reports was not documents or reliable reports but clearly entertainment and polemic. Such texts were frequently written in simple rhyming verses, not only in relationship to their entertainment value but in order to facilitate their oral transmission, for example, Nicolaus Kessel, Newe zeittung. Und erschreckliche straffen Gotes / welche sich haben zugetragen am tag der Himmelfart Christi dieses 87. jars, Jena 1587. Sometimes a melody was even suggested for their transmission, for example, in Zwo warhafftige und erschröckliche newe Zeitungen. Die erste / am tag Simoniß und Judae / hat in der Statt Feldkirch eines Hauptmanns Weib seines Namens Bernhardt Schmid / dises Weib hat in jhrer Geburt drey bösen Geister gebracht / welche gestalt / wie ein Mensch / aber langen Schwaif / wie die Schlangen / die leben noch auff den heitigen Tag / unnd die Pfarrherrn haben sie beschwören wöllen / warumb sie da seyen / hat einer auß jhnen angefangen zusagen / mit Worten / warumb sie da seyen / biß jhrer Mutter sechs Wochen fürüber kommen / was nun weitter geschehen ist / werdet jhr in disem Gesang ferner vernemmen. Im Thom: Hilff Gott daß mir gelinge. Hohenems 1623. The entertainment value could often derive from the goal of producing shock or even Schadenfreude in the reader, for example, Newe Zeittung auß dem Bayerland. Von einem schöcklichen Ungewitter / so sich daselbsten mit Hagel / Schawer / und einem Wolckenbruch / auch unseglichem Schaden derselben gegen / den letzten Monats tag Julij dieses 82. Jars zugetragen, Nürnberg 1582; judging by the collection included in the Herzog August Bibliothek, storms and floods seem to have been particularly popular topics, but miracles or pious stories for the support of faith in general and doctrine in particular were also disseminated: for example, Newe Zeitung: Eine Warhafftige Historia / so sich am heiligen Ostertage [...] zu Alberhofen ... mit einem jungen Gesellen ... / und zweyen Männern / von Angesicht und weissen Kleidern gantz schön und herrlich anzusehen & zugetragen, Schweinfurt 1581. Monstrous birth literature also bordered on this genre and was generally excluded from chronicles after the mid sixteenth century, for example, as were stories of witches, ghosts, and malformed animals (an interesting collection of forty two interesting mixed such reports is found at the HAB in Alvensleben Dn 251 8°).

[35] Johns, Nature of the Book, 5.

[36] Sleidan, Vorrede to Warhafftige Beschreibung, B [i] verso.

BIBLIOGRAPHY

[Alting, Menso, et al.], Gründtlicker Wahrhafftiger Bericht Van der Evangelischen Reformation, der Christlicken Kercken tho Emden un in Ostfrießland van 1520 beth up den hüdigen dag, Bremen 1594.

Andreae, Jakob, Dreyzehen Predigen vom Türcken, Tübingen 1568.

Avis, Paul, Foundations of Modern Historical Thought: From Machiavelli to Vico, London 1986.

Barnes, Robin, Prophecy and Gnosis: Apocalypticism in the Wake of the Lutheran Reformation, Stanford 1988.

Boettcher, Susan R., Martin Luthers Leben in Predigten: Johannes Mathesius & Cyriakus Spangenberg, in: Rosemarie Knape (Hg.), »von daher bin ich« – Martin Luther und der Bergbau im Mansfelder Land, Eisleben 2000, S. 163-183.

Bünting, Heinrich, Braunschweigische und Lüneburgische Chronica, Magdeburg 1584.

Dickens, A.G. et al., The Reformation in Historical Thought, Cambridge (Massachusetts) 1985.

Eisenstein, Elisabeth L., The Printing Press as an Agent of Change: Communications and Cultural Transformations in Early-Modern Europe, 2 vols., Cambrige 1979.

Eisenstein, Elisabeth L., The Printing Revolution in Early Modern Europe, Cambridge 1983.

Fisch, Stefan, »Auf dem Weg zur Aufklärungshistorie: Prozesse des Wandels in der protestantischen Historiographie nach 1600,« in: Geschichte und Gegenwart 23 (1997), S. 115-133.

Iggers, Georg, Historicism: The History and Meaning of the Term, in: Journal of the History of Ideas 56 (1995), S. 129-152.

Garrelts, Heinrich, Die Reformation in Ostfriesland nach der Darstellung der Lutheraner in 1593, Aurich 1925.

Giesecke, Michael, Der Buchdruck in der frühen Neuzeit, Frankfurt 1998

Gordon, Bruce, The Changing Face of Protestant History and Identity, in: idem (Hg.), Protestant History and Identity in Sixteenth Century Europe: The Later Reformation, Aldershot 1996.

Grochowina, Nicole. Durch historische Erinnerung zur konfessionellen Identität, in: Steffen Bruendel et al. (Hg.), Kulturelle Identität, Berlin 2000, 88-106.

Johns, Adrian, The Nature of the Book: Print and Knowledge in the Making, Chicago 1998.

Kelley, Donald, Faces of History: Historical Inquiry from Herodotus to Herder, New Haven 1998.

Donald Kelley, »Johann Sleidan and the Origins of History as a Profession,« in: Journal of Modern History 52 (1980), S. 573-598.

Kessel, Nicolaus, Newe Zeittung. Und erschreckliche straffen Gotes / welche sich haben zugetragen am tag der Himmelfart Christi dieses 87. jars, Jena 1587.

Kessler, Eckhart, Theoretiker humanistischer Geschichtsschreibung, Munich 1971.

[Kirchner, Timotheus], Gründtliche Warhafftige Historia von der Augspurgischen Confession [...], Leipzig 1584.

Landfester, Rüdiger, Historia magistra vitae: Untersuchungen zur humanistischen Geschichtsschreibung des 14. bis 16. Jahrhunderts, Geneva 1977.

[Ligarius, Johannes], Warhafftiger Gegenbericht der rechtgläubigen Predicanten in Ostfrießland auff des D. Petzels Vorrede, Emden 1593.

McKitterick, Rosamund, Books and sciences before print, in: Marina Frasca-Spada and Nick Jardine (Hg.), Books and the Sciences in History, Cambridge 2000, S. 13-34.

Menke-Glückert, E., Die Geschichtsschreibung der Reformation und Gegenreformation, Leipzig 1912.

Muhlack, Ulrich, Geschichtswissenschaft im Humanismus und in der Aufklärung, Munich 1991.

Newe Zeittung auß dem Bayerland. Von einem schöcklichen Ungewitter / [...] den letzten Monats tag Julij dieses 82. Jars zugetragen, Nürnberg 1582.

Newe Zeitung: Eine Warhafftige Historia / so sich am heiligen Ostertage [...] zu Alberhofen ... mit einem jungen Gesellen ... / und zweyen Männern / von Angesicht und weissen Kleidern gantz schön und herrlich anzusehen & zugetragen, Schweinfurt 1581.

Pohlig, Matthias, Lutheraner vor Luther? Modelle protestantischer Geschichtsdeutung am Beispiel von Vitensammlungen der zweiten Hälfte des 16. Jahrhunderts, Magisterarbeit, Humboldt University 1999.

Reske, Christoph, Die Produktion der Schedelschen Weltchronik in Nürnberg, Wiesbaden 2000.

Scherer, Emil, Die letzten Vorlesungen Melanchthons über Universalgeschichte, in: Historisches Jahrbuch 47 (1927), S. 359-366.

Schilling, Heinz, Calvinismus und Freiheitsrechte: die politisch-theologische Pamphletistik der ostfriesisch-groningischen »Patriotenpartie« und die politische Kultur in Deutschland und in den Niederlanden, in: Bijdragen en Mededelingen betreffende de Geschiedenis der Nederlanden 102 (1987), S. 403-434.

Schmidt, Heinrich, Politische Geschichte Ostfrieslands, Leer 1975.

Sleidan, Johann,Warhafftige Beschreibung aller Geistlichen unnd Weltlichen sachen / so sich unter dem jetzigen Grosmechtigsten Keyser Carolo V. verlauffen haben. [...], Basel 1557.

Smid, Menno, Ostfriesische Kirchengeschichte, Pewsum 1974.

Spangenberg, Cyriakus, Mansfeldische Chronica. Der Erste Theil, Eisleben 1572.

Spangenberg, Cyriakus, Newe Zeittung. [...] vom dem Beylager eines Mönches mit einem Marienbilde / Von der Barfüsser Holtzschuch / Wovon die gemacht, Eisleben o.D.

Vogel, Klaus A., Hartmann Schedel als Kompilator. Notizen zu einem derzeit kaum bestellten Forschungsfeld, in: Stephan Füssel (Hg.), 500 Jahre Schedelsche Weltchronik, Nürnberg 1994, S. 73-98.

White, Hayden, Metahistory: The Historical Imagination in Nineteenth-Century Europe, Baltimore 1973.

White, Hayden, Tropics of Discourse: Essays in Cultural Criticism, Baltimore 1978.

Zwo warhafftige und erschröckliche newe Zeitungen. Die erste / am tag Simoniß und Judae / hat in der Statt Feldkirch eines Hauptmanns Weib seines Namens Bernhardt Schmid / dises Weib hat in jhrer Geburt drey bösen Geister gebracht [...], Hohenems 1623.

Abstracts

ROGER BROMLEY: NARRATIVES FOR A JOURNEY OF HOPE: STORIES OF GLOBAL TRANSITION

This paper focuses upon themes of migration, human displacement and communication in a globalised world. Using Sebastiao Salgado's *Migrations: Humanity in Transition* and Michael Haneke's *Code Inconnu*, the paper explores the relationship between representation and reality in the context of a world in which there are, currently, 22 million refugees, with a further 24 million displaced by civil war or famine. The paper is principally concerned with the ways in which the digital and postmodern era, rather than witnessing the eclipse of stories, opens up powerful ways of thinking about narratives, and it also investigates narrative forms which invest the Other, conventionally seen by the West as image or object, with the possibilities of recognition and subjectivity.

VITTORIA BORSÒ: THE BODY OF WRITING AND THE MATERIALITY OF THE IMAGE: NARRATIVE PRODUCTIONS AND VISUALITY IN GUSTAVE FLAUBERT'S »SALAMMBÔ«

Given that writing is a medium, two complementary aspects defining writing are discussed, namely its technological surroundings and phenomenological time insofar as it determines perception. Photography produces narratives that block chronological story-telling and problematize mimetical pictures, foregrounding the visual experience made possible by the surface of pictorial space. Visuality turns out to be a hinge between subject and the other, an interval into which traces of difference (of the cultural other, of the body) inscribe themselves. Opaque, non-mimetic pictures weaken the epistemic subject which, nevertheless, is able to open up with regard to the aesthetical experience of the other. Such are the theoretical preconditions behind Gustave Flaubert's discourse of crisis with regard to the mimetical implications of the picture. *Salammbô* shows his orientalism which exhibits the (historically and culturally) unfamiliar and prompts visual experience by narrative means. Such experience can lead to an reflective turn, thematizing one's own attitude (»Einstellung«), a term which can also carry a technical connotation, referring to a visually or narratively mediated frame that is grounded in the capacities of the eye and delimited by the aesthetics of modernity.

TOM KINDT: »ERZÄHLERISCHE UNZUVERLÄSSIGKEIT« IN LITERATUR UND FILM. ANMERKUNGEN ZU EINEM BEGRIFF ZWISCHEN NARRATOLOGIE UND INTERPRETATIONSTHEORIE

This paper attempts to demonstrate the possibility to conceptualize narratology as a heuristic procedure which might be useful for cultural studies. I precede by developing a definition of Wayne C. Booth's concept of »unreliable narration« which can serve as an instrument in different methodological contexts, and with regard to media such as fiction film, drama, etc. My point of departure is the clarification of the frame of reference for the attribution of »unreliability«. Opposing the traditional definition, I propose to conceptualize the »reliability« of a narrator as part of a general textual interpretation which may vary depending on the interpretive approach chosen (1.1). It is shown that clinging to Booth's definition on the one hand, and using his examples of application on the other, made the concept of »unreliability« ambiguous. My suggestion is to differentiate between narrators that present the events of a story in a misleading way and narrators that are morally deficient and non-exemplary (1.2). Thus the definition of »unreliability« results in a concept which can serve not only to qualify narrators, but also to describe ways of narrating. Against this background it is possible to apply the concept of »unreliability« to film (2).

STEFANIE DIEKMANN: ALLES AUF ANFANG. ANMERKUNGEN ZU CHRIS MARKER, *LA JETÉE* (1962)

This text is not so much an integral reading of Chris Marker's famous film but a collection of notes and observations focusing on issues of film and photography, media mythology, museology, and theories of memory and remembrance. It begins with a comment on the narratological paradoxa of time travel and repetition, and moves on to a comparison of *La Jetée's* organizing principles with those of the photo album on the one hand, and the museum on the other.

HILDEGARD HABERL: WISSEN ERZÄHLEN. DIE ENZYKLOPÄDIE IM LITERARISCHEN TEXT

What is at stake in this article is the question of how the »encyclopaedia« is, as a medium of storing and classifying knowledge, represented in literary texts. On the basis of an analysis of two texts, namely the fragmentary *Bouvard et Pécuchet* by Gustave Flaubert (1881) and *Alizès* by Michel Rio

(1984), the changes in dealing with and shaping of the encyclopaedia are examined. I try to show where different sorts of texts – the novel and the encyclopaedia – resemble one another and where generic boundaries between them are transgressed. The motif of the encyclopaedia is discussed on two distinct levels: content and form. In the first part I examine explicit references to encyclopaedias in both texts (the presence of real and fictional encyclopaedias in the texts). Secondly, I try to show on the basis of the keywords classification/order, document/nomenclature, visualisation/illustration how the pattern or model of the encyclopaedia implicitly shapes the text. In both texts can be noticed a changing conception of encyclopaedia, which calls into question the claim to fixed and absolute knowledge systems and emphasises the cultural and discursive dependence of knowledge.

TAMAR ASHURI: NARRATIVES AND MEDIA CHANGE: MAKING ›NATIONAL‹ DOCUMENTARIES IN A GLOBAL TELEVISION ERA

This paper looks at television documentaries, as cultural manifestations of the tension and contradictions between nationalism and globalization, from the vantage point of a particular mode of production, namely International Co-production. It argues that despite the considerable loosening of the symbiotic ties between nation-states and the national broadcasters operating in them, filmmakers are still committed to adjusting the contents of their products to what they perceive to be the specific »consciousness« of their national target audience. In the final analysis, films are made to reflect a certain »national narrative«, even in cases where they are made through international co-productions. This argument is made through the examination of a particular television documentary, which was produced through an international co-production by three networks, under the title *The Fifty Years War: Israel and the Arabs.* To make this series possible, funding from three separate sources was secured, with each funding source given the right to use the produced footage to construct its own version of the final product. The completed series thus exists in three distinct versions, British (BBC2), American (PBS) and Middle-Eastern (MBC). Given the splitting of the final product of these co-productions into several »national« versions, this contents-dependence becomes translated into ›reality‹ being presented differently in the different national versions.
Analysing the similarities and differences among the three national narratives, this paper offers some reflections on the contradictions and ambiguities in processes of globalization.

ERNST LANGTHALER: DENK-ORTE: EIN DORF ERZÄHLT SEIN GEDÄCHTNIS

The article summarizes the results of a research project on the narrative, interactive, and retrospective construction of collective memories in a village community in Lower Austria at the end of the 20th century. The fieldwork combines several methods in order to reconstruct the complex process of ›doing memory‹: the interpretation of narrative-biographical interviews with villagers; the publication of a commented selection of these life narratives on CD; the interpretation of a group discussion with a heterogenous sample of the village population on the reception of the published CD. On the one hand the actors affirm ›non-political‹ images of the past like sociability, nativeness, diligence, and modesty that represent a collective memory of the village. On the other hand they criticize political-ideological images of past periods, especially the Nazi era, that represent collective memories of different generations. The latter must be excluded or at least neutralized in order to include the whole village population in the former. However, rigid images of the past are set in motion by the memory discourse that is both condition and consequence of the reflexive fieldwork.

CAROLINE GAY: *LEIDKULTUR* OR *LEITVERANTWORTUNG*? THE LEGACY OF THE THIRD REICH IN THE NATIONAL MEMORY NARRATIVES OF THE ›BERLIN REPUBLIC‹

The Schröder cabinet elected autumn 1998 was considered to be a turning point with regard to Germany's attitude towards its Nazi past. Representative of a generation without direct memories of the »Third Reich« it reflects a change from »communicative« to »cultural« memory of this past. The present contribution discusses national memorial narratives about Germany's NS-past in the context of the »Berliner Republik«. Firstly, those narratives are considered against the backgroud of international narratives. The German variety is marked by »Leitverantwortung« which recognizes the crimes of »Nationalsozialismus«, but emphasises the need to take actual responsibility for the present. This does not exclude numerous references to the Holocaust and to German guilt, particularly within the media. Debates concerning »Leitkultur« and »Nationalstolz«, involving questions of identity and patriotism, will in this context be discussed as examples of a »Leidkultur«. I conclude by examining a change in form and function of national memorial narratives in Germany, focussing on current problems, e.g. the political movement of the extreme right.

ROLF F. NOHR: NARRATION UND FERNSEHKARTOGRAPHIE

At first glance, cartography on TV is not a narrative system but a quasi-objective writing system for spatial event configurations. My analysis shows that this understanding is ›naive‹. I demonstrate how far cartography in general contains narrative moments, and how far narrative functions of cartography in the special field of media cartography are essential characteristics of the media event. As such, these functions contribute in both discursive and functional ways to the production of a specifically narrative moment on TV. TV and in particular its news coverage can be understood as a mediator between the huge common sense narrations of society which are accepted as »super vision generating« factor for the implementation and constitution of discourses of truth. In this perspective, TV is not the initiator of reality constructions but part of the discursive production of norms, values and truths in a sense of bardic television. In the analysis of the interdependence of the cartographical signs we can also see the production of naturalizing effects of common sense structures. One effect of this naturalization is indeed the construction and stabilisation of a certain kind of ideological truth. But these effects of truth are on the one hand essentially related with contextual effects of TV and news coverage – but on the other hand integral parts of cartography itself from the earliest forms of mapping till today.

SONJA NEEF: ZITAT UND RAHMEN. *LEONARDO DA VINCIS CODEX ÜBER DEN VOGELFLUG* DIGITAL

In this paper, I concentrate on the concepts central to this volume, »narrative« and »media change,« by analyzing a CD-ROM entitled *The Multi-Media Manuscripts of Leonardo da Vinci* which contains Leonardo's *Codex on the Flight of Birds*. The aim of this paper is to understand how the contemporary digital medium of the computer transcribes this renaissance manuscript by a set of interventions grounding on the concepts of »quoting« and of »framing.«

As Leonardo was left-handed, this codex was originally written mirrorwise. In the hypertextual system of the CD-ROM, this »left« writing can be reversed by a click of the mouse into readable »w/ri(gh)ting«. I make this gesture of reversing left and right productive for questioning an encompassing set of binary oppositions constituting the differences between the digital monitor-writing and the renaissance codex, oppositions such as present and past, writing and image, surface and depth, readability and unreadability. I seek to understand how the difference between the »original« and its »quote« is generated by the »frame« of the digital graphics – its symbols, its icons, and its cursors – and how this difference invites new perspectives on the concept of media change.

KARIN HARRASSER: COMPUTERHYSTORIEN. SZENARIEN DER DIGITALISIERUNG UND IHRE BÜHNEN IN DEN 80ER JAHREN

In this paper I discuss some theoretical approaches to the question of how culture, technologies and the social interact. These considerations result from my research on the genesis of »digital cultures« in the 1980ies. I start with a brief discussion of some of the most influential approaches within cultural studies of technology, and I continue by sketching out the relationship between SF-narratives and technological developments. I end with a little sample of an analysis that combines narratological and discourse analytical methods with practice-oriented cultural theories. What is at stake here is twofold: Firstly – a question of causality: Do culture and society determine technological developments or is it technology itself that triggers social and cultural change? I am arguing for a reciprocal – circular approach that relies on the analysis of narratives to arrive at a »thick description« of digital technologies and their cultures. Secondly: How power enters this process and how interventions for a more equal distribution of cyberpower could look like.

ANNA SCHOBER: POLITIK DER FORM. KORRELATIONEN UND BRÜCHE IM LESBAREN TEXT DER AVANTGARDE

Avant-garde movements such as the Dadaists, the surrealists, the expanded cinema and neo-avant-garde movements in Ex-Yugoslavia since 1989 use certain aesthetic tactics – such as the montage technique, alienation or parody – in order to refresh perception, to get rid of »false« ideologies and to gain a »more emancipated« view of things. Older, linear forms of narration or naturalistic forms of visual representation and other contemporary forms of narration are thereby rejected as »outdated«, as »conformist« or, as impregnated with a »bourgeois ideology«. The new forms of narration established by these groups are described as expressions as well as agents of a transformation of perception and of a belief in the western urban world since the 19th century. Avant-garde movements react to these transformations of perception – and are at the same time also pushing them forward – by trying to make »politics« with visible forms in their own particular way. Inside such a »regime of perception« aesthetic interventions of avant-garde groups can be seen as »doubled«: even if they are guided by certain narrative utopias and myths and directed against other narrative myths and ideologies, they escape the subject's control and establish connections that surprise everybody.

BARBARA ZIMMERMANN: ERZÄHLTE GESCHICHTE IM BILD. DIE NARRATIVE DARSTELLUNGSWEISE DER TRAJANSSÄULE ALS VERMITTLUNG HISTORISCHER EREIGNISSE

The terrible events of the 11th of September 2001 have engraved themselves into our memories and the seemingly unbiased reports by modern media – showing us realtime pictures – have stamped our western world's perception and created a kind of collective reality. The people of the antique period also lived with the power of pictures dominating their life. Different media presented historical events under certain predetermined ideological points of view. To build up this illusion of reality they did not use film or photos of events but a certain narrative-documentary form. The reliefs of the Trajan column show to which extent the narrative form established this illusion of reality by connecting the events to a certain sequence of time and space. The question is whether the combination of this form of narration together with the »new media« of continuosly illustrated rotulus has been created especially for this purpose. The ideological message of this ›unbiased‹ report has influenced society's thinking and acting then as much as today.

URSULA REBER: INFORMA(K)TIONEN. *METAMORPHOSEN* ALS INTERTEXTUELLES PRINZIP

For an analysis and description of antique intertextuality, Bloom's categories, which situate a given author in the light of his predecessors and in agon with them, as well as Bachtin's *chronotopos* and *dialogicity* prove to be quite useful and provide a descriptive model tantamount to an agon-society. The category *clinamen* in particular allows »antique work on the mythos« to be effectively outlined. Mythos in a two-fold sense: as a narrative and as an explicit narration of a »precursor«, since each specifically activated narrative is subject to constant reinterpretation. Ovid's *Metamorphoses* with their metamorphous narration of transcending archi-genres and of sequencing individual narrratives are situated in the middle of this specific feature of Roman agon that is held together by the common context of myths. Intellectual wordplay and wit on the one hand, but also familiarity with Roman everyday life and the Augustean involvement in re-establishing marginal religious cults on the other hand are characteristics of Ovidian poetry. In using myths Ovid's main interest lies in the shift of emphasis regarding the sudden change of form as a sort of *fatum* that is prior to the situation of the psychosomatic crisis, which has caused the *metamorphosis*. Ovids »pictures« of changing bodies are compared to movie pictures, esp. to chrono- and opto-signs as they are described by Gilles Deleuze. This sort of metamorphous images are characterized by oscillating demarcation lines of two bodies in one image – an image, that shows a moment of pure alterity between two forms. The non-narrative dynamic of this alterity is located in a narrative within the spaces of myth.

STEFANIE RINKE: »GEISTIGES GEBÄREN« ALS NARRATIV DER FRAUENMYSTIK: DIE TRANSPOSITION DES GENIESSEN GOTTES DURCH MECHTHILD VON MAGDEBURG

This article is concerned with the analysis of female mystic's narration of the 13th century, who understood themselves as »medium of god«. On the one side these women obey to the ideology of the female mystic common sense, on the other side they transform these structures by their enjoyment of god. Their narration consists of the idea that they give birth to the mystic book in a quite physical way. For this experience Maria was an important model, because the whole mysterium of giving birth to Jesus Christ by her flesh could be regarded as a manufacture of a text. By analysing Mechthild von Magdeburg's book »The fluid light of god«, which contains metaphors of fluidity and of the enjoyment of god, it becomes clear, that Mechthild mediated her mystic book instead of giving birth to Jesus Christ like Maria did. So you can say that Mechthild was a »translation machine«. As a kind of a prospect the article shows that the technical transposition of the fluid enjoyment of god into the book by female mystics becomes later an important model for the reproductive technique of the printing press.

SUSAN BOETTCHER: PRINTING PRESS AS AGENT OF CHANGE REDUX: A THOUGHT EXPERIMENT ABOUT THE ORIGINS OF OBJECTIVITY IN REFORMATION HISTORICAL NARRATIVES

Drawing on material from important chronicles of the Reformation Age a hypothetical link between the change of narrative patterns as well as historiographic methodology and printing technology in the early modern Age is established and discussed. Some similarities to historicist historiography are pointed out. Johannes Sleidan's history of the reformation exemplifies several strategies used by authors to address the awareness of their readers and to manipulate their products (and their own »objectivity«) as commodities or »selling points« on the market of historical narratives. In conclusion the current paradigm for understanding the printing press and its importance to European intellectual life (manifest in the work of Elisabeth Eisenstein, Adrian Johns and Michael Giesecke) is presented and discussed in the light of the findings reported.

Autorinnen und Autoren

Tamar Ashuri, London School of Economics and Political Science (LSE)
t.ashuri@lse.ac.uk

Susan R. Boettcher, Department of History, University of Texas at Austin
susan.boettcher@mail.utexas.edu

Vittoria Borsò, Lehrstuhl Romanistik I, Universität Düsseldorf
borso@phil-fak.uni-duesseldorf.de
http://www.phil.fak.uni-duesseldorf.de/rom1/

Roger Bromley, Nottingham Trent University
roger.bromley@ntu.ac.uk

Stefanie Diekmann, Fakultät für Kulturwissenschaften, Europa-Universität-Viadrina, Frankfurt/Oder
stefanie.diekmann@t-online.de

Caroline Gay, Institute for German Studies, Birmingham (UK)
cmg822@bham.ac.uk

Hildegard Haberl, Universität Wien und École des Hautes Études en Sciences Sociales (EHESS), Paris
hi.haberl@free.fr

Karin Harrasser, Bundesministerium für Bildung, Wissenschaft und Kultur / Institut für Germanistik der Universität Wien
karin.harrasser@culturalstudies.at
http://www.sinn-haft.at

Herbert Hrachovec, Institut für Philosophie, Universität Wien
Herbert.Hrachovec@univie.ac.at
http://hrachovec.philo.at

Tom Kindt, Forschergruppe Narratologie, Universität Hamburg
Tom.Kindt@Narrport.uni-hamburg.de

Ernst Langthaler, Ludwig Boltzmann Institut für die Geschichte des ländlichen Raumes
ernst.langthaler@univie.ac.at
http://mailbox.univie.ac.at/ernst.langthaler

Wolfgang Müller-Funk, Institute for German Studies, University of Birmingham und Universität Wien
Wolfgang.Mueller-Funk@univie.ac.at

Sonja Neef, Europäische Medienkultur, Bauhaus Universität Weimar
sonja.neef@medien.uni-weimar.de

Rolf F. Nohr, HBK Braunschweig, Institut für Medienforschung
r.nohr@hbk-bs.de

Ursula Reber, Mitarbeiterin (Redaktion, Organisation) »Kakanien revisited« (Internet Plattform)
usha.reber@kakanien.ac.at

Stefanie Rinke, Promovendin an der Humboldt Universität zu Berlin
Stefanie.Rinke@student.hu-berlin.de

Anna Schober, FWF. Der Wissenschaftsfonds, Wien
annaschober@t0.or.at

Birgit Wagner, Institut für Romanistik. Universität Wien
Birgit.Wagner@univie.ac.at
http://www.univie.ac.at/romanistik

Barbara Zimmermann, FWF. Der Wissenschaftsfonds, Wien
barbara.zimmermann@univie.ac.at